Matter of North

Matter of North

Essays on Glenn Gould and *The Idea of North*

Edited by

BRENT WETTERS *and*
ANTHONY CUSHING

Cover photo: Sunset with "Churchill Trees" (2004), Brent Wetters.

Published by State University of New York Press, Albany

© 2025 State University of New York

All rights reserved

Printed in the United States of America

No part of this book may be used or reproduced in any manner whatsoever without written permission. No part of this book may be stored in a retrieval system or transmitted in any form or by any means including electronic, electrostatic, magnetic tape, mechanical, photocopying, recording, or otherwise without the prior permission in writing of the publisher.

Links to third-party websites are provided as a convenience and for informational purposes only. They do not constitute an endorsement or an approval of any of the products, services, or opinions of the organization, companies, or individuals. SUNY Press bears no responsibility for the accuracy, legality, or content of a URL, the external website, or for that of subsequent websites.

EU GPSR Authorised Representative:
Logos Europe, 9 rue Nicolas Poussin, 17000, La Rochelle, France
contact@logoseurope.eu

For information, contact State University of New York Press, Albany, NY
www.sunypress.edu

Library of Congress Cataloging-in-Publication Data

Name: Wetters, Brent, editor. | Cushing, Anthony, 1979– editor.
Title: Matter of North : essays on Glenn Gould and the Idea of North / edited by Brent Wetters and Anthony Cushing.
Description: Albany : State University of New York Press, [2025]. | Includes bibliographical references and index.
Identifiers: LCCN 2024053738 | ISBN 9798855803136 (hardcover : alk. paper) | ISBN 9798855803143 (ebook) | ISBN 9798855803150 (pbk. : alk. paper)
Subjects: LCSH: Gould, Glenn. Solitude trilogy. Idea of North. | Gould, Glenn—Criticism and interpretation. | Documentary radio programs—Canada, Northern. | Experimental radio programs—Canada—History and criticism. | Soundscapes (Music)—Canada, Northern—History and criticism. | Canada, Northern.
Classification: LCC ML417.G68 M406 2025 | DDC 791.44/72—dc23/eng/20241113
LC record available at https://lccn.loc.gov/2024053738

Contents

Foreword   vii
    Ethan Kleinberg

Acknowledgments   xiii

Introduction   1
    Anthony Cushing and Brent Wetters

Essays

1. A Conflicted Soundscape: Glenn Gould's *Idea of North*   21
    Lucille Mok

2. Glenn Gould and the Non-Imagined North   45
    Jeffrey van den Scott

3. Rails of Protest   71
    Christopher DeLaurenti

4. "That Incredible Tapestry": Revisiting *Pilgrimage to Solitude*, *The Idea of North*, and the Landscapes of Glenn Gould   95
    Mark Laurie

5. When a Fugue Isn't a Fugue: Glenn Gould's Musical Semiotics of Contrapuntal Radio and *The Idea of North*   113
    Anthony Cushing

6. North, History, and the Shadow of Hanslick: Glenn Gould's Ideal of Musical North and Northern Listening   145
   Markus Mantere

7. The Genius Is in the Genesis: Demythologizing the Idea of Gould as Creative Outsider   165
   Anthony Cushing and Brent Wetters

8. De-Northing *North*: Thematic Continuity in Glenn Gould's *Solitude Trilogy*   187
   Paul Sanden

9. Monstrous North   203
   Brent Wetters

Appendix   221

   1. Letter from Jim Lotz Accepting Gould's Interview Request (7 September 1967)   221
   2. Gould's Interview Questions for Jim Lotz   222
   3. Introduction to Transcripts   223
   4. Jim Lotz Interview Transcript   225
   5. Walter "Wally" Maclean Interview Transcript   241
   6. Frank Vallee Interview Transcript   256
   7. Robert Phillips Interview Transcript   271
   8. Marianne Schroeder Interview Transcript   286
   9. Gould's Preliminary Sketch of Form   293
   10. Janet Somerville's CBC Publicity Memo (15 November 1967)   294
   11. Scene-by-Scene Analysis   295
   12. "Eskimo at the Piano" ["Eskimo am Flügel"]   300
   13. Anthony Cushing in Conversation with Marianne Schroeder   303

Bibliography   319

List of Contributors   329

Index   333

Foreword

Ethan Kleinberg

In his introductory remarks to *The Idea of North*, Glenn Gould announces the work as a product of one who has long been fascinated by the north but has had "no real experience" of it; Gould states, "The north has remained, for me, a convenient place to dream about, spin tall tales about, and, in the end, avoid."[1] And yet, Gould does not avoid the north at all, composing a soundscape comprised of voices that, in his view, belong to people who have had "real experiences" of it. Here, we stumble into the first of several conundrums, because while Gould tells us about both his lack of experience and avoidance of the north in contrast to the "experts" he has assembled, it is he who has staged the interviews and assembled the dialogue curating an idea of north that is very much his own: an experience of north he conveys to the audience. "The north isn't finding," we are told about halfway through the program, "it is seeking."[2] The contrapuntal voices and varied perspectives then serve as evidence that the idea of north that Gould offers to his audience is something that always resides just out of reach. But is it the north that draws us in or Gould's idea of it? Is it the north that remains forever out of reach or Gould's presentation of it?

I see this as a compelling lens through which to view Brent Wetters and Anthony Cushing's assembled collection of essays and materials that take up Gould's fascination with the north and our fascination with Gould. The two are inextricably bound together, and this leads to the question around which Wetters and Cushing frame the volume: Why do we remain fascinated by the north as both a concept and as a destination and why do we remain fascinated by Gould? What is the enduring allure and attraction of north and what is the allure and attraction of Gould? As in Gould's composition, it is the seeking that motivates the work enabling the editors to compose a scholarly whole from the varied voices and perspectives that make up the chapters and source materials while also empowering the reader to navigate between the idea of north and Gould himself without overdetermining either. The volume, however, is no hagiography. It is a testament to the scholarly precision of the editors and contributors that the fascination with the north and with Gould is not a tale of endless attraction but also a story about repulsion, which is, frankly, what I find so attractive about it.

In a piece called "True North," I discussed how the concept of north serves as both a vertiginous empty wasteland and a means of orientation via the North Star or North Pole.[3] The emptiness represents a space yearning to be filled, and beacons serve as a compass offering surety of direction. One of Gould's experts, Jim Lotz (the geographer), goes so far as to say, "In the north, we are seeing one of the final playings-out of those two great dreams of man: El Dorado [and] Utopia," echoing and modifying an argument from his book *Northern Realities*.[4] Lotz identifies Utopia with the American West and manifest destiny. He identifies El Dorado with the Spanish conquest of the Americas. In both cases, the territories are considered "empty spaces" to be used to secure a better future through the acquisition of property, the acquisition of resources, or both. This understanding of north is conditioned by two preconceptions: first, a belief that the territories were open and somehow promised to the settlers and colonizers; second, an understanding of nature as unchanging and unlimited. In her chapter, Lucille Mok discusses this preconception in terms of the emptiness of silence that yearns to be filled with sound.[5] The north is, in the trope of polar explorers or Gould's own presentation, an empty space waiting to be occupied, if only temporarily: "Of course I am fascinated by the look, feel and smell of the land. Because there are fewer people there, I find that my powers of observation are sharper. . . . The North has been a filter for my thoughts. Some of my clearest, sharpest thinking has been done there. The only powers you sharpen among the pacemakers, the leaders, are rhetorical powers. Decisions that shape your life are best made alone."[6] In Gould's telling, one goes north to obtain these powers and then return to the place from where one came. I see this as akin to the directional power we have long afforded the North Star and the North Pole—beacons that guide us not only through space but also through time in pursuit of a better future. As recently as December

2023, President Dr. Sultan Al Jaber concluded the COP28 United Nations Climate Change Conference with these remarks: "We leave Dubai with our heads held high. And our work goes on. In unity and solidarity, we will walk the new path that the UAE Consensus has set for the world. Together, we will follow our North Star. We will follow it from here to Baku and from Baku to Belem. And together, we will secure the future of this beautiful planet for the many generations to come."[7] Here, we see that the compass or beacon of orientation the north provides is also meant to be a moral one, a star of redemption. The truth is that while the North Star and North Pole are each stable and effective enough to guide a traveler in need, it is the idea of north that gives them their power and status as paragons of orientation and direction just as it serves to sharpen Gould's powers of observation and clarify his thinking. This idea, sure direction and guidance secured by the promise of north, is fixed in our imagination and beliefs.

As Wetters and Cushing make clear in their introduction:

> There is perhaps no better sign of the persistent allure of the north than the continued relevance of . . . his landmark 1967 *Idea of North* (hereafter referred to simply as *North*). There are many reasons for the interest in this documentary, not least the cultlike status accorded to Gould, the so-called eccentric genius. But if the interest were just about Gould, why so much focus on *North* rather than the other documentaries like *The Latecomers* (1969) and *The Quiet in the Land* (1977)?[8]

Wetters and Cushing assert that it is not Gould alone who has sustained interest in *The Idea of North*, but they also point us toward his cultlike status and so-called eccentric genius. There is no doubt that Gould's life and work make him an attractive figure worthy of scholarly investigation on his own. Gould's virtuosity, originality, and idiosyncrasies are fascinating as this volume surely shows. But one of those idiosyncrasies is Gould's own obsession with the north and the power of solitude. Here, we reach a second conundrum because Gould's assertion of a general or cultural fascination with the north is conditioned by his quite personal or individual fascination with it and the power he believes it to have. Gould and the north are problematic subjects as well.

To begin with there is the cliché of the solitary individual genius whose actions are justified by the quality of *his* artistic work. Gould crafted an image of himself as the creative outsider and solitary genius, which has made a lasting impression on his audiences and reception. The contributors approach this critically and with skepticism as in Cushing and Wetters's chapter "The Genius Is in the Genesis: Demythologizing the Idea of Gould as Creative Outsider."[9] This is an important correction because, as noted earlier, Gould's self-presentation is linked to his idea of north as a site of emptiness, isolation, and solitude. But, as Jeffrey van den Scott and others make clear in their chapters, the north is not empty, and the projection of isolation and solitude disregards the inhabitants who reside in the territories Gould calls the north. "*North* exclusively contains the voices of those who go north by choice and lacks the voices of those who live their entire lives there. The Indigenous northern voice is, despite Gould's fascination with 'the Eskimo,' outside the scope of his philosophical exploration of the Canadian North."[10] There is something of a feedback loop here as Gould's erasure of the Indigenous northern population in the service of his promotion of solitude can be retrospectively justified by his genius, which he claims is heightened and sharpened by the solitude of the north. In the case of Gould, the sharpening powers of the north are assuredly effective, if his creative output is the measure, but also illusory and, in some ways, pernicious. The idea of north always comes at a cost.

We should be distrustful of any narrative of the solitary genius and *his* singular vision and voice. The contributors and supporting materials show that even the multiple perspectives offered by the differing voices in *Idea of North* were guided by a series of leading questions deployed by Gould to lead them toward responses about solitude. The multiple possible understandings of north are thus reduced to one, and I see this as akin to the way the use of north as a directional guide likewise limits and restricts our movements even as it appears to offer orientation. "The freedom of openness" that the north promises is impeded by the "danger of getting lost in all the expanse."[11] The unbridled openings and possibilities are curtailed or cut off by the fear of that very openness, lest we lose orientation and wind up lost. It is in this sense that I argue the directional *poros* or path that north provides us is also an *aporia*, or trap, because it ultimately limits where we might let ourselves go.[12]

This volume navigates between the *poros* and the *aporia* by offering positive contributions to our understanding of Gould, his soundscape, and north in a critical, unflinching way. In reading through the chapters and assembled source materials, I came away with a determined sense that the power of Gould's *Idea of North* does not lie in the "idea of north" at all nor in his particular presentation of it. It is the contrapuntal and thus polyphonic structure of his soundscape, however flawed, that enables the work to say more than it says. Markus Mantere cites Edward Said in his chapter "North, History, and the Shadow of Hanslick," contending the soundscape works "not univocally, but *contrapuntally*, with a simultaneous awareness both of the metropolitan history that is narrated and of those other histories against which (and together with which) the dominating discourse acts."[13] The contributors work with and against the grain to draw out that which is most compelling in Gould's *Idea of North*—not to fetishize it or laud it as exemplary but as an opportunity to hear and to listen for that which is present and that which is absent. These are the voices that the volume brings forth to compete with Gould's experts and with Gould himself opening space for multiple and conflicting logics of how we encounter the north and how we might encounter music. *Matter of North* compels us to hear multiple notes and multiple voices beyond that which is most immediate or present, an attunement not only to that which is close but also to what is other.

Notes

1. Glenn Gould, *The Idea of North* (1967), in Glenn Gould, *Glenn Gould's Solitude Trilogy: Three Sound Documentaries*, CBC Records, 1992. This and other documentaries have been released in several formats over the years, including an LP Release (1971), and *North* has occasionally been available streaming from the CBC. Throughout the present volume, citations for timings will be based on the 1992 CD release. The shortened citation *North* will always refer to this work as audio document, and other related documents will be given clarifying citation.

2. Gould, *North*, 29:08.

3. Ethan Kleinberg, "True North,*" *History and Theory* 63 (2024): 151–165, https://doi.org/10.1111/hith.12344.

4. Gould, *North*, 34:37. See also Jim Lotz, *Northern Realities: Canada-U.S. Exploitation of the Canadian North* (Chicago: Follet, 1971), and Wetters, "Monstrous North," in the present volume.

5. Lucille Mok, "A Conflicted Soundscape: Glenn Gould's *Idea of North*," in the present volume.

6. "Glenn Gould's Idea of North," press release from CBC-FM Radio, 13 December 1967, Item 1979-20 51 13 2, Glenn Gould fonds, Library and Archives Canada, Ottawa.

7. Sultan Al Jaber, "COP28 President Delivers Remarks at Closing Plenary," COP28UAE, 13 December 2023, https://www.cop28.com/en/news/2023/12/COP28-President-Delivers-Remarks-at-Closing-Plenary.

8. Cushing and Wetters, introduction to the present volume, 2.

9. Cushing and Wetters, "The Genius Is in the Genesis: Demythologizing the Idea of Gould as Creative Outsider," in the present volume.

10. Jeffrey van den Scott, "Glenn Gould and the Non-Imagined North," 00. See also Mickey Vallee, "Glenn Gould's *The Idea of North*: The Cultural Politics of Benevolent Domination," *Topia* 32 (Fall 2014): 21–41.

11. Gould, *North*, 24:10.

12. Kleinberg, "True North.*"

13. Edward Said, *Culture and Imperialism* (New York: Vintage Books, 1994), 51, cited in Markus Mantere, "North, History, and the Shadow of Hanslick," in the present volume.

Acknowledgments

Brent Wetters Interviews Brent Wetters and
Anthony Cushing About Glenn Gould

bw: The present volume has had a more than ten-year path to publication. As such, the number of people we need to thank or who have had a hand in various parts of this book is extensive. Additionally, with two editors, finding the right voice for this section was challenging—third person seemed awkward and first-person plural was unworkable because both authors were involved at different points in the process. The present solution may be silly, but I submit that a book on Glenn Gould should have a bit of silliness (see, for example, Glenn Gould's CBC promos spoofing, among others, Karlheinz Stockhausen, Sir Thomas Beecham, and Marlon Brando, or his many interviews with himself). Brent, when did you first encounter the music of Glenn Gould?

BW: That would have been, I think, during high school, probably in 1992 or 1993. I was a mediocre piano player and was probably learning one of the Bach two- or three-part inventions. My brother Kirk is three years older than me and has always been more of a music collector than I am. I would ask him for suggestions of good performances, and he got me a recording by Gould. Things got serious when I learned the Mozart K. 332 and started emulating Gould's performances.

bw: That couldn't have gone over well with your teacher?

BW: I remember my teacher shrugging it off, but when I played an imitation of Gould's Mozart at local juries, let's just say they were a bit baffled. Through Gould, I also found Schoenberg and the Second Viennese School, which did little to encourage the local piano community that I was anything other than a provocateur.

bw: Before we get to the *Idea of North*, I will ask you, Anthony, the same question. When and how did you encounter Gould?

AC: It's hard to pinpoint the exact moment I first encountered Gould, having grown up in Canada. I was quite young when Gould died in 1982, so for a long while his music was ubiquitous both in our home and on CBC radio. I'm sure there must be a clause in the CBC's broadcast license that they *must* play at least one Gould recording a day lest their license be revoked. It would have been impossible for me to *not* encounter his music at some point early on. The first moment I consciously remember hearing his recordings was in middle school. I found a copy of the Brahms 10 Intermezzi in my father's vinyl collection after my cello teacher disparaged Gould's humming in the recordings. The Brahms album set me about on a whole new world of listening.

bw: Would I be correct in assuming that both of you only found the *Idea of North* somewhat later? It doesn't seem like many people find the documentary without first exhausting most of Gould's other work.

BW: In my case, that's certainly true. About the time I started listening to Gould's recordings, I also purchased a copy of *The Glenn Gould Reader* (ed. Tim Page). When I think about where I ended up, not as a performer or even a composer, but as a musicologist, that book was decisive. Gould's writing showed me, even if I'm not always able to emulate it, how to combine evocative musical descriptions, technical rigor, and no small amount of charm. But for the topic at hand, it was surely in that book that I first read the chapters pertaining to the documentary and learned of its existence. It would be a few years before I tracked down the CBC *Solitude Trilogy*—this was still before Amazon, eBay, and streaming made this sort of thing instantly available. I want to say it was late in my undergraduate (1994–1999) or during my two-year sojourn in Belgium (1999–2001).

bw: Belgium? That sounds interesting.

BW: It was! I ended up in Belgium almost by chance after I graduated from the University of Michigan, and I went to Ghent where I continued my composition studies with an experimental composer named Godfried-Willem Raes. From Raes I learned about the wider world of *Hörspiele* by composers like Ferdinand Kriwet and Mauricio Kagel and began composing my own. More important, however, was the arrival of another American composer, Jonathon Kirk, who (if this is possible) may have been a bigger Gould-nut than I was. Together we listened to and discussed the *Idea of North*; this, I think, marks the beginning of my critical engagement with the documentary. After Belgium, I ended up back in the states, in the Wesleyan University composition program, studying with Alvin Lucier and Ron Kuivila. Kuivila, in particular, was already very interested in Gould and radio montage and pushed me to dig deeper into the documentary and my own relationship to it. During my second year at Wesleyan, I traveled to Churchill, Manitoba, along the same train route as Gould, making field recordings and interviews that culminated in my "response," titled *Saturn and Jupiter*, and a chapter in my thesis, traces of which survive in my chapter here. In Churchill, I stayed at the Churchill Northern Studies Centre where I spent a week talking with researchers and scientists (especially Michael Goodyear and Roger "Starman" Woloshyn) who greatly influenced my thinking about the north. Two other teachers from Wesleyan deserve special mention: musicologist Jane Alden and intellectual historian Ethan Kleinberg. They were both on my degree committee, and both noted in my writings and compositions a trajectory that seemed to be taking me away from composition toward musicology. Kleinberg, in turn, seems to have been infected by my northern obsession and, in addition to writing the foreword to the present volume, also recently published an article titled "True North" for *History and Theory* (2024).

bw: Anthony, when did you encounter *The Idea of North*?

AC: Shortly after I found some of Gould's albums at home, the CBC broadcast François Girard's *Thirty Two Short Films About Glenn Gould* and one of the vignettes depicts Gould in a studio booth, conducting along with the *North* prologue before his spoken introduction. Whoa! The overlapping voices, the distinct vocal timbres, the sheer musicality of it! It wasn't until later when I was an undergrad that a friend showed me a vinyl recording in the school's library. There was immediate recognition in the moments after the stylus found the groove. I listened to the documentary in its entirety twice that day. Much later, in grad school, I "rediscovered" *North* when I was researching mashups and mashup production as a kind of counterpoint exercise. My copy of *The Glenn Gould Reader* was the keystone for decoding both the mashup research *and* laying a path to exploring Gould's radio works writ large.

bw: When did you decide to write a book on *The Idea of North*?

BW: I'm not sure that I ever did "decide" as you say, and it's not entirely accurate anyway, seeing as this is an edited volume. However, the idea for a book, as well as many of the contributors, came from a conference in 2013. The American Comparative Literature Association conference that year was announced to be in Toronto, with the overall theme of GPS (as in "global positioning system"), encouraging panels broadly on the topic of topography. The idea of north struck me as a fantastic fit, so I organized a panel on the idea of north (not, however, *The Idea of North*, though I knew that several papers would be about Gould). In the end, there were eleven papers, five of which were focused on Gould. After the conference, I started looking into the possibility of collecting them into a book. I initially asked Jeffrey van den Scott to coedit, but our first publisher contact suggested narrowing the book's focus from the north generally to Gould's *North*. It was at that point that Jeff bowed out and I asked Anthony, a Gould specialist, to take on that role. A notable absence in the book, at least as a contributor, is sociologist Mickey Vallee, who gave a fantastic paper at the ACLA panel. His paper, "Glenn Gould's *The Idea of North*: The Cultural Politics of Benevolent Domination," was published in *Topia* (2014) and so is not included here. The title on the panel, however, was "Matter of North" and Vallee agreed to gift us that title for the present volume.

bw: What were the other papers on that panel?

BW: Here is the full program: Anthony Cushing, "Listening to Solitude: The Idea of North as Music"; Mickey Vallee, "The Matter of North"; Nesrin Eruysal, "The Idea of North in Glenn Gould and Kenneth White's Creative Trajectories"; Lucille Mok, "A Conflicted Soundscape: Glenn Gould's *Idea of North*"; Jeffrey van den Scott, "Arctic Dreams: Musical Imaginings of the Canadian North and Its People"; Paul Krejci, "Developing Perceptions of the Eskimo in Music: Late 19th to Mid-20th Centuries"; Jeroen Gevers, "Musico-Sonic Representations of the European North on ECM Records"; Iain Gillis "Le nuit le froid la solitude: The Idea of Poulenc and the Idea of North"; Alfred Viktor Sjödin, "Locating the North in Swedish 18th-Century Representations of Global Commerce"; Brent Wetters, "Nordseits der Menschen: Tropes of Northernness in the Poetry of Paul Celan"; Stefan Donecker, "Wicked Witches of the North: The Medieval and Early Modern Roots of a Literary Archetype."

bw: Do I hear that correctly that your paper wasn't even about Glenn Gould?

BW: Gould played a fairly significant role in that paper, but it was, as its title suggests, mostly about Paul Celan's book of poetry *Atemkristall*. The early drafts of my chapter in this book were derived from that paper, but eventually I realized that I was trying to combine two papers. I've since split the Celan material into a separate paper ("Celan's *Winterreise*," AMS, 2020), although I do consider the two essays complementary.

bw: For both of you, is there anyone else you'd like to thank?—this is an acknowledgments section after all.

BW: I think I've covered most of the people who had a hand in the production of the book, but yes, there are a few others I need to mention. Denise Von Glahn and Sabine Feisst were especially helpful with early drafts of the book, and although that first version didn't work out, Feisst remained committed and interested. I had just about given up on finding a publisher when she found me in the lobby of the 2023 (Denver) American Musicological Society (AMS) meeting. She asked (as was our custom by that point) if anything ever came of the book and then dragged me down to the book room to introduce me to Richard Carlin of SUNY Press. The rest, as they say, is history. Having done some work as a copyeditor, I also don't want to fail to mention all the people at SUNY Press, Carlin included, who have joined the project only at this final stage: production by Diane Ganeles, copyediting by Dana Foote, interior design and composition by Sue Morreale, and cover design by Steve Kress.

Maybe the most important people to thank, however, are the contributors in this volume. In addition to their fine contributions, I need to thank them for their abundance of patience. When the project had stalled, I would occasionally get a gentle nudge but never the scolding I (heartily) deserved.

I must also thank David Josephson, one of my professors at Brown University. When I was ambivalent about attending an AMS meeting, David would encourage me by offering up the extra bed in his hotel room. And although it took a while, being present at AMS meetings proved decisive. Finally, I would like to thank my family, Carrie most of all, but also my mother, and my two sons Jude and Hendrik; they have had to listen to me talk about "working on a book about Glenn Gould's *Idea of North*" for years without giving up on me or the project—even if at times I was close.

AC: I heartily second Brent's thanks to the contributors to this volume! Working with them has been both enlightening and humbling. I would be remiss not to mention my dissertation supervisor Norma Coates from Western University. Though she knew little to nothing about Gould or *North*, she believed my research into the "*Solitude Trilogy* as music" had some traction, even when other faculty members on my committee thought Gould's concept of contrapuntal radio was empty and a dead end. My parents and siblings, all of whom had inquired for years about when my dissertation would be done, turned their questions around to ask when the book would be done. Further, a hearty thanks to Faye Perkins and Samantha Rhulen at Primary Wave Music 1 and Emma Baril at CBC Archive Sales and Licensing for their gracious assistance in chasing down the rights to use a good deal of our primary source material.

Introduction

ANTHONY CUSHING AND BRENT WETTERS

Why must we keep going north? The geographical north, while in no sense "densely populated," has very little mystery left to it. Circumpolar flights now routinely cross the Arctic, and reaching the North Pole is no longer the unattainable test of human perseverance that it was during the nineteenth century. To reach the far north in 2024 is a matter of economic privilege and takes a certain amount of dedication. In Norway, for example, it is possible to drive right up to the Arctic Ocean at the town of Nordkapp. Getting from there to the pole requires booking passage on either a flight, an ice-breaker ship, or getting first to an ice station at Barneo and then taking a helicopter the final hundred kilometers. There are companies happy to sell just such tours for upward of twenty thousand euros; thus, while going to the North Pole is not something feasible for most people, it has become eminently *possible*, and this fact stands at odds with the original motivations for going there. The nineteenth-century explorers who first sought the poles, both north and south, went precisely because the journeys seemed impossible.

Canada, and Canada's "north," spans six time zones, from St. Johns, Newfoundland, in the east, to Victoria, British Columbia, in the west, with stops along the way at Canada's largest cities: Toronto, Montreal, and Vancouver. Even allowing for a few outliers like Edmonton, Alberta, 90 percent of Canada's population lives within one hundred miles of the US-Canada border. Much like its southern counterpart, as Canada took shape in the nineteenth-century post-Confederation, construction of the railroad pushed to broaden the country from the Atlantic to Pacific. Even today, travel within Canada often emphasises the east/west axis rather than north/south. Effects of climate change notwithstanding, the north remains geographically inhospitable and the climate even more so. Agriculture is not sustainable north of the sixtieth parallel due to temperatures and short growing season. Food and other supplies must be imported from the "south" at great expense. Yet there are some established small "urban" communities in the three northern territories. Though there is little mystery left, the north having been explored extensively for television, magazine photo essays, and film documentaries, few Canadians make the trek north to the Arctic Circle. It is fair to say that there is a romance to the north and the impression remains of vast tracts of unspoiled tundra.

And yet we remain fascinated by the north as both a concept and as a destination. There is perhaps no better sign of the persistent allure of the north than the continued relevance of a documentary by Canadian pianist Glenn Gould, his landmark 1967 *The Idea of North* (hereafter referred to simply as *North*).[1] There are many reasons for the interest in this documentary, not least the cultlike status accorded to Gould, the so-called eccentric genius. But if the interest were just about Gould, why so much focus on *North* rather than the other documentaries like *The Latecomers* (1969) and *The Quiet in the Land* (1977)? Why indeed does the present volume seek once again to "go north" as it were, instead of broadening the scope of work on Gould's radio compositions?

One might expect to find one of the other two documentaries in the *Solitude Trilogy*, the aforementioned *Latecomers* or *Quiet in the Land*, to have occupied *North*'s position. They both have the advantage of being in stereo rather than mono, a significant benefit for the contrapuntal layering techniques used in all three. We might discount *Quiet in the Land* because of its somewhat less "sexy" topic of rural Mennonite communities, but why not *Latecomers*? Its subject, Newfoundland, is no less exotic than the environments described in *North*.

A quick survey of academic work on Gould's radio documentaries confirms *North*'s status as not only the magnum opus of the collection, but the example par excellence of any presumed discussion of Gould as composer rather than piano virtuoso. Kevin Bazzana's comprehensive biography, for example, devotes a full fifteen pages to the exposition of *North* and only one or two paragraphs each to *Latecomers*, *Quiet in the Land*, and the documentaries on Pablo Casals and Leopold Stokowski.[2]

North has also found its way into other scholarly work in other disciplines not directly concerned with the figure of Gould. Several works use *North* as an example and starting point for deconstructing the Canadian conception of the north. A 2005 book by Peter Davidson went so far as to borrow Gould's title for his exploration of "north" as a cultural construct.[3] Sherrill Grace, in her book *Canada and the Idea of North*, takes its jumping off point from *North* and, indeed, she opens her first chapter with an extended quote from Gould's spoken introduction to the documentary.[4]

These last two books indicate the importance of the topic (i.e., north) over other concerns. What attracted Davidson and Grace to *North* was its topic, not technical concerns or its importance to our understanding of Gould's artistic trajectory. *North* resonated (and resonates) in these cases because it touches a nerve and captures something essential about the north. Whether these authors ultimately agree or disagree with Gould's characterization of the north, it has maintained its position of relevance on the strength of that characterization.

The reasons for *North*'s ascendency over the other documentaries that are related to Gould's biography are also compelling. For those who are interested first and foremost in Gould himself, *North* represents a pivotal moment, almost as important as Gould's decision to exit the concert stage in 1964. According to the fictionalized version in François Girard's 1993 film, *Thirty Two Short Films About Glenn Gould*, he signed an autograph before a concert while cheerfully announcing that he'd never sign another, because he would never play another public concert. In truth, it was not widely known that Gould had in fact "quit" until 1966, merely that his concert activity had ceased.[5]

Over the previous twenty years, Gould established himself as Canada's most famous musical export, known for his inspired performances of Bach and his many personal eccentricities. Distaste for the concert stage led him to prefer the meditative seclusion of the recording studio. He had come to believe, ever since his first experience recording for the Canadian Broadcasting Corporation (CBC), which he would later recall as beginning his "love affair with the microphone," that musicmaking of the future would be in recorded media, even predicting the demise of the traditional concert.

During the years from 1964 to his death in 1982, Gould embarked on a series of ambitious recording projects, many of which required the technological possibilities afforded by the recording booth. Most famously, his late re-recording of Bach's *Goldberg Variations* includes precise metrical relationships between the thirty-two movements, each being related to the other by ratios such as two to one, three to two, and so on. Such correspondences might be possible in a live performance, but not with the precision envisioned by Gould. In another case, Gould transcribed and recorded a piano version of the overture to Wagner's *Die Meistersinger* but found himself unable to cover all of the parts himself. To make it work, he simply recorded the extra notes on another track and mixed them together. Where others might have found this solution to be "cheating," Gould embraced it as a form of "creative lying."[6]

Another reason frequently cited for Gould's abandoning the concert stage was that he wanted to devote himself to composition, writing, and other projects; Bazzana characterizes him as properly a "Renaissance man."[7] Gould had already tried his hand at composition, writing an "opus 1" string quartet in 1955. The self-conscious application of "opus 1" seems to have been a calculated step to announce his intentions to become a composer, or to announce that he already was one. By the time the string quartet was recorded for commercial release, he expressed ambivalence about the importance of this initial step into composition, concluding the liner notes with the exclamation, "It's Op. 2 that counts!"

His postconcert retirement, however, never did fulfill that promise, and there was no opus 2 despite a copious trove of sketches and unfinished projects.[8] That is, unless one takes a broader view of what counts as musical composition. One could, for example, see his composerly side at work in his studio approach to something like the 1981 *Goldberg Variations*. The careful manipulation and planning led to a conception of the final product as a "work" unto itself—all of which count as composition in other contexts.

If we were to imagine that Gould did produce an opus 2, however, it would have to be *North*. In other contexts, notably the European avant-garde, such a work would have counted as a musical composition. One need only look to the electronic music of the Darmstadt school, and especially the text-based experiments by Luciano Berio and Bruno Maderna at the Studio di Fonologia Musicale di Milano della RAI, to see similar "compositions," as is discussed in greater depth in chapter 7. For both Gould and his North American audiences, however, "composition" likely meant the kind of instrumental music that had cemented his reputation as a performer. Without those instrumental compositions, the radio documentaries, particularly *North*, give the clearest insight into Gould as creator.

North began as a highly personal exploration of a topic that had long fascinated Gould. He embarked on a two-day train trip north from Winnipeg to Churchill, the so-called Muskeg Express, in June 1965. On the protracted trek Gould made the acquaintance of Walter "Wally" Maclean, a surveyor with whom he struck up a conversation on the north and its various manifestations.

Leading up to the Canadian centennial celebrations in 1967, the CBC commissioned several radio and television works to mark the occasion.[9] Radio producer Janet Somerville approached Gould to produce a work for the program *Ideas*. In 1967, the program was only two years into its run. Originally aired in 1965 as "The Best Ideas You'll Hear Tonight," *Ideas* featured documentaries, interviews, and panel discussions on a wide range of topics. For the princely sum of $1,500 CDN (approximately $13,000 CDN in 2023), Somerville commissioned the work from Gould that became *The Idea of North*.

Having received the commission, Gould's methods for finding his interview subjects was rather unsystematic. Robert A. J. Phillips, a bureaucrat, anthropologist and geographer James "Jim" Lotz, and Frank Vallee, a sociologist and academic, were extensively published on matters of the north, each having published at least one book on the topic. Marianne Schroeder, a nurse and the only female subject, was only two degrees of separation from Gould.[10] Last, Gould drew from his experience of meeting Wally Maclean on the train and invited him to participate. Perhaps by a matter of serendipity, all Gould's interviewees have distinct vocal timbres and varied experiences in the north. Schroeder's voice, with a mild German accent, follows a slow lilt with short, thoughtful pauses at each phrase's cadence but is melodic in breadth and contour. Frank Vallee, a sociologist and academic speaks in a short, shotgun staccato that flows in bursts between long pauses and phrases punctuated by "Uh" and "y'know." Lotz, an English expat from Liverpool, offers a calm contrast to Vallee. Phillips's somewhat nasal voice with narrow contour complements Lotz and Schroeder's calm demeanors. The combination of vocal rhythm, cadence, and timbre are effective in rendering their voices distinct, though in audio production, the volume level adjustments and frequency filters significantly affect vocal independence.

In his article "Radio as Music," Gould suggested that he initially conceived of the work as five one-hour programs presumably dedicated to each of his interview subjects or to sundry topics on the north and solitude.

As late as November 1967, just over a month before the work's premiere in December, Janet Somerville wrote to the CBC publicity department that the program would occupy two one-hour broadcasts. Whether by post facto mythmaking or genuine genesis, Gould conceived of the contrapuntal form of *North* sufficiently early in the production process to whittle the final product down to just under fifty-eight minutes. He referred to his studio production techniques as "contrapuntal radio" in response to his critics. "When 'The Idea of North' first came out in 1967, the fashionable word was 'aleatory,' and some critics were quick to apply this term to my work. *Nothing* [original emphasis] could have been further from the truth, and to counter this impression, I began to speak of 'contrapuntal radio,' implying a highly organized discipline."[11]

Before Gould began his work in the editing suite, he ventured into the information-gathering stage for interviews. His questions of the interview subjects were wide-ranging, probing topics personal to professional. Two lists of questions are extant in the fonds of the Gould archives in Ottawa, one for Jim Lotz and the other for Wally Maclean. In his near-indecipherable, cramped autograph he scrawled one question after another, often with marginalia as follow-ups, all numbered to make post-interview editing easier. Gould traveled to Winnipeg to conduct Wally Maclean's interview, the first of the five interviews; it spanned three tape reels and the results likely formed the grounds for questions for the other interviews. Jim Lotz's interview came late in the gathering stage in September 1967. In his interview with Lotz, conducted in the CBC radio studio at the Chateau Laurier hotel in Ottawa, Gould used more leading questions. "What prompted you to go north—Was it just the opportunity to study a very unique people and their confrontation with civilization or was it in fact an inclination to feel out the north itself?"[12] This question is clearly inviting Lotz to explore only one of the two options: Did he go for anthropological pursuits or for the sake of going north? Only a response to the first option yielded a satisfactory response for Gould.

North has three clearly articulated sections: an introduction, followed by a main section, followed by an epilogue. Gould further conceived of the middle section as a series of five "scenes," each dealing with different topics and featuring different configurations of the five interview subjects. Anthony Cushing's chapter in this volume details the formal structure and musical devices used throughout. The documentary fades in with Schroeder describing her first experience coming north, looking out over the Hudson Bay and hoping to see polar bears or seals. She is then joined by Vallee, who seems ready to dismiss the whole project. He "doesn't go in for this northmanship bit at all" and identifies himself as the northern skeptic. Phillips enters next, and he and Vallee share the spotlight, speaking simultaneously at roughly the same volume, while Schroeder fades out. (Lotz and Maclean do not appear until the main part of the documentary.) Vallee and Phillips then fade into a background texture, while Schroeder comes back to the front, offering a lilting melodic reflection on the northern environment before all three fade to near silence.

After a significant pause, Glenn Gould himself enters to introduce the documentary:

> This is Glenn Gould, and this program is called *The Idea of North*. I've long been intrigued by that incredible tapestry of tundra and taiga which constitutes the Arctic and sub-Arctic of our country. I've read about it, written about it, and even pulled up my parka once and gone there. But like all but a very few Canadians, I've had no real experience of the North; I've remained, of necessity, an outsider, and the North has remained for me a convenient place to dream about, spin tales about, and in the end, avoid.[13]

He continues to introduce the participants, giving particular attention to Wally Maclean, telling the story of meeting Maclean and their subsequent day-long conversation. He says that having had the conversations, "when it came time to organize this program, and to correlate the disparate views of our four other guests, I invited Wally Maclean to be our narrator, and to tell me how, in his view, one can best attain an idea of north." The veracity of this final statement by Gould is somewhat in doubt. It is true that Maclean is given a place of privilege throughout the documentary—his voice is never treated polyphonically—but other evidence and personal testimony suggest that Maclean was not the last interview conducted and may have even been the first. In any case, it does not seem that Maclean was accorded any special status until *after* the interviews had been collected. It could be said, then, that Gould composed *North* from its material rather than the material being collected with a preconceived sense of its final form.

Some critics have found the presence of Gould's voice jarring in *North*, and he notably opted not to include similar introductions in the subsequent documentaries. Bazzana, in particular, objects to the "overwritten prose" and its "autobiographical" content.¹⁴ One wonders, however, if part of the appeal of *North* over the other documentaries might have to do precisely with the lack of authorial distance, and the sense in which the documentary offers autobiographical insight into Gould himself.

When Gould first mentions the train, the background voices of Schroeder, Vallee, and Phillips are replaced with train sounds that fade up over the remainder of Gould's soliloquy. Coinciding with Gould's conclusion, the train sounds come to the fore with a prominent bellringing. The train remains a constant feature throughout the rest of the documentary, until the very last section. Maclean introduces the subject of the north by describing the experience of taking the thirty-six-hour train to Churchill. Thereafter, reflections by Maclean are interspersed with contrapuntal treatments of Lotz, Schroeder, Vallee, and Phillips. At the end of the main section, space is given once more for an extended clip of train sounds; the last section is announced by the abrupt interpolation of the finale from Sibelius's Fifth Symphony, which then becomes the backdrop for one last monologue by Maclean.

The epilogue amounts to a philosophical meditation on the meaning of north as a window on humanity and the relationship of humanity to nature. Brent Wetters devotes the final chapter in the present volume to a close reading of this section, examining the extent to which Gould constructs a thesis about the north. Gould presents the north often as utopia, but a subterranean thread in *North* conjures a monstrous dystopia.

The CBC is as much a looming figure in the creation of *North* as perhaps the north itself. Having been born out of the ruins of the Canadian Radio Broadcasting Corporation in November 1936, the first three years of the CBC were spent largely in building itself out as a coast-to-coast national broadcaster, with content often taking a back seat to nation building.¹⁵ In the beginning it aired American content but also created programs that were sent south to air nationally on American networks, which served to validate the corporation as a producer of quality content. The corporation grew and its focus shifted more toward homegrown national and regional programming while also striving to improve technical capability and reach. Former CBC news host Knowlton Nash, in his seminal work on the corporation's importance, opines, since its creation, the CBC "has reflected to mass audiences the spirit and reality of this country as nothing else could, and without it, Canada would be a soul-starved nation, hiccupping the cultural values and history of our southern neighbour."[16] To that end, the corporation played an invaluable role in 1967 during the centennial celebrations, sharing programming from all regions around the country to feed, as Nash might comment, Canadians' collective soul. The corporation was only thirty-one years old when *North* premiered and was still growing its cultural programming, having long established its status as a news broadcaster.

The contrapuntal elements of *North* were demanding and complex not just for Lorne Tulk and Gould in the editing suite but also for listeners in 1967 and for contemporary listeners. It marked a milestone for the CBC almost as a new genre of content, certainly establishing a new style of production that would be used several more times over the following decades, especially in Gould's own radio productions, including the other two works in the *Solitude Trilogy* and the documentaries on Leopold Stokowski, Pablo Casals, and Richard Strauss.

That *North* continued to live on as an important marker of Canadian culture is evidenced by its later adaptation to video. In 1970, the CBC deemed the original sufficiently successful that it commissioned a joint production of *North* with the local PBS station in Buffalo, New York, WNED-TV. The video version was broadcast simultaneously on Canadian and US television. This version never did have the cultural impact of the original, but it does offer an interesting comparison. The most notable change is the imposition of a narrative structure to the documentary, which may have been implied in the original but was in no way determined. The video presents the documentary as a train journey undertaken by a young man who meets and converses with the documentary's narrator, Wally Maclean. Before Marianne Schroeder's voice enters (where the radio version begins), the video shows a montage of the protagonist departing from Toronto's Union Station for Winnipeg and then taking the so-called Muskeg Express to Churchill.

Another significant change to the television version is a completely recast sound effects layer. The train basso continuo is replaced by sound effects that track closely to the video. The video, in turn, follows the audio of the documentary such that verbal references with any kind of strong visual association usually precipitate corresponding video and sound effects accompaniment. For example, when Jim Lotz says he received a phone call offering him to go on an arctic expedition, the video shows a man answering a telephone that also rings in the sound effects layer. Video and sound effects are directly linked and synchronized but are triggered by the interviews, which are the primary driver of the images and sound.

Most of the changes in the television version seem to be aimed at making *North* more conventional. The narrative structure and the video cues guide the viewer in terms of what to follow. Moreover, the contrapuntal sections, which in the original had an abstract and musical quality, are generally passed off as being the result of sitting in a crowded train. This may have been at least partially the conceit in the radio version as well, but the visual images of a crowded dining car encourage the viewer to understand the contrapuntal voices as something expected—and to attend to whatever voice seems primary as one would when conversing in a crowded environment.

The seeds for the genesis of *North* were planted in 1965 when Gould's close friend John P. L. Roberts, then head of English radio music at the CBC, invited the recently retired pianist to contribute more regularly. He gave Gould a modest office space at the CBC headquarters on Jarvis Street in Toronto. Though Gould was mostly nocturnal and was not in the building during standard business hours, the office gave him the opportunity to network with producers and technicians and keep up with technical matters and other projects happening elsewhere in the building.

Apart from the occasional live radio performances, Gould's works for CBC radio were limited to standard, "linear" documentaries with little contrapuntal content. Gould described his first documentary, the two-hour-long *Arnold Schoenberg: The Man Who Changed Music* (1962), as an unsatisfying effort due to the limited documentary techniques of the time.[17] Later in January 1965 he hosted a panel-style documentary, *Dialogues on the Prospects of Recording*, loosely based on an article of the same title. Additionally, the *Art of Glenn Gould* series of radio shows featured performances, recordings with commentary, and lectures on sundry topics with musical examples. Notable is *The Search for Petula Clark*, which aired in December 1967, shortly before *North*. A somewhat bizarre and self-indulgent exegesis on popular music with Clark as his foil, it marked his first collaboration with CBC audio engineer Lorne Tulk. Gould and Tulk formed a close friendship and worked together on several projects over the years in addition to many late-night recording sessions at Eaton Auditorium in Toronto.

What makes *North* all the more extraordinary is where it stands in relation to his future efforts. *North* is the only one of Gould's experimental works in monaural (mono) sound. Further, all the work was completed without the use of multitracking or automation. In the studio, Gould and Tulk worked with multiple tape players that fed into a mixing console, connected to a single-track mono tape recorder. All the manipulation was realized by tightly choreographed movements of starting and stopping the tape machines and turning dials for volume and frequency filters. Tulk was tasked with translating Gould's musical concepts into practical audio production techniques. By Gould's reckoning this work required upward of 150 hours of studio time and weeks of trial and error. All the scenes had to be recorded in a single take, which may have been relatively easy in the linear scenes with only one person speaking at a time accompanied by the train sound effects; however, the highly contrapuntal scenes like the prologue (up to three simultaneous voices) and the dining car scene (up to four aural streams) pushed the limits not only of contemporary audio production, but the limits of what is physiologically possible.

North was the first of his eight experimental radio documentaries over the following twelve years. Technological developments at the CBC aided production of those future works. His next work, *The Latecomers*, was the first to make use of stereo and two-track tape recorders. Commissioned by the CBC to take advantage of three new stereo FM broadcasting locations in Montreal, Toronto, and Vancouver, Gould's cast of interview subjects expanded from five in *North* to twelve in *Latecomers*. True to form, the production process required countless hours of studio time and careful production choreography but made full use of the technology available, using the full 180-degree stereo separation and several scenes with contrapuntal layering of voices in addition to the ocean wave sound effects. Later, multitracking allowed Gould to pursue works with better synchronization of aural streams, including overlapped music as in *Stokowski: A Portrait for Radio* (1971), *Casals: A Portrait for Radio* (1974), *Schoenberg: The First Hundred Years—A Documentary Fantasy* (1974), and *Strauss: The Bourgeois Hero* (1979). Perhaps the work in which contrapuntal radio reached its apotheosis was *The Quiet in the Land* (1977) in which Gould interviewed more than twenty subjects. Though these later works highlight *North*'s limitations, they also reveal how resourceful Gould and Tulk were at making the most of the technology available to them.

For all the technical and aesthetic merits of *North*, the work is not without issues. There is the matter of journalistic integrity in which the notion of "*North* as documentary" is cast into doubt. One need only compare each interview subject's transcripts with what appears in the final cut to reveal the heavy hand with which Gould mediated the interviews in the editing suite. As is the case with any producer working with hours of recorded interviews and a limited block of time to fill, Gould culled the bulk of the material into small segments. The transcripts are marked frequently for exclusions, segments of the interviews selected for inclusion in the final work. Sometimes the exclusions are single sentences, entire thoughts, or, indeed, incomplete thoughts and sentences. These segments are then juxtaposed either linearly or contrapuntally with exclusions from other interviews. This in itself does not pose an ethical or moral quandary, as the meanings are not being changed substantially. However, what changes is the context, which is cause for concern. Further, "Our five guests were . . . interviewed separately. They did not at any time during the making of 'North' have occasion to meet, and whichever dramalike juxtapositions came about were achieved through some careful after-the-fact work with the razor blade on tape and not through any direct confrontation among our characters."[18] By removing his own voice from the interview, Gould leaves only the subject's responses. Gould uses this method in his other works, notably in *Latecomers* when he brings two voices into dialogue that appear to be embroiled in an argument. One voice, a male, opines on the Thoreauvian lifestyle while the other, the work's only female subject, appears increasingly agitated by his responses. We know, however, that she is responding not to the voice in the documentary as implied, but to Gould's interview questions. What appears is not just dialogue but Gould's own figurative voice, speaking through that dialogue. The same is true of *North* in the dining car scene, which is discussed later in this introduction.

Following the issue of juxtaposition and dialogue, there remains the issue of representation. Though there are no extant archival materials that suggest as much, the interview subjects are at Gould's whims in terms of how they are presented in the final work. Wally Maclean became a philosophical narrator whose voice never appears in dialogue with the others. Vallee often appears confrontational when in dialogue, yet there is nothing in Vallee's transcript that suggests confrontation. An interview subject for *Quiet in the Land*, Roy Vogt, an economics professor at the University of Manitoba and an ordained Mennonite pastor, expressed his concern about representation in the documentary:

> Your approach to the present project leaves me somewhat baffled. You seem to be intent on capturing the "spirit" or Zeitgeist of a group, a rather abstract object in which the human beings

> you are interviewing become primarily a means to an end. Several times in our conversation I was led to believe that my ideas would be used not as the expression of an individual but as a foil for the ideas of others. . . . The musical analogy of counterpoint which you used very often reinforces this impression. Each person becomes a note in a larger symphony, which in social terms is perhaps as good a way as any of describing the underlying assumptions of a totalitarian state. The dictator is a social composer.[19]

Vogt's concerns are applicable retroactively, as Gould used the same techniques in *North* to create the foil and the dialogues.

Though *North* is about solitude, some of the scenes come across as crowded. The aural space of mono forced Gould into a corner when trying to place his subjects in the sound field. With only two real options for spatializing mono, presence and depth (affected by changes in volume and frequency filtration), the scenes in which more than two speakers appear at any given time become nearly unintelligible. As the listener contends with the appearance of simultaneous voices, much like at a cocktail party, they must privilege one voice over another until Gould changes the volume level of one voice to the detriment of the other. Immediately, at the work's opening, Gould challenges the listener with just such a scene. Though it starts with only one voice, the others enter shortly thereafter. While some voices are shuttled deeper into the sound field, one is privileged with presence in the forefront. Finally, Gould's voice enters at the three-minute mark while the other three voices are backgrounded in a tape loop. Cushing describes the prologue in his chapter as it regards textural density and the number of simultaneous voices. Further, Lorne Tulk illustrated the progression of voices in a "performance sketch" that has been reproduced several times.[20]

The infamous dining car scene is even more crowded. Gould describes the scene as a train porter attending to different tables, eavesdropping on two conversations (four spoken voices). As one voice is faded to the background, another is foregrounded. At any given time, there are only two simultaneous voices; however, there is also the matter of the train basso continuo and the sound effects that one might expect in a dining car: flatware hitting the plates, ice clinking in glasses, and the occasional murmur of people elsewhere in the dining car. This makes for a challenging listen.

> It's perfectly true that in that dining-car scene not every word is going to be audible, but then by no means every syllable in the final fugue from Verdi's *Falstaff* is, either, when it comes to that. . . . I do believe most of us are capable of a much more substantial information intake than we give ourselves credit for, I would like to think that these scenes can be listened to in very much the same way that you'd attend the *Falstaff* fugue.[21]

Gould justifies the scene perhaps based on his own perceptual prowess and ability to process multiple simultaneous aural streams. The unprepared listener may find themselves lost in the crowd.

Assuredly the most glaring issue with *North*—and the one for which it and Gould receive the most criticism—is the missing voice of the Inuit people of Canada's north, the true northerners, often referred to as "Eskimos" throughout the work. Relative to their experiences of the north, Gould's interview subjects are interlopers and southerners. Van den Scott addresses this issue extensively in his chapter, though it bears mention again here because, despite good-faith efforts, our volume remains complicit with the issue: we have no chapter written by an Inuit scholar. One reason for this could be that the much-needed Indigenous critique of Gould and his *North* would represent yet another instance of an oppressed minority being asked to redress an injustice perpetrated against them. It is our hope, however, that we have allowed space and invite precisely the critiques that have been lacking in previous scholarship. We do not look away from nor paper over those aspects of *North* that bring discomfort, and we look forward to future scholarship that will fully address its failings and blind spots, as well as our own.

༄

The opening essay of *Matter of North* from Lucille Mok provides insightful archival research into the genesis of Gould's project, situating *North* in the context of other Canadian soundscape artists of the period. She argues that the contrapuntal structure of Gould's documentary holds several competing interpretations and views of the north in delicate balance: it is a work where the north refuses to submit to a unified meaning. Ethnomusicologist Jeffrey van den Scott critiques Gould's vision of the north by considering the missing aboriginal voice that haunts the documentary. Chris DeLaurenti's "Rails of Protest" examines *North* through the lens of tactical media to rehear it as a soundscape of political struggle. Mark Laurie's essay is an analysis of his film *Pilgrimage to Solitude*, an homage to Gould and contrapuntal radio using interviews from Gould's personal and professional acquaintances. Anthony Cushing's reading of *North* focuses on the ways that Gould constructs a musical semiology to depict the north and its solitude. Markus Mantere takes a concept from *North* about "northern listening" as a pretext for understanding "north" and "south" as aesthetic categories in Gould's thought and their resonances in the European tradition. Next, the volume's editors coauthor a chapter considering the relationships, or lack thereof, between Gould and European radio art produced in parallel at the important electronic music studios in Cologne and Milan, addressing the persistent question of what genre *North* falls into. Paul Sanden looks beyond *North* to the other *Solitude Trilogy* documentaries to find that *North* often says more about Gould than it does the north itself, and—with the other documentaries—forms a cohesive intertextual discourse. Wetters concludes the volume with a close reading of *North* as literary text with a focus on Maclean's final soliloquy.

The appendix collects relevant source material and previously unpublished archival documents ranging from interview transcripts from all five participants, an internal CBC memo regarding publicity for *North*, a detailed scene-by-scene formal analysis of the work, and a conversation with Marianne Schroeder, among other items.

Again, we return to the question, "Why must we keep going north?" In the years since *North*'s premiere, the question of the north has become ever more urgent, in part because the deleterious effects of climate change are felt most acutely there. As ice melts, new contested spaces open for exploration, travel, and research. Gould's *North* is also situated on its own contested terrain. It does not fit neatly into any generic categories: Is it a documentary, drama, music, or some combination of the three?[22] Our volume brings together essays reflecting a variety of approaches and disciplines—musicology, ethnomusicology, composition, aesthetics, and cultural studies—each to understand Gould's north from a different perspective.

Indeed, there is no disciplinary claim to the "north" as a field of study, just as no single nationality can make uncontested claim to the polar regions. To engage with the north is to simultaneously address questions of geography, philosophy, politics, history, and aesthetics. Gould's *North*, while probing the geographic north, never underestimates the extent to which north is also a cultural construct. While the present volume focuses on Gould's *North*, many of the contributions were first presented at an interdisciplinary panel about the north in general at the 2013 meeting of the American Comparative Literature Association in Toronto. Among the papers was a provocative critique of the colonialist tendencies at work in Gould's documentary titled "Matter of North," by sociologist Mickey Vallee. His essay has since been published as an article in the journal *Topia* under the title "Glenn Gould's *The Idea of North*: The Cultural Politics of Benevolent Domination."[23] Vallee is, incidentally, the grandson of Frank Vallee, one of Gould's interview subjects and the one (mentioned previously) who is positioned as a "northern skeptic." He asserted during the discussions that his grandfather's comments about "not going in for this northmanship bit" were suspect; he recalled memories of Frank Vallee bragging about his northern expeditions and frequently showing off the souvenirs of his travel, like Inuit spears.

With Vallee's blessing, we adopted his title "Matter of North" for this book because it plays on the double meaning of "matter" as both physical presence and as "problem" or "situation," while it maintains a resonance with Glenn Gould's work. The interview transcripts, published here for the first time—form the tangible "material" of Gould's work. We do not situate our book as a comprehensive historical study of *North* but as a companion to the work itself. By including a section of primary source material, including letters, formal schemes, and sketches, we provide readers with multiple perspectives. We invite the reader to "travel north" with us, remaining open to the discoveries that remain to be uncovered in Gould's documentary and the north itself. As Gould tells us: "Something really does happen to most people who go north—they become at least aware of the creative opportunity which the physical fact of the country represents and—quite often, I think—come to measure their own work and life against that staggering creative possibility: they become, in effect, philosophers."[24]

Notes

1. For clarity, we have instituted the following formatting rules regarding the word "north": 1. Capitalization and italics are used to refer to the documentary; 2. all other instances of north or northern, except as part of a proper noun (i.e.,

"North America" or "North Pole"), are presented in lower case; 3. quotations and interview excerpts generally preserve the capitalization scheme of their source.

2. Kevin Bazzana, *Wondrous Strange: The Life and Art of Glenn Gould* (Toronto: Oxford University Press, 2004), 292–313.

3. Peter Davidson, *The Idea of North* (London: Reaktion Books, 2005), 7. In the introduction, Davidson reveals that the title, while ultimately derived from Gould's documentary, was taken first from a sculpture that sat on his desk during the writing of the book, bearing "the idea of north" as an inscription. Davidson described it as "translucent, so that it can be held up to catch a landscape in its lens. Whatever place embodies your own idea of north, you can always see it through the clear glass, with the red compass needle always indicating the north of what you see" (7).

4. Sherrill E. Grace, *Canada and the Idea of North* (Montreal: McGill-Queen's University Press, 2001), 1.

5. Robert Hurwitz, "The Glenn Gould Contrapuntal Radio Show," *New York Times*, 5 January 1975, https://www.nytimes.com/1975/01/05/archives/the-glenn-gould-contrapuntal-radio-show-the-glenn-gould.html (accessed 26 November 2023).

6. Andrew Kazden, *Glenn Gould at Work: Creative Lying* (New York: E. P. Dutton, 1989).

7. Bazzana, *Wondrous Strange*, 269–275.

8. Among the works either in embryonic form or extant only in writing are a song cycle titled *Letters from Stalingrad*, a piano trio, and an idea for an opera titled *Mr. Strauss Writes an Opera*, about composer Richard Strauss.

9. Canadian singer-songwriter Gordon Lightfoot was commissioned to write his song "The Canadian Railroad Trilogy," a musical depiction of the building of the Canadian Pacific Railway, perhaps a matter of serendipity given Gould's use of the train as a foil for his program.

10. Schroeder babysat for the family of singer and vocal coach Joan Maxwell, who was a friend of Gould's.

11. Glenn Gould, "Glenn Gould in Conversation with Tim Page," in *The Glenn Gould Reader*, ed. Tim Page (New York: Vintage Books, 1990), 457.

12. "Idea of North | Interview Questions for James Lotz," 1967, Item 1979-20 4 94 1, Glenn Gould fonds, Library and Archives Canada, Ottawa.

13. Gould, *North*, 3:00–3:33.

14. Bazzana, *Wondrous Strange*, 298.

15. Sean Graham, "As Canadian as Possible: The Canadian Broadcasting Corporation, 1936–1939," PhD diss., University of Ottawa, 2014, 11.

16. Knowlton Nash, *The Microphone Wars: A History of Triumph and Betrayal* (Toronto: McClelland and Stewart, 1994), 11.

17. Gould, "Radio as Music," in *The Glenn Gould Reader*, 374.

18. Gould, "'The Idea of North': An Introduction," in *The Glenn Gould Reader*, 393.

19. Roy Vogt to Glenn Gould, 17 July 1971, Item 1979-20 35 1 25, Glenn Gould fonds, Library and Archives Canada, Ottawa.

20. See, for example, Tim Page, *Glenn Gould: A Life in Pictures* (Buffalo, NY: Firefly Books, 2007), 153.

21. Gould, "'The Idea of North': An Introduction," 393.

22. See Friedemann Sallis, "Glenn Gould's *Idea of North* and the Production of Place in Music," *Intersections: Canadian Journal of Music* 25, no. 1-2 (2005): 113-137; Anthony Cushing, "Glenn Gould and 'Opus 2': An Outline for a Musical Understanding of Contrapuntal Radio with Respect to *The Idea of North*," *Circuit: Musiques contemporaines* 22, no. 2 (2012): 21-35.

23. Mickey Vallee, "Glenn Gould's *The Idea of North*: The Cultural Politics of Benevolent Domination," *Topia: Canadian Journal of Cultural Studies* 32 (2014): 21-41.

24. Gould, "'The Idea of North': An Introduction," 392.

Essays

1

A Conflicted Soundscape

Glenn Gould's *Idea of North*

Lucille Mok

> This . . . makes drama out of life itself, expressed by the living, and welded by the artist into an art, an art of today, but wholly by sound—spoken sound, musical sound, noise.
>
> —Pat Pearce[1]

The Canadian-Finnish anthropologist Vilhjámur Steffánson became a pioneer in Canadian arctic exploration when he documented his expeditions and his life among the Inuit beginning in 1913. His prolific writings contain evocative descriptions; statements about his encounters with sound are striking in their depth and detail. Consider, for instance, this excerpt from his 1915 collection, *The Friendly Arctic*:

> In the far North not only is the ground continually cracking when the temperature is changing and especially when it is dropping, but near the sea at least there is, not always but on occasion, a continuous and to those in exposed situations a terrifying noise. When the ice is being piled against a polar coast there is a high-pitched screeching as one cake slides over the other, like the thousand-times magnified creaking

of a rusty hinge. There is the crashing when cakes as big as a church wall, after being tilted on edge, finally pass beyond their equilibrium and topple down upon the ice; and when extensive floes, perhaps six or more feet in thickness, gradually bend under the resistless pressure of the pack until they buckle up and snap, there is a groaning as of supergiants in torment and a booming which at a distance of a mile or two sounds like a cannonade.[2]

Shackleton's men now and again commence their diary entries with the words "din, Din, DIN." The literary north is barren, dismal, and desolate. Here we are dealing with words of indefinite meaning into which each of us reads our own significance.

Steffánson documents firsthand a moment in which his audition reigns supreme, calling into question what has been the status quo in the imaginary sonic north. In the Arctic, he witnessed a resonant body host to a constant battery of noises and sounds. Almost a century after Steffánson's daring journey into the northern topography, this vignette is the reverse of what remains characteristic of sonic interpretations of the north—stillness, starkness, silence, and solitude still prevail.

Like Steffánson's description, Glenn Gould's rumination on solitude and the north is clamorous and full of utterances; the "basso continuo" of the railway converges with human voices and Sibelius's Fifth Symphony. Steffánson's narration is striking in juxtaposition to Gould's program, because they both observed sound as central to their understanding of the north. But Gould's "north" was imagined as much as experienced; he never traveled past the last stop on the Muskeg Express—Churchill. Yet, as I will argue, Gould expressed reverence toward the concept of north. As his subsequent two documentaries from the trilogy attest, the north was merely a point of access to the broader issue of solitude, a theme for which he offered no real conclusion, but which he invited his audience to explore with him—by listening.

Although Gould is best known for his piano performances, his most significant artistic and intellectual contribution was to challenge traditional ideas about music and sound. He did so by embracing technology while turning his attention to sound and his sonic environment, both of which came together in the production of his radio documentaries. Gould's controversial perspectives on the potential of studio recording and his work with radio documentaries both emerge from the impulse to use technology to push his creative limits, to create rather than interpret, and to explore sound and the act of listening. In this realm Gould's philosophical and musical approach is, notably, not far removed from the work of his Canadian contemporaries: musicians and artists who, in the 1960s, were also rethinking their changing relationship to sound.[3]

I argue for a sound-centered study of Gould's *Idea of North*. This chapter explores how Gould responded to changes in his everyday sonic experience impacted by urban life and the mass media, expanding traditional radio programming to include a nontraditional approach to sound. To that end, I examine *North* as a response to solitude within the context of a greater awareness of the spoken word, environmental sound, and noise by intellectuals in the 1960s and '70s. In conjunction with a close analysis of *North*, I examine primary source material from the Glenn Gould fonds at Library and Archives Canada. Providing an examination of the sonic confrontations of documentary, music, and radio drama within this work, I situate *North* within the context of a culture shaped by what Canadian journalist Robert Fulford deemed Canada's "radio generation." Between the scant sounds of a barren arctic landscape, Gould's fabricated Nordic soundscape, this documentary is what I call a "conflicted soundscape," to borrow a term from Canadian composer R. Murray Schafer. The north has traditionally been portrayed as remote and therefore silent, but *North* goes against that trend, presenting a populated and noisy setting replete with multiple simultaneous voices and the mechanical sounds of the locomotive.

Scholars have observed that Gould's radio documentaries incorporate conflicted perspectives on the issues of solitude and sound. In 1996, Kevin McNeilly began a conversation about the plurality of ideas contained within Gould's contrapuntal radio, writing, "Gould's North is not a single topos, a functional 'idea' of North, but a site at which many voices and 'ideas' coalesce, antagonize, support, subvert, mingle, and separate. The North acts, for Gould, as a name for a certain multiplicitous music, an imaginative zone in which the voices, noises, and ideas of the human community entangle and sound themselves out."[4] Indeed, McNeilly assessed *North* as an exploration of artistic interiority, acknowledging that it possibly expressed a state of internal conflict.

Gould biographer Kevin Bazzana and radio scholar Howard Fink observed that Gould's radio documentaries incorporate the influence of contemporary developments in sound and technology. Howard Fink, reflecting his approach from the field of radio studies, argues that Gould's *North* is a new "syncretic" genre, situating the program at the intersection of documentary, drama, and music.[5] Bazzana's assessment of *North* picks up on Fink's argument, suggesting that at its heart it is a "synthesis of three principles: documentary, drama, and music. . . . It *is* a documentary about the North, but the documentary material is dramatically charged, conveyed through confrontations of characters with different perspectives, blended evocatively with other sounds."[6] My analysis begins with Bazzana and Fink's premise that Gould's documentary is a hybrid genre of several influences relating to music, technology, and sound. Rather than completely displace the obvious musical components to Gould's work in radio production, I suggest that sound and technology had an overwhelming impact on Gould and his intellectual and artistic contemporaries, including his Canadian contemporaries who, during the 1960s and '70s, while not in direct communication with Gould, nevertheless took a similar interest in traditionally nonmusical and environmental sounds. Then, I turn to a discussion of solitude, its relationship to the act of listening, and how they relate to Gould's northern ruminations.

The Radio Generation

The new and ubiquitous sonic presence of radio broadcasting in the 1920s and '30s played a powerful role shaping the everyday soundscape and deeply influenced Gould's approach to the *Solitude Trilogy*. Timothy Taylor describes this major cultural shift as follows: "It's impossible to explain the impact that radio had on the world to anyone who didn't live through that time. Before radio, people had to wait for the newspaper to learn what was happening in the world. Before radio, the only way to see a performer was to see a performer."[7] The increased prominence of radio programming during Gould's formative years made an indelible mark on his everyday sonic environment and encouraged a greater awareness of auditory sensation and its relationship to technology and sound. What were the broad cultural forces at play in the establishment of a national radio service in Canada during Gould's early life? What was its impact on his relationship to radio broadcasting, and furthermore, what role did it play in the conception of his experimental documentaries?

Symbolically and culturally, radio's relevance to the everyday experience of North Americans was matched only by its geographical reach and impact across social class. Radio made its cultural mark in the United States very soon after World War I, but it wasn't until the 1920s that its popularity rapidly grew among the general public.[8] Canadians saw a rapid development of a national wireless infrastructure especially in the 1930s, alongside an increased demand for radio sets and licenses. Sales of radio licenses doubled from 1938 to 1941, triggering the greatest period of active growth in radio's popularity among Canadian households.[9] Writing in 1955, radio conductor Geoffrey Waddington reflected on the first two decades of Canadian radio, attributing its considerable influence to the nation's population and physical characteristics: "In these days of mass communication, the influence of radio upon the intellectual life and cultural character of a community can be said to be of unusual importance in Canada, by reason of its small population in an extremely thin distribution."[10] Attaching significance to radio as a Canadian cultural phenomenon, Waddington's reflections about the interaction between technology and national characteristics resonates in comments by other Canadians on the role of radio technology and communication on their everyday lives in the 1930s and '40s, including Gould and his contemporaries.

As documented by Gould's childhood friend and Canadian newspaper columnist Robert Fulford, this rapid growth in radio's popularity coincided with Gould's early life in Toronto. Fulford described his early childhood experiences with radio broadcasting, many shared with Gould, as life changing. Fulford reveals that the dramatic cultural shift felt across Canada as a result of radio's pervasive social and cultural presence was also felt in the domestic sphere, in family dens and living rooms: "When you think of Glenn and the idea of sound, you have to think of him as a kid who grew up with radio. The phonograph was important too, but at that time, you are talking about the 10- or 12-inch 78 RPM variety which had to be constantly turned over if you wanted to hear a whole piece of music. So, the first time you actually heard a great classical symphony was on the radio."[11] As Fulford notes, Canadians born in the early 1930s grew up during the CBC radio's nascence, arguing its central place in Gould's relationship to radio broadcasting.

Both Fulford and Gould shared excitement and awe in response to this cultural phenomenon: "I remember once saying to Glenn, 'You know, I'm embarrassed to say this but I'm thrilled by the idea that we can be here in Toronto listening to a live broadcast by the Winnipeg Symphony Orchestra on a Sunday night,' and he'd say to me, 'Don't be embarrassed by it. It IS thrilling!'"[12] Arguing that a greater attention to *listening* was specific to his and Gould's generation, Fulford directed attention to the development of radio in Canada. Their experience centered on listening to the radio before the pervasiveness of the home television, influencing them down to the primacy of their corporeal senses. Fulford wrote: "Members of the radio generation developed an aural sensibility, and an aural dependency, that were both new in the world. We were the first to grow up with radio all around us, and pretty well the last to grow up without television. Radio provided the sound track of our lives, and as we grew toward maturity we began slowly to understand its effects on our way of thinking. It was an alternative centre of existence."[13] This paradigm shift alerted their generation to the possibilities of the mediated aural experience. Gould's focus on the relationship between radio entertainment and the aural senses surely influenced his enthusiasm to experiment with the radio medium later in his life.

Contrapuntal Radio and "Radio as Music"

In addition to being thematically experimental, Gould's radio documentaries were sonically innovative, demonstrating a new technique he called "contrapuntal radio." By layering multiple tracks of spoken word, sound, and musical recordings, Gould achieved multidimensional and dramatic sound environments, heightening the narrative of the radio programs. By broadening the texture of the radio documentary to include several voices at once, he challenged the listener to actively attend to multiple meanings of the interviews. Canadian broadcaster and journalist Barbara Frum noted the importance of Gould's contribution to the radio documentary genre, particularly because of his application of contrapuntal techniques, what she interpreted as a groundbreaking innovation. After its 1967 broadcast she wrote: "The usual radio documentary . . . by now has been refined to a formula. And perhaps it takes an outsider like Gould to redirect. The likelihood of course, is that Gould's undoubted imitators won't have his sense of rhythm or balance and will obliterate in technique the flow of ideas that must still be the basis of a documentary."[14] Much like he aspired to do with his piano recordings, Gould challenges his listeners to engage with the radio documentary rather than just hear it as a passive receiver.

Although Gould sought to decode the documentaries for his listeners by way of musical terminology, his explanations indicate that he was also reluctant to cast them as strictly musical. In "Radio as Music" Gould admitted that by using the terms "contrapuntal radio" and "basso continuo," for instance, Gould was grappling with the pragmatic concerns of how to discuss the various sound elements of his programs. Musical terminology, as he discussed, was one way to communicate legibly and specifically about different aspects of the programs: "(So) it's not just a question of dealing with musical forms. Sometimes one must try to invent a form which expresses the limitations of form, which takes as its point of departure the terror of formlessness. After all, there are a limited number of rondos you can exploit in the radio documentary; then you find you have to invent according to the criteria of the medium, which is essentially what we ended up doing."[15] While musical form was one tool that Gould used to describe his radio goals, he also resisted the limitations of such terminology.[16]

Gould's reference to contrapuntal radio likely initiated this conflation between musical counterpoint and Gould's radio production technique that mingled simultaneous spoken word, music, and sound. Listeners picked up on Gould's musical perspective, often relating his (and his technical assistant Lorne Tulk's) hours of laborious editing and splicing to an extended compositional process. Record producer Robert Hurwitz, for instance, invoked vocabulary that suggested the radio documentaries were on par with large-scale musical compositions, calling *North* a "symphony."[17] In 1985, Darrel Mansell discussed Gould's contrapuntal radio technique as creating the impression of "two entirely different pieces of music that just amazingly happen to cross, recross, and harmonize with each other like motorboats cavorting around a lake."[18] In 1988, Richard Kostelanetz referred to Gould as a radio *composer*, in a single sentence comparing Gould's performances as "a masterful interpreter of fugues" to his role as producer of radio work as "a masterful creator of fugues."[19]

Western music concepts dominate these statements, demonstrating the challenge of discussing sound-based art independent of established musical paradigms. Dan Lander, a Canadian composer with an interest in sound art and the radio medium, reasons that the dominance of musical concepts rooted in Western art music has been partly to blame for the perceived limitations of radio art: "The imposition of a borrowed musical discourse applied to all sound phenomenon, [it strips] away any social and/or cultural referentiality, thus creating a situation in which aurality in general is perceived as music, as if the origin, context and phenomenology of any given sound or noise can be measured only by its contribution to a renovation of western art music."[20] The inclination to use musical vocabulary to discuss the *Solitude Trilogy* has hindered discussions about Gould's radio programs. In light of Lander's statements, Gould's innovative use of the radio medium to manipulate sound and the perception of time and space cries out for discussion beyond the sometimes-stubborn fixation on Western music's rigid analytical frameworks.

Gould's interview with John Jessop, published in 1971 as "Radio as Music" in *The Canadian Music Book*, reveals that issues pertaining to music and radio technology were nevertheless inescapable. The title alone suggests that musical understanding took precedence in Gould's perspective of his work for radio. Evidence from the interview alludes to the deeper role that radio broadcasting played in the *Solitude Trilogy*. Gould explained that radio dramas "came out sounding 'Over to you, now back to our host, and here for the wrap-up . . .'—in a word, predictable."[21] Contrapuntal radio allowed Gould to break free from the "linear" radio documentary, to borrow a term from his intellectual contemporary Marshall McLuhan:

> It seems to me terribly important to encourage a type of listener who will not think in terms of precedence, in terms of priority, and collage is one way in which to do it. I think, at the same time, it ought to be possible to play around with the time sense, the time scale in relation to an individual voice, to hear only one voice and yet receive separate and simultaneous messages, you know, from the statement it offers. That's something that, as far as I know, has not really been done in radio. I think it should be done.[22]

The practical constraints of the sixty-minute radio program also contributed to Gould's development of a contrapuntal radio technique. Gould's original plan for *North* was to create five different documentary programs, one based on the material from each respective interviewee.[23] The temporal constraints of the radio schedule, however, forced Gould to think in contrapuntal terms by finding a way to use the voices simultaneously. Responding to Gould's revelation about the birth of contrapuntal radio, John Jessop described it as "pretty inauspicious."[24]

Contrapuntal Radio and Solitude

Throughout his life Gould's statements about the role of music and technology were remarkably consistent, but on the issues of solitude and his concept of north, his statements and actions were conflicted. Gould expressed a firm personal view about the importance of solitude, stating that "isolation is the indispensable component of human happiness . . . for every hour you spend in the company of other human beings, you need x number of hours alone."[25] Initiated by Gould's own suggestion, *North*, more so than the other two programs in the *Solitude Trilogy*, has been regarded as a form of an artist's statement: "Yes, it's [*North* is] very much me, in terms of what it says . . . it's about as close to an autobiographical statement as I am likely to make at this stage of my life."[26] As newspaper columnist William Littler observed, Gould played into the "reclusive image," as he did in an interview with Elyse Mach for her volume of interviews with pianists: "The recording studio and the kind of womblike security that it gives is very much integrated with my life style. I guess it's all part of my fantasy to develop to the fullest extent a kind of Howard Hughesian secrecy."[27] Such statements became part of Gould's self-perpetuated myth—that he was solitary by choice, a state that he preferred—and was a crucial part of his public persona during his life and beyond. Photographs, films, and literary accounts depict and describe his affinity to the north and the state of solitude.[28]

Gould expressed this point so emphatically that biographers understandably wove this personality trait into narratives of his life. Fink, for instance, wrote: "*The Idea of North* was clearly autobiographical for Gould, in the sense of playing out his own development: he abandoned the definition of himself as a stage performer, a definition forced on him by our urban civilization; he left the concert stage and turned inward, to the solitude of the studio which led him to fulfill his urge to create by means of his contrapuntal documentaries."[29] Peter Ostwald, a Gould biographer, wrote that "solitude was for Glenn a cherished state of existence. He preferred being alone."[30] In a 1985 article about the *Solitude Trilogy*, Darrel Mansell drew connections between Gould, the "solitary, strange, cold, cerebral genius,"[31] and another twentieth-century icon with whom Gould had already expressed a personal resonance: "He saw himself as isolated in a cold, remote and lonely arctic circle—an anchorite, the self-proclaimed brother-in-solitude of that other modern misanthrope, Howard Hughes."[32] Connecting Gould's personality back to his radio documentaries, Mansell stated that *North* was "really a documentary about Gould himself."[33]

Although Gould fostered an image of himself as a hermit, reflections by his friends and colleagues have sought to debunk the widespread solitude myth surrounding his life and work.[34] They, in contrast, described Gould as sociable. Their accounts reveal that he even tended to reach out to strangers. In a 2013 interview with Gould's lawyer Stephen Posen, former CBC radio producer Larry Leblanc states, "The enduring myth that Glenn Gould was a recluse [also] isn't true." Posen, in agreement with Leblanc, responded that he overheard a conversation with a man who described Gould as "the most gregarious guy I had ever known. I used to see him in the park all of the time, and he was very talkative and very chatty."[35] More recent interviews with his romantic partner Cornelia Foss suggest that he sought out romantic affection and a traditional family life, even if it was something he never fully pursued.[36] Increasingly, scholars have mitigated the overwhelming attention on Gould's personality in discussions about the radio documentaries. In 1996, Kevin McNeilly nuanced the oft-stated idea that "Gould's life and art testify to his own obsession with isolation and with the connections between solitude and creativity," elaborating that Gould's withdrawal from the concert hall was, in fact, in the service of "greater intimacy with his audience."[37]

Gould glorified solitude, fetishizing it throughout his career. Despite this initial disconnect between Gould as social and solitary, I suggest an understanding of these opposing perspectives not as a conceptual impasse but as a dialectic, connected by Gould's interest in technological mediation. Gould's friends describe him as talkative and describe his infamous propensity to call them late at night and talk for hours at a time.[38] Gould's preference for social contact over the telephone channeled his affinity with the mediated reach of the radio broadcast.

If Gould felt as if his radio documentaries communicated from a deep well of personal artistic conviction, his minimal audible presence in *North* is worth noting. Gould biographer Otto Friedrich noted that if the radio documentary reflects a personal perspective, Gould's voice is conspicuously absent from most of it. Gould's only aural appearance is in the introduction, where he describes the premise and characters—hardly a statement of a personal or revelatory nature. He almost immediately leaves the documentary, never to return. As Friedrich puts it, "In the way Gould presented 'The Idea of North,' he made it seem that these were his own ideas, his own creation. And yet he never signed the check."[39] Kevin Bazzana's opinion about Gould's short introduction to *North* notes that Gould's narrative interjection is out of place in the radio program: "It was his only misstep in *The Idea of North*. . . . The autobiographical comments, the introduction of the characters, and the tone of Gould's overwritten prose . . . are jarring in this context."[40]

Bazzana highlights the incongruity between Gould's manner of directly addressing the listener and the sense of "listening in" that he wished to simulate with his contrapuntal technique. Gould's general absence from his radio documentaries contributes to the idea that he intended to achieve the same goals with them as he aspired to in his musical recordings: to encourage active listening without the performer's intervention. Without Gould's guiding voice, he encouraged listeners to engage more actively and, in turn, gather their own interpretation from the material. A firsthand account by Barbara Frum offers insight following the initial broadcast of *North*: "I found myself listening at two levels simultaneously—to the stream of ideas, but just as compelling in this production, to the pattern of sounds Gould wove out of his speakers' voices."[41] Whether intentional or inadvertent, by drawing listeners into active listening, Gould's contrapuntal radio became an exercise in community building rather than isolation.

Gould discussed a concept of "active listening" in the context of his musical recordings, but his contrapuntal radio documentaries offered yet another medium that pushed the idea to its limits, forcing the listener to deeply engage with the multilayered sonic environment. Recordings appealed to Gould because they placed responsibility onto the listener, yielding an unprecedented shift from the concert hall where the responsibility fell on the performer. Gould frequently returned to the idea that simultaneous aural stimuli sharpened the listener's ability to discern a single melody or voice. For instance, he recalled from his early musical development that he could achieve an increased focus on the music if his mother vacuumed the house while he played the piano.[42] The simultaneous sound source of the machine drone goaded him to concentrate more fully on the contrapuntal structures of the music. In a way, Gould sought to create a similar ideal listening environment for the listeners of his radio documentaries.

Gould's own enjoyment in hearing, parsing, and performing contrapuntal music was related to his desire to re-create this experience for his listeners. Contrapuntal radio encouraged the listener to simultaneously attend to individual voices yet hear them all together. Gould's interest in the idea of "active listening" was not unlike Marshall McLuhan's concept of "hot media," in which the listener is forced to engage more actively with the content of the media format as a result of its low-fidelity qualities.[43]

Active listening is also crucially important to Gould's evocation of acoustic space in that his listeners only experience it when they fully attend to the layers of sound within his radio documentaries.

Radio and Acoustic Space

Like others in the field of radio drama, Gould relied on sound to evoke physical and imaginary spaces. Gould specifically cited the CBC writer and producer of *Sunday Night Stage* program, Andrew Allan, as a major influence: "I used to listen to the inevitable 'Sunday Night Stage' something-or-others for which, in those days, Andrew Allan and Company were responsible. I was fascinated with radio. A lot of that kind of ostensibly theatrical radio was also, in a very real sense, documentary-making of a rather high order. At any rate, the distinctions between drama and documentary-making were quite often, it seemed to me, happily and successfully set aside."[44] Allan and his colleagues were particular about the physical space where they broadcast their live drama program. As Allan recalled in his memoir, the studio where they recorded—an old CBC concert studio on McGill Street in Toronto—had a unique acoustic stamp that was as much a part of his show as its other sonic elements. He wrote, "What we liked was the acoustical variety we could get there. It came to have an atmosphere of its own [for us]."[45] Because acoustical effects were an important part of the production, the physical space of the studio played a key role in the age of limited postproduction. In Allan's experience the relationship between the tactile qualities of the physical world were inseparable from sound itself. *Stage* dramatist Gerald Noxon, Gould noted, was another key innovator who imported cinematic concepts of montage into the radio studio from his work in film production; Gould heard, for instance, some "very sophisticated microphone placement," which inspired his own later efforts to convey "space and proximity" in radio.[46]

This concern with the relationship between sound and physical space is one he shared with R. Murray Schafer and Marshall McLuhan. Schafer's writings—as they pertained to the World Soundscape Project (WSP)—frequently foregrounded the relationship between acoustic space and sound. The concept of the soundscape so central to Schafer's projects relied on the physical setting and its role in the acoustic experience. According to Schafer, the soundscape consisted of sounds and their relationship to "geography and climate: water, wind, forests, plains, birds, insects and animals."[47] Schafer's observations about acoustic space were not limited to the natural. He also discussed technology in terms of its impact on the soundscape and the personal sound experience.

Like Schafer, McLuhan was also influenced by the concept of space, a concept that extended into all aspects of his philosophy. Literature scholar Richard Cavell argues in his 2002 monograph that Marshall McLuhan's body of thought is best understood from a spatial understanding and that, despite McLuhan's many subjects of interest, space in all of its diverse forms is a common concept to all of them.[48] Influenced by McLuhan, Schafer regarded the radio as "extended acoustic space," though his understanding departed from McLuhan's in that for Schafer, radio technology was an interruption of natural acoustic spaces, provoking anxiety in response to its fragmentary nature.[49] Schafer envisioned sound technology—specifically, the ubiquity of sound as a result of technology—as a wall that enclosed "the individual with the familiar and excluding the enemy."[50] Reminiscent of Gould's fascination with solitude and sound recording, Schafer also expressed the idea that new technology enabled the listener to isolate one's self, shielding sonic distractions with more noise.[51]

Gould likened the modern recording process to filmmaking, particularly as it pertained to the use of multiple takes and the postproduction editing process. Defending his position that a modern musician should be free to produce his performance, he stated that if in film, "many takes are the rule, not the exception," then the same should hold true without stigma in the recording studio.[52] Gould's wishes were never fully embraced among classical musicians, but the cross-genre influences between filmmaking and sound production pushed him to think about the relationship between the perception of acoustic and spatial dimensions in his various projects in the late 1960s and early 1970s.[53] Among his conventional musical recordings, his experimentation with quadrophonic microphone placement allowed him to play with multitrack recordings and a microphone technique he called "acoustic orchestration."[54] Gould used this approach, strongly influenced by a dimensional awareness that he regarded as similar to that of a filmmaker, in his recordings of Scriabin's fifth sonata and other works by Scriabin and Sibelius.[55] Four microphones positioned around the studio allowed extreme control over the musical "shots" as a result of greater accessibility to separate tracks, giving him creative freedom to convey a new sense of space and environment.[56]

The Idea of North (1967) —
A Sonic North and a Conflicted Soundscape

For Gould, the allure of radio originated with its most basic function, to carry sound wirelessly and alert listeners to the simple pleasure of the audio experience. To overcome the challenges of reaching across Canada's geographic expanse, radio was as important to national unity as the railway, reaching the far north as well as east and west. Radio's geographical reach piqued Gould's interest, a point he reiterated in his introduction to the broadcast of *North* by the CBC Northern Services. In contrast to his more utilitarian lead-in for the national broadcast of the program, Gould waxed philosophical in his Northern Services introduction, contemplating the sensorial interface that existed in the radio-listening experience between human and machine:

> It seems to me astonishing that radio, the simplest, best and most direct means of recording our auditory impressions of the world, should have largely ignored this aspect of its function. In its desire to provide for us clear concise portraits of the events which transpire in our world, radio is perhaps by-passing its own mirror-like function.
>
> When those first fascinated listeners sat wired to their crystal sets and recognised another human voice from five miles away, it was the fact of the voice, and not the message it presented that was important . . . and access to information of news, or the weather, or any other reportage no matter how vital—was at that moment and in relation to the sensory experience of recognising another human voice, secondary.[57]

Was Gould suggesting that the themes that emerged from linguistic meaning were less important than sound itself? His attention to thematic organization and editing of the interview suggest otherwise, but Gould reveals that sound is part of the message and that the act of listening might reveal more than the words alone.

Sound and its relationship to the north has long figured into myths and identity narratives for citizens of Nordic nations. Daniel Grimley, for instance, has studied the influence of Nordic landscapes in the music of Edvard Grieg and Carl Nielsen, particularly as they pertain to concepts of nationhood. Grimley explains that Grieg has been heralded by his countrymen as a "founding father" of Norwegian music, largely because of his appeal to landscape imagery and use of folk tune material.[58] The connection between Norwegian national identity and interpretations of the land is characterized by a particular cultural trope that Grimley identifies as "a sense of remoteness and inaccessibility that serves as a symbol of perceived Norwegian isolation," not unlike the barren desolation perceived of the Canadian Arctic.[59] In the case of Nielsen, Grimley argues that the tension between an opposing idea of Danishness and modernism is "central to a proper understanding of Nielsen's life and music."[60] The land was emblematic of Nielsen's national identity and the provincial origins and rural upbringing that were central to his persona legitimized him as a result.

Like Grieg and Nielsen, Gould's relationship with the north was tied to the idea of nationhood. Aware of the powerful influence of iconic landscape images from his childhood, Gould recalled the "romanticized, art-nouveau-tinged" paintings by members of the Group of Seven that "in my day adorned virtually every second schoolroom."[61] These images, as Gould explained, forged his early associations between Canada and the land. Detecting a kinship between Gould's artistic impulse and that of Group of Seven founding member Lawren Harris, Paul Hjartarson's 1996 analysis of *North* juxtaposes Gould's documentary alongside Harris's paintings and philosophical ruminations, arguing that their commonality lies in their similarly complex perspectives on Canadian north. Hjartarson claims that they both were particularly taken with what the north represented. "For Gould, the North was less a landscape than a figure for solitude and isolation; his particular concern was the effect of solitude on those who venture north."[62]

Gould was as interested in the north as a physical place as a symbol of isolation. In a press release announcing the first broadcast of *North* Gould stated that his north was intimately bound to the idea of solitude, a theme that became the connective thread for the trilogy: "Of course I am fascinated by the look, feel and smell of the land. Because there are fewer people there, I find that my powers of observation are sharper. . . . The North has been a filter for my thoughts. Some of my clearest, sharpest thinking has been done there. The only powers you sharpen among the pacemakers, the leaders, are rhetorical powers. Decisions that shape your life are best made alone."[63] But Gould also communicated affection for the physical aspects of the north: "the look, feel and smell of the land." To Gould, the physical and the metaphysical north were inseparable concepts—two sides of the same Nordic coin. Others, such as environmental historian Peter A. Coates, have also shared this association between wilderness settings and solitude. Coates cites the 1964 Wilderness Act in his sound-centered research of environmental history, arguing that a greater awareness of sound can be of benefit to environmental historians: "Silence is an implicit ingredient of solitude and contemplative recreation, central to the definition of wilderness. The 1964 Wilderness Act refers to 'outstanding opportunities for solitude' and to 'the earth and its community of life untrammeled by man.'"[64] Much like Schafer's advocacy for preserving the wilderness for its visual beauty as well as its aural serenity, Coates implies that environmental preservation is intimately tied with the experience of silence. It seems incongruous, then, that Gould would convey his ideas about the north using his contrapuntal method. The north, a place supposedly barren and quiet, is clamorous and full of utterances in *North*—the "basso continuo" of the railway converges with a multitude of human voices and a recording of the final movement of Sibelius's Fifth Symphony.

The cacophony of voices is particularly chaotic in the opening sequence of the program. In the first three minutes, Marianne Schroeder, Robert Phillips, and Frank Vallee ruminate on their northern experiences, and Gould's contrapuntal editing reflects the dissonance of their accounts. Here, Gould constructs an exposition about the collapse of expectation, a metaphor for Gould's intentions to deconstruct this "idea" of north. The cultural trope that often emerges in discussions of the north, combining both awe and anxiety, emerges in all three voice parts; indeed, it appears in some form by all five of the characters in the documentary. Schroeder is the first to speak, blissfully recalling the north's physical vistas. She remembers her initial flight into the Arctic, only to confess that the polar bears and seals she had expected to see were absent from the landscape. Vallee's voice enters, skeptical of what he perceives as a fictional virtuous "northmanship." Phillips completes the trio, admitting the difficulty for those who have experienced the north and letting go of that enduring first impression.

Whereas in previous sonic interpretations the human presence in the north has been expressed through appropriations of Inuit language or wordless expressions of anxiety about the north's wild unpredictability, the land in its untouched state is frequently regarded as an empty, resonant space. Composers have gravitated toward high-pitched, sustained notes and minimalist techniques to depict these physical characteristics of the northern regions.[65] Gould challenges these ideas. Rather than portraying a serene Nordic landscape, his imaginary space is one of human encounter.

At once we go from hearing phrases, then words, and eventually, an incomprehensible tumult. In the sonic clutter, Gould's north is heavily populated. Gould's use of three simultaneous tape loops on the mono recording amplifies this claustrophobic spatial effect; this is especially true in contrast to Gould's subsequent radio pieces in which the stereo recording creates a sense of three-dimensional space.

Technology not only enables Gould's imagined north, it also infiltrates the soundscape itself. The aural penetration of sounds from the Muskeg Express is the setting for the narrative of Gould's encounter with Wally Maclean, the program's narrator. It also functions as a sonic signifier, neutralizing the fear that often characterizes the southerner's encounter with the Arctic. Gould referred to the constant rumble as a basso continuo and it functions similarly to its musical counterpart: the listener becomes habituated to its progression—it provides, both in terms of register and theme, a grounding for what goes on above it.

At the opening of this chapter, I proposed a connection between *North* and Schafer's concept of the soundscape. Hildegard Westerkamp, a founding member of the WSP, described the soundscape as an "intimate reflection of the social, technological, and natural conditions of an area," and Gould's contrapuntal technique might effectively be referred to, in the context of the concept, as a conflicted soundscape.[66] Although Gould probably did not completely align himself with the political stances of the members of the WSP, his interest in the practice of listening coincides with their interest in sound environments. Schafer and his colleagues turned to technological innovation, mediating sound through their practice of acoustic ecology, electroacoustic techniques such as granular synthesis, and soundscape composition. For this group of musicians and thinkers, technological mediation presented a new avenue to transform sound and challenge the very nature of their listening culture.

If Schafer were to describe Gould's fabricated soundscape, he might call it "schizophonic," that is, a collection of sonic incongruities that have little to do with one another, and no relationship within a "natural" setting. In *The Tuning of the World*, Schafer quotes Hermann Hesse from his 1927 novel *Der Steppenwolf* to illustrate the violence that characterizes schizophonic sound:

> It takes hold of some music played where you please, without distinction or discretion, lamentably distorted, to boot, and chucks it into space to land where it has no business to

> be. . . . When you listen to radio you are a witness of the everlasting war between idea and appearance, between time and eternity, between the human and the divine . . . radio . . . projects the most lovely music without regard into the impossible places, into snug drawing-rooms and attics and into the midst of chattering, guzzling, yawning and sleeping listeners, and exactly as it strips this music of its sensuous beauty, spoils and scratches and beslimes it and yet cannot altogether destroy its spirit.[67]

To Schafer, radio broadcasting is a culprit, causing a maniacal collision between foreign noises and the beautiful harmony of human sounds. Gould's contrapuntal radio is a complete rejection of Schafer's ideal, pitting voices and sounds against one another with very little effort invested in maintaining natural conversational rhythm or group dynamic. Gould does very little to unite the voices into conversational harmony. Every player speaks almost in monologue, without any indication to whom they are addressing their statements, providing an even greater sense of aural disorientation. The polyphonic voices in *North*, while seemingly contradictory to themes of solitude, silence, and the north, are instead, symptomatic of Gould's rumination on solitude. Individually, they convey the solitary nature of human contact with the north while together, they became a sonic representation of the north, encompassing Gould's obsession with solitude, enabled by radio broadcasting.

Gould continued to be fascinated with the themes of northernness and solitude even beyond his exploration in *North*. Almost fifteen years later, he planned a sound documentary that was to be included on his 1981 *Silver Jubilee Album* entitled "A Glenn Gould Fantasy," but only made it to the preliminary planning stages. As revealed in a series of primary source documents that include a track list and the script for a comic scene entitled "Hysteric Return," Gould intended to use eight tracks of music, sound, and dialogue.[68] The scene enacts a fictional scenario: his triumphant return to the concert stage on an oil-drilling rig in the Arctic region Beaufort Sea. Once again, Gould imagined himself in isolation and in the north.

Gould turned to contrapuntal technique, this time including a dense sonic collection of prerecorded sounds: the arctic wind, seagulls, splashing water, and a barking seal. CBC radio announcer Byron Rossiter describes the events, interviewing the chairman of the oil company, voiced by Gould. A restless audience joins him on the rig. Like the train sounds that rumble throughout *North*, the continuous sound of a turbine underlies in this contrapuntal mix. These sound effects provide the accompaniment to Gould's performance of the last few measures of Weber's *Konzertstück* in F Minor (he used the recording from a 1951 CBC radio broadcast of his performance). In "Hysteric Return" Gould returns to the ideas of solitude and north, exploring their connection to sound, and like *North* he fabricates a soundscape that again, curiously, interprets an environment conducive to physical isolation with a dense mix of sounds of people, animals, and machinery.

Conclusions

The year 1964 marked a significant career change for Gould when he retired from live performance and focused on the process of musical recording and radio broadcasting. The resonance Gould felt with the recording medium had ramifications beyond piano performance. The period immediately following his retirement was creatively fruitful not only with respect to his musical recordings but also in his endeavors as a radio producer and presenter.

Gould's approach to sound was inextricably linked to his philosophy of sound recording, specifically the new directions he saw in the ability to edit and splice his recordings, thereby altering the live recording and shaping the final outcome. His projects in both realms are evidence of the creative transference from musical performance to his projects in radio broadcasting. Nowhere is this intermingling of creative influence more apparent than in Gould's radio documentaries where this cross-fertilization of influences—of drama, of radio broadcasting, and musical performance and composition—bridge Gould's approach to his musical practice and his radio work. Anyssa Neumann alluded to this connection in her reading of the aesthetic of the sublime in *North*. Neumann argues that Gould's "barren, desolate" north represents a Hegelian "state of mind . . . an object whose positive body is just an embodiment of Nothing," not unlike what Bazzana described in his observation that in Gould's approach to music, "the physical aspect of music [was] subservient to the conceptual."[69] Beyond his idea of north, however, these radio works allowed Gould to apply techniques and ideas inseparable from his concept of the musical work and his role as performer and composer. Both genres of recorded sound were, in Gould's mind, very much connected.

The textual richness and musical aspects of Gould's *North* have understandably held the imagination of listeners and scholars for decades, but examining Gould's work within the realm of sound yields a new perspective on its significance as a composition and as an intellectual pursuit. Gould's interest in sound and his use of technology to execute this exploration, moreover, was contemporaneous with similar concerns within Canada's artistic community, including the World Soundscape Project and active discussions within the Toronto School of Communication. To stretch this argument further, this exploration of sound through technology could be regarded as a form of frontier exploration, not unlike the northern frontier that Steffánson braved almost one hundred years ago—though, rather than physically pursuing the physical abyss, Gould ventured further into sound—to not only hear, but also to listen.

Notes

1. Pat Pearce, "What We Can Learn from Gould's 'Aleatoric' Documentary," *Montreal Star*, 9 February 1968, Item 1979-20 42-2-2, Glenn Gould fonds, Library and Archives Canada, Ottawa.

2. Vilhjámur Steffánson, *The Friendly Arctic* (New York: Macmillan, 1921), 19–20.

3. Gould was part of a community of Canadians that included composer R. Murray Schafer and public intellectual Marshall McLuhan, who reflected in their work on the impact of radio's ubiquity on their everyday perception of sound. While Schafer's World Soundscape Project emerged from a political impulse to preserve aspects of the natural environment through the preservation of an environmental acoustics, McLuhan's interest in mediated sound was part of a larger project of understanding the role of media and its role in cultural transformation.

4. Kevin McNeilly, "Listening, Nordicity, Community: Glenn Gould's 'The Idea of North,'" *Essays on Canadian Writing* 59 (Fall 1996): 87.

5. Howard Fink, "Glenn Gould's Idea of North: The Arctic Archetype and the Creation of a Syncretic Genre," *Glenn Gould* 3, no. 2 (Fall 1997): 35–42.

6. Kevin Bazzana, *Wondrous Strange* (Toronto: McClelland & Stewart, 2003), 301.

7. Timothy Taylor, "Radio: Introduction," in *Music, Sound, and Technology in America*, ed. Timothy Taylor, Mark Katz, and Tony Grajeda (Durham, NC: Duke University Press, 2012), 238.

8. During this period an infrastructure that could support radio's popularity expanded, including the establishment of radio broadcasting stations and the growth in radio sales. Taylor, "Radio," 241.

9. David Skinner, "Divided Loyalties: The Early Development of Canada's 'Single' Broadcasting System," *Journal of Radio Studies* 85, no. 1 (May 2005): 144.

10. Geoffrey Waddington, "Music and Radio," in *Music in Canada*, ed. Ernest MacMillan (Toronto: University of Toronto, 1955), 131.

11. Interview with Robert Fulford by Rhona Bergman in Bergman, *The Idea of Gould* (Philadelphia: Lev, 1999), 9.

12. Bergman, *The Idea of Gould*, 9.

13. Robert Fulford, "Glenn Gould in the Age of Radio," *Glenn Gould* 6, no. 1 (Spring 2000): 18.

14. Barbara Frum, "Gould Documentary the Best of Ideas," *Toronto Daily Star*, 30 December 1967, 26, Item 1979-20 42-1-14, Glenn Gould fonds, Library and Archives Canada, Ottawa.

15. Glenn Gould, "Radio as Music: Glenn Gould in Conversation with John Jessop," in *The Glenn Gould Reader*, ed. Tim Page (New York: Vintage, 1990), 379.

16. See also chapter 5 in this volume, "When a Fugue Isn't a Fugue" by Anthony Cushing.

17. Robert Hurwitz, "Towards a Contrapuntal Radio," in *Glenn Gould Variations*, ed. John McGreevy (Toronto: Macmillan, 1983), 256.

18. Darrel Mansell, "Glenn Gould: The Idea of South by North," *Iowa Review* 15, no. 3 (Fall 1985): 60.

19. Richard Kostelanetz, "Glenn Gould as Radio Composer," *Massachusetts Review* 29, no. 3 (Fall 1988): 561.

20. Dan Lander, "Radiocasting: Musings on Radio and Art," in *Radio Rethink: Art, Sound, and Transmission*, ed. Diana Augaitis and Dan Lander (Banff: Walter Phillips Gallery, 1994), 13.

21. Gould, "Radio as Music," 374.

22. Gould, "Radio as Music," 380–381.

23. Cushing and Wetters question the veracity of some of these claims by Gould in chapter 7 in this volume.

24. Gould, "Radio as Music," 376.

25. Quoted in Otto Friedrich, *Glenn Gould: A Life and Variations* (New York: Random House, 1989), 204; Peter Ostwald, *Glenn Gould: The Ecstasy and Tragedy of a Genius* (New York: W. W. Norton, 1997), 231.

26. Quoted in Friedrich, *A Life*, 205, and Bazzana, *Wondrous Strange*, 300.

27. Quoted in William Littler, "The Quest for Solitude," in *Glenn Gould Variations*, ed. John McGreevy (Toronto: Macmillan Canada, 1983), 218.

28. See, for instance, François Girard's 1993 biopic *Thirty Two Short Films About Glenn Gould*, which features several scenes depicting Gould as a solitary figure in various settings: in the northern tundra, listening to music as a teenager at his family's summer cottage, contemplative and sitting alone in a room. *Thirty*

Two Short Films About Glenn Gould, DVD, directed by François Girard, Columbia TriStar Home Video, 1993; Sony Pictures, 2001.

29. Fink, "Glenn Gould's Idea of North," 37.
30. Ostwald, *The Ecstasy*, 230.
31. Mansell, "The Idea of South by North," 65.
32. Mansell, "The Idea of South by North," 61.
33. Mansell, "The Idea of South by North," 62.
34. The foremost "myth" associated with Gould concerned his sexuality, possibly fueled by speculation on the part of his colleagues and friends. See, for instance, Kazdin's reflection that Gould might be "a kind of [sexual] neuter" in Andrew Kazdin, *Glenn Gould at Work: Creative Lying* (New York: E. P. Dutton, 1989), 61. The 2008 PBS *American Masters* documentary made headlines for including an interview with Cornelia Foss, wife of American composer Lukas Foss, who described her torrid affair with Gould in the late 1960s, effectively debunking rumors that Gould was "asexual" or homosexual. See also *The Genius Within: The Inner Life of Glenn Gould*, DVD, directed by Michèle Hozer and Peter Raymont, Lorber Films, 2011. Michael Clarkson's *A Genius in Love* (Toronto: ECW Press, 2010) also aims to dispel rumors about his sexuality and personal relationships by presenting interviews from a string of former lovers and girlfriends.
35. Larry LeBlanc, "Industry Profile: Stephen Posen," in *In the Hot Seat with Larry LeBlanc*, http://www.celebrityaccess.com/members/profile.html?id=630&PHPSESSID=21hdlqtighrfqulao06p5driu1 (accessed 30 January 2013).
36. Hozer and Raymont, *The Genius Within*.
37. McNeilly, "Listening, Nordicity, Community," 88.
38. Cott wrote in his account of his professional relationship with Gould: "In 1974, I had the opportunity of talking to Gould on the telephone for six hours over a three-day period, the results of which were published as a two-part interview in *Rolling Stone* magazine. . . . It was, in fact, during these phone conversations that Gould and I became friends—the phone made it easier for the pianist to make contact and keep in touch with people he liked." Jonathan Cott, *Conversations with Glenn Gould* (Boston: Little, Brown, 1994), 23. See also Kazdin, *Creative Lying*, 29. Kazdin includes accounts of his and Gould's long telephone conversations pertaining particularly to the editing of Gould's recordings. Journalist and artist Richard Kostelanetz similarly describes Gould's insistence that he conduct his interviews over the telephone. As Kostelanetz put it, "He not only does as much business as possible by phone but he would sooner telephone his family and friends—extend himself literally into their ears—than visit them or even have them visit him." Richard Kostelanetz and Oriana Leckert, eds., *Three Canadian Geniuses* (Toronto: Colombo, 1999), 10.
39. Friedrich, *A Life*, 206.
40. Bazzana, *Wondrous Strange*, 298fn.
41. Frum, "Gould Documentary," 26.

42. Gould, "Advice to a Graduation," in *The Glenn Gould Reader*, 6–7. This anecdote is also discussed at length in Ostwald, *The Ecstasy*, 76–77.

43. For discussion about this concept, see "Media Hot and Cold" in Marshall McLuhan, *Understanding Media: The Extensions of Man* (New York: McGraw-Hill, 1964), 24–35.

44. Gould, "Radio as Music," 374. Also quoted in Geoffrey Payzant, *Glenn Gould: Music and Mind* (New York: Van Nostrand Reinhold, 1978), 134.

45. Andrew Allan, *Andrew Allan: A Self-Portrait* (Toronto: Macmillan Canada, 1974), 108–109.

46. Bazzana, *Wondrous Strange*, 302.

47. R. Murray Schafer, *The Tuning of the World* (New York: Alfred A. Knopf, 1977), 9–10.

48. Richard Cavell, *McLuhan in Space: A Cultural Geography* (Toronto: University of Toronto Press, 2002), xiii–xiv.

49. Schafer, *Tuning*, 92.

50. Schafer, *Tuning*, 93.

51. Schafer, *Tuning*, 95.

52. Glenn Gould, *The Art of Glenn Gould*, "On Records and Recording," Radio Broadcast, 13 November 1966, AIN 661113-6, CBC Radio Archive.

53. This point has also been raised by Kevin Bazzana in *Wondrous Strange*, 265.

54. Bazzana, *Wondrous Strange*, 265. As Bazzana points out, Gould sometimes referred to it as "acoustic choreography."

55. Gould released his recordings of Sibelius's Three Sonatinas (Opus 67) and *Kyllikki* in 1977 to mixed reviews. Andrew Kazdin mixed Gould's recording of Scriabin's Fifth Sonata for release in 1986 in a conventional stereo format. Kazdin reflects on the process of Gould's quadrophonic recording in his memoir, *Creative Lying*, 137–142. These Scriabin and Sibelius recordings were mastered by Paul Théberge and released in 2013 as Glenn Gould, *Acoustic Orchestrations: Works by Scriabin and Sibelius*, Sony Music B008L8OFJU.

56. Bazzana, *Wondrous Strange*, 265–266.

57. Glenn Gould, "Introduction to an Idea, CBC Northern Services," Item 1979-20 9-32, Glenn Gould fonds, Library and Archives Canada, Ottawa.

58. Incidentally, Gould claimed ancestral relation to the Norwegian composer Edvard Grieg. Bazzana, *Wondrous Strange*, 30.

59. Daniel Grimley, *Grieg: Music, Landscape and Norwegian Identity* (Woodbridge, UK: Boydell Press, 2005), 2.

60. Daniel Grimley, *Carl Nielsen and the Idea of Modernism* (Woodbridge, UK: Boydell Press, 2010), 2.

61. Gould, "'The Idea of North': An Introduction," 391.

62. Paul Hjartarson, "Inward Journeys and Interior Landscapes: Glenn Gould, Lawren Harris, and 'The Idea of North,'" *Essays on Canadian Writing* 59 (Fall 1996): 66.

63. "Glenn Gould's Idea of North," press release from CBC-FM Radio, 13 December 1967, Item 1979-20 51-13-2, Glenn Gould fonds, Library and Archives Canada, Ottawa.

64. Peter A. Coates, "The Strange Stillness of the Past: Toward an Environmental History of Sound and Noise," *Environmental History* 10, no. 4 (October 2005): 649.

65. Among orchestral repertoire, especially by Canadian composers, examples include John Weinzweig's *Edge of the World* (1946), the opening to the first movement of Harry Somers's *North Country* (1948), and Harry Freedman's *Tableau* (1952). More recently, several jazz artists have become associated with a "Nordic sound," including Norwegian saxophonist Jan Garbarek, Swedish pianist Jan Johansson, Norwegian trumpeter Nils Petter Molvær, and other recording artists associated with the ECM record label.

66. Hildegard Westerkamp, "Bauhaus and Soundscape Studies—Exploring Connections and Differences," lecture delivered at the Goethe Institut Tokyo, October 1994, https://hildegardwesterkamp.ca/writings/writings-by/?post_id=16&title=%E2%80%8Bbauhaus-and-soundscape-studies—-exploring-connections-and-differences- (last accessed 30 September 2024).

67. Schafer, *Tuning*, 92.

68. Some of this material was printed in the journal *Glenn Gould*. "'Glenn Gould's Hysteric Return': A Recently Recovered Manuscript from the Library and Archives Canada," *Glenn Gould* 12, no. 2 (Fall 2007): 56–57.

69. Anyssa Neumann, "Ideas of North: Glenn Gould and the Aesthetic of the Sublime." *voiceXchange* 5, no. 1 (Fall 2011): 39.

2

Glenn Gould and the Non-Imagined North

Jeffrey van den Scott

For Glenn Gould, *The Idea of North* served as a vehicle to explore the human condition, highlighting the solitude and remoteness that he valued in his own life. Each of the work's five interviewees lived in the Canadian north for some period prior to Gould's intervention in their lives. Within the program and in archival documents, they each express aspects of the remote, isolated existence Gould associated with this region. While the voices overlap and intertwine, fading in and out, clear statements resound, defining the character of the north and its people. Each interviewee, however, is a "southerner," one who goes *to* the north. Colonial attitudes prevail throughout much of the work. Gould himself uses the north to his own end, joining a long line of southerners before and after him who exploit the region with little attention paid to the interests (or existence) of the Indigenous Inuit populations. By carefully choosing excerpts of the interview transcripts to include in *North*, Gould created contradictions about the north and helped to cement enduring stereotypes of Inuit.

North exclusively contains the voices of those who go north by choice and lacks the voices of those who live their entire lives there. Including an Inuit voice is, despite Gould's fascination with "the Eskimo," outside the scope of his philosophical exploration of the Canadian north—a representation closely aligned with his comment: "It was a program about the Canadian North, ostensibly. What it was really about . . . was 'the dark night of the human soul.' It was a very dour essay on the effects of isolation upon mankind."¹ While Gould "never pretended to offer indigenous perspectives of the North and Northerners,"² he does present a view on the Inuit from the south. He weaves the interviewees' words to create a portrait of "The Eskimo" when Inuit culture was just beginning the planned change from nomadic life to life in settlements.³

In this chapter, I consider the implications of the missing Indigenous voice in Gould's *North*. The north characterized in the documentary is far removed from the daily experience of those whose lives are bound inextricably to this non-imagined, and not always isolated, place. I reflect briefly on Gould's role in Canadian nationhood, in particular this work's presentation of nationalist sentiments in the centennial year, including the use of auto-exoticism as a marker of Canadian identity. My central discussion explores Gould's presentation and characterization of the Inuit (the Eskimo).⁴ I focus my discussion particularly on *North*'s "Dining Car" scene, the moment when Inuit issues come to the fore. The very presence of an Indigenous population problematizes Gould's choice to characterize the north as a place of solitude. Finally, I draw on my own fieldwork in Nunavut to reflect an Indigenous northern voice in this discourse. My informants highlight the problems of misrepresentation, demonstrating that Gould's imaginary north is an impossibility for the inhabitants who live in its reality. Gould's north is completely fictitious, so the actuality of a nonfictive north is problematic to the entirety of *North* as understood fifty years later. Gould's *Idea of North* continues to be celebrated for its portrayal of isolated living, contrary to the experiences of so many Inuit, thus perpetuating stereotypes of northern life for *North*'s audiences.

Glenn Gould and Canadian Nationalism

Gould's legacy places him as a national figure in Canada and one of the country's most well-known musicians. Ten years into his concert career, conductor Ettore Mazzoleni points to the need to assert Gould's uniquely Canadian character: "Glenn Gould, surely one of the most remarkable of young musicians and pianists, was trained entirely in this country. For some time he has confined his performances to this country. In Canada we have a basic distrust of our own ability to produce anything really outstanding, and as a result we either pay the artist a wholly meaningless and harmful lip-service or treat him with condescension until he has been accepted in New York or London or Paris."⁵ After Gould's retirement from public concerts, he remained an institution of sorts, as noted by Gilles Potvin: "Even if, for a few years now, his admirers have no longer been able to applaud him as a result of the premature retirement which he has imposed upon himself, they can console themselves by listening to his numerous records, by watching him on television or by reading his articles in the leading magazines."⁶ Through his recordings and relationship with the microphone, Gould became a legendary figure in his own right, not only for his skill as a pianist and his poignant writing, but as a mystical artistic hermit. The attraction to the isolated, solitary life still fuels the Gould myth, parallel to the myth of the Canadian north. Gould found solace in solitude through the twin media of radio and recording. He explains:

> In January 1950, I took part for the first time in a CBC broadcast and made a discovery that influenced in a most profound way my development as a musician. I discovered that in the privacy, the solitude, the womb-like security (Freudians, stand clear!) of the studio it was possible to make music in a more direct, more personal manner than any concert hall would ever permit. I fell in love with broadcasting that day, and I have not since been able to think of the potential of music (or for that matter of my own potential as a musician) without some reference to the limitless possibilities of the broadcasting and/ or recording medium.⁷

Like Gould, *North* contributes to the intellectual and public discourse on the role of the north in Canadian mythology, a role that garnered increasing attention at the time of the Canadian centennial celebrations in 1967. While the program premiered late in the year, in retrospect *North* and the ideals it represents recur regularly in Canadian scholarship fifty years later. The title, too, is co-opted for two significant monographs on the geographic north generally and on Canadian culture more specifically.⁸ But, as Gould acknowledges, it is not *the* north that serves as the topic or goal of this program, but the *idea* of north—an idea that, for Gould, links the north with the condition of solitude. Gould contemplates his link between north and isolation in the introduction to the documentary, which he wrote for the CBC's Northern Services broadcast:

> In the end, however, this programme is not about techniques which have gone into its making. It is no matter how metaphorically treated, about the North, or about the experience of isolation which the North helps us to understand. It is inevitably limited by being a southerner's nostalgic look at the north, and despite all attempts to give it balance and ballast it is perhaps handicapped by that envy with which we in the South who think about the fascinating contradictions of a social being who voluntarily seeks a situation which superficially at least minimizes the responsibilities of society, regard those of you who reside in Northern Canada.
>
> This may well seem an odd and naïve thing to say, especially since for those of you who will hear this programme on the Northern Services outlets, an envy of the comforts and facilities offered by life in the South is a more accustomed state, but bringing together just such disparite [sic] views is what this programme was meant to do and if we can just find a form which would harness in some viable way that mutual envy of ours, think what contrapuntal radio that could make.[9]

Here, Gould acknowledges some of his limitations; namely, that *North* represents a southern gaze and the experience of isolation is his focus. But he also overlooks several limitations in his statement. Most directly, he admits that his concern is with southerners who voluntarily seek this situation, thus marginalizing (before the work even begins) the experience of an Indigenous population who did not choose their life in the north. Gould's elision is made easier by the fact that this part of the country's population already exists at the margins of political discourse while simultaneously residing at the geographic margins.[10] By the time *North* aired, several notable works had appeared based on the experiences of southerners living among Inuit populations, including Farley Mowat's *People of the Deer* (1952) and Edward Keithahn's *Eskimo Adventure* (1963). Duncan Pryde's *Nunaga: Ten Years of Eskimo Life* was not published until 1972, but the author's story begins with the trek to Baker Lake in 1958. Gould's work ultimately plays into the discourse of these southerners' exploration of the north for their own benefit—a stance that still contributes to the exoticization of the region. In essence, this exoticization is simultaneously intensified through a process of auto-exoticism because southerners present the north as an element of Canadianness—the north distinguishes

Canada from its southern neighbor. Gould's draft for *North* includes a section titled "The Deromantizing North [*sic*],"[11] but his efforts to this effect achieve the opposite; Gould creates the north he wants, values, and subsequently romanticizes: the solitary north.

Auto-Exoticism

Despite Gould's claimed efforts to deromanticize the north, the program serves rather to auto-exoticize Canada's northern regions. While in many cases auto-exoticism involves marketing one's own culture so that it is attractive to another, Gould's auto-exoticism marks a "psychological condition" in which he privileges isolation and suggests this as an ideal moral state not only for himself but for any upstanding Canadian.[12]

Sherrill Grace, in *Canada and the Idea of North*, succinctly points to Gould's north as a southern creation and exposes the problems exoticized through this lens: "Inevitably each 'character' turns to the question of the relationship of the North to the rest of Canada, to the idea of nation, and to the way the North shapes the southern individual who goes there. These reflections flow smoothly into observations about some of the harsh realities of the North—poverty, alcoholism, starvation, racism, and sexism."[13] Grace argues that Gould's idea of the north—and even the idea of Canada—is a white idea proffered by Euro-Canadians, and it is thus a singularly Euro-Canadian Utopia. She nevertheless concedes: "Gould's North is, in fact, contrapuntal and multiple, just as are the voices that we hear. These refuse to be reduced or distilled to a single vision, a unifying idea, or a master narrative, despite the apparently privileged voice of one of the speakers [Wally Maclean]."[14] Yet, the disparate voices do offer a homogenous vision—that of the southerner (or Westerner). The privileged voice is not Wally Maclean, as Grace suggests, but rather Gould himself, proclaiming the all-encompassing views of the south over the Canadian north. As is frequently noted in the present volume, Gould presents his thesis through the accumulation of voices. Using the selected words of his interviewees, Gould exoticizes the north as a place for his imagination but keeps it close, as though in his backyard. Grace's "harsh realities of the North" are significant: for Gould, the problems ("poverty, alcoholism, starvation, racism, and sexism") are obstacles to be overcome by southerners, but he never admits the possibility that they may be caused by the colonial activities of the south. I discuss those realities later in considering

Gould's "Eskimo." Gould emphasizes solitude while minimizing perceived Inuit "problems" such as sexism and racism, even if his audio production techniques, including layering voices for "contrapuntal radio" may suggest a clamorous and noisy north.[15]

Even the term "north" has a peculiar resonance for Gould, when viewed from his perspective as a Torontonian. Geoffrey Payzant, Gould's first biographer, notes, "Torontonians use the expression 'up north' in a special way."[16] Uptergrove, near Orillia on Lake Simcoe, represents "cottage country" a mere one-hundred-minute drive north of Toronto, where cottages are too close for isolation. Payzant continues: "There is not much real solitude there."[17] "North," in this context, means vacation, relaxation, and quiet but not necessarily isolation. Gould, rather than drawing on his own experience of solitude, seeks his interviewees' experience of solitude. In doing so, he conflates their experiences as southerners in the north with the isolation he sought but could not find in either Toronto or cottage country. As such, Gould needed to press his search for solitude farther to the north.

Gould's choice of the last movement of Sibelius's Fifth Symphony for the closing minutes of *North* universalizes this region, by suggesting an allegiance with Scandinavia. Payzant tells us that, for Gould, this symphony is the musical equivalent of independent northern living and that part of this association is the correlation of "northerliness with moral rectitude."[18] Payzant quotes a 1974 article written by Gould in which he "equates 'separation from the world' with latitude: the higher the latitude the greater the degree of separation or isolation."[19] By drawing on a Scandinavian composer, whose works often reference Finnish mythology, Gould builds on pan-northern themes described by Anka Ryall and colleagues as "arcticism," in the vein of Edward Said's *Orientalism*.[20] Said's work discusses the Orient as having "a special place in European Western experience."[21] Through his concept of "orientalism," Said identifies a "distribution of geopolitical awareness into aesthetic, scholarly, economic, sociological, historical, and philological texts" as a means to "control, manipulate, even to incorporate, what is a manifestly different (or alternative or novel) world."[22] In short, Said claims that Western interests, be they scholarly, political, and so forth, present a patronizing and romanticized view of the Orient that is bound to processes of imperialism. Ryall and colleagues advance similar claims in discussing the north. Like the Orient, which has "less to do with the Orient than it does with 'our world,'" the southern view of the Arctic is filled with self-perpetuating tropes, usually as an isolated paradise, or an icy wasteland.²³ While the latter trope bears the weight of truth—there are large swaths of uninhabited lands to the north—in arcticist manifestations, the trope presents a heightened version of the truth through the eye of the southern imagination.

By placing his "polylogue" (Grace's term) or contrapuntal radio (Gould's term) within the psychological condition of solitude and the geographic north, Gould brings listeners to his ideal north: an empty and isolated space leading to what Gould might consider the paradise of solitude. This characterization is troublesome in that, while these spaces exist, Gould and his participants spent their time living with native populations in these northern reaches; Gould largely ignores this fact in his presentation, even though the interviewees regularly mention their living circumstances. Gould and his participants present a view of the Inuit population through this southern gaze, particularly in the fourth scene (per Cushing's formal breakdown of the work included in the appendix), labeled in archival documents simply as "The Eskimo."²⁴

Gould and "The Eskimo"

Through Gould's choices as an interviewer and editor, he presents Canada's northern Indigenous population entirely through the voices of his interviewees. Gould leaves us with a portrayal filled with colonial attitudes that describe "the Eskimo" as extremely patriarchal and slow to adopt Western ways; the trope of the noble savage, skilled at hunting and survival in the harshest of conditions, flows throughout.

Gould's interviewees regularly refer to the Indigenous inhabitants of the north, "the Eskimo," in the singular. Further, they let the masculine pronoun, him, stand in for the group. Privileging the male and coloring Inuit culture as patriarchal does not entirely correlate with historical records and oral history. In 2004, John Bennett and Susan Rowley compiled and edited *Uqalurait: An Oral History of Nunavut* from sources including the publications of explorers such as Knud Rasmussen, government documents, and Inuit sources such as articles in *Inuktitut* magazine, local historical societies, and publications of Nunavut Arctic College. I do not suggest that traditional Inuit roles were ungendered; rather Gould and his interviewees perhaps missed the subtleties of these roles. The conspicuous deficit of a female presence in the interviewees' discussions of "the Eskimo" further heightens the suggestion of solitude, particularly for the male participants who might miss the presence of family, or of unattached women, while stationed in the north.

Marianne Schroeder, a nurse and the only woman among Gould's interviewees, provides some interesting insight, although much of her speech was obscured in the editing room. Gould uses her voice to present the gendered "Eskimo" in scene 4. Her voice figures prominently at 38:36 in *North*, just long enough for the following phrase to stand out: "because the Eskimo society is definitely a patriarchial [sic] one."[25] Gould features her voice again a minute later (39:46): "The man is definitely the head of the household . . . the head of the society. A woman is only a woman. She has to stay in the background and never do you find a woman under those circumstances in a position of authority. [At this point in the recording, Schroeder's voice disappears into the background, obscuring what follows.] So this was extremely difficult for a man to accept. We had an Eskimo employee who was sometimes rather resentful."[26] In the obscured speech, Schroeder refers to Inuit men having difficulty following orders from women, based on her own experience as a woman in a position of authority. At the time, many southern women went north to follow and support a husband; as a single female, Schroeder was an anomaly. Despite a difference of four decades between Schroeder's experience of the north and my own, Gould's manipulation of her interview resonates with events I witnessed. It also speaks to powerful stereotypes of Inuit driven by lingering colonial attitudes.

The power structure within Gould's gendered society contrasts with material presented by Inuit voices in the volume *Uqalurait*. Stories recorded before, during, and after Gould's work show a more fluid view of gender roles in Inuit social life. While these roles often relate to outdoor and indoor work, Bennett and Rowley share more subtle differences, demonstrating these roles as parallel and integrated rather than one serving the other:

> Although children often acquired other skills, their gender determined the nature of their education. Boys . . . learned the skills of the outdoors: hunting, travelling, making tools and other equipment, and so on. Girls . . . learned the *complementary skills* of the home: preparing skins, making clothing, tents and *qajaq* coverings, and the like. Once their sons and daughters knew the basics—and had an *equally competent* spouse—parents could be confident that their children had what they needed to begin making their own way in the world.[27]

Note the attention to phrasings that mark the shared partnership of men's and women's work. The "complementary skills" and "equally competent" spouse reflect power-sharing rather than the woman staying in the background. Furthermore, these roles were not and are not absolute. Inuit society appreciated and supported dissolving these boundaries. In 1979, James Muckpah, an elder from the Pond Inlet area of northern Baffin Island, commented:

> Sometimes if a girl had often gone hunting with her father at an early age, she would be as capable a hunter as any man. *She would also be respected* as such. . . . Some men also were good at sewing and could do housework themselves. They would reach the same level of skill as any good woman. So, a woman could catch a seal as well as a man, and a man could do housework as well as a woman. This was not considered bad at all. As a matter of fact, *it was considered all for the good*.[28]

Muckpah recollects a story from his childhood that preceded the northern intervention of Gould's interviewees. During my time in Arviat, Nunavut, from 2004 to 2014, I witnessed female hunters admired by others for their abilities and men who took on the domestic responsibilities of sewing and child-rearing who also earned peer respect. This could be attributed to recent changes in gender roles, but Muckpah's story suggests a longer trend of fluidity in gendered work roles. While I witnessed these role reversals, the introduction of permanent housing perpetuates Schroeder's view, as the traditionally feminine roles were relegated to indoor, back rooms, out of the public view. Conversely, men's roles were on display in the community.[29] In the previous nomadic life, lived in igloos and tents, gendered roles were treated more equally, each done publicly.

Gould's male interviewees also failed to mention Inuit women during their interviews, which reinforced the idea of a masculine society. It may be that they simply did not pay attention to female Inuit. Their oversight highlights this aspect of their northern gaze. Some notable selections from *North* underscore these views. James Lotz, the "anthropologist and geographer," overlaps voices with Schroeder during "the Eskimo" scene. His voice wavers in his characterization of "the Eskimo." He speaks regularly to the singular, masculine "Eskimo" with phrases like, "if we can only look on him as a sort of human being," which, while couched in a discussion of admiration, Gould presents in the voice he describes as that of the "limitless capacity for disillusionment."[30] Lotz's voice in combination with this description of his role in the documentary raises questions of the authenticity of this admiration; are Inuit truly worthy subjects for admiration or merely another source of disillusionment in the north?

Western Administration and Leadership

The colonial attitudes of Gould's interviewees emerge most strongly when referencing Western institutions, such as government and even settled living, despite their best efforts to critically examine these views. Consider Frank Vallee, the "cynic," a sociologist who opens a more extensive discussion of the Eskimo in the interview transcript but is not present in *North* itself:[31]

> It was said it wasn't in their nature to work in the mines . . . *it wasn't in their nature to observe the time schedules that we have* and so on and so I found it fascinating to actually live in that community for 3 or 4 weeks, while it was the centre of controversy among those people who engage in the art of Northmanship . . . debates that is about the souls and culture of the Eskimos are to be saved.[32]

Several voices present the idea that certain southern habits and customs are "not in their nature." Robert Phillips, a bureaucrat with the Ministry of Northern Affairs, addresses the prevailing allusion that the Eskimo are unprepared to adapt to a southern and cosmopolitan lifestyle. His voice overlaps with Vallee's preceding quote, "we've often tended to do a dis-service to Northerners . . . by *putting them in places they shouldn't quite be.*"[33] Specifically, Phillips references committee work and challenges the notion of affirmative action, such as including the native population in decision-making processes in the name of addressing discrimination. For him this negative consequence of a paternal attitude trumps good intentions.

> By having on your Board of Directors . . . a tame Negro or a tame female or a tame Indian. . . . It comes from the noblest of motives, the very absence of racial prejudice but there is behind it a sort of . . . paternalism. We tend to say look . . . we're terribly good fellows and broadminded we whites, and we do

want to turn things over to you Eskimos so come and sit on our Board so to speak. . . . And then there's such a tendency for the . . . the Eskimo, the Northern Indian to be a kind of showpiece . . . and this doesn't do anybody any good.[34]

Gould and his interviewees also ascribe to "the Eskimo" an inability to adhere to Western conventions of time and scheduling. Beyond the imposition of a definite colonial approach to how Inuit *should* spent their time, this dismissal of Inuit as frustrating and without a concept of time voids any potential Inuit agency in using time to fight this very imposition of colonial time.[35]

In her interview transcript, Schroeder describes the frustration of locals seeking medical attention at all times of day: "You are in that station and when somebody knocks at the door you go and answer it regardless of what time it is. This of course was one of the frustrating things, because the Eskimos just didn't seem to have any conception of time."[36] The notion that "Eskimos [don't] seem to have any conception of time" suggests that the Eskimo should conform to a westernized schedule, and Schroeder places responsibility for adaptation on the shoulders of the Eskimo. Phillips, in the preceding quotation, recognizes this conflicting juxtaposition, and in the elided section of the quote, he comments on the number of people who watch the "tame" Eskimo, thinking, "he doesn't know anything, how can he contribute?"

The entire framework of Western leadership and administration was foisted on this population within the period that Schroeder and the other interviewees worked in the north, with no expectation for the Western administration to adapt themselves to Inuit culture. It was a period that an attitude of "helping the Eskimo" was prevalent, but as Schroeder herself—a naïve young woman just out of nursing school—notes in *North*, it was she herself who was "more in need of help . . . than anyone."[37] Inuit resist the idea of the nine-to-five work day and practice their "informal time" (required of a life of sustenance living) whenever possible as a means of resisting the imposed framework.[38]

Colonial attitudes and institutionalized racism still pervade Nunavut's healthcare system. Stories of staff refusing to see Inuit patients or respond to after-hours emergencies are common. A high-profile case from November 2014 addressed the difficulties faced by territorial residents in accessing healthcare. In a case in Cape Dorset, on Southampton Island, a nurse was alleged to have refused to treat an infant following a late-night telephone call from the mother. Regulations state explicitly that on-call nurses must open the health center after hours for cases involving children under the age of two. The nurse advised the family to give the child a bath and report back in the morning. The infant died hours later. The nurse admitted to wrongdoing two years after public knowledge of the case.[39] Admittedly, I do not present a fair comparison to Schroeder's case. Schroeder makes no mention of an emergency. However, the case demonstrates that colonial attitudes and stereotypes have continued since *North*: "the Eskimo" is somehow ill-prepared to attend to health problems, or to understand Western constructs of time management. Schroeder's comments may not indicate quite so deep a problem as this case, but they do, in Gould's presentation, use the same racialized and alienating language.

One reason why Inuit have been seen as stubborn is their resistance to submitting to government assistance and integration programs. Vallee identifies the early signs of "the Eskimo" fitting into "settlement living." This was a government goal evidenced in the 1972 report "Eskimo Housing as Planned Culture Change" by the Northern Science Research Group of the Department of Indian Affairs and Northern Development.[40]

> The people who have committed themselves to settlement living, and particularly those who have received more than let's say a grade 5 education which is equivalent to a university degree in the Arctic . . . these people are becoming keys in the networks of communication in the North. The outsider has to . . . pass through the screen of these people . . . to get at the others . . . and . . . these are the people who're becoming conscious of being not only members of a settlement or members of a given band but are conscious of being Eskimo as contrasted with White.[41]

Vallee uses the term "nationalists" to describe those Inuit who have a basic education, act as gatekeepers to "the Eskimo," and provide access to the larger population; they were and remain a small part of the population. In my ethnomusicological study of music in Arviat, Nunavut, there are a small number of Elders with the capacity to organize a community. Drum dances, where people gather to sing and dance to songs that contain the oral history of the Inuit, were once commonplace. In 2004, my first year living in Arviat, the community held drum dances monthly, sometimes several times per week. On a research trip in the winter of 2013–2014, one of the Elders who organized these events passed away, and another was ill. It was the first time during a ten-year period in which I was unable to participate in a drum dance. This illustrates that the preservation of traditional practices relies to a great extent on a few dedicated community members. Additionally, the education system pays Elders to teach traditional skills (such as the song repertoire) in the schools. As a result, traditional knowledge becomes a commodity that has only a tenuous connection to the members of the community who may be more focused on daily activities.[42]

Vallee describes some of the acculturation methods used in Inuit communities. The church, trading posts, and health centers each play a role in changing Inuit culture. The new settlement life ensnared the Eskimo with church services or by requiring him to take an English name to perform official tasks or to buy bullets for his rifle. Vallee, however, warns of the loss of Inuit identity through settlement: "As to playing a concrete role . . . which ties you to the settlement, that's a different matter, then you get identified with the networks . . . in the settlement . . . and to the extent you do that, so much of your selfhood is given to the life there."[43] The loss of selfhood reflects the federal government's planned cultural shift from a nomadic to settled life among Inuit.[44] Whereas the fallout of a problematic residential school system and decaying reservations are major concerns for many of Canada's First Nations populations—and subject to great efforts toward reconciliation in political rhetoric—the Inuit case is distinct and different in notable ways. Inuit were nomadic peoples who, in the central Arctic that Gould focuses on by evoking Churchill, were forcibly relocated into communities dotting the arctic shorelines in the 1950s. For some, this included relearning hunting patterns in new areas, sometimes hundreds or thousands of kilometers from their ancestral lands. What Gould attempted to address—the possibility of isolated living and solitude—is impossible. Instead, the north would be better represented by communities of cohabiting people that usurp smaller family units and clans. Rather than traveling in groups of tens, they reside in hamlets of hundreds—or thousands. Vallee articulates a fear that these conditions could lead to a changing Inuit identity: "They don't want to get themselves locked into dependency situations with them. It's almost as if they fear some inner core of selfhood or something would be lost."[45]

Despite Vallee's acknowledging the fear of identity loss among Inuit populations, Phillips's lone voice closes the discussion of the Eskimo in the dining car scene with a reminder of the work still needed to bring "the Eskimo" up to the standards of the governing Western institutions: "We used to say in the early days of the new administration . . . that our work would in effect show signs of success . . . when for the first time an Eskimo stood up and said 'no.'"[46] Gould excerpted this comment from a longer quotation, which builds a little more context. In the interview transcript, Phillips goes into more detail on the goal of "revolution" in the state of "the Eskimo." He also preaches the importance of patience on behalf of those trying to instill this revolution. "We want to see them be real citizens, no longer just a kind of well, a practical ward, although theoretically they have full rights of citizenship. We used to say in the early days of the new administration that our work would in effect show signs of success when for the first time an Eskimo stood up and said 'no.'"[47] Phillips emphasizes the problematic human side of the north—in the interview transcript he discusses the "ugliness" of tuberculosis.[48] As he discusses his hope that "the Eskimo" will accept the full rights and responsibilities of citizenship, Phillips also invokes long-standing tropes of aboriginal peoples, and thus of the north: the noble savage.

Admiration and the "Noble Savage" Trope

The trope of the noble savage persists in the West particularly when one looks to its others, be it the Orient, the Western Frontier of the United States, or in this case the Northern Frontier of Canada. The idea of a frontier is the necessary pretext for colonization (or imperialism)—the land is either empty or not being used in ways that are worthy of consideration—and marginalization of local, Indigenous populations, as in American westward expansion. Phillips articulates the idea of frontiers most succinctly. He contrasts the then-current Canadian north to the historic American west: "There's a wonderful cliché, which I hope I may be forgiven for mentioning once more, that a nation is great only so long as it has a frontier. Now we've got that frontier. Other people are nostalgically having to dip back a hundred years to find their frontier and vicariously become part of it—we've got it."[49] Jim Lotz most clearly articulates the admiration and sense of wonder that situates "the Eskimo" in the noble savage trope:

> I'm inclined to think if we will only look at the Eskimo, not as the quaint funny little . . . hunter or as an artist or all those

ghastly clichés that clutter up our literature . . . and if we can only look on him as a sort of human being . . . and adapt some of his ways of doing things . . . his culture, his values . . . for instance in child rearing, permissiveness rather than authoritarianism . . . a sense of community . . . rather than a sense of individualism.[50]

By contextualizing Lotz this way, Gould develops a sense of drama between Lotz's admiration and Phillips, Vallee, and Schroeder's respective ideas about the perceived trouble of Inuit adaptation to Western institutions. In the first section of Lotz's interview transcript, the excerpt of which Gould places in the dining car scene, he discusses the survival of "the Eskimo" and challenges elements of the trope, like the hunter-gatherer. He suggests that "we," the West, also have something to learn from "the Eskimo," rather than focusing on the ways in which "the Eskimo" resists adaptation to "his" new culture.

Lotz also examines reception of "the Eskimo" and the public image in Canada as a whole. He expresses Canadians' strong admiration for Inuit, built, he claims, not on stereotype but on the ability to survive in harsh conditions.[51] And yet, stereotypes persist in the Western portrayals of Inuit.

Inuit culture remains on display for international consumption, most visibly in the form of the Inuksuk—stone cairns in the shape of humans that served as markers across the Arctic. The 2010 Vancouver Olympics chose the Inuksuk as the official logo, and Inuksuit (the plural form of Inuksuk) are available in gift shops across the country engraved with "Calgary, Canada" or "Niagara Falls"—cities with no historic relationship to Inuit.[52] In November 2015, a fashion designer based in the United Kingdom courted controversy by using a design from a well-known, sacred Inuit shaman's jacket.[53] The designer appropriated the patterns without consultation of the shaman's family. These examples, which remove Inuit culture from its context, demonstrate that in contrast to what Lotz may have hoped in 1967, Inuit are more stereotyped than ever, reduced by the south to a series of artifacts and re-creations without reference to a vital, living culture.

Lotz admires Inuit capacity for survival in isolation, suggesting they would be ideal for sending to the moon. He also proposes that "the Eskimo" could be placed into positions of influence, particularly in education, where he could tell life "as it really was in the past and how it has changed . . . rather than this second-hand Gutenberg gibberish," in reference to whitewashed, out-of-date histories of the printed word.[54]

Phillips offers his own views that break from the trope of the noble savage. For him, the elements that we celebrate today made "the Eskimo" un-Canadian. Canadian life is defined by the south, by places like Gould's Toronto home. Those aspects of Inuit living, however exotic and appealing, are not "Canadian" because they do not conform to living standards deemed acceptable in the south. For Phillips, the treatment of Canada's Indigenous populations is no worse than anywhere else and he states that we should not judge the actions of the past by morality of today:

> We weren't any nastier to the native peoples *there* . . . than we were to the rest of the world. But for today . . . it's not good enough to treat . . . native peoples as native with that kind of snarl in our voice or that kind of paternalism in our voice either. These are Canadian citizens and let's face it, the igloo . . . is not a part of Canadian life, because the life expectancy of 27 years . . . isn't part of Canadian life.[55]

Note Phillips's use of "there" rather than "then" to discuss the treatment of Indigenous America, separating his past temporally and geographically from his present, and from Canadian life.

Ultimately, as Gould notes, *North* is not about the north itself, but the solitary life and imagined isolation in that region. As a result, he partakes of myth, the noble savage trope, uses it to *evoke* the solitude he so valued, because Gould's work fundamentally disavows actuality in favor of ideas.

The Solitary North

In discussing his "characters," Gould reasons that each of his interviewees experienced isolation while living in the north, but also that their isolation was an attractive feature of northern life: "The five people we used as characters in this play-documentary were all people who had experienced isolation in some very special way, and had things to say about it. By the time we were about half-way through that hour, we had a fair notion as to which aspect of isolation had attracted each of them."[56] Despite Gould's projected impression, even a cursory examination of transcripts reveals isolation did not emerge as a theme during interviews with his participants. In the interview guide Gould uses with Lotz and Maclean, we see that Gould elicited mention of the experience of isolation through direct questions. His guides show a series of leading questions in which Gould asks directly about aspects of solitary life. Gould does not ask about the *advantages* of solitary living, as these are likely self-evident. During the Lotz interview, Gould asks:

> Do you or did you while in the north or indeed at any other times in your life think of yourself as solitary? . . .
>
> What aspects of the solitary life attract you—what are its disadvantages? . . .
>
> What type of solitary (kabloona) division is attracted to the north? Are there special characteristics of the Eskimo that would relate to the solitary experience / Does the Eskimo in fact change his spots depending on the extent of his . . . ?[57]

Each question presumes that Lotz was attracted to the north for its solitude, rather than for the vocational opportunity afforded him. Furthermore, Gould asks of the Inuit relationship with solitude during the period when they were forced into communities. In that respect, the relocation removed an aspect of physical solitude. Talking to his "narrator," longtime northern resident Wally Maclean, Gould asks similar questions, adding one that equates environment with solitary life: "One can appear to lead a very solitary life in a megalopolis. Does the true solitary search out an environment—any atmosphere—that accords with his personality in some fashion?"[58] The questions expose Gould's own experience and affection for solitude. He actualizes his interior in the form of the north and mediated through radio. Darrel Mansell, now professor emeritus of English at Dartmouth College, offers: "That solitary, strange, cold, cerebral genius had found a way to carry on a passionate friendship, a shy romance, with the sprawling, unkempt, bustling world outside, *though he'd probably never go there*: the blandishments the world had for him, his for it, going back and forth for the most part through a thin wire."[59] Mansell points out that Gould did not travel to the north—the train to Churchill, a bustling military town and port at the time of the documentary, was the closest he went. For Gould, however, it was far enough to give him a taste of northern life, but there was a deeper need that fueled his desire for solitude. Geoffrey Payzant draws a connection between Gould's quest for solitude and Immanuel Kant's ideas of the sublime. In order to be heroic, one needs to be self-sufficient. For Kant, "to be sufficient for oneself, and consequently to have no need of society, without at the same time being unsociable, i.e., without flying from it, is something bordering on the sublime, as is any dispensing with wants."[60] Payzant argues that this stands against Canadian culture, in which musicians and artists are not self-sufficient but need to compete, at all times, against each other.[61] Self-sufficiency, and thus solitude, is a requirement for Gould: "Solitude is the prerequisite for ecstatic experience, especially the experience most valued by the post-Wagnerian artist—the condition of heroism. One can't feel oneself heroic without having first been cast off by the world, or perhaps by having done the casting-off oneself."[62] Kant, of course, wished to avoid being unsociable while Gould advocates casting off from society to be valued as an artist-hero. The progression from mythical "Eskimo" (the noble savage) to an integrated member of Canadian society mirrors this dichotomy between heroic isolation and nonheroic community. In both cases, a mythical ideal is played against a less-glamorous reality.

Phillips offered his perspective on solitude in the north in two excerpts that Gould did not include in the final edit of *North*. He stressed the importance of trying to get involved with his northern community and, further, the difficulties he encountered. The following excerpts appear at different locations in the Phillips interview transcript,[63] but Gould pieced them together in a document titled "Exclusions."

> If you don't become partners with the rest of society in this extraordinarily remote and self-centered little village then you have to live entirely on your own. You may think you're strong enough to live on your own and if you lived in an igloo really a thousand miles from nowhere you might live on your own but you can't live on your own with twenty neighbors. I don't want to claim to be an authority on the kind of personality and profile of an arctic village because I have never lived there. I've travelled a very great deal but I can never be anything but an outsider.[64]

Phillips undermines Gould's idea of casting oneself off—Phillips's own sense of isolation is personal, not related to physically removing oneself from the company of others. To him, isolated living can be advantageous, but yet again, isolation in the north is something to be achieved only as an outsider to that community.

As I have stated, each of Gould's interviewees was an outsider to the northern community. The essence of *North* is from this perspective—the south looking north—and this is why it represents an *idea* but not the actual north. In the closing section of this chapter, I wish to approach the idea of solitude in the north from an insider's perspective, using the words and experiences of Inuit who have lived their entire lives in the north.

Filling a Void: Northern Voices of Today

While today's Inuit experience varies greatly from what the interviewees observed a half-century ago, Gould's work made a significant impression on the Canadian imagination of the north. As such, introducing the small sampling of Inuit voices helps communicate the impact of such mythologizing and its profound effect on the Indigenous population.

My fieldwork in the hamlet of Arviat, Nunavut, the first town north of Churchill along the coast of Hudson Bay, reveals a starkly different view of the north. While I do not suggest that I can offer a true insider perspective, I hope that through the voices of my research participants, I can present views closer to an Inuit perspective than Gould chose with *North*.

Peder,[65] a middle-aged, Inuk[66] government worker, explains what the north means to him. He projects his ideas on the outsider's view, too:

> I think it just means where I'm from. Where my home place is. But, to others it means something very different. For instance, it's a place to exploit resources and that's it. And also to claim it—to claim it against other countries. That's kind of what it means to me to the outsiders . . . It has no meaning of gold, or diamonds. It's just where I can continue my traditional way of hunting and living off the land, and appreciating what it is without it being exploited.[67]

Whereas Gould and his interviewees focus on what's lacking for "the Eskimo" and the north, Peder focuses his comments on what *is* in the north; it is not a place of isolation but rather, home. Gould imagines a solitary north, where someone goes to live in isolation. For native inhabitants, by contrast, interdependence on other people makes this a home. This, alongside a hope for noninterference, makes Gould's vision of "going north" seem increasingly colonial in that his vision directly contradicts the native experience of north.

Salka, an Inuk woman who works closely with Inuit and southerners, says "they [southerners and Inuit alike] talk a lot about the north,"[68] and within this "talk" regular phrases recur both within interviews and in daily conversation. Such phrases identify their reality of the north and communicate a common understanding, but quickly shift to personal experiences. When asked what the north is, Theo, a young high school graduate, laughs and says, "North of sixty. The north is where I'm from and where I've lived all my life. And I don't want to move anywhere 'cause it's my tradition, you know?"[69]

People and culture play vital roles in identifying the north as a lifeplace for Arviammiut (the people of Arviat) and are largely lacking in Gould's vision. Marina notes "there's a difference between up north and down south . . . She's proud of where she's living, where there's people keeping their culture strong, and everyone knows everyone."[70] Likewise, Olga contrasts the past of her childhood with the present, noting the people's ability to survive in this place: "For her what Arctic or Up North means is that they used to live in *iglus* back then, they used to make all their clothes by hand. What north means to her is very cold back then, but now we have a shelter like this [gesturing at her single-story house]. She's happy about what she went through and what life was back then."[71] Wendela, in her early forties, highlights the difference between the life of her mother's generation and her own. When asked what the north means to her, she said, "The north—people. Inuit. Living up north, in the cold. Trying to survive. It's different now. How my mom grew up on the land—her way of survival and my way of survival is different. She lived off the land, I don't."[72] Raukka brings together the cold, people, and music: "North is very cold. There's cold temperatures, like you go out and you freeze, but, there's all kinds of talents with Inuit with musicians and throat singers, and they do a lot of activities . . . all over north."[73]

During an informal conversation with friends in Arviat, a different idea of isolation arose, far removed from what Gould explored in *North*. Isolation, in that conversation, meant being stuck with the same people all the time, rather than being alone or solitary. This sense of being "stuck together" is also reflected in Robert G. Williamson's monograph, *Eskimo Underground*. Williamson, who served as a member of the Legislative Assembly for the Northwest Territories around the time of *North*, had also taught at the University of Saskatchewan and established the Eskimology section of the Department of Northern Affairs. In his 1974 dissertation on Inuit in Rankin Inlet, Williamson drew a map of the community circa 1959. In this case, the "Eskimo Settlement" is visibly separated from the rest of the town, creating a greater sense of isolation from the community, creating an inside and outside (which group is out and which is in, I cannot say). Williamson's map (fig. 2.1) certainly gives an impression of being stuck with the same people.

Figure 2.1. Map of Rankin Inlet from Williamson, *Eskimo Underground* [n.p.]. *Source*: Robert G. Williamson, *Eskimo Underground: Socio-Cultural Change in the Central Canadian Arctic* (Uppsala: University of Uppsala, 1974). Used with permission.

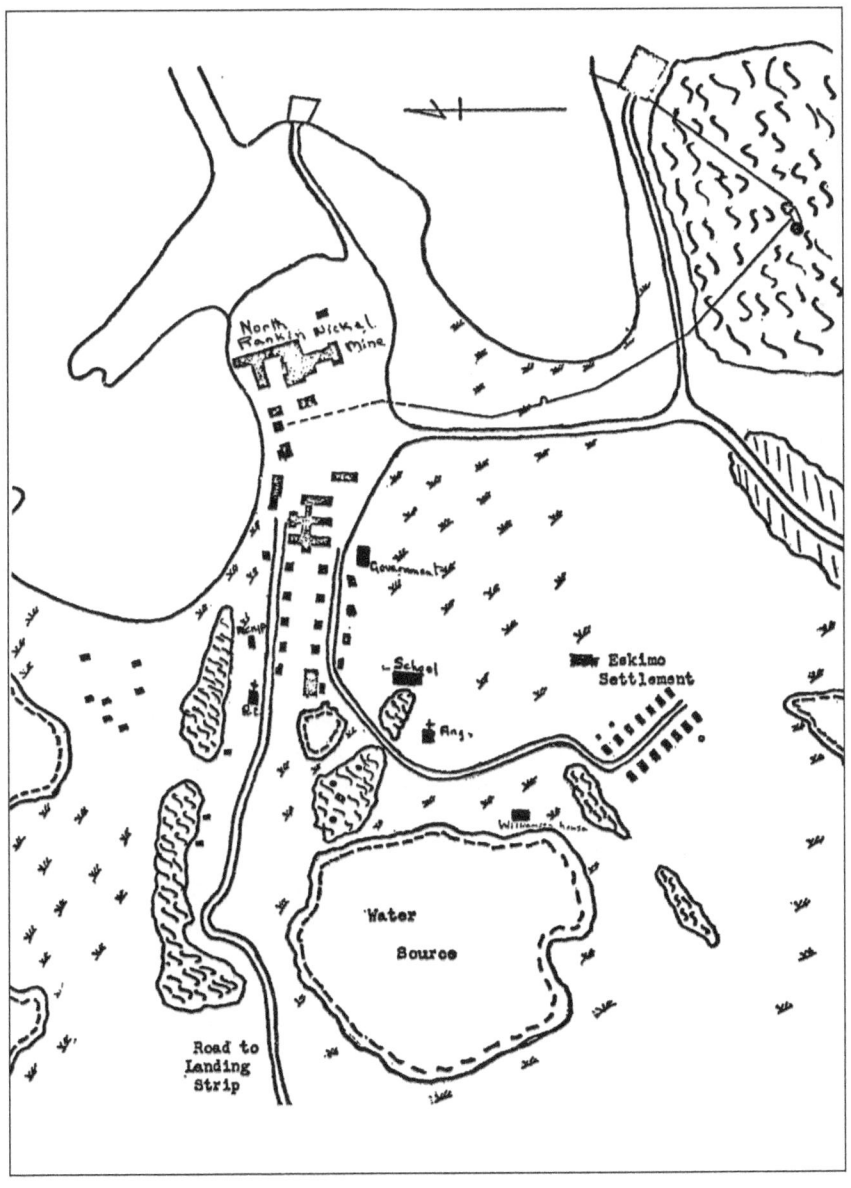

Conclusions

In *The Idea of North*, Gould attempts to project his own ideals of isolation and the heroism of solitude onto the Canadian north, a region known as much for its imagined qualities as its reality. In doing so, he projects stereotypes of "the Eskimo" that remain in place as a challenge facing today's Inuit population. Whether intentionally or not, he overlooks the fact that this harsh environment cannot be a place of isolation—the people who live there, be they the modern northern nomads, his interviewees, or the settled former nomads (i.e., Inuit)—rely and depend on each other for survival. Though the Inuit population lives generally beyond the scope of Gould's program, *North* presents a portrait of "the Eskimo," through the voices of his five interviewees.

The men—Robert Phillips, Jim Lotz, Frank Vallee, and Wally Maclean—make general observations about the impact the north had upon them. Marianne Schroeder provides a more reflective voice, including her experiences with the Inuit. In all cases, however, colonial attitudes prevail. "The Eskimo" is reduced to a singular, male example intended to reinforce the idea of solitude in this region. Paradoxically, efforts to colonize and "civilize" the population removed any semblance of isolation from the Inuit existence. Formerly nomadic groups were forcibly relocated by government initiative throughout the 1950s and finally entrenched in hamlets by 1967.

For Inuit, then, the residents of the north, Gould's interpretation of isolation and solitude is impossible. His "idea of north" is imagined, idealized, and problematic. The very skills necessary to live and survive in such an environment necessitate a reliance upon others—this holds both for Inuit and visitors from the south. The northern environment fosters a sense of home—a place of survivors, and a place of action, where people do things together. That Gould did not perceive, or seek, this aspect of northern life in his interviews is not surprising for a work about solitude. As today's consumers of this work, however, we must take a moment of reflection to remind ourselves that *The Idea of North* is merely that—an idea.

Notes

1. Kevin Bazzana, *Wondrous Strange* (Toronto: McClelland & Stewart, 2003), 299.
2. Bazzana, *Wondrous Strange*, 299.

3. D. K. Thomas and C. T. Thompson, "Eskimo Housing as Planned Culture Change," Northern Science Research Group Department of Indian Affairs and Northern Development, Ottawa, 1972.

4. In the course of this chapter I often use the term "Eskimo" rather than today's accepted autonym, Inuit, in deference to Gould and his interviewees, for whom the term was in common usage.

5. Mazzoleni cited in Ernest MacMillan, ed., *Music in Canada* (Toronto: University of Toronto Press, 1955), 109.

6. Potvin cited in Arnold Walter, ed., *Aspects of Music in Canada* (Toronto: University of Toronto Press, 1969), 156.

7. Gould cited in Walter, *Aspects of Music in Canada*, 185.

8. Peter Davidson, *The Idea of North* (London: Reaktion Books, 2004); Sherrill E. Grace, *Canada and the Idea of North* (Montreal: McGill-Queen's University Press, 2001).

9. Glenn Gould, "Introduction to an Idea: CBC Northern Services," 1967, Item 1979-20 32 1, 4–5, Glenn Gould fonds, Library and Archives Canada, Ottawa.

10. James Parakilis, "How Spain Got a Soul," in *The Exotic in Western Music*, ed. Jonathan Bellman (Boston: Northeastern University Press, 1998).

11. Glenn Gould, "The Deromantizing North," 1967, Item 1979-20 4 123, 1, Glenn Gould fonds, Library and Archives Canada, Ottawa.

12. Assaf Shelleg, *Jewish Contiguities and the Soundtrack of Israeli History* (Oxford: Oxford University Press, 2014), 16.

13. Sherill E. Grace, *Canada and the Idea of North* (Montreal: McGill-Queen's University Press, 2001), 14.

14. Grace, *Canada and the Idea of North*, 13.

15. See Lucille Mok's chapter, chapter 1 in this volume.

16. Geoffrey Payzant, *Glenn Gould: Music and Mind* (New York: Van Nostrand Reinhold, 1978), 55.

17. Payzant, *Music and Mind*, 55.

18. Payzant, *Music and Mind*, 55.

19. Payzant, *Music and Mind*, 55–56.

20. Anka Ryall, Johan Schimanski, and Henning Howlid Wærp, *Arctic Discourses* (Newcastle upon Tyne, UK: Cambridge Scholars, 2010), x.

21. Edward Said, *Orientalism* (New York: Random House, 1979), 1.

22. Said, *Orientalism*, 12.

23. Said, *Orientalism*, 12.

24. Glenn Gould, "Idea of North | Draft 1, the Deromantizing North," 1967, Item 1979-20 4 123, Glenn Gould fonds, Library and Archives Canada, Ottawa. In interviews and essays, Gould referred to the scene as the "Dining Car."

25. Glenn Gould, "Idea of North Transcript A," 1967, Item 1979-20 5 25, 37, Glenn Gould fonds, Library and Archives Canada, Ottawa.

26. Gould, "Transcript A."

27. John Bennett and Susan Rowley, eds., *Uqalurait* (Montreal: McGill-Queen's University Press, 2004), 13, emphasis added.

28. Bennett and Rowley, *Uqalurait*, 14–15, emphasis added.

29. Lisa-Jo K. van den Scott. *Walled-In: Arctic Housing and a Sociology of Walls* (Lanham, MD: Lexington Books, 2024), 105.

30. Gould, "Transcript A," 39; Gould, "Introduction for CBC Northern Services," 1, emphasis added.

31. Gould, "Transcript A," 1; Grace, *Canada and the Idea of North*, 13

32. Gould, "Transcript A," 35.

33. Gould, "Transcript A," 35, emphasis added.

34. Gould, "Transcript A," 36.

35. Lisa-Jo K. van den Scott, "Time to Defy: The Use of Temporal Spaces to Enact Resistance," in *Oppression and Resistance: Structure, Agency, Transformation*, ed. Gil Richard Musolf (Bingley, UK: Emerald, 2017), 144ff.

36. Glenn Gould, "Schroeder Transcript Tape 2," 1967, Item 1979-20 4 114, Glenn Gould fonds, Library and Archives Canada, Ottawa.

37. Gould, "Transcript A," 30.

38. Van den Scott, "Geographies of Identity and Knowledge," 221.

39. See Amber Hildebrandt, "Nunavut Put Community's Health 'At Risk' by Mishandling Nurse," *CBC News*, 31 October 2014, updated 7 November 2014, http://www.cbc.ca/news/multimedia/nunavut-put-community-s-health-at-risk-by mishandling-nurse-1.2818184 (accessed January 22, 2015). Also Thomas Rohner, "Ell Orders Independent Review of Nunavut Nurse Scandal," *Nunatsiaq Online*, 7 November 2014, http://www.nunatsiaqonline.ca/stories/article/65674ell_orders_independent_review_of_nunav__nurse_scandal/ (accessed 22 January 2015).

40. Thomas and Thompson, "Eskimo Housing as Planned Culture Change."

41. Gould, "Transcript A," 40–41.

42. Field Notes.

43. Field Notes, 38.

44. Thomas and Thompson, "Eskimo Housing as Planned Culture Change."

45. Gould, "Transcript A," 37.

46. Gould, "Transcript A," 42.

47. Glenn Gould, "Idea of North | Transcript of R. A. J. Phillips Interview, Tape 1," 1967, Item 1979-20 4, 9, Glenn Gould fonds, Library and Archives Canada, Ottawa.

48. Gould, "Transcript of R. A. J. Phillips Interview Tape 1," 5.

49. Gould, "Transcript A," 24.

50. Gould, "Transcript A," 38–39.

51. Gould, "Transcript A," 37–38.

52. The Inuksuk rose to mainstream consciousness in Canada in the 1990s, owing in part to its use in a well-known government-sponsored Heritage Minute television spot. Its use, as well as the examples noted, display the appropriation of

this Inuit symbol by a largely middle-class, Anglo-Canadian population without regard for its original intent and meaning.

54. Sima Sahar Zeheri, "KTZ Fashion Under Fire for Using Inuit Design Without Family's Consent," *CBC News*, 25 November 2015, 15, http://www.cbc.ca/news/canada/north/ktz-fashion-inuit-design-1.3337047 (accessed 15 December 2015).

54. Gould, "Transcript A," 41.

55. Gould, "Transcript A," 39–40.

56. Glenn Gould, quoted in Payzant, *Music and Mind*, 132.

57. Glenn Gould, "Idea of North | Interview Questions for James Lotz," 1967, Item 1979-20 4 94, Glenn Gould fonds, Library and Archives Canada, Ottawa.

58. Glenn Gould, "Idea of North | Interview Questions for Wally Maclean," 1967, Item 1979-20 4 104, Glenn Gould fonds, Library and Archives Canada, Ottawa.

59. Darrel Mansell, "Glenn Gould: The Idea of South by North," *Iowa Review* 15, no. 3 (Fall 1985): 65, emphasis added.

60. Immanuel Kant, quoted in Payzant, *Music and Mind*, 57.

61. Payzant, *Music and Mind*.

62. Payzant, *Music and Mind*, 56.

63. Gould, "R. A. J. Phillips Interview, Tape 2," 3, 5.

64. Glenn Gould, "Idea of North | Exclusions," 1967, Item 1979-20 4 122 1, Glenn Gould fonds, Library and Archives Canada, Ottawa, 3. The "exclusions" were the interview excerpts Gould wanted to appear in the finished version of *North*. He numbered each exclusion and constructed every scene in the work from them.

65. All names of my research participants are pseudonyms to protect anonymity.

66. Inuk is the singular form of the plural, Inuit.

67. Interview with the author, December 2013.

68. Interview with the author, December 2013.

69. Interview with the author, December 2013.

70. Interview with the author, through an interpreter, December 2013.

71. Interview with the author, through an interpreter, December 2013.

72. Interview with the author, December 2013.

73. Interview with the author, December 2013.

3

Rails of Protest

CHRISTOPHER DeLAURENTI

> Was not writing poetry a secret transaction, a voice answering a voice?
> —Virginia Woolf, *Orlando: A Biography*

Any examination of Glenn Gould's *The Idea of North* must implicitly absorb an irretrievable loss, a haunting absence that compels those of us huddled together within the tiny Venn diagram of radio nerds and Glenn Gould fans to accept a *North* that has become something else: a fixed, born-again digital work irretrievably culled from its origin as a Canadian Broadcasting Corporation (CBC) radio broadcast on 28 December 1967.[1] Rather than burnish Gould's place in the pantheon of radio producers,[2] in this essay I examine the possibility of recuperating *North* as a radio broadcast and then explore *North* as an invitation to radical listening of a work whose gaps, absences, and nearly crushed fissures of silence not only foreshadow tactical media but offer an instructive, inspiring soundscape of dissent. *The Idea of North* invites us to remake the world.

Today, *North* exists as an exalted digitized echo, sampled then replicated for compact disc[3] and compressed into streaming audio from the CBC.[4] But before its limited distribution on LP[5] and CD, *North*—considered by Gould to be music and deeming it his opus 1[6]—was made for radio, commissioned by the CBC Radio program *Ideas* to celebrate the Canadian Centennial.[7]

Obliging Gould's role as a national icon, Canadian newspapers reviewed the broadcast premiere, praising *North*, as, for example, a "poetic and beautiful montage."[8] But listeners heard something else too; the medium, specifically the sonic aspects of radio broadcasting, conveying or at least perturbating the message.

Peter Shewchuk, one of the CBC audio engineers who helped edit *North*, remembered "when the program was first aired, it was logged as crosstalk,"[9] entangled or indecipherable voices heard when one radio station's coverage (sometimes referred to as a "broadcast footprint") coincides with another. Shewchuk added, "There was much criticism over the fact that voices were sounding simultaneously."[10]

Whether the listeners who complained and reported Gould's contrapuntal radio as crosstalk heard actual radio interference remains unclear. The polyphonic and structural complexity of *North*[11] surely confounded expectations and identification of signal and noise as much in 1967 as it does today. How much of what radio scholar Margaret Ann Hall describes as "early radio's distinct qualities: the chaos from a listener's perspective of random and broken narratives, feedback, and static"[12] permeated the soundscape of the average listener? What kind or how much of *North* could someone with a tiny radio speaker with possibly haphazard reception hear? Airing across CBC-FM on stations in Toronto, Montreal, Ottawa, Winnipeg, and Vancouver,[13] *North* might have been received in outlying areas much differently, perhaps faintly and not quite deciphered.

One outlying earwitness, Roger Saydack, caught *North* by chance "on the car radio while on a long drive in Michigan"[14] and remembered

> some static and crosstalk during the broadcast but it didn't at all interfere with my experience of the piece. Static was expected on car radios then. And crosstalk was part of the package on cold, clear nights as signals from distant AM stations bounced off the ionosphere and ricocheted around the cloudless sky and the broad, flat Michigan landscape. I remember what I think was a bit of square dance music intervening at one point, which just added to the real life/real time experience of hearing *North* on the radio as I drove along.[15]

No amateur airchecks—recordings of the CBC's original radio broadcast—of *North* are known to exist. On 30 June 1999 I attempted to investigate and recuperate the broadcast soundscape of *North* on my radio show,

The Sonar Map, on KSER 90.7 FM.[16] Months earlier, Barbara Brown of the CBC's Licensing Department had kindly granted permission and waived the broadcast fee[17] for KSER, one of the few remaining noninstitutionally affiliated, nonprofit community radio stations in the United States. With a studio-quality microphone and digital audio tape (DAT) deck placed in front of a tiny speaker embedded in a cheap clock radio, I hoped to capture a *North* bound by limited bandwidth, hiss, distortion, intermodulation, and other interference. I wanted to know what my listeners heard. What would happen to the voices? Could listeners identify the speakers, their words? Might my rerecording of the broadcast capture an ever-elastic continuum ranging from noise to Gould's fastidiously calibrated contrapuntal radio?

The resulting aircheck was indeed noisier than the compact disc of *North*[18] played on the air that night. Listeners reported via phone calls and subsequent conversations something similar to what I had recorded: some masking hiss and occasional interference along with an anomaly or two. My attempt to re-create the circumstances of *North*'s radio reception proved naïve and flawed, in retrospect. I failed to note that KSER broadcasts with an FM transmitter in stereo—CBC Radio did not have a stereo FM network until 1975[19]—which could result in greater crosstalk and increased noise inherent in stereo FM broadcasting.[20] Assuming that most listeners would tune in with solid-state, transistor-based radios, I failed to imagine that part of the audience might tune in with a venerable vacuum tube radio, which has a distinct, at times musical, kind of distortion.[21] In 1999, like most radio stations in the United States, KSER used a digital multiband processor to regulate the modulation of the FM signal; this technology did not exist in the late 1960s.[22] I also forgot a central aspect of radio listening: tuning in. Media theorist Manuel Cirauqui suggests, "The leisurely hand on the dial is responsible for the subtle oscillation between a place and a non-place, open and encrypted soundscapes, recognition and phantasm."[23] Without sporadic fiddling and cajoling of the radio dial to tune in toward a clear signal, my recording documented an immobile, casually ambient hearing, not exploratory listening. My microphones, unlike real human listeners, did not move.[24] Where were the phantasms of radio reception such as intruding voices and storms of static that might answer and reshape how *North* could be heard over the airwaves? Somewhere far away from the broadcast booth and adjacent transmitter tower. My aircheck of *North* merely exemplified Marshall McLuhan's axiom of "the continuing process by which new technologies create new environments for old technologies."[25] Historically, Gould's initial foray into contrapuntal radio remains a radiophonic work.[26] I could air *North* as many times as I wanted, but without similar technical equipment (and compensating for geographical proximity and physical barriers that help or hinder FM radio reception), an analog *North*, an original version born of the uncertain soundscape of broadcast radio, is lost to us. What remains is a work sonically denuded of its origins in radio, an example of radio artist Gregory Whitehead's contention that "the investigation of radio has disappeared into the investigation of *sound*."[27] How can we listen to *North* anew?

"Listening is never natural," declares the radical art collective Ultrared. "It requires and generates literacy."[28] Where might a listener begin to "read" *North* away from the radio? Certainly not in the canonical genre of post–World War II electroacoustic music.[29] Unlike Schaeffer, Henry, and Stockhausen who all aspired to the concert hall,[30] Gould's deliberate composerly choices thwart any tidy collocation within the avant-garde. The exclusive use of dense, accented English-language interviews erect an effective barrier to listener comprehension of concert performances and radio broadcasts outside the English-speaking world.[31] With a running time of fifty-eight minutes and fifty-four seconds—*North* was allotted a generously uninterrupted bloc of prime-time radio—nonetheless the near-hour length is a concert programmer's nightmare. *North* is longer than a typical thirty-five- to forty-five-minute half of a concert program and too short for an entire concert. The filtering Gould employed on the voices in *North*[32] is subtle and elegant, however the lack of unusual timbres and dazzling sonic transformations banish *North* as an outlier among contemporaneous milestones rooted in the human voice such as *Bye Bye Butterfly* (1965) by Pauline Oliveros, whose lush tape delays propelled a mythic clash of grand opera and live electronics; Berio's polyvocal prototype for his signature *Sinfonia* (1968–1969) and *Laborintus II* (1965); the ring-modulated voices of Stockhausen's *Mikrophonie II* (1965); *Next Stop Mars*, released on LP in 1966 by Sun Ra,[33] who launched his ensemble's thrilling voyage into extended techniques with a chanting chorus drenched in reverberation; and the yelping, babbling, dive-bombing tape loops of "Tomorrow Never Knows" from the Beatles' 1966 album *Revolver*.

Heard on the home stereo system, *North* is spatially primitive, an atavistic remnant more suited to an antique tombstone radio than a hi-fi console embedded in a table-wide credenza—where speakers sit far enough apart for the bifurcated stereo mixes common in 1960s jazz and pop recordings to suffuse a room with instruments in distinct spaces. In

Making Easy Listening: Material Culture and Postwar American Recording, media historian Tim J. Anderson reminds us that "stereo technologies not only rendered new pieces of domestic furniture," such as the hi-fi console,[34] but also opened up "a once-unthinkable proximity to audio spaces" that was "beyond a realism that embraces the strict obsession with the perfect reproduction and representation of any particular audio event."[35]

Bifurcated mixing assigns one group of instruments mostly to the left channel and another group of instruments to the right channel. Up close, the instruments sound separated, for instance, piano in the left channel, rhythm section in the right. Further away in the room, the listener hears great spatial clarity.[36] In his liner notes to the LP *The Black Saint and the Sinner Lady* (1963), Charles Mingus wryly observed, "That's what's good about stereo. You can turn the channels up that make it and off if they don't."[37] One example is Rudy van Gelder's 50/50 system employed on the classic 1960s Blue Note albums.[38] When the stereo mix is collapsed to mono during an AM radio broadcast or playback on cheap record players, all instruments are present.

Where was Gould's first foray into contrapuntal radio amid the flowering of stereophony in all genres of audio production and multispeaker presentations by the avant-garde? Mixed down into dowdy monaural sound, necessitated by the "FM mono" format of CBC Radio. Although Gould mocked "stereophonically marshaled speaker platoons,"[39] he accepted the limits of mono,[40] which makes the clarity of voices an even more impressive achievement by engineer Lorne Tulk. During her research in the 1980s, Gould discographer Nancy Canning conferred with Tulk and, as an admirer of *North*, found out that, "after recording all the voices and effects separately, Tulk lined up four Studer tape decks and wired the switches so two or more could be simultaneously played while yet a fifth Studer took down the entire mix."[41] Instead of focusing on technological invention, Tulk innovated with the comparatively primitive technology available at the CBC. According to *North* radio producer Janet Somerville, "Lorne generously loved, admired and served the infinitely demanding Gould through weeks of eighteen-hour sessions that would have made Tulk's union apoplectic, had it been informed."[42]

North could be consigned to the obscure realm of text-sound works, where many text-sound poets, focused on the grain of the voice, typically work at the subatomic level of phonemes, syllables, and words. "Gone is the word as the word," wrote the pioneering sound poet Bob Cobbing in 1969, "though the word may still be used as sound or shape. Poetry now resides in other elements."[43] By contrast, throughout *North* and the two successive works in what the CBC marketed as "The Solitude Trilogy,"[44] *The Latecomers* (1969) and *Quiet in the Land* (1977), Gould preserved the semantic content of his speakers molecularly, discernibly reordering sentences and phrases as well as culling what linguists call fillers and voiced pauses such as "um" and "uh."[45] In his conversation with pianist Arthur Rubenstein, Gould, who had an expert knowledge of the recording studio,[46] recounted editing interviews for *The Latecomers*: 1,600 discourse markers and other "syntactical fluff" were painstakingly edited out in one interviewee's recording that, as a result, "we made a new character out of him."[47] A search of a transcript made of *North*[48] reveals that only ten of sixty-three spoken segments contain more than a half-dozen utterances of "uh," mostly spoken by Frank Vallee and heard in Wally Maclean's thousand-word soliloquy that electrifies the work's final eight minutes.

Discernible phrases and sentences constitute nearly the entire text of *North*. Yet in his landmark anthology *Text-Sound Texts*, Kostelanetz groups Gould with Charles Amirkhanian, Charles Dodge, Philip Glass,[49] and in a later essay hails the "text-sound art" of Milton Babbitt[50]—a group so sonically and thematically heterogeneous as to make the category bafflingly broad. Other text-sound taxonomies[51] are so similarly expansive that writing a collaborative social history[52] or hewing to a firmly reductionist dividing line such as Nancy Perloff's dictum "sound poetry rejects meaning"[53] may be the only path to map the disparate aural and formal differences in sound poetry.

Before addressing how to read *North* anew, this formerly radiophonic work should be examined in its most widely distributed tangible medium, the compact disc. The CBC released the complete *North* on CD twice, first in 1992 on a three-disc set labeled *Glenn Gould's Solitude Trilogy* and then in 2007 on a five-disc set, *Glenn Gould: The Radio Artist*. According to WorldCat.org, ninety-one libraries worldwide hold the 1992 edition while thirty-two libraries worldwide hold the 2007 set.[54] Regrettably, WorldCat is not complete and a few cataloguers of *North* have conflated the categories of "Sound Recording" with "Compact Disc"—thus the number of libraries holding these discs is likely higher.[55] Digitally extracting and comparing these two CD iterations of *North* reveal subtle visual and thus digital differences between the waveforms. Both 1992 and 2007 releases are exactly 155,869,980 samples long,[56] however they do not share an identical CRC32 or MD5 checksum, which indicates subtle bit-for-bit differences between the files. The shared exact sample length implies—but does not prove—that the digital file of Gould 1992 might have been the basis of Gould 2007, and furthermore that Gould 2007 was not a new transfer (and subsequent digital mastering) of the analog master tape. These two tangible digital iterations of *North* prophesy the work's ultimate status as what philosopher Yuk Hui calls a "digital object."

Hui defines digital objects as "objects on the Web," photos, videos, text, files—anything that exists as data amid a group of relations, "schemes or ontologies that one can generalize as metadata."[57] You can tag, link to, click on, stream, and (if you are Web-savvy) download *North* as a digital object. But what about *North* on compact disc? Again McLuhan proves prescient, for the personal computer and web as "new technologies create new environments for old technologies,"[58] in this case the analog master tape and compact disc of *North*. Without *North* on CD, *North* could not have become a digital object; it is reasonable to assume that the various YouTube uploaders only had access to a compact disc, not the analog master tape of *North*. Following McLuhan, Hui discerns that "the relations that were once in a physical form are now turned into another material form, which is code or data."[59] The *where* and *when* of *North* exists continually for anyone online who finds or seeks it; the Web has transformed CDs of *North* into nearly identical—yet remote—nodes in a network. Those CDs are now just data that do not circulate, except when loaned or sold.

Tellingly, the brief history of *North* as a digital object echoes its analog, radiophonic counterpart: the statistics tallying the broadcasts of *North* on radio and online streams remain incomplete and inaccessible. CBC Radio does not track broadcast history or licensing information for *North*. A senior media librarian of the CBC Content Sales and Licensing Division replied to my email inquiry for licensing along with streaming data spanning any available, nonproprietary time frame, "I truly don't think that information is available anywhere."[60] This is surprising considering that "to this day the CBC maintains its copyright on the work."[61] And while performing rights organizations (PRO) worldwide such as ASCAP, BMI, and SESAC in the United States and the Society of Composers, Authors and Music Publishers of Canada (SOCAN) might collect royalties when *North* is aired, the randomized surveying of stations precludes the collection of precise numbers. A thornier issue is whether *North* gets logged as music or as spoken word or another category, which absolves a PRO from collecting royalties.

As a maker of several similarly lengthy sound works that have aired on radio stations around the world,[62] I can attest that reported playlists and PRO-conducted broadcast surveys almost never match the playlists compiled and sent to me directly by radio DJs. As algorithmic snapshots and "best-guess" sets of statistics compiled without independent oversight of a neutral third party, worldwide royalty figures are not a reliable guide. Online, *North* has a similarly fugitive digital life on streaming sites based in Eastern Europe and Russia as well as on video aggregators, notably YouTube, where three separate uploads of *North* attracted 9,377, 6,647, and 30,906 views respectively.[63] The earlier uploads of *North* I saw in previous years are no longer available online, either removed by the uploader or lost in the fog of DMCA takedown notices. The Lumen database, formerly known as chillingeffects.org, contains no DMCA takedown notices submitted to Google for *North*, though this does not preclude the possibility of other takedowns.[64] In any case, all YouTube "views" are approximate, not necessarily actual, complete views of *North* from 0:00 to 58:54. YouTube uses a mysterious proprietary algorithm to count views with some verification done by Google employees.[65] Yet given the randomized logging practices of SOCAN and other PROs, I believe it fair to assert that *North* has been heard on well-linked websites (albeit sporadically) including the CBC since the late 1990s, YouTube, and elsewhere[66] much more often than a decades-old, fifty-eight-minute "sound documentary" on compact disc. Born analog, *North* will live a much longer digital existence. Yet if *North* is a digital object when we find it, what is it when we hear it?

North begins aloft, high in the air and *lontano*. Marianne Schroeder's recessed voice recalls what she saw while flying over the Canadian north, "a tapestry of tundra and taiga" as Gould later describes it.[67] While "forever looking out," she notes "some of the lakes were frozen around the edges, but towards the center of the lake you still could see the clear, clear water"[68] and other remote sights resplendent with color and shape. Tellingly, we hear Schroeder's voice solo with no sound effects. *North* begins not with a radiophonic soundscape but with a monologue, a recollection so visual, so distant, that sounds are not mentioned, only muted. No buzz of an airplane, thunk of thawing ice, or splashing of polar bears or seals. We only hear a voice. Gould lures the listener toward imaginatively "looking" or envisioning in order to intensify the effect of the oncoming vocal polyphony, the "sort of trio sonata,"[69] which introduces listeners to the contrapuntal radio that permeates the work. This initial inversion of sound and sight offers a rich clue, for listening to *North* within the first minute is certainly not, to echo Ultra-red's words, natural and generates, if not inspires, a literacy that can only be understood by examining the voices, sound effects, and silences within the digital object of *North* as a soundscape.

Despite the bland appropriation of "soundscape" to sell dreamy relaxation CDs[70] or as a diluted byword brandished in ethnographies addressing the aural aspects of a society,[71] R. Murray Schafer's pithy definition of the soundscape as "the sonic environment"[72] remains potent, flexible, and radical. One of Schafer's fiercest critics even concedes that "the term's popularity rests precisely on its ability to evoke a whole complex set of ideas, preferences, practices, scientific properties, legal frameworks, social orders, and sounds."[73] In *The Tuning of the World*, Schafer proclaims: "The Soundscape is any acoustic field of study. We may speak of a musical composition as a soundscape or a radio program as a soundscape or an acoustic environment as a soundscape."[74] The soundscape is a place of exploration; in a 1990s radio interview Schafer proposed the soundscape as a way "to see the landscape with one's ears."[75] For Schafer, a contemporary of Gould—the two shared the same piano teacher, Alberto Guerrero[76]—the soundscape remains an inherently political space. "Wherever Noise is granted immunity from human intervention, there will be found a seat of power,"[77] observes Schafer. Gould understood this intuitively and sought to protect himself: "Until physical and verbal aggression are seen as simply a flip of the competitive coin, until every aesthetic decision can be equated with a moral correlative, I'll continue to listen to the Berlin Philharmonic from behind a glass partition."[78] As the chief boundary and sole point of visual contact, the partition, usually of dual-pane glass, divides the typical recording studio bicamerally: music is made in the live room while being recorded, monitored, and edited in the control room.[79] Though transparent, Gould's partition erects a safe barrier, a true and sonically hermetic refuge.

Behind that glass partition Gould dissents, offering an explicitly radical invitation at the beginning of *North* with what Kostelanetz, at once alluding to Grand Opera and text-sound, calls a "speech-trio."[80] He also describes it as "a fugue of three people talking about their personal experience of the Canadian north,"[81] however the lack of distinct, discrete entities moving against one another with rhythmic simultaneity and measured evasion mitigates against this label. Despite the persuasive contours of Lorne Tulk's analog graph of the prologue to *North*,[82] the temptation to categorize *North*'s beginning as a canon should be resisted as well; the lines depict amplitude measured in volume units (VU), however the VU meter "does not give a true indication of perceived audio level"[83] and should be employed with caution as "it's an analog, mechanical device that could easily be knocked out of calibration."[84] Intended to measure the average of a signal, VU meters tend to ignore or underreport extreme, transitory peaks[85] such as the plosives and fricatives that punctuate speech. Tulk's graph does not chart any semantic content and does not reflect a perception of what is understood. Nevertheless, the diagram is invaluable for tracing the voices' general contour and guiding the ear to listen through what Gould called "an exercise in texture and not a conscious effort to regenerate a musical form."[86] The radical, protesting essence of *North* resides elsewhere.

Sound artist and media theorist Sabine Breitsameter connects Gould's "exercise" to Schafer's notion of the soundscape, contending that listeners of *North* are "called on to follow a way of listening that leans heavily on Schafer's model in that it demands a conscious sensitivity to one's full environment rather than a selective listening attention."[87] As a digital object, we can rehear *North* up close from the grains in and around Schroeder's voice to the concluding *tuttis* of Sibelius punctuating the wry peroration of Wally Maclean. Listening to digital objects, especially uncompressed digital audio—with detailed, digital means—affords a different kind of listening, a repetition under the listener's close control and choice, which fulfills Gould's prophecy of "participational possibilities which the listener will enjoy once current laboratory techniques have been appropriated by home playback devices."[88] But do digital objects spawn artifacts? "Digital audio," contends radio producer and programmer Martin Spinelli, "has been almost exclusively about silencing technology in order to achieve a better delivery of something else: more direct access to the human voice, less noise, less distortion, less evidence of process."[89] The flatter frequency response and wider dynamic range of digital audio only silences its own traces, except in the case of data-compressed audio such as MP3 at low bitrates.[90] Artifacts and residue as well as reduced frequency response induced by interposed computer speakers or earbud headphones from the analog realm pervade digital audio. Despite such limitations, we can listen between gaps, absences, and fissures of silence digitally; this "tactical poetics of ambience"[91] can alert our ears to potentially revelatory gaps and absences in *North*. Let's relisten.

In the short introduction to *North*, Schroeder shifts from the remote, overheard, and poetic to the direct and intimate. *North* begins aloft and *lontano* with no audible frequencies below 140Hz or above 2000Hz. Marianne Schroeder's voice—distant as if turned away from us—describes what she saw while flying over the Canadian north, but after thirteen seconds her voice brightens, not with enthusiasm at "some of the lakes were frozen around the edges,"[92] but with an opening up of an audio filter that expands the timbral range and richness of her voice down below 100Hz and above 2500Hz. She is closer, becoming less distant; the gradual fade-in raises not only the loudness of her voice but its proximity. A poem of overheard fragments becomes a conversation.

We can't reply to Marianne, but we respond. Gould masterfully has broken up the phrases of her monologue with ten gaps, leaving enough time for the listener to voice or think of an affirmative vocal filler. The gaps last about or just a little longer than one second, excepting three gaps of a half-second or shorter. These seeming silences frame her words in segments lasting 2.2, 4.1, 3.2, 6.5, 9.1, 4.5, 1.0, 2.1, 4.2, 1.6, and 2.6 seconds respectively.[93] The first segments of 2.2 and 4.1 suggest a dramatic poetic demarcation. The subsequent segments expand and contract somewhat proportionally—3.2, 6.5, 9.1, and 4.5 then 1.0, 2.1, and 4.2—suggesting a transition from the declamatory to the elastic push-pull of conversational English. The remaining times of 1.6 and 2.6 hasten the punch line "I was always looking for a polar bear . . ."

We also hear the grain of her voice. The pops heard and seen in the spectral view of digital audio software are not radio anomalies or artifacts of LP surface noise or digital glitches. These "grains" originate from the analog master tape. Between 20.385 and 21.822 seconds[94] there is a quiet pop followed by a quieter thump. It could be what audio engineers call a "mouth noise," the lip- and/or tongue-smacking heard when some singers, actors, and voice-over artists are recorded up close.[95] The next significant pause in Schroeder's recollection from 30.944 to 31.844 contains no such mouth noises. The thump is likely a tape splice, possibly a purposeful one. "One cannot ever splice style," Gould ventured, "one can only splice segments which relate to a conviction about style."[96] What we remember is tempered by what cognitive scientists call sensory adaptation,[97] the rapid subsuming of ambient sound to the periphery of our attention and memory.[98] Both sounds may have been left in to prepare the ears for the various mouth noises made by Schroeder in the words "most" at 28.798 and "fascinating" at 29.378. Mouth noises by Gould noticeably appear at 3:13.920 and 4:22.265. Even when barely noticed, mouth noises convey authenticity—the conviction of a real person, not a produced, radio voice.

Sensory adaptation also regulates how we hear what Kostelanetz calls the "cantus firmus"[99] of *North*, the ambient bed of railroad and railcar sounds that Gould deems a "basso continuo"[100] and Sallis derides as "acoustic *décor*" whose "sounds fall out of our immediate consciousness relatively quickly."[101] To my ears, this ambient bed swerves in and out of awareness. Cushing cannily asserts that "the continuous train is not just sound, but sound with inflection,"[102] notably at 5:06.066 when the ambiance of the train station punctuates Gould's introduction of Wally Maclean on the word "be," the last syllable of "our narrator," and placed a distant "hey" under the first syllable of "his view." The next railyard exclamation, recessed with its upper frequencies rolled off in order to create the same kind of distance we heard at the beginning of *North*, appears one beat before Gould says "an idea" and continues in a series of exclamations that almost mask Gould's "of North." Additional examples abound: the train toot at 6:10.415 bisects Maclean's rhetorical question "What finally, you ask, uh" and "i-is done about it?," which continues to inure the listener to Maclean's stuttered, trepidatious questions throughout *North* and foreshadows the hortatory conclusion of the work. Passage through and out of architecture is also implied by the mysteriously momentary fade-out at 18:55.412; the train races along the tracks only to reemerge barely a second later after this fissure of near silence with somewhat higher frequency content as if exiting the muted acoustics of a tunnel. More dramatically, the sudden truncation of the train rocketing along at 35:57.216 crucially shifts the scene to back the crisp tinkling of glasses. Other gradations of dislocation are too numerous to catalogue here, yet any close analysis of any section or scene must entail a conscious sensitivity to the soundscape of *North*.

The soundscape model, according to Schafer, offers a fulcrum for political listening by implicitly asking: "Who is heard?" "What are they listening to?" "What are they ignoring or refusing to listen to?"[103] We hear Gould's guests, though our attention to—as well as agreement with—the semantic content will be dissimilar. We listen, perhaps unknowingly, from multiple vantage points in *North*, including direct address, third-person presence, overhearing, and the indecipherable (or masked). We are meant to hear Gould's "guests" at different distances. "And this detachment," recalled Gould, "was abetted by the totally different sound perspectives for each speech."[104]

As mentioned earlier, *North* begins with us overhearing Schroeder. But most voices veer from direct address to a third-person presence, where listeners are proximate spectators; we are not spoken to directly and the conversation fosters opportunities for contemplation, but not verbal interjection. With a few exceptions in *North*, Wally Maclean's voice sounds up close; he faces us and speaks to us directly, folksy and at times petulant. The sudden fade-out of his voice at 7:47 suggests a leaning or turning away toward R. A. J. Phillips, but the speaker does not leave; you do, or at least your attention does. The clipped nasal tone of this "geographer by training"[105] bobs and sinks beneath in the rhythmic clack of the train cruising along the rails. Phillips drones on about his first attempt to "go north" during a summer vacation[106] and our attention wanders. As third-person listeners—we're not spoken to directly—we can reflect upon or ignore what's being said, until the jolting terraced increase in volume at 8:31.632. Suddenly, Phillips's voice clearly and forcefully addresses the listener until 9:36 when his voice fades out and Maclean's returns.

Masked voices also permeate *North*, mainly in the sections of overtly contrapuntal radio such as the trio starting at the fifty-two-second mark and accumulating fugal voices in the "Dining Car" section at 36:04.772. Masking also covers Schroeder's voice entirely in a section starting at 32:45.059; we listen in the third person only to hear her voice drowned out at 33:04 by an adjacent onrushing train passing by for twelve seconds. These are just a few of many examples in *North* of what Spinelli calls "a self-conscious processing or digital occluding of the radio voice"[107] that mediates meaning through distance, juxtaposition, and the occasional overlapping words, phrases, and sentences. Gould was sanguine about such concerns, "I don't honestly believe that it is essential in radio that every word is heard."[108] A commanding formal diagram such as the figures in Cushing[109] could not measure the powerful and subversive rhetoric of juxtaposition and accumulation in *North*. The listener becomes immersed, not in the "negative dialectic"[110] posited by Porter, but amid a community of voices. The varying distances of these voices grant the listener liberty—the semantic space to ponder the experiences and ideas of Gould's guests. Fashioning such a subjective diagram might also perturb *North*'s place as an ancestral model of tactical media, which is "not oriented toward the grand, sweeping revolutionary event; rather, they engage in a micropolitics of disruption, intervention, and education."[111] Furthermore, "tactical media signifies the intervention and disruption of a dominant semiotic regime, the temporary creation of a situation in which signs, messages, and narratives are set into play and critical thinking becomes possible."[112] The disruption becomes distinctly individual and perchance personal not only because of the scale of *North*, but because of *North*'s transformation into a digital object. Unmoored from the temporal treadmill of radio broadcasting, the listener can, with "a leisurely hand on the dial"[113]—or more likely a mouse, trackpad, or touch screen, press the pause button, adding a tiny DIY aspect of tactical media.[114] In his radio program *Dialogues on the Prospects of Recording*, Gould insisted that listeners "have opportunities for analytical judgment which afford them a responsible role in the recreative process. This responsibility exists because of the physical circumstances through which the listener can control and modify the nature of his experience."[115] Such homemade modifications along with the other gaps and fissures in *North* accumulate into what artist Jordan Crandall has labeled "the hidden substrata of the technology" whose "raw immediacy"[116]—here, the gaps inflicted imposed by the listener and composer, what Gould descried as "the integral use of cessation in a texture as a component of that texture"[117]—pries open "a direct access to the real. The reality of representation is substituted for the representation of reality."[118]

Gould opens a direct access to the "real" of our world—its colossal form and navigable expanse—through polyphony and duration. Contrapuntal as well as geological, Gould's polyphonic soundscape not only encompasses voices answering other voices, but it offers poetic, contrapuntal pathways to multiple viewpoints and listener attention. In a 1975 interview Gould explained, "In my radio work, you'll find that every line is meant, at least, to stack up with every line opposite. So that there is, indeed, a great deal of data, a great deal of information being given, but that the lines are intended to contradict each other and to supplement each other in some fashion."[119] The radically directive pathways in *North* fulfill the classic objective of counterpoint as articulated by Kent Kennan in his standard textbook *Counterpoint*, which is to make listeners "sensitive to the forces of opposition and agreement, tension and relaxation, direction, [and] climax."[120] For Gould, these forces always remained rooted in the human voice, a credo that antedated his retirement from the concert stage. "The music which I play, Bach and Schoenberg and points in between, I play in a contrapuntal manner. My approach is essentially a vocal approach, trying to make certain unities out of independent lines."[121]

Improvisor and scholar Ajay Heble maps Gould's counterpoint onto the listener where it "works to unsettle such processes of identity formation, and to encourage us to reconceive the relationship between the whole and its parts."[122] Heble probes further, proposing, "If identity, as Gould's contrapuntal method invites us to see, is multiple, dialogic, and ever-evolving, then what is at issue, is, in large part, an attack on forms and structures of authority, on constructions and representations, which authoritatively claim to be able to have access to some pure, definitive, or whole truth about, say, the identity of Canada."[123] Or for that matter, the idea—your idea—of north.

Composer and playwright Gregory Whitehead's incantatory call for radio art to "begin in a radio dreamland, end in a radio war"[124] aptly encapsulates Gould's invitation to remake the world. If form is a kind of memory, then *North* as a networked, nodal, massive digital object offers perpetual access and an endless stream of revolutionary data to be punctuated and distributed seamlessly at will by the listener. In the epilogue of *North*, Gould proffers an exemplar, Wally Maclean, who makes a final stand athwart the surging horns and strings from Sibelius's Fifth Symphony. He prophesies:

> No longer do humans combine: To defy, or to measure, or to read, or to understand, or to live with, this thing we call Mother Nature. Our number one enemy instead of being Mother Nature, is of course—human nature.
>
> It's crept stealthily from the South; not necessarily by steel—all these long and endless miles that we've sort of passed. And now it's infecting. It's infecting the North with a contagion that's hunh, I don't know what you—what it's like. I don't dare tell this person—that it's, that it's that bad. I just indicated: He's a nice fellow.
>
> You know, I don't want to destroy his—dream. Also, I don't want to smash my own, which is, uh, paper thin at times.
>
> So, we're up against this William James—uh, moral equivalent of war, the equivalent of this war now is now the North. This William James that wrote in Harvard this many years ago whenever he did uh . . .[125]

Gould's protesting, apocalyptic herald battles the hectoring *tuttis* of Sibelius. The grainy, folksy doubt in Maclean's querulous, railing voice is pummeled and ultimately punctured by the disciplined bombardment of the Berlin Philharmonic smashing through Gould's—and our—glass partition: "I suppose he meant really, that, not war: The moral equivalent for us is going north."[126]

Notes

1. Nancy Canning, *A Glenn Gould Catalog* (Westport, CT: Greenwood Press, 1992), 169.

2. See the uncredited roundtable, "Extra BEHIND THE SCENES: A Collection of Reflections on Glenn Goul [sic]," at http://www.thirdcoastfestival.org/explore/article/f-23e38 for an example (accessed 22 December 2023).

3. Glenn Gould, *The Idea of North* (1967), in Glenn Gould, *Glenn Gould's Solitude Trilogy: Three Sound Documentaries*, CBC Records, 1992; and Glenn Gould, *Glenn Gould: The Radio Artist*, five compact discs, PSCD20315, CBC Records, 2007.

4. *The Idea of North* has been erratically available on the CBC website (CBC.ca) in excerpted as well as complete form since the late 1990s.

5. The 1971 LP of *North* released by CBC Learning Systems catalog number T-56998 remains a rarity: According to WorldCat.org, sixteen libraries have the LP in their collection; fifteen of them are in Canada according to https://search.worldcat.org/title/933169951?oclcNum=933169951 and https://search.worldcat.org/title/316146744 (accessed 22 December 2023). Listening to *North* on LP precipitates a host of additional compromises, notably a steadily diminishing frequency response within the inner grooves in tandem with the ticks, pops, and possible skips that sooner or later mar LP playback on even the best systems. Bisecting *North* to fit on two sides of an LP injects another formal shift—the necessity of changing an LP side, a performative element discussed in László Moholy-Nagy, "New Form in Music: Potentialities of the Phonograph" [1923], in *Moholy-Nagy*, ed. Krisztina Passuth, 291–292 (New York: Thames and Hudson, 1985); Charles Mudede, "The Turntable," *CTheory*, 24 April 2003, https://web.archive.org/web/20191101211508/http://www.ctheory.net/articles.aspx?id=382; and elsewhere.

6. Kevin Bazzana, *Wondrous Strange: The Life and Art of Glenn Gould* (Toronto: McClelland & Stewart, 2003), 303.

7. Janet Somerville, "The Gould Radio Documentaries: Some Birth-Memories," CD booklet included in Gould, *Glenn Gould's Solitude Trilogy*, three compact discs, PSCD 2003-3, CBC Records, 1992.

8. Otto Friedrich, *Glenn Gould: A Life and Variations* (New York: Vintage, 1990), 189.

9. Penny Johnson, "Stories Untold: An Interview with *The Idea of North* editor, Peter Shewchuk," Glenn Gould Foundation, 12 April 2010, https://web.archive.org/web/20160429212033/http://www.glenngould.ca/stories-untold-an-interview-with-the-idea-of-north-editor-peter-shewchuk/ (accessed 22 December 2023).

10. Johnson, "Stories Untold."

11. Anthony Cushing, "Glenn Gould and 'Opus 2,'" *Circuit: Musiques contemporaines* 22, no. 2 (2012): 29–32.

12. Margaret Ann Hall, "Radio After Radio: Redefining Radio Art in Light of New Media Technology Through Expanded Practice," PhD thesis, University of the Arts, London, 2015, 50.

13. These FM radio stations and their respective frequencies are listed on a CBC advertising poster for *North* now held in the Glenn Gould fonds, Library

and Archives Canada, Item 1979-20 51, 31, 4 at https://www.collectionscanada.gc.ca/glenngould/028010-1040.03-e.html (accessed 23 December 2023).

14. Roger Saydack, "GG: ST on LP," listserv post, 11 February 2000, http://www.glenngould.org/f_minor/msg04587.html (accessed 22 December 2023).

15. Personal correspondence, 25 November 2018.

16. I hosted 191 broadcasts of *The Sonar Map*, later renamed *The Sonic Stratosphere*. This two-hour radio show aired weekly on KSER 90.7 FM from 1998 to 2001 with the tagline "probing the far-flung frontiers of adventurous music."

17. Personal correspondence, 13 March 1999.

18. Gould, *North*.

19. See Peggy Lynn Kelly, "Dorothy Livesay and CBC Radio," in *Boundaries of Daring: The Modernist Impulse in Canadian Women's Poetry*, ed. Di Bandt and Barbary Godard (Waterloo: Wilfrid Laurier University Press, 2009), 231. Kelly, however, contradicts Lorne Tulk, "Glenn Gould: Some Journeys into Isolation," in Gould, 1992. Some *individual* Canadian stations did broadcast a stereo FM signal before 1975; the debut of Gould's *The Latecomers* "inaugurated the new stereophonic program of Ottawa's CBO-FM in 1969 [on 12 November]." Phillipe Despoix, "Radio as Music: A Video Document by (and with) Glenn Gould," *Intermédialités: Histoire et théorie des arts, des lettres et des techniques* 19 (2012): 178.

20. Lawrence Der, "Frequency Modulation (FM) Tutorial" (Austin: Silicon Laboratories, 2008), 9; and Paul Thurst, "FM Stereo vs. station coverage," posted 8 August 2011 at the blog *Engineering Radio*, http://www.engineeringradio.us/blog/2011/08/fm-stereo-vs-station-coverage/ (accessed October 6, 2016).

21. I am grateful to Anthony Cushing for suggesting the possibility of listeners tuning in with tube-based radios.

22. In this regard, digital is not necessarily preferable to analog processing. See part 3 of "A History of Audio Processing" by Jim Somich and Barry Mishkind at https://www.thebdr.net/a-history-of-audio-processing-part-3-the-era-of-multiband-processing-begins (accessed 27 December 2023).

23. Manuel Cirauqui, "Thanatophonics: From White Noise to Forensic Radio," *PAJ: A Journal of Performance and Art* 104 (2013): 20.

24. See Andrew Crisell, *Understanding Radio* (New York: Routledge, 1994), 12, for a brief discussion of mobile radio listening.

25. Marshall, McLuhan, "New Media and the Arts," *Arts in Society: The Avant-Garde Today* 3, no. 2 (1965): 239, http://digital.library.wisc.edu/1711.dl/Arts.ArtsSocv03i2 (accessed 27 December 2023).

26. Sabine Breitsameter, "Ways of Listening, Figures of Thought," in *Ways of Listening, Figures of Thought*, ed. Sabine Breitsameter and Eric Leonardson (Darmstadt: Hochschule Darmstadt, 2013), 18. Breitsameter defines radiophonic as "the full range of audio techniques and tools which can be utilized for the creation of acoustic formats that appear on radio, especially field recorded, environmental sounds, music and spoken word."

27. Gregory Whitehead, "Out of the Dark: Notes on the Nobodies of Radio Art," in *Wireless Imagination: Sound, Radio and the Avant-Garde*, ed. Douglas Kahn and Gregory Whitehead (Cambridge: MIT Press, 1992), 253, emphasis in original.

28. Ultra-red, *Five Protocols for Organized Living*, self-published pamphlet, 2012, 4, http://www.ultrared.org/uploads/2012-Five_Protocols.pdf (accessed 27 December 2023).

29. For a contrasting viewpoint, see "The Genius Is in the Genesis: Demythologizing the Idea of Gould as Creative Outsider," in the present volume.

30. Radio broadcasts of *musique concrète, elektronische Musik*, and their respective culminations in the Acousmonium and various multispeaker presentations (e.g., the quadraphonic array of Stockhausen's *Kontakte*) suggest that radio broadcasts of these works were intended merely as a waypoint toward live concert presentation.

31. Howard Fink, "On the Trail of Radio Drama: Organizing a Study of North American and European Practices," *Journal of Radio Studies* 6, no. 1 (1999): 130. Fink states *North* "was rebroadcast in 1991 in Klaus Schöning's *Akustische Kunst* series from Cologne, Germany."

32. Glenn Gould, "Radio as Music: Glenn Gould in Conversation with John Jessop," in *The Glenn Gould Reader*, ed. Tim Page (New York: Vintage Books, 1990), 385.

33. John F. Szwed, *Space Is the Place: The Lives and Times of Sun Ra* (New York: Pantheon, 1997), 199. Szwed notes that *Next Stop Mars* was recorded in 1963 but not released on LP until 1966.

34. Keir Keightley, "'Turn It Down!' She Shrieked: Gender, Domestic Space, and High Fidelity, 1948–59," *Popular Music* 15, no. 2 (May 1996): 162–163 and 167, explores the gendering of hi-fi stereo systems as furniture (feminine) or free-standing components (masculine).

35. Media historian Tim J. Anderson distinguishes two approaches to stereo, the "realistic" and the "melocentric." Anderson, *Making Easy Listening: Material Culture and Postwar American Recording* (Minneapolis: University of Minnesota Press, 2006).

36. Eric Barry, "Mono in the Stereo Age," in *Living Stereo: Histories and Cultures of Multichannel Sound*, ed. Paul Théberge, Kyle Devine, and Paul Everrett (New York: Bloomsbury, 2015), 142.

37. Charles Mingus, *The Black Saint and the Sinner Lady* (untitled liner notes) ITC 308 (insert A), New York, Impulse! Records, 1963.

38. Richard Capeless, "How They Heard It—Blue Note Records and the Transition from Mono to Stereo," *LondonJazzCollector* [sic], https://londonjazzcollector.wordpress.com/2014/07/24/guest-post-how-they-heard-it-blue-note-records-and-the-transition-from-mono-to-stereo 23 October 2014 (revision of July 24, 2014, blog post) (accessed 27 December 2023).

39. Gould, "The Prospects of Recording," in *The Glenn Gould Reader*, 345.

40. On 26 September 1970, Gould wrote to R. A. J. Phillips regarding *North*, "We're going to attempt to stereoize it prior to its release in that form [on LP], and although this will, in itself, be a major undertaking, it will, I think, render into still more cogent counterpoint the multitrack sequences and thereby ensure it a long life in recorded form." I am grateful to Anthony Cushing for finding and providing this fascinating document.

41. Canning, *A Glenn Gould Catalog*, xv.

42. Somerville, "The Gould Radio Documentaries," 1.

43. Bob Cobbing, "Some Statements on Sound Poetry," in *Sound Poetry: A Catalogue*, ed. Steve McCaffery and bpNichol (Toronto: Underwhich Editions, 1978), 39.

44. See the cover of Gould, *North*, 1992.

45. Gould, "Rubenstein," in *The Glenn Gould Reader*, 288, describes editing interviews for *The Latecomers*.

46. Johnson, "Stories Untold."

47. Gould, "Rubenstein," 288.

48. Mary Jo Watts, *The Idea of North* by Glenn Gould, transcript of *The Idea of North*, https://web.archive.org/web/20010224012530/http://www.rci.rutgers.edu/~mwatts/glenn/ion.html 24 February 2001 (accessed 27 December 2023).

49. Richard Kostelanetz, "Text Sound Art: A Survey," in *Text-Sound Texts* (New York: William Morrow, 1980).

50. Richard Kostelanetz, *The New Poetries and Some Old* (Carbondale: Southern Illinois University Press, 1991), 32.

51. See Dick Higgins, "A Taxonomy of Sound Poetry," http://www.ubu.com/papers/higgins_sound.html 1980 (accessed 23 December 2023); and Cathy Lane, "Voices from the Past: Compositional Approaches to Using Recorded Speech," *Organized Sound* 11, no. 1 (2006): 3–11, for other taxonomies of sound poetry and composing with recorded speech.

52. Exemplary collaborative histories of twentieth-century avant-garde movements include *A Power Stronger than Itself* by George E. Lewis; *The San Francisco Tape Music Center* edited by David W. Bernstein; and *Dub* by Michael Veal.

53. Nancy Perloff, "Sound Poetry and the Musical Avant-Garde: A Musicologist's Perspective," in *The Sound of Poetry / The Poetry of Sound*, ed. Marjorie Perloff and Craig Dworkin (Chicago: University of Chicago Press, 2006), 97–98.

54. Accessed 15 March 2020.

55. See Jay Weitz, "Defending Differences from Duplicate Detection," *OCLC Next*, https://blog.oclc.org/next/defending-differences/, 2016 (accessed 4 December 2024) for details on the process of culling duplicates in WorldCat.org.

56. This number, 155,869,980, divided by the standard CD (aka "Red Book") sample rate of 44,100 samples per second, equals 3534.466 seconds or 58.9 minutes, that is, 58 minutes and 54 seconds.

57. Yuk Hui, "What Is a Digital Object?," *Metaphilosophy* 43, no. 4 (July 2012): 380.

58. McLuhan, "New Media and the Arts," 239.

59. Hui, "What Is a Digital Object?," 393.

60. Personal correspondence 6 February 2017.

61. Friedemann Sallis, "Glenn Gould's *Idea of North* and the Production of Place in Music," *Intersections: Canadian Journal of Music* 25, no. 1–2 (2005): 117.

62. See http://delaurenti.net/protest/ (accessed 23 December 2023).

63. See https://www.youtube.com/watch?v=ry5MUnZoeGI uploaded 30 September 2014; https://www.youtube.com/watch?v=Tsux27kMwjc uploaded 5 February 2015; and https://www.youtube.com/watch?v=TwIbUdbVqQE uploaded 28 September 2014 (all accessed 27 December 2023). *North* is not known by its equivalent title in Francophone Canada; a Google video search of "Idée du Nord" together with "Gould" on 9 November 2018 yielded eleven results. A reprise of the same search on 27 December 2023 yielded no results. None linked to *North*. A search without terms delimited by quotes yielded "about 11,400 results" according to Google with the top two results linking to the televised version and radiophonic *North* respectively.

64. See https://lumendatabase.org (accessed 27 December 2023).

65. See https://support.google.com/youtube/answer/2991785, especially "How Views Are Counted" (accessed 27 December 2023).

66. A complete stream is also available on Spotify.com, Amazon.com, and NaxosMusicLibrary.com (accessed 27 December 2023).

67. Gould, *North*, 3:08.

68. Gould, "Prologue from 'The Idea of North,'" in *The Glenn Gould Reader*, 389, mistranscribes the second mention of "lakes." Schroeder actually says "lake."

69. Gould, "Prologue from 'The Idea of North,'" 393.

70. A search of Amazon.com for "soundscape" results in titles such as *Music for Stress Relief*, *Music to Journal By, Vol. I—Soaking Music Soundscapes for Hearing God's Voice*, and *Soundscapes for Relaxation, Meditation, Healing and Sleep*.

71. See Tim Ingold, "Against Soundscape," in *Autumn Leaves* (Paris: Double Entendre, 2007); and Ari Y. Kelman, "Rethinking the Soundscape," *Sense and Society* 5, no. 2 (2010), for a critique of Schafer's concept and those who (mis)use the term.

72. R. Murray Schafer, *The Tuning of the World* (New York: Alfred A. Knopf, 1977), 274.

73. Kelman, "Rethinking the Soundscape," 228.

74. Schafer, *Tuning of the World*, 7.

75. Breitsameter, "Ways of Listening," 24.

76. Breitsameter, "Ways of Listening," 18.

77. Schafer, *Tuning of the World*, 76.

78. Gould, "Glenn Gould Interviews Glenn Gould About Glenn Gould," in *The Glenn Gould Reader*, 325.

79. Alten discusses the desirably dry objective acoustics of the recording studio control room. Stanley R. Alten, *Audio in Media*, 10th ed. (Boston: Wadsworth, 2014).

80. Richard Kostelanetz, "Glenn Gould as Radio Composer," *Massachusetts Review* 29, no. 3 (Fall 1988): 562.

81. Kostelanetz, "Glenn Gould as Radio Composer," 561.

82. Reproduced in Sallis, "Glenn Gould's *Idea of North*," 123 and Cushing, "Glenn Gould and 'Opus 2,'" 24.

83. Michael Dorrough, "The VU Meter," paper presentation 1794, 69th Audio Engineering Society Convention, May 1981, http://www.aes.org/e-lib/browse.cfm?elib=11960&rndx=242582 and http://www.aes.org/e-lib/browse.cfm?elib=11960 (accessed 23 December 2023), 3.

84. Bobby Owsinski, *The Mastering Engineer's Handbook*, 4th ed. (Burbank: BOMG, 2016), 56.

85. Dorrough, "The VU Meter," 1; and Owsinski, *The Mastering Engineer's Handbook*, 56–57. Most contemporary audio production employs peak Metering and true peak metering in tandem with LUFS (loudness units full scale); VU meters remain in recording studios rooted in vintage analog technology. Today, most users encounter VU meters in audio software plug-ins that model classic analog gear.

86. Gould, "Radio as Music," 379.

87. Breitsameter, "Ways of Listening," 19.

88. Gould, "The Prospects of Recording," 347.

89. Martin Spinelli, "Electric Line: The Poetics of Digital Audio Editing," in *New Media Poetics: Contexts, Technotexts, and Theories*, ed. Adalaide Morris and Thomas Swiss (Cambridge: MIT Press, 2007), 103.

90. But this is perceptible only at low bitrates; see Jonathan Sterne's *MP3: The Meaning of a Format* (Durham, NC: Duke University Press, 2012). Greater obstacles are posed by earbud headphones and computer speakers.

91. David C. Jackson, "Militant Sound Investigation," conference paper read at Circuits of Struggle, Ontario, 2 May 2015, 6.

92. See note 69 in this chapter.

93. These lengths cannot be rendered in exact milliseconds as many of the phrases end with a fricative "ff" or "h," which may or may not be audible depending on the listener's volume level.

94. Time is measured here in minutes:seconds.milliseconds; 1,000 milliseconds = 1 second.

95. John Purcell, *Dialogue Editing for Motion Pictures: A Guide to the Invisible Art* (Burlington, VT: Focal Press, 2007), 194.

96. Gould, "The Prospects of Recording," 338.

97. Juan G. Roederer, *The Physics and Psychophysics of Music* (New York: Springer Verlag, 1995), 96, uses the term "adaptation" without the common prefixes "audio" or "sensory."

98. Carryl L. Baldwin, *Auditory Cognition* (Boca Raton: CRC Press, 2012), 36.

99. Kostelanetz, "Glenn Gould as Radio Composer," 560.

100. Gould, "'The Idea of North': An Introduction," 393.

101. Sallis, "Glenn Gould's *Idea of North*," 119.

102. Cushing, "Glenn Gould and 'Opus 2,'" 30.

103. R. Murray Schafer, "Open Ears," *Soundscape: The Journal of Acoustic Ecology* 4, no. 2 (Fall/Winter 2003): 14.

104. Gould, "Radio as Music," 379.

105. Gould, *North*, 8:13.

106. Gould, *North*, 7:59.

107. Martin Spinelli, "Rhetorical Figures and the Digital Editing of Radio Speech," *Convergence* 12, no. 2 (2006): 209.

108. Gould, "Glenn Gould in Conversation with Tim Page," in *The Glenn Gould Reader*, 457.

109. Cushing, "Glenn Gould and 'Opus 2,'" 31.

110. Jeff Porter, "Radio as Music: Glenn Gould's Contrapuntal Sound," in *Lost Sound: The Forgotten Art of Radio Storytelling* (Chapel Hill: University of North Carolina Press, 2016), 166.

111. Rita Raley, *Tactical Media* (Minneapolis: University of Minnesota Press, 2005), 1.

112. Raley, *Tactical Media*, 6.

113. Cirauqui, "Thanatophonics," 20.

114. Eric Kluitenberg, *Legacies of Tactical Media* (Amsterdam: Network Notebooks, 2011), 17.

115. Edward Jones-Imhotep, "Malleability and Machines: Glenn Gould and the Technological Self," *Technology and Culture* 57, no. 2 (April 2016): 303.

116. Jordan Crandall, *Under Fire 1: The Organization and Representation of Violence* (Rotterdam: Witte de With Center for Contemporary Art, 2004), 15.

117. Gould, "Radio as Music," 382.

118. Crandall, *Under Fire 1*, 15.

119. John Thompson, "There Is a Strong Visual Component in Radio" [Interview with Glenn Gould conducted in 1975], *Intermédialités* no. 19 (Spring 2012): 183–184.

120. Kent Kennan, *Counterpoint*, 4th ed. (Englewood Cliffs, NJ: Prentice-Hall, 1999), 1.

121. Alfred Bester, "The Zany Genius of Glenn Gould," *Holiday*, April 1964, 150.

122. Ajay Heble, "New Contexts of Canadian Criticism: Democracy, Counterpoint, Responsibility," in *New Contexts of Canadian Criticism*, ed. Ajay Heble, Donna Palmateer Pennee, and J. R. Struthers (Peterborough, ON: Broadview Press, 1997), 90.

123. Heble, "New Contexts of Canadian Criticism," 90.
124. Whitehead, "Out of the Dark," 256.
125. Gould, *North*, 57:25–58:36. Transcription by Watts with corrections and emendations by the author.
126. Gould, *North*, 58:37–58:45.

4

"That Incredible Tapestry"

Revisiting *Pilgrimage to Solitude*, *The Idea of North*, and the Landscapes of Glenn Gould

MARK LAURIE

"What more can be said about Glenn Gould?" This refrain, which I encountered with discouraging frequency during the production of *Pilgrimage to Solitude* (2009), my documentary about Gould's life, mind, and music, was, perhaps, to be expected. By 2007, when I began photographing the Toronto-area sites most closely associated with Gould, an enormous volume of commentary already existed about the enigmatic pianist. Indeed, few twentieth-century performers have been the focus of so much enduring admiration (with as much enduring controversy). Writers, like Kevin Bazzana, have come to speak of the emergence of a veritable Gould "industry."[1] This industry has produced a vast number of commemorative works, including several major biographies, which each emphasizes a different dimension or employs a different mode of analysis (musical, philosophical, psychological).[2] Arguably the only area where Gould's influence is comparatively muted is in the relative dearth of pianistic imitators. As the *Toronto Star* music critic William Littler noted when I interviewed him for *Pilgrimage*, those lacking the unparalleled technical abilities of Gould come off as mere "caricature . . . and nobody wants to go through life as a caricaturist except a caricaturist."[3]

The unique memorializing impulse that fuels the Gould industry reflects his exceptionally broad impact on contemporary cultural life. He is, of course, celebrated for his pathbreaking interpretations of the piano repertoire, above all his hyperarticulated Bach, but also his irreverent Beethoven, technicolor Mozart, and deeply expressive Byrd, Brahms, and Schoenberg. Artists and theorists have also long admired his multidisciplinary approach (as pianist, composer, critic, conductor, and documentarian), his blurring of traditional artistic boundaries and categories, and his visionary embrace of new technologies. In Canada, Gould occupies a particularly exalted stature, with his ubiquity on the airwaves of the Canadian Broadcasting Corporation (CBC) and his fascination with the country's north serving as indicators of his quintessential Canadianness.

No matter the underlying reasons, Gould has become the object of a particularly cultlike archival obsession, as even those portions of his personal ephemera bearing dubious relation to his creative output are meticulously catalogued, preserved, and periodically displayed (in the manner of religious relics) by Library and Archives Canada; sifting through and enumerating the contents of his personal archival fonds is a favorite pastime for biographers. In the first posthumous biography of Gould, Otto Friedrich observed that the seventy-two meters of shelving devoted to Gould's personal effects included "a box containing four pairs of sunglasses and another with three wristwatches, one stopped at quarter past one, one at quarter past five, and one at quarter past six. And a box containing nothing but 'miscellaneous keys,' dozens and dozens of them, on rings and chains and various bits of string, door keys, car keys, trunk keys, keys to God knows what forgotten cupboards and closets."[4] It is difficult to ignore the voyeuristic overtones of this passage with its painstaking scrutiny of the banal possessions of an artist known for his reclusive lifestyle. Such voyeurism is not limited to Friedrich. According to Bazzana, pilgrims visit the library "often not to study Gould's papers as much as to see and touch them," asserting that the institution's staff "have always been uneasy with the library's status as a *de facto* Gould museum."[5] In recognition of this, a 2007–2009 exhibition at the Canadian Museum of Civilization entitled *Glenn Gould: The Sounds of Genius* allowed the public an opportunity to view a sampling of the sunglasses and keys (each one carefully numbered in miniscule handwriting) alongside framed Bell telephone bills, pens, and cufflinks. Nonetheless, despite this broad-based and enduring public obsession, or perhaps because of it, the question remains: "What more can be said about Glenn Gould?" Less and less, it would seem, especially since the living memory of Gould is finally starting to dissipate, an inevitability considering the passage of more than four decades since his death, in 1982, at age fifty. One might speculate that the looming disappearance of the firsthand, living testimony of his personal friends and professional acquaintances will signal the demise of the Gould industry's first, "documentary" phase; it is still unclear what will succeed it.

It was into this context, crowded and yet uncertain, that I placed my own documentary, *Pilgrimage to Solitude*. The film employs Gould's own "contrapuntal radio" technique of layered voices (taken from interviews) to examine the mind of its originator, with particular emphasis on Gould's personal geography and sense of place. *Pilgrimage* is a personal response rather than an attempt to produce a comprehensive synthesis of a complex life and its equally complex posthumous reverberations. As someone born in the historical moment of Gould's death and raised among the Toronto places and institutions where his mythology resonates most strongly, I framed *Pilgrimage* as a journey to reimagine those sites familiar to Gould as he might have seen them. Through experimentation with Gould's creative methods (while avoiding the picked-over archive altogether), I hoped to inscribe my own voice within the elaborate counterpoint that has become Glenn Gould's posthumous life.

Landscapes of Glenn Gould: The Genesis of *Pilgrimage to Solitude*

Pilgrimage to Solitude explores geographical places of significance from Gould's biography, above all in Toronto and the northern Ontario town of Wawa, where he assembled the script for his first contrapuntal radio documentary, *The Idea of North*. Visually, *Pilgrimage* takes the form of an extended montage of long-held, mostly static views of the Gould sites, shot on Super 8mm film, an anachronistic and disappearing cinematographic medium. The use of film—as opposed to video—evokes memory, the intimacy of home movies, and other personal modes of filmmaking, among them the characteristically Canadian "landscape film."[6] The documentary soundtrack interweaves the spoken reminiscences of Gould's friends and colleagues using his contrapuntal radio technique, taking a number of structural and stylistic cues from *North*.

As a landscape film, *Pilgrimage* focuses on the geographical backdrop of Gould's life—spaces and places where his former presence is, for the most part, unmarked and thus imperceptible. Its genesis depended on the realization that Gould, despite being an artist working almost exclusively in the domains of sound and language, is inextricably linked in the popular Canadian imagination with the visual image of the landscape. Gould exercised a significant degree of control over his own representation in promotional and journalistic photographs and played a role in creating the now-familiar motif of himself as a solitary man set against a barren winter scene. During the 1950s, Jock Carroll photographed Gould negotiating craggy shards of ice against the deep blue horizon of Lake Ontario, in compositions recalling the paintings of Caspar David Friedrich.[7] Two decades later, Don Hunstein, the Columbia Records staff photographer, followed Gould to a snowy park, resulting in the iconic image of the pianist huddled contemplatively on a bench looking outward at a landscape of bare trees and yet more ice.[8] Recalling one such photo shoot, Hunstein noted, "Glenn stopped the car, got out, and stood looking over a frozen lake surrounded by pines, under a heavy sky. Once again, he had found his landscape."[9] John McGreevy's film, *Glenn Gould's Toronto* (1979), part of McGreevy's *Cities* series, highlights Gould's affinity for solitary spaces by placing him in the opposite environments: crowded urban spaces such as the Canadian National Exhibition and the then-new Eaton Centre shopping mall where the pianist seems genuinely ill at ease. McGreevey portrays Gould as a city-dweller whose sanity depended on finding rare places of escape *within* the chaos. In the film, Gould finds one such refuge at the Metropolitan Toronto Zoo, where he sings Gustav Mahler's "Des Antonius von Padua Fischpredigt" (from *Des Knaben Wunderhorn*) to the elephants. Since his death, the image of Gould as a solitary figure against the landscape has become a dominant motif in a number of commemorative works, such as François Girard's *Thirty Two Short Films About Glenn Gould* (1993) as well as the painted portrait of Gould by Yana Movchan commissioned by the Glenn Gould Foundation in 2007. However, despite Gould's visual self-fashioning, I argue that the cultural persistence of this image stems, above all, from his renderings of the landscape in the realm of sound: the radio documentaries of the *Solitude Trilogy*, particularly *North*. It was in these works that he most thoroughly elaborated his philosophy of solitude, and that he explored the complex and often contradictory reactions of the psyche to the isolated spaces where he felt most at home.

To explore the intersection of Gould's art and sense of place in *Pilgrimage*, I adopted the contrapuntal radio technique that Gould pioneered in *North*. In this work, Gould experimented with simultaneously overlaying discrete vocal lines (as spoken by his interviewees) to create a "musical" effect. In *Pilgrimage*, I used contrapuntal radio along with static or slowly moving images of the Gould sites to suggest affinities between his creative personality that expressed itself through sound and his physical environment. Following Gould's musical semiotic, as Cushing discusses in this volume in chapter 5, the visual imagery acts as a kind of basso continuo, providing a sense of rootedness (in the landscape) to the contrapuntal vocal lines above it.

Documentaris personae

The contrapuntal soundtrack for *Pilgrimage* features four speakers, friends and colleagues of Gould during the period of his creative maturity. All were associated with the CBC and, as such, had firsthand experience of Gould's innovations in broadcasting. Nevertheless, they represent a range of contrasting perspectives on Gould's mind and music and thus were well suited for the contrapuntal treatment.[10]

William Littler, a writer and broadcaster, began his long tenure as classical music critic for the *Toronto Star* in 1966. Himself a pianist, he wrote countless reviews and articles on Gould for the newspaper, including its multiple obituary tributes that drew together the main themes of Gould's life.[11] Littler paid a late-night visit to the studio where Gould edited *North* and explored the connections between the radio documentaries and Gould's personality in his essay, "The Quest for Solitude," published in John McGreevy's 1983 anthology, *Glenn Gould Variations: By Himself and His Friends*.[12] Littler was also Gould's neighbor at the Park Lane Apartments on St. Clair Avenue West in Toronto, and they occasionally drove home together from the CBC. Littler recalled to me, "As befitted my humbler station in life, I was on the third floor, while Gould was in the penthouse."[13]

Margaret Pacsu, an American-born broadcaster, worked as a television news anchor and hosted a music show, *Listen to the Music*, on CBC Radio. Pacsu collaborated with Gould on his *Silver Jubilee Album* in 1980. For that record, she acted as a moderator in a scripted discussion between Gould's various comic personae and her own alter ego, Márta Hortaványi, a Marxist musicologist from Hungary.[14] Pacsu also makes an appearance in *Thirty Two Short Films*, whose twenty-fourth vignette consists of a brief interview on the topic of Gould's dependence on prescription drugs.

Vincent Tovell represents the voice of the previous generation. A decade older than Gould, Tovell (who died in 2014) was a prominent producer of arts and history television programming for the CBC, working on documentary series such as *Images of Canada*, that, in collaboration with thinkers like Northrop Frye, explored Canadian history and identity through landscape, architecture, and visual culture.[15] Tovell interviewed Gould several times, and produced various musical programs with the pianist during the 1960s. After Gould's death, Tovell codirected the first posthumous documentary on the musician, *Glenn Gould: A Portrait*.[16]

Among the four interviewees whose voices appear in *Pilgrimage*, Lorne Tulk was one of Gould's closest friends. Tulk first met Gould on Christmas Eve 1950, when he cut an acetate record of the pianist's first radio recital in his father's recording studio.[17] He reconnected with Gould seventeen years later, working on Gould's humorous radio essay *The Search for Petula Clark*. He subsequently edited *North* and later documentaries. Though an employee of the CBC throughout the 1970s, Tulk worked after-hours for Gould on piano recordings at the Eaton Auditorium in downtown Toronto.

The Contrapuntal Soundtrack in *Pilgrimage to Solitude*

The idea of adopting Gould's contrapuntal radio technique to accompany the visual imagery in *Pilgrimage* evolved initially from the practical decision to conduct audio-only interviews with Gould's friends rather than undertake the interviews onscreen; I reasoned that one-on-one audio interviews would be more intimate, with less self-consciousness and greater candor. However, once adopted, I considered the contrapuntal soundtrack to be determinative of the work's overall structure, with the visual imagery playing a supporting role. The resulting work is perhaps better described as a sound documentary with images than as a film. In this regard, I was influenced by Judith Pearlman's film version of *North* (1970), which sets Gould's original radio documentary to a series of evocative images (some overlapping to kaleidoscopic effect), illustrating the divergent perceptions of northern Canada as related by Gould's five interviewees. Pearlman characterizes her film as an early example of the "music video,"[18] a modest label for such a substantial work, but one that speaks to the intricate, musical construction of Gould's soundtrack. Like a musical work, Gould's *North* was so dependent on the subtle, momentary interactions of spoken words that it would not permit any significant reediting of sound in the service of pictures. Similarly, during the production of *Pilgrimage*, I worked toward a final "sound lock" and edited the pictures to fit the soundtrack's themes, harmonies, and rhythms.

Gould's contrapuntal radio works are described variously as documentaries and as musical compositions;[19] Vincent Tovell favored the term "operas,"[20] whereas Geoffrey Payzant's nuanced description encompassed "hybrids of music, drama, and several other strains, including essay, journalism, anthropology, ethics, social commentary, [and] contemporary history."[21] This range of descriptors points to the technique's most remarkable feature: its ability to evoke simultaneously both the linguistic-communicative and musical facets of spontaneous human speech. In defiance of long-standing broadcast conventions that accorded supremacy to a single vocal line, lulling the audience into passive agreement with its singular message, Gould believed that contrapuntal radio should present a challenge to his listeners. At the same time, he believed listeners could absorb multiple streams of information at once, while appreciating the "musical" whole created by their overlapping textures.[22] Gould was hesitant to make the claim that contrapuntal radio involved the transposition of highly regimented musical *forms* such as fugue onto spontaneous human utterances taken from interviews; he preferred to speak of creating musical textures.[23] The experience of contrapuntal radio varies from listener to listener, and from first to subsequent listenings, wherein lies its power. On first hearing, the multiple spoken lines can induce aural fatigue, but after repeated listenings the fatigue subsides and the listener may uncover previously hidden contrasts and connections of argument, emphasis, wording, accent, harmony, and rhythm. In essence, the listener may perceive the work's balance of music and meaning differently with each audition. For this reason, one could argue that *radio*—where programs in progress could be "happened upon" by listeners unprepared for the technique and repeated broadcasts were not available "on demand"—was perhaps not the ideal medium for presenting the contrapuntal sound documentary.[24] By contrast, sound recordings (tape, vinyl records) afforded listeners the opportunity for complete personal listenings, even repeated listenings, of such challenging works and would perhaps have been better suited to provide the full spectrum of the contrapuntal experience.

One reason for adopting the contrapuntal radio technique in *Pilgrimage* was that it proved ideal to raise questions about received mythologies, whether about the Canadian north or about the cliché-encrusted figure of Gould himself. By assigning equal sonic weighting to differing opinions and interpretations, I emphasize the relativity and subjectivity in our perceptions of a documentary subject. I also can chip away at the monolithic biographical representations that attempt to elide or rationalize apparent contradictions and construct a singular account out of a necessarily fragmented memory. Paul Hjartarson suggests that it was through contrapuntal radio that Gould could question "both the idea of North he and other Canadians had inherited and his own propensity 'to draw all sorts of metaphorical allusions based on what was really a very limited knowledge of the country and a very casual exposure to it.'"[25]

Kevin McNeilly observes that Gould's objective was not to suggest "a single topos, a functional 'idea' of north, but a site at which many voices and 'ideas' coalesce, antagonize, support, subvert, mingle, and separate."[26] Quoting Gould, Hjartarson similarly asserts that Gould shed his romantic preconceptions about his subject by creating "a space within which 'discordant ideas' about the north could 'be emphasized in all their jarring dissonance.'"[27] Dissonances beg resolution, and Hjartarson argues compellingly that Gould's resolution of his documentary's contrapuntal fragmentation, through Wally Maclean's moving epilogue set against Sibelius's Fifth Symphony, "unwittingly reinscribes the conception of North he [Gould] set out to question."[28] I attempted to address this problem in the concluding section of *Pilgrimage*, allowing the contrapuntal layering to increase in density until, for the first time in the work, all four voices sound simultaneously: no attempt is made to privilege a single interviewee's testimony over the other three for the sake of constructing some dramatically satisfying synthesis.

My documentary about Gould turns contrapuntal radio technique back upon itself to examine the mind of its originator. It seems fitting that *Pilgrimage* should begin with a discussion of Gould's own first foray into the technique, *North*. The choice of *North* as both model and subject was not difficult. Compared to his later, stereo works in the *Solitude Trilogy*, the monaural *North* is somewhat restrained in its contrapuntal explorations, some of which, Gould later asserted, first emerged as a practical way of fitting excess content within his limited allotment of airtime.[29] *North* is nevertheless a singularly powerful work that achieves a fine balance between clarity and complexity—and between the musical and linguistic properties of spontaneous speech. It is perhaps the most celebrated item in his entire nonpianistic oeuvre. It also reflects a core preoccupation of Gould's, central to his self-identification: artistic solitude. Gould's passion for northernness manifested itself in his musical tastes, which skewed toward the Scandinavian and Germanic and away from the Mediterranean. It may also have motivated him, in 1965, to board the Muskeg Express train and head north from Winnipeg 1,015 miles to Churchill, Manitoba, on a journey that inspired his concept for *North*.[30] Gould undertook his northern journey at a pivotal point in his life, having just retired from the concert stage. As such, the voyage marked an important dividing line in his biography, between his youthful fame as an international virtuoso and the reclusive maturity in which he explored new technological means of achieving, as Littler put it, "communication in isolation."[31] In light of the significance of *North* within Gould's creative evolution, and the centrality of its themes and methods to his self-identification, the soundtrack in *Pilgrimage* begins with a ten-minute "Return to North" that introduces Gould by way of his fascination with northern solitude and then discusses the origins of his first documentary and the impact it made on its first listeners in 1967. Furthermore, the opening section of *Pilgrimage* takes a number of structural, thematic, and stylistic cues from *North* while departing from Gould's model in several significant ways.

For *Pilgrimage*, I sought to create a contrast with the opening of Gould's *North* prologue. In *North*, Marianne Schroeder delivers her gently lilting opening line, "I was *fascinated* by the country as such," which emerges almost imperceptibly from the silence and begins a monologue on the young nurse's first impressions of the Canadian Arctic.[32] At the outset of *Pilgrimage*, Margaret Pacsu's statement, "The North is *not* my favorite place in the world," immediately recalls Schroeder's voice in pitch and meter, while opposing Schroeder in its negativity. Pacsu's next spoken lines reveal a more nuanced and ambivalent view of the northern experience, more closely aligned with Schroeder's mixture of awe and anxiety than Pacsu's first line would suggest. In *North*, the first contrapuntal texture is the baroque trio sonata of the prologue, as the male voices of Frank Vallee and Robert Phillips join Schroeder.[33] Likewise, *Pilgrimage* features a trio of staggered entrances, as speakers offer perspectives on Gould's relationship to the north: Vincent Tovell tempers Pacsu's initial skepticism with a philosophical meditation on "the arctic dimension" of Gould's imagination and its religious overtones, and then Lorne Tulk counters abruptly, "It had nothing to do with north . . . what it had to do with was solitude."

The second half of the opening transitions from a general discussion of the Canadian north to a series of recollections about the production of

North specifically. The speakers recount their initial impressions of contrapuntal radio technique and offer some speculations as to its workings upon the listener's mind. I conceived of this passage as a "process about a process," in which each speaker discusses counterpoint while simultaneously becoming a part of it. This follows Gould's example in his clever multipart vocal piece "So You Want to Write a Fugue?," a "fugue about the writing of fugues."[34] In this passage, Littler describes the way Gould edited the voices of interviewees to create simulated conversations between them; next, Tulk enters to offer an analysis of how contrapuntal radio worked on various cognitive levels; finally, Pacsu enters and exclaims above them, "Yes, it was polyphony!" Soon after this climax, Littler's voice fades away, and then Tulk follows, leaving Pacsu to end the "Return to North" on a bittersweet note: "I had never heard anything like that before. And I hear it and it doesn't have the same impact on me, of course, now . . ."

The next two sections are less contrapuntal, which allows each speaker more time to reminisce unchallenged and provides the listener a temporary break from the challenging superimposition of what Gould called "elements in a state of flux, interplay, [and] nervous agitation."[35] These two sections explore the themes of "Performance and Its Perils" and "Conversations with Gould." In the former, the four speakers discuss Gould's anxiety about the stage and his desire to replace a culture of live, public performances with a new paradigm centered on studio-based recording. This segment explores the tensions between seeing and listening in the experience of music. The speakers also discuss the hybrid space of the televised concert, and the prevailing view of Gould's aversion to live performance is offset by counterexamples. In the latter section, which is the least contrapuntal and meant to evoke a telephone exchange, Pacsu, Littler, and Tovell each describe memorable conversations they had with Gould. The three debate the meaning of his alter egos and emphasize his affinity for the telephone instead of direct human contact.

The fourth and final section departs from the example of *North*, whose epilogue consists of the stirring soliloquy of Wally Maclean set to the finale of Sibelius's Fifth Symphony, in which he expounds on the human struggle against hostile nature and its importance as a unifying tie with which civilization binds itself. Although contemplated in the early stages of scripting, I dispensed with the soliloquy concept in favor of a recapitulation of the first section's dense contrapuntal texture. In this section, Tulk and Pacsu remember the shock of Gould's death, followed by a sober assessment of the musician's legacy from Littler. Following the example of *North*, in *Pilgrimage*, we hear music: Gould playing Brahms's Intermezzo in A Major, op. 118, no. 2. I chose that recording, one of Brahms's final works, for its elegiac lyricism that complemented the nostalgic reminisces of my interviewees. It is a stark contrast to the triumphant bombast Gould achieves with Sibelius; whereas Brahms wrote the introspective intermezzo to reflect back on a long career, Gould's optimistic use of Sibelius looks forward to the future of the north. It is at this moment that Gould, the absent figure in the landscape, becomes present and embodied in the soundscape. Each speaker offers one last statement on Gould, and for the first time in the work, we hear four-part spoken counterpoint: Tulk remembers an impromptu lunchtime concert Gould gave toward the end of his life, Littler contemplates Gould's importance in the history of music, Pacsu discusses the local Toronto places that remind her of Gould, and Tovell returns his thoughts to the vast spaces of the north. Mirroring the opening, Pacsu and Tovell are the last two audible speakers. He expresses the Frye-inflected idea of a journey without arrival: "I keep remembering, he was only fifty. He was still discovering himself as he got older. Most of us, I hope, do." Pacsu, speaking about Gould's gravesite in Toronto's Mount Pleasant Cemetery, says: "That whole little area of his with the tree . . . that's a beautiful place." With this statement, she evokes a peace that was noticeably absent in the statement that began the work: "The North is *not* my favorite place in the world."

Tissue of Memory:
The Super 8mm Imagery in *Pilgrimage to Solitude*

Along with the use of contrapuntal radio, my decision to shoot the project on Super 8mm film represented a key moment in the evolution of *Pilgrimage* toward a final form. Initially, I proposed shooting *Pilgrimage* on high-definition (HD) video. However, after undertaking HD shoots at the Phillips Collection in Washington, DC,[36] and at Gould's cottage at Uptergrove on Lake Simcoe in central Ontario, I was dissatisfied with the results, feeling that, for a project whose goal was to conjure a sense of memory and fleetingness, the extreme visual sharpness and clarity of HD could achieve little more than a banal indexicality. HD, it seemed, was so crystalline in its rendering of the present that it overwhelmed any contemplation—nostalgic or otherwise—of the film's unseeable subject, the departed figure of Gould. By contrast, Super 8mm film intrinsically possessed the visual qualities amenable to my objectives: the prominent film grain, high-contrast look, and imperfect, slightly jittery registration serve to imbue even long-held, stationary takes with movement, rhythm, and a sense of fleeting time. Addressing the fundamental qualities that make film, as opposed to video, a quintessentially memorial medium, the Canadian experimental filmmaker Rick Hancox, whose work often engages with themes of landscape, memory, and absence, suggests, "The idea of the latent image—exposed film waiting for development—is one of the key differences between film, and its bond with the past, and video, with its window on the present."[37] Quoting Babette Mangolte, he adds, "[Grain] in film 'constantly trades spaces and places from one frame to the next . . . reinforcing the demonstration of time passing,' and yielding a sense of temporal difference that is perceived by the viewer as a kind of 'pathos.' "[38] In addition to its evocation of passing time and pathos, the Super 8mm medium is contemporary to Gould's maturity, having been introduced in 1965, the year of his voyage north to Churchill on the Muskeg Express, and in steep decline by the time of his death in 1982. At this historical moment, Super 8mm seems to be a medium in a reprieve of unknown duration; camera equipment for the film gauge has not been manufactured on a significant scale for more than thirty years, and the discontinuation, in 2005, of the legendary Kodachrome-40 reversal stock was widely regarded as the medium's death knell. As a vulnerable medium on borrowed time, the act of filming in Super 8mm is now always an act of remembrance, of looking backward, especially since the future looms uncertainly. As such, it is suited not only to evoking the past in its projected images but also to reenacting the past through its antiquated process: it is a good medium for a pilgrimage.

Visually, *Pilgrimage* consists of long, stationary shots, slow pans and tracks, and time-lapses, documenting the sites in which Gould lived and worked, with particular emphasis on those places to which he returned in search of solitude. Some of the sites depicted include Toronto's Beaches neighborhood, the quiet lakeside enclave on the city's eastern fringe where Gould spent his formative years; his winterized cottage at Uptergrove, where he recuperated from the early concert tours and recording sessions; and the now-defunct Inn on the Park, where Gould maintained a studio toward the end of his life, which commanded a high point over the wooded ravines of Toronto's Don River valley.[39]

An important influence for me in using landscape and architectural cinematography to evoke memory was Claude Lanzmann. His seminal work, *Shoah* (1985)—although dealing with a much more somber subject—similarly combines oral testimony with the physical passage through an empty space in contemplation of its inaccessible human past. In *Pilgrimage*, landscape serves as a ground for conjuring what Bill Nichols has aptly termed the "fantasmatic subject."[40] The work is propelled by dual impulses: the archaeologist's zeal in discovering and documenting environments of historical significance and the pilgrim's compulsion to project into these now-abandoned vistas a sense of the "lost object that haunts the film."[41] Sound, the aural medium, conjures the spectral presence. The contrapuntal lines of spoken remembrances in *Pilgrimage* largely resist imposing a single meaning on the interpretively open landscapes over which they drift, never quite coming to rest. At the same time, a discernible pathos pervades the gulf between image and sound; the processes of reminiscence and visual exploration are both haunted by an awareness of absence, of the unrecoverable "fantasmatic subject" at the film's center.

In contemplating the work's structure, I considered depicting Gould's spaces in an order reflecting the chronology of the musician's life. However, as noted, the contrapuntal soundtrack made the images subordinate in the work's final structure. Thus, the opening "Return to North" is accompanied by images of Wawa's winter landscape: the frozen lake, the snowbound main street dotted with faded motels, the goose statue overlooking Highway 17 as it winds along the north shore of Lake Superior. The section on "Performance and Its Perils" has at its center the Eaton Auditorium where Gould performed and recorded over so many years, and the discussion of his death brings the viewer finally to the flat grave marker in Mount Pleasant Cemetery, adorned with the opening of the aria from the *Goldberg Variations*. Throughout the work, the camera, responding to thematic cues in the contrapuntal soundtrack, travels searchingly across Gould's personal geography. It lingers in those places where Gould could have found a measure of the anonymity and the restorative isolation that he explored so richly in *North*: remote Wawa, quiet Uptergrove, the ravines and beaches of Toronto. In *The Idea of North*, Gould explored the condition of solitude existing on the distant margins of northern Canada; *Pilgrimage* finds it closer to home, in Glenn Gould's own landscapes of memory.

Editors' Epilogue

Laurie revisited *Pilgrimage* in 2017, adapting the soundtrack into a radio version to mark the fiftieth anniversary of *North*'s December 1967 broadcast premiere on CBC's *Ideas*. Working with *Ideas* executive producer Greg Kelly, Laurie was provided the use of an editing suite at the CBC Vancouver studios in summer and fall 2017. The aim of the radio project was to "smooth out rough edges . . . [and] create a more audience-friendly sound documentary."[42] The new work is titled *Return to North: The Soundscapes of Glenn Gould* and is notable for its extensive use of music, which Kelly encouraged. Whereas *Pilgrimage* used the combination of visuals and audio to delineate the work's sections, Laurie relied on music as a sectioning device (see table 4.1)

In *Return to North*, the only sections where spoken voices and music overlap texturally are the first and the last. In the first, Laurie

Table 4.1. Formal Diagram of *Return to North*

Section	Thematic Material
Intro	Spoken introduction by *Ideas* host Paul Kennedy.
I	Largely about contrapuntal radio. Contrapuntal texture with at least two voices and music. Music: William Byrd's *Hughe Ashton's Ground*, Glenn Gould, piano.
Music	J. S. Bach, *Well-Tempered Clavier Book I*, A-flat Major fugue, Glenn Gould, piano.
II	Gould's performance career and recordings. Linear with no contrapuntal elements in speech.
Music	J. S. Bach, *Well-Tempered Clavier Book II*, C Minor fugue, Glenn Gould, piano. Music fades to background and host reintroduces *Return to North*, Laurie, and four interviewees.
III	Gould's humor, quirks, and need for control.
Music	J. S. Bach, *Well-Tempered Clavier Book I*, F-sharp Minor fugue, Glenn Gould, piano.
IV	Reminiscences on Gould's hospitalization and death. Contrapuntal with at least two voices.
V	Gould's legacy. Music: Richard Strauss, *Morgen!*, op. 27, no. 4., Elisabeth Schwarzkopf, soprano; Glenn Gould, piano.
Music	J. S. Bach, "Aria," *Goldberg Variations* (1981 recording), Glenn Gould, piano.

uses William Byrd's *Hughe Ashton's Ground* as a major-inflected foil to the discussion of Gould's conception of counterpoint and contrapuntal radio. In the last section, Laurie incorporates Richard Strauss's *Morgen!*, which accompanies William Littler's and Vincent Tovell's reflections on Gould's professional and personal legacy. The first line of the Lied's text reads, "Und morgen wird die Sonne wieder scheinen" (And tomorrow the sun will shine again), reminding the listener that there may be pause for mourning and reflection but also an opportunity to ponder future possibilities. As noted earlier in this chapter, in *Pilgrimage* Laurie used Johannes Brahms's A Major Intermezzo, op. 118, no. 2 for the last scene; in preparing his adaptation for broadcast, he considered the Brahms work to be too dense and hard to decipher for the radio audience and decided to substitute the comparatively spare Strauss Lied for a more impactful ending with a stronger sense of finality.

The inner sections of *Return to North* are marked by Laurie's choice of three fugues from books 1 and 2 of J. S. Bach's *Well-Tempered Clavier*. "The main point of using fugues was to provide some good examples of musical counterpoint and further reinforce what Gould was trying to do with contrapuntal radio."[43] Indeed, the fugues provide not only a sectional foil but also meaning; Laurie used the solemn f-sharp minor fugue from book 1 before the section about Gould's death.

While *Pilgrimage* was Laurie's personal statement and project, *Return to North* is a broader and more accessible work and a lasting testament to the power and creative influence of Gould's contrapuntal radio.

Notes

1. Kevin Bazzana, *Wondrous Strange: The Life and Art of Glenn Gould* (Toronto: McClelland & Stewart, 2003), 9.

2. Beyond scholarly writing, other recent tributes to Gould include the 2009 film *Genius Within: The Inner Life of Glenn Gould*, directed by Michèle Hozer and Peter Raymont; the 2014 Toronto revival of David Young's play *Glenn*; and Sandrine Revel's graphic novel *Glenn Gould: A Life Off Tempo* (2016).

3. William Littler, interview with the author, 17 September 2008.

4. Otto Friedrich, *Glenn Gould: A Life and Variations* (New York: Random House, 1989), 8.

5. Bazzana, *Wondrous Strange*, 7. Since the publication of Bazzana's account, Library and Archives Canada has imposed certain restrictions on public access to Gould's papers.

6. Bart Testa notes that Canadian experimental filmmakers have long taken a great interest in the landscape, reflecting an earlier preoccupation in Canadian painting as well as a national cinematic culture characterized by a strong inclination toward the documentary genre and "on-location" filming. Testa further observes that many prominent Canadian film artists, including Jack Chambers, Joyce Wieland, Rick Hancox, and Richard Kerr, among others, have adopted a painterly approach to their filmmaking practices while making use of the temporal, spatial, and kinetic qualities specific to cinema. See Bart Testa, *Spirit in the Landscape* (Toronto: Art Gallery of Ontario, 1989), 4–5.

7. Attila Csampai, *Glenn Gould: Photographische Suiten* (Munich: Schirmer/Mosel, 1995), 54–56. See also Jock Carroll, *Glenn Gould: Some Portraits of the Artist as a Young Man* (Toronto: Stoddart, 1995).

8. Tim Page, *Glenn Gould: A Life in Pictures* (Toronto: Doubleday, 2002), 6–7.

9. Rhona Bergman, *The Idea of Gould* (Philadelphia: Lev, 1999), 110.

10. According to Lorne Tulk, Gould was known to compartmentalize his relationships to the extent that his friends often had little sense of whom else he numbered among them. Lorne Tulk, interview with the author, 19 December 2008.

11. William Littler, "His Curiosity Made Label of Pianist So Inadequate," *Toronto Star*, 5 October 1982, E1. See also William Littler, "Glenn Gould: Inside the Mind of a Genius," *Toronto Star*, 9 October 1982, F1.

12. John McGreevy, ed., *Glenn Gould Variations: By Himself and His Friends* (New York: Doubleday, 1983).

13. William Littler, interview with the author, 17 September 2008.

14. Pacsu notes that she modeled Hortaványi after her own mother, a Hungarian-born pianist and "Bartók groupie." Margaret Pacsu, interview with the author, 4 February 2009.

15. David Hogarth makes a strong case for the exceptionality of Tovell's films, noting that they had an abstract style between "visual essay" and "poetry," and rather like Gould's own radio work, they challenged "the indexical authority claimed by [National Film Board of Canada] documentaries and even journalistic and vérité television reporting at the time." David Hogarth, *Documentary Television in Canada: From National Public Service to Global Marketplace* (Montreal: McGill-Queen's University Press, 2002), 84. See also Vincent Tovell, dir., *Journey Without Arrival: A Personal Point of View from Northrop Frye*, Images of Canada series, Canadian Broadcasting Corporation, 1975.

16. Vincent Tovell and Eric Till, dirs., *Glenn Gould: A Portrait*, Kultur Video, 1985, videocassette.

17. Bergman, *The Idea of Gould*, 68.

18. Judith Pearlman, "The Idea of North," director's introduction, *The Idea of Gould*, Cinemathèque Ontario, Toronto, 26 April 2008.

19. Bazzana, *Wondrous Strange*, 301.

20. Vincent Tovell et al., "Gould, the Communicator," panel discussion, National Library of Canada, Ottawa, 25 May 1988, Glenn Gould Archive, https://www.collectionscanada.gc.ca/glenngould/028010-4020.08-e.html (accessed 1 September 2024).

21. Geoffrey Payzant, *Glenn Gould: Music and Mind* (Toronto: Van Nostrand Reinhold, 1978), 131.

22. Glenn Gould, "Radio as Music: Glenn Gould in Conversation with John Jessop," in *The Glenn Gould Reader*, ed. Tim Page (New York: Vintage Books, 1990), 380.

23. Gould, "Radio as Music," 379.

24. Moreover, AM radio, with its limited spectral content, whose audio fidelity was subject to any number of factors, weather included, would have further impacted the listening experience.

25. Paul Hjartarson, "Of Inward Journeys and Interior Landscapes: Glenn Gould, Lawren Harris, and 'The Idea of North,'" *Essays on Canadian Writing* 59 (Fall 1996): 83–84.

26. Kevin McNeilly, "Listening, Nordicity, Community: Glenn Gould's 'The Idea of North,'" *Essays on Canadian Writing* 59 (Fall 1996): 87.

27. Hjartarson, "Of Inward Journeys," 84.

28. Hjartarson, "Of Inward Journeys," 84.

29. Gould, "Radio as Music," 376. See also chapter 7 by Wetters and Cushing in the present volume, which calls much of "Radio as Music" into question as an example of Gould building his own mythology.

30. Bazzana, *Wondrous Strange*, 294.

31. William Littler, "The Quest for Solitude," in *Glenn Gould Variations: By Himself and His Friends*, ed. John McGreevy (Toronto: Doubleday, 1983), 223.

32. Gould, "Prologue from 'The Idea of North,'" in *The Glenn Gould Reader*, 389.

33. Cushing discusses the "trio sonata" construct in greater depth in his chapter in the present volume.

34. Gould, "So You Want to Write a Fugue?," in *The Glenn Gould Reader*, 234.

35. Gould, "Radio as Music," 380.

36. The site of Gould's US debut performance in January 1955.

37. Rick Hancox, "Film—Is There a Future in Our Past? (The Afterlife of Latent Images)," keynote speech at Is Film Dead? A Symposium on the State of Celluloid, Atlantic Filmmakers Cooperative, Halifax, 23 March 2007.

38. Hancox, "Film."

39. The journalist and critic Robert Fulford, one of Gould's closest childhood friends, asserted that such ravines "are the heart of the city's emotional geography," as canals are to Venice and hills to San Francisco, observing that, "[because] of the ravines, a Torontonian can explore nature with an ease that's impossible for many

people living in the country." Robert Fulford, *Accidental City: The Transformation of Toronto* (Toronto: Macfarlane Walter & Ross, 1995), 37–38.

40. Bill Nichols, "Documentary Reenactment and the Fantasmatic Subject," *Critical Inquiry* 35 (Autumn 2008): 73.

41. Nichols, "Documentary Reenactment," 74.

42. Mark Laurie, email to editor, 12 April 2024.

43. Mark Laurie, email to editor, 12 April 2024.

5

When a Fugue Isn't a Fugue

Glenn Gould's Musical Semiotics of Contrapuntal Radio and *The Idea of North*

ANTHONY CUSHING

It somehow seems an exercise in futility to debate the merits of *The Idea of North* as music, drama, or theater. Gould gives proponents of each discipline enough material to formulate a persuasive argument within their respective analytical frameworks.

As a documentary, it falls short if only because the source interviews are extensively mediated by post facto editing. One only need compare interview transcripts and the final script to understand the extent to which Gould manipulated the participants' speech and recontextualized their responses by juxtaposition with comments from others. Even if this practice of extensive editing does not conform to the expected ethical standards of journalism, the work's dramatic characteristics in the form of dialogues and scenes provide the redeeming artistic virtue.

North employs theatrical techniques by presenting its material in scenes and acts, juxtaposed interview excerpts comprising ersatz dialogues, and backgrounded sound effects reminiscent of scripted radio dramas. By extension, there is a cinematic element to Gould's work in the appearance of movement and his primary influence for the work's construction. "For *North* he frequently made reference to *The Ship of Fools* (a movie he adored), because it, though in a far less complicated [way], it sort of conceptualized visually what *He* [original emphasis] was trying to do aurally."[1] As the movie's title suggests, the boat, an ocean liner bound for Germany from Mexico, is inhabited by an unusual lot of passengers. What may have influenced Gould was not so much the film's narrative content, but the contrapuntal layering of stories. The film weaves several threads for the viewer to absorb, process, and retain as the focus shifts between several different dialogues. The film challenges the viewer to parse the numerous conversations as opposed to the overlapped speech favored by Gould.

The most ambitious scenes in the film transpire in the ship's dining room, at the captain's table. Six passengers carry out at minimum two sustained conversations. Though there is no simultaneous speech, one dialogue is interspersed with another. Passengers A and B form one dialogue, and C and D form another. The respective conversational threads overlap linearly, making it difficult to keep segments of each conversation in their rightful sequence. Their conversation topics are unrelated, which renders the viewer's task that much more difficult. Whereas the visual element of the film helped to parse the conversational threads, in *North* Gould relied on aural trickery to achieve similar effects.

For the purpose of this chapter, I put forward a musical analysis of *North* because it provides a compelling point of entry. By a simple count, the bulk of Gould's expository discourse on *North* involves musical analogies. He uses the comparisons as a semiotic system to explain much of the work's compositional process and final product. I base my discussion of semiotics on Ferdinand de Saussure's system of semiotics, rooted in linguistics; it is a dyadic system based on signs and syntax. At its most basic, it involves a *sign*, like a word or image, and a signified object or concept inasmuch as the sign, a symbol, implies an arbitrary correspondence with a particular thing. Discussions of semiotics often center on the idea of making meaning; the word "solitude" might mean "being alone," though it may or may not be predicated on other influences, that is: Is the person alone in a crowded environment or one devoid of others?

Gould applies common musical terms—ternary, binary, fugue—to connote sounds and concepts divorced from their conventional, art-music application.[2] Arnold Schoenberg adopted a similar system for some of his early post-tonal and twelve-tone works. His piano suite, op. 25, self-consciously uses titles for the individual movements—gavotte, minuet, gigue—modeled on J. S. Bach's instrumental suites. However, Schoenberg's suite does not conform to the same harmonic conventions. The dance titles indicate meter and form, which Schoenberg used for sectional and textural delimiters. He adopts a semiotic approach to music composition that indicates a meaning that is different from its conventional use. Gould, in the case of *North*, chooses idiosyncratic musical terminology like "basso continuo" and "contrapuntal" that sometimes applies equally to both traditional notated music and the results of audio production practice.

Gould superimposes his musical semiotics onto various compositional elements of *North* with the expectation that the listener also makes the connection between the musical sign and the sonic signified. He draws his terminology entirely from common-practice, tonal theory—counterpoint in particular. In the liner notes to *North*'s record release in 1970, he explains that he employs "a number of techniques which I would be inclined to identify as musically derived. . . . [The prologue is] the first of several instances of a technique I've grown rather fond of dubbing 'contrapuntal radio.' . . . And there are other, perhaps more complex occasions, which simulate musical techniques as well."[3] Contrapuntal radio is a series of compositional techniques akin to the devices and techniques required of composers in notational music in the style of, say, Palestrina, J. S. Bach, or Paul Hindemith. Gould appends the adjective "contrapuntal" to "radio" to distinguish his brand of radio composition from the commonplace, linear use of radio in which events flow from one to another. Moreover, contrapuntal radio is more than just a series of techniques. I contend that Gould uses it as the name for his semiotic system and, in his definition, provides the disclaimer that it only *simulates* musical techniques. In this respect, Gould at once acknowledges the strengths and weaknesses of his analogies.

Even after producing several other increasingly complex radio works—the *Art of Glenn Gould* radio shows notwithstanding—Gould's descriptions of *North* rely heavily on musical semiotics with few inclusions of more technical terminology idiomatic to radio production. The first published mention of contrapuntal radio appears in the *North* vinyl record release liner notes a full three years after the work's premiere. Surely, contrapuntal radio took root before the work's inception as a concept if not as a concrete toolbox of techniques or semiotic system. The three-year gap between conception and exposition prompts the question as to whether Gould relied on his semiotics to *guide* composition or as a means of *explaining* his compositional process. If the former, he could have expounded on his musical semiotic in place of reliance on interdisciplinary terms. If the latter, an accessible use of technical language would have provided a clearer explanation in place of an incomplete system of musical analogies.

Lorne Tulk, the CBC audio engineer who worked most closely with Gould on *North*, recalls trying to process and translate the aesthetic goal into a method workable by contemporary audio production techniques. In my correspondence and interviews with Tulk, he does not mention any specific incidences during the production of *North* in which Gould used specific musical terminology.

> If it took an hour or even a half a day he would explain, using (where possible) examples to get me to fully understand, his or the situations' need for such a presentation . . . I can remember one or two occasions when we crossed swords. Generally . . . no always it was when Glenn wanted to do something, which was technically not feasible. i.e., Like wanting to have an effect too Hot (or loud) . . . and I would, with great difficulty, have to explain the transmitters simply couldn't handle that. ". . . Besides if we present erratic levels . . . compressors at the transmitters will readjust all the levels. Thus defeating your carefully orchestrated presentation."[4]

Gould may have relied on demonstrations and protracted explanation without *actual* musical terminology because Tulk was unfamiliar with the vocabulary. It appears that Gould chose to use more "practical" instructions by way of technical directions or by examples.

The language of contrapuntal radio, however piecemeal, establishes the foundation for analysis in a musical framework, but it is also an incomplete analytical system. The intrepid analyst easily identifies the musically derived production techniques, but the scenes idiomatic to audio production techniques are problematic. In the instance of the "Dining Car" scene, Gould tries to simulate the illusion of movement; he creates a sonic illusion whereby the interviewee's voice appears to move on the proximal plane between the listener (closeness) or away in the distance. Without a close musical analogy for this technique to flesh out his semiotic, Gould instead draws from theater or cinema. By drawing from other disciplines, he frustrates a complete *musical* analysis.

Anecdotes from his CBC colleagues throw into question Gould's familiarity with parallel compositional trends in the international community. Germany by 1967 had a rich history of experimentation in their public radio *Hörspiel* genre. In France, Pierre Schaeffer and Pierre Henry had all but codified the notion of *musique concrète*.[5] John Cage, in New York City, held frequent events to perform his experimental works involving tape recorders, turntables, and radios. Given Gould's frequent trips to New York for recording sessions in addition to his professional and social contacts in the city, it is not unreasonable to assume that he may have come in contact with some contemporary audio experimentation either in recital or private listening. If Gould had exposure to those other works, he may have used similar compositional techniques or, at the very least, more contemporary or idiomatic language in his musical semiotic. Brent Wetters and I explore this topic in more depth later in this volume, but I introduce it here only as it pertains to the discussion at hand.

Semiotics

Gould's use of the musical semiotic system is a clever and accessible entry point for both the casual listener and analyst. For an audience unfamiliar with the complex elements of audio production and psychoacoustics, but who—as fans of Gould's piano recordings—would have had fairly generous musical knowledge, musical terminology would have been easier to understand. There are only a few direct analogies between musical concepts and audio production, though they are often intertwined in practice. Audio production in the 1960s involved a network of activities: a collected process of recording sound to a storage medium (tape), editing lengths of tape by physically cutting and taping segments together, and manipulating the audio content by applying effects like reverberation or dynamics processing.[6] This was accomplished with electromechanical devices (audio tape recorders and playback equipment) and manual sleight of hand. The language of audio production is rooted in the science of acoustics and mechanics with terms like "decibels," "volume units," "frequency filters," and, for tape, "centimeters-per-second" (cps). An explanation of the more complex scenes in *North* using language idiomatic to audio production would give a greater level of detail to those familiar with the processes, but it would make little sense to the average listener or analyst. Likewise, the realm of psychoacoustics, the study of how we perceive sound, bears its own distinct vocabulary. It is not appropriate for describing the compositional process, only how and why we hear the final work as Gould intended. For the purpose of exposition in this chapter I approach psychoacoustics as a means of creating sonic illusions insomuch as Gould manipulates audio to simulate the "appearance" of depth, movement, and ambience.

I want to contextualize my discussion of the so-called traditional musical terminology versus the electromechanical "other" of audio production with several composition and performance/recording binary comparisons. When Gould applies the musical terms to the recorded equivalents in contrapuntal radio, he creates an opposition of something that is infinitely variable (performance) and infinitely repeatable with no variation (recording). This reduces further to the human/machine binary.

In the realm of composition and live performance, the elements of performance are all relative. A performer's pianissimo is only quiet relative to the same performer's forte or fortissimo. The same applies to tempi where "slow" is only relative to "fast" unless otherwise directed by the composer's tempo markings. As in Gould's case, however, the noted tempi are not so much directions as prescriptions. Human frailty introduces variability into the performance and, sometimes, the recorded performance.

By contrast, a tape composition like *North* does not involve live performers, only recorded interviews based on spontaneous responses to Gould's questions. Once committed to tape, the interview segments represent only sounds with meaning embedded in the speech, manipulated into meaning something else. As opposed to the live performance of notated music, *North* did not require a notated score or live performers to actualize a score. Gould assembled the work using fixed elements, sounds suspended in time, existing only as electromagnetic impulses on magnetic tape. The metrics of compositional elements here are not qualitative, but quantitative. The producer measures "dynamics" in decibels (dB). A decrescendo is not a relative volume decrease as in performance. It is a quantitative decrease in decibels over a given measure of time. Further, to change the timbre of a voice, the engineer does not follow an abstract interpretative marking like sul ponticello. Instead, the timbral change involves, say, a high-pass frequency filter set at five kilohertz.

Though *North* is a tape composition and not a recorded performance, per se, it required a measure of real-time human intervention to actualize the final recording. Whereas some elements of modern audio production involve automated processes (volume increases, panning, dynamics processing), midcentury production involved real-time, manual intervention to produce the same results. In effect, Lorne Tulk and other CBC engineers with whom Gould worked are performers and the work, a live performance, but only insomuch as the performers are audible in the corporeal sense.[7] When in a traditional live performance, the listener experiences the sounds emanating from voices or instruments, which are the results of the performer's actions, the body. In the tape composition, the engineer's body is disconnected from the sound they control by their mixing board.

With these comparisons and the following case studies, I demonstrate the structural deficits in Gould's incomplete musical semiotic. The listener and analyst alike will find some direct analogies as well as those that are "close but not quite." Consequently, as Gould strains his use of musical analogies, he resorts to theatrical and cinematic idioms to illustrate his point, which reveals the cracks in his system. Gould could have codified a robust musical semiotic had he the time or desire, but contrapuntal radio is, first and foremost, born of practice. As such, he prioritized the completion of *North* and subsequent radio works rather than contemplate a systematic, discursive terminology. The terms he uses to describe elements in *North* imply preconceived musical parameters such as harmony, form, and texture. Perhaps the most frustrating element of examining contrapuntal radio is that Gould sometimes hints at a meaning but moves on to another concept without elaboration. Chief among these elements is harmony.

Semantic Harmony

> Every voice leads its own . . . life and adheres to certain parameters of harmonic discipline . . . how the voices came together and in what manner they splashed off each other, both in the actual sound and in the meaning of what was being said.
>
> —Tim Page, *Glenn Gould: A Life in Pictures*

This fleeting mention of harmony is Gould's only nod to one of the primary pillars of Western tonal music. With little elaboration, the key words "sound" and "meaning" provide at least a starting point for an exploration of contrapuntal radio's harmonic system. His choice of words indicates action and a relation to semantics as regards interaction and meaning. It establishes an element of theatricality in addition to harmony. Theatrical analogies do not advance a discussion of the harmonic system.

I posit semantics as a more productive avenue of exploration for Gould's "harmonic discipline." Because Gould does not use traditional music content as a structural element of *North*, the question turns to the formulation of harmony without musical pitches or, rather, how one accomplishes such a feat.[8] Here, I focus not so much on the speech but on speech content. I focus on Gould's suggestion of what the voices "say" and how they interact in each section or scene. These interactions, speech content, and vocal inflection cumulatively form the harmonic system. As the speech content changes by theme or topic area, so too does the harmony akin to a shift in the work's "tonal center." In scene 2, the interview participants share recollections about their early days in the north while in scene 3 the topic shifts to the reality of northern living and deromanticizing the north. The topic and sentiment changes markedly between scenes, not just in topic but also in tone.

Contrapuntal radio's roots in the study of counterpoint also come with preconceived notions of what constitutes counterpoint. A cursory examination of several texts reveals extramusical descriptions.[9] It requires a minimum of two voices interacting in point-against-point (*punctus contra punctum*) and with them, the forces of tension and release, consonance and dissonance. These forces are not the exclusive domain of music.

For the purpose of this discussion, composer Hugo Norden offers a compelling definition of counterpoint, in which

> contrapuntal lines are played or sung against, not with, each other so that the prevailing spirit is one of conflict or stress. This requires skillful construction of the separate melodic lines to insure smooth effective operations. . . . This is not conflict in the violent sense. It is . . . that of the two or more lines, each with a characteristic design of its own, functioning simultaneously with a common artistic purpose . . . this constantly surging activity of two or more contrapuntal lines moving at once is often compared to that of *quite unlike people working together* [emphasis added]. Discord and its ensuing concord are integral ingredients of the phenomena both of living and of music.[10]

Norden's perspective on counterpoint aligns nicely with Gould's apparent compositional intent. The emphasis is not so much on harmony as the notion of conflict and resolution, tension and release. These conditions occur between the voices of their own, unique design. Norden refers to musical voices as notated, independent melodic strands running in tandem while Gould works with literal voices, speech. In *North*, Gould brings together five interviewees from varying professions and disciplines, distinct vocal timbres, and different experiences of northern living. In each scene, however, the interviewees' speech is brought together for the common purpose of putting across Gould's narrative. As the voices appear in dialogue, they create the concord or discord by the semantics representing alike or opposing viewpoints. The voices in *North* never appear to interact directly as do the voices in Gould's future works. Rather, the listener is left to pick out the alike or opposing content and make conclusions. Semantics, however, are not the only determinant of tension. Vocal inflection and specific keywords emphasize a perspective, as does the rhythm and tempo of the speech. In scene 5, Phillips discusses the future of the north. In earlier scenes, Phillips's vocal delivery is evenly measured with words emphasized only after he takes a breath.

The dialogues and ensemble casts of the ambitious contrapuntal scenes do not occur naturally, in real time. Gould "composes" them in the editing suite by splicing together lengths of tape and mixing multiple voices down to the monaural audio channel. Just as a composer of notational music writes musical voices that run in tandem, Gould assembles preexisting voices to create an equivalent mix of musical voices. The contrapuntal vocal layering occurs in only four of the work's seven sections. In the remaining sections voices proceed linearly in a call-and-response delivery, yet there are always at least two voices sounding at any given time: none of the scenes are monophonic. Gould relies on an underlying harmonic device that accompanies single spoken voices in the absence of a second or third spoken voice.

Basso Continuo

Literally, the "continuous bass," the continuo is a harmonic device used commonly to unify the local-level harmonic system and provide direction for the upper "voices." It is a stalwart element of much baroque music, an era of music with which Gould was amply familiar. As in notational music, the continuo establishes the harmonic foundation while one or more upper voices embellish and emphasize the tonal center. For *North*, train sounds stand in for the continuo. Gould qualifies the continuo concept in this work: "Anyone who has had the experience of the organ feels that need for a bass foundation of some kind. . . . That may in fact be the reason that I've always felt the necessity of a continuum of some kind in everything that I've done in radio."[11] Using the train as continuo proved a clever compositional choice in several respects. It offered Gould a practical solution to mitigate the work's appearance as a disjointed collection of themes unified only loosely by the theme of northern living. It brings together the inner five scenes as a cohesive whole. Subsequently, the train establishes a theatrical premise wherein Gould and his collection of interviewees transpire on the "Muskeg Express" en route to Churchill, Manitoba.

Functionally, the continuo gives aural relief to the listener between the contrapuntal sections with two or more spoken voices. Listening and processing multiple simultaneous vocal threads produces a condition known as aural fatigue that tires the listener's ears. It does not produce temporary deafness so much as dull the listener's perception and aural processing abilities. While the train provides the respite, it also serves as a unique voice with its own means of creating tension and resolution as it interacts with the spoken voice above it.

Finally, though Gould may not have made the connection during conception or production, the train may stand in as an allegory for Canadian nationalism. Canada's first prime minister, John A. Macdonald, pushed to unify the country—thousands of miles between the east and west coasts—by railroad. During the country's centennial year celebrations for which the CBC commissioned *North*, Gould's train could evoke the country's early history and allude to its only remaining frontier, the north, as open and mysterious as the west had been only a century earlier.

Gould's use of the basso continuo is unusual in that it establishes a two-way relationship with other audio content in the scenes. Like a traditional basso continuo that establishes a harmonic foundation for the musical voices above it, Gould's continuo provides the thematic premise and establishes the dramatic framework for the upper voices. It creates for the listener an expectation as to the speech content. Simultaneously, the continuo takes specific "harmonic" cues from the speech content. This inverts the basso continuo role in which the upper voices elaborate the bass harmony.

I identify three instances in which Gould makes novel use of the continuo and, in one case, requires of the listener a measure of indulgence to recognize a continuo in lieu of the train. Gould presents *North*'s prologue as a kind of trio sonata, though it does not contain a clearly identifiable continuo. In scene 3, all of the work's participants appear at some points with most repeating at least once, however Gould does not juxtapose the speech. All the spoken segments follow one from the other while the continuo runs the duration of the scene. Last, the dining car scene employs two distinct continuo voices to establish the scene's harmonic center.

Gould calls the prologue a trio sonata more than once.[12] The analogy is apt with an exception: there is no "fixed" basso continuo. Instead, the scene's three voices share the role of providing the bass line, the harmonic support for the others. The voices, one female and two male, undulate by volume, level but there is no particular dominant voice to carry through the scene.

Lorne Tulk's iconic illustration of the prologue reveals a map of three voices—Marianne Schroeder, Frank Vallee, and Robert Phillips—that fade in and out of the foreground by adjustments in volume. The effect of sharing the continuo role is audible by prominence of whomever Gould foregrounds or pushes to the audible background. The voice with the lowest volume level takes on the continuo role and exchanges the role only when another voice's volume level drops to become the lowest. The frequency content of the voices—whether "high" or "low" voice—is irrelevant to the role of continuo. As with a traditional continuo, this technique maintains a flow of sound, a *voce continuo*. This is the only function that Gould retains in his adaptation of the device in the prologue. The dynamic continuo does not provide a harmonic support for the upper voices as with the train continuo throughout the rest of the work.

The voice exchanges through the prologue (table 5.1) occur between individual voices until 2:00 when the pairing of Phillips's and Vallee's respective voices merge to form a compounded continuo while Schroeder occupies the foreground as the "upper voice." At the prologue's conclusion,

Table 5.1. List of Vocal Exchanges in the Prologue

Exchange	Time	Changes in the role of voce continuo
1	0:50	From Schroeder to Vallee
2	1:06	From Vallee to Schroeder
3	1:25	From Schroeder to Vallee
4	1:41	From Vallee to Phillips
5	1:56	From Phillips to Vallee
6	2:00–3:00	Alternate between Phillips and Vallee
7	3:00	Voices combine; Gould's voice enters as foreground

Schroeder's voice joins the continuo with Phillips and Vallee; Gould's voice assumes the foreground with the multivoice basso continuo below.

It seems a stretch of the imagination to even refer to a continuo in the prologue if only because it bears little resemblance, if any, to the commonly accepted notion of the device until Vallee's and Phillips's respective voices merge. From then until the end of the scene there is a plain distinction between the "upper voice" and "lower voice" continuo. I include this discussion here only because Gould insists on referring to the prologue as a trio sonata, which, in turn, implies the presence of a continuo. This device is put to more effective use later in scene 3.

In contrast to the prologue that used only voices, scenes 1 through 5 employ the train sound effects for the continuo. Gould uses the train to great effect in scene 3 and with great subtlety. His continuo emulates the musical technique of "word painting," idiomatic to vocal music, in which the composer illustrates the lyric text in music.[13] This is not the purpose of the continuo per se but it is a compelling use nonetheless. The following two examples verge on the side of too subtle to be perceptible as a harmonic device in this context.

In the first instance, James Lotz recalls the exhilaration of realizing he made the trip north successfully. "My God! I am here. I live here, I live—I breathe, I laugh, I walk . . ."[14] This was his momentary celebration of being alive and experiencing the mythical north. Approximately thirty seconds before Lotz's voice enters the scene, the train runs over a switch, resulting in a percussive rattle. Immediately after, the continuo simulates a heartbeat by a regular pulse rhythm. In this respect, the train serves as an aural embodiment of Lotz's heart as he lives, breathes, laughs, and walks. The volume level of the voice is sufficiently high that the listener must focus intently to hear the specific train effect. Gould used professional studio monitors during production to render the train and voice distinctly. Current listeners benefit from the sonic clarity of high-fidelity recordings to hear the train and voice in tandem. However, the sonic characteristics of FM radio often dull subtle audio effects and the pulsing continuo may have been hidden by the broadcasting medium.[15]

The second example highlights some element of self-indulgence or cleverness for its own sake on Gould's part. Word painting is effective only when it complements the sung or spoken voice. In this instance, the continuo masks the voice, rendering it entirely inaudible. Near the conclusion of scene 3 Schroeder reflects on her disillusionment at the end of her tenure in Coral Harbour. As her speech goes on, the train gets louder until her voice gets lost in the metal-on-metal thrashing of wheels on rail switches. Only the work's complete transcript reveals the train's harmonic inflection, the word painting. Just as Schroeder's voice gets lost, she reflects, "I would like to go north again . . . because although there are many disadvantages people mean something there. You're not just one of so many who walk on the street as in a big city . . . sometimes I've been lonelier in a big city than I ever was in the North."[16] By the time Schroeder gets to "walk on the street," her voice is entirely inaudible. To the casual listener the loud train is an annoyance because it effectively interrupts the speech at a crucial juncture in her story. The noise stands in for the overwhelming street-level din of the "big city" and illustrates the loneliness of disappearing into the chaos of urban life as opposed to the clarity and openness of the quiet north.

The end of scene 3 dovetails with scene 4, the "dining car." A short dialogue between Phillips and Lotz follows the call-and-answer format of the previous scene but includes an additional continuo voice as in the dining car. By the reckoning of Gould's final "script," this dialogue belongs to scene 3. I mention it here only because of the curious use of continuo that carries into the dining car. In this case the continuo includes two aural streams, but they meld together to form a compound continuo. As the two men converse on the topic of "Eskimos" and alcoholism, Gould introduces the sounds of ice clinking in scotch glasses. The effect is subtle, and most listeners might not hear the clink or, if they do hear it, may not make the link between the sound and speech. Again, the continuo mirrors the "upper voices."

Later, as he brings Schroeder and Vallee into the scene, Gould introduces the occasional clink of flatware on plates and the faint murmur of generic background chatter. This serves to fortify the theatrical premise of the "dining car." The train is relatively quiet through this scene so as to not overwhelm the additional voices.

Examining local-level harmony is only part of an analysis. Contrapuntal radio encompasses broader concerns beyond ephemeral harmonic devices. Specifically, if Gould's techniques are to stand on their own as an autonomous compositional process, semantic harmony must sustain a high-level harmonic teleology.

Gould composed *North* in seven discrete sections. For the purposes of my high-level harmonic analysis, I consider only the central five sections (table 5.2) because they make the clearest arguments for consideration as musical entities rather than stand-alone narratives or theatrical pieces.

Table 5.2. Scene-by-Scene Synopsis

Scene	Synopsis
Prologue	Personal reflections on the north
Scene 1	Descriptions of the characters' "early days" in the north
Scene 2	First experiences of northern living with reflections on emotional and community connections
Scene 3	Reality of northern living and deromanticizing the north
Scene 4	Conversation in the "dining car" about "Eskimos" and colonial attitudes toward the north
Scene 5	Contemplation on the future of the north
Epilogue	Narrator's soliloquy on the north's philosophical meaning and relationship to Canada, and what role the north will play in Canada's future

There is a clear progression in programmatic content that points to the notion of tension and release, consonance and dissonance. Scenes 1 and 5 reflect optimism, albeit in different ways, while the inner three scenes are decidedly not optimistic. The harmonic structure translates into a pattern not unlike a tonic-dominant-tonic relationship:

optimism > disillusionment > nostalgia/optimism for the future of the north

or

rest > unrest, demanding resolution > rest.

The large-scale, almost symphonic structure unifies all its constituent movements, forming a cohesive harmonic whole. I do not mean to suggest a direct correlation between this element of semantic harmony and the specifics of major/minor tonalities. Nor do I attempt to quantify these elements of as specific chord functions if only because Gould did not make that connection himself. I merely draw attention here to similarities to highlight the parallel functions in semantic harmony. I derive my analysis from the scant details available in writing in tandem with a close examination of the recording and script.

The discussion of high-level harmony lends itself to a discussion of form, as the latter is, generally, discernible by the former: formal sections are usually marked by prominent harmonic shifts. When harmonic centers shift and change, there goes with it an accompanying sectional change. Indeed, Gould devotes significant space to issues of form in "Radio as Music" and his liner notes to the documentary's vinyl record release.[17] The following analysis elaborates on Gould's sometimes frustratingly brief descriptions of individual scenes and glossing over of large-scale form.

Form

> One must invent a form, which expresses the limitations of form, which takes as its point of departure the terror of formlessness. . . . There are a limited number of rondos you can exploit in the radio documentary; then you . . . have to invent according to the criteria of the medium.
>
> —Gould, "Radio as Music"

Cracks in Gould's music semiotic start to emerge from his discourse on form. Though he discusses several facets of form in *North*, he does not discuss it in sufficient depth to clarify or qualify his use of particular labels. Form in music is fundamentally different than in radio works based, in Gould's language, on the criteria of the medium. It is not only a matter of formal division but also content as in traditional, pitch-based, notational musical materials. What works in music, like, for example, a sonata-allegro form with a development section, does not make sense in the context of a radio documentary where speech is the primary content. At times, there is no direct way to apply musical developmental techniques in creating an audio documentary as one would in a "traditional" music composition. In *North*, development is a rhetorical device, as in the development of an argument, but this is not how a composer develops musical materials by breaking down a theme into motives, expanding and transforming them by various means, and presenting the themes again in their original form with slight differences. Unlike the developmental progression in a sonata form, the documentary form as Gould perceived it in 1967 followed a linear, sectional progression.[18] The typical call-and-response narrative teleology with the "introduction, discussion, climax, resolution" formal distinctions was not Gould's ideal proving ground.

Gould uses the commonplace terms associated with Western tonal music to identify formal demarcations, though it does not appear that he uses those terms strictly or with a great deal of rigor. Quite the opposite, he frequently uses ambiguous terms such as "kind of," "similar," and "not unlike" to sidestep discrepancies in the theory and compositional practice. What emerges via Gould's system is a hybrid of traditional forms and those idiomatic to the radio. Why would Gould draw from traditional terminology to bolster his semiotic rather than derive his own vocabulary rooted in the modern and traditional media? Did Gould follow traditional forms to guide his compositional process? Subsequently, did Gould allow the criteria of the medium to dictate the form that happens to align approximately with the tried and trusted?

A clear formal pattern emerges at both the local and macro levels no matter the semiotics Gould uses for his descriptions. A harmonic teleology, guided by semantics, affects the form and guides the documentary from scene to scene. However, local-level form follows a logic entirely divorced from macrolevel form.

Gould described the traditional radio documentary form as a series of linear binaries with all the structural limitations therein. He does not mince words about his opinion of the call-and-response style between interviewer and interviewee. The listener in *North* never hears Gould apart from his short introduction. Rather, the back-and-forth binary becomes a series of somewhat disconnected statements from the five interviewees rather than questions and direct responses.

Interview transcripts reveal long responses to very short probing questions. Gould allowed his interviewees the luxury of waxing rhapsodic with few, if any, interruptions to break their respective trains of thought. This gave him a large body of material from which to draw his samples and, subsequently, sufficient leeway to edit together the dialogues that constitute each scene. Gould laments the limited number of rondos available for exploitation, although, in practice, it appears he makes a concerted effort to find them all. Scenes 1 and 3 both take the shape of generously mutated rondos that maintain some element of symmetry, befitting their traditional namesake. The seven-part "classical" rondo follows a clear pattern of key areas through the ABACAB^{1}A structure. The second instance of "B" repeats in the tonic rather than the dominant. Gould's scene 1 rondo is a significant departure from that form but maintains an element of symmetry that bears analysis here. The local-level progression of voices follows an ABABABAB-C-DBDBDB-C-A pattern. Each of the letters

When a Fugue Isn't a Fugue | 129

represents a different voice: Lotz (A), Maclean (B), Phillips (D), and "C" is an overlapped dialogue of Maclean and Lotz. The opening "AB" linear pairing is between Lotz and Maclean and the "DB" pairing is between Maclean and Phillips. The contrapuntal "C" provides some aural relief and interrupts the monotony of the preceding binaries.

The duration of each section decreases as the scene unfolds, which negates the traditional notion of proportion and temporal balance in form. The sections get shorter and shorter until they become isolated statements rather than complete thoughts or sentences. This literal sectional breakdown (table 5.3), following only the progression of voices, does not make sense in the context of semantic harmony.

Alternately, the scene's form might be reimagined as ABCBA[1] if the opening AB dialogue constitutes one section (A); the overlapped dialogue

Table 5.3. Scene 1 Sectional Divisions and Durations

Section	Duration
A	2:37
B	1:46
A	0:25
B	1:19
A	0:41
B	1:02
A	0:25
B	0:41
C	0:52
D	0:47
B	0:24
D	0:20
B	0:17
D	0:20
B	0:26
C	0:43
A	0:50
Silence	0:06

maintains its autonomy as a section (B); the second dialogue, DB, becomes (C); and the final A section stands on its own (A^1). The sectional proportions in this model are more drastically aberrant but make sense when taking into consideration the semantic harmony. Lotz begins the scene describing himself as a captive audience for a young man engaged in idle chatter. The back and forth with Maclean outlines the act of going north and early experiences there. Later, the discussion between Phillips and Lotz consists of observations on government studies and *how* Canadians were involved in the north. The second instance of overlapped speech consists of Maclean's rumination on a young man in search of himself, interspersed with interjections by Lotz. The scene closes as Lotz poses the question as to whether a man can get along with himself. Gould follows that query with a pregnant pause of six seconds before the train continuo resumes. Lotz's final appearance is only fifty seconds long, but the question, the theme that runs through the whole work, is significant enough to warrant its own section.

A local, literal sectional analysis does not yield a satisfying analysis. It is somewhat surprising that Gould employed for his explanation the ungainly, literal sectional form rather than the tidy, symmetrical form. In this respect, his discourse on form again reveals problems with the musical semiotic. Gould makes himself vulnerable for scrutiny by using disclaimers about inventing idiomatic forms that divert from traditional forms. This in itself is not an issue. His effort to tie together the new and the traditional here is counterproductive and confusing, and it is all the more perplexing when stepping up one level to a middle ground, reexamining scene 1 with new sectional delimiters. This approach ties together dialogues into their respective sections and reveals a connection with the semantic harmony even if it ignores the elements of proportion. Moreover, the progression of ideas through the scene presents *North*'s grand narrative in microcosm. By the alternate perspective, the macrolevel form is a large-scale elaboration of scene (table 5.2).

Macrolevel form, even by Gould's reckoning, reveals a more cohesive, traditional formal model. Semantic harmony plays a more active role in distinguishing sections, not the voice-by-voice delimiters Gould employed at the local level. Once again, he sets aside his music semiotic in favor of the theatrical analogies and describes the form as an introduction, five scenes, and an epilogue or soliloquy.[19] However, the narrative arc does not follow the theatrical model of rising action, climax, and resolution with the predictable cast of protagonists and antagonists. The five-fold sections reveal another symmetrical narrative form.

An examination of large-scale form necessarily recalls the parallel discussion of teleology in semantic harmony. Scene 1 is largely positive, scenes 2 through 4 highlight a crack in the patina of Utopian fantasies. Scene 4 in particular casts a negative pall over the work in its discussion of colonial "us-versus-them" as relates to the north's Indigenous population. (Jeffrey van den Scott discusses the scene's narrative extensively in his chapter in this volume.) A more positive, if wistful, theme rounds out the work with hopeful contemplations of the region's future.

Though Gould talks only of the five scenes, the semantic content indicates a simpler ternary form (table 5.4).

The prologue and scene 1 indicate a romanticized notion of the north, the middle three scenes are about disillusionment and deromanticization, and scene 5 and the epilogue reflect positive reminiscence without romanticism but remain hopeful.

Gould's rationale of form at the local level evades a serious comparison with traditional forms. However, the macrolevel in this context resonates with a traditional form, at least at the high level. In this respect, it may only be a matter of coincidence that my formal analysis connects with a traditional form that validates Gould's semiotic.[20] His discussions of form are flawed but worse, still, are his explanations of texture. His semiotic, as it relates to texture, takes some substantial liberties in its linkage with tradition.

Texture

The following discussion highlights a deficit in Gould's semiotic system and this is largely the result of the composition medium. Terms like "trio sonata" and "fugue" function as smoke screens that simplify, or trivialize,

Table 5.4. Reduction to Macro Level, Ternary Form

Section	Scene	Semantic Content
A	Prologue and 1	Positive/Consonance
B	2–4	Negative/Dissonance
A¹	5 and epilogue	Positive/Consonance

the complex underpinning of audio production techniques and psychoacoustic phenomena. To use a well-worn cinematic analogy, the "Gould of Oz" wants the listener to ignore the man behind the curtain splicing tape and turning dials. I invoke the literary wizard not to criticize Gould but to illustrate that his semiotic system falters under scrutiny. With this in mind, my discussion of texture requires an explanation of the intersection between "texture," the technical elements of audio production, and accompanying sonic effects.

Some results of audio production technique are explained easily under the auspices of musical terminology—a decrescendo is affected by decreasing volume—while other techniques, idiomatic to the recording studio, lack a parallel technique or terminology in notational composition practice. In these instances, it would be difficult to imagine how Gould could translate traditional (pre-electronic) musical concepts into the more complex scenes in *North*. It is possible that Gould explained his ideas to Lorne Tulk who, with some negotiation, re-created the idea to the best of his abilities with tape and dial manipulation. Before production of *North* began in 1967, Gould already had some knowledge of radio production through previous work with the CBC, including his earlier collaboration with Tulk on *The Search for Petula Clark*. It is likely that Gould applied some of his knowledge from those experiences to supplement his musical explanations in the composition/production process. Moreover, Tulk likely retained and recalled the knowledge from their *Petula* work to help expedite the translation process.

The portion of Gould's theatrical discourse on *North* may be explained by his familiarity with radio theater. It was a significant early influence for Gould in shaping how he worked for radio.[21] He credits the CBC show *Sunday Night Stage* with the formation of early childhood memories. The show, which ran for the ten years spanning Gould's teens and early adulthood (1943–1953), was created by Scottish expat Andrew Allan, the head of radio drama at the CBC. Allan featured the works of Shakespeare in addition to his own creations and commissioned works from several other Canadian playwrights. The sonic theater was as much an influence as the cinema. The theatrical and cinematic analogies represent not only the technical aspects of the production but also the *results* of those techniques. How and why we hear those effects as we do is explored in the discipline of psychoacoustics, the study of sound perception that encompasses both physiological and psychological responses to sound. These are effects created by judicious application of audio production techniques such as adjusting volume, equalization of particular frequency bands, using panoramic potentiometers to create the illusion of horizontal placement or movement in stereo.

A significant device in *North* is Gould's use of space, or the illusion of space: "The sense of area, the sense of space and proximity in the technology is just not being used at all. . . . The moment you define a character as doing something . . . people assume that they ought to be more or less close, more or less distant from the listener. . . . Thoughts have been disengaged from action and movement."[22] Gould expresses a measure of dissatisfaction with the then-current state of affairs in radio production. At the time, at least in radio drama, depth and space were communicated by the subjects' proximity to the microphone, and the resulting artifacts of room noise. Gould, however, recorded his interviewees in close proximity to a microphone and in an acoustically dry booth designed to dampen extraneous room noise. As such, Gould's affect of space in *North* transpires entirely in production by adjustments in volume and frequency filters. He uses these to create the perception of depth, presence, and vocal independence.

By combining multiple simultaneous, independent melodies in music, a composer creates the illusion of multiple "voices" as in, say, a four-part fugue; however, it is not enough to create a work with multiple voices. The rules of counterpoint emphasize the need to avoid formulations such as parallel fifths and octaves that render the voices less distinct. Because Gould used recorded speech and not notated melodies, he achieved the illusion of polyphony and vocal independence by other means.[23] By employing space, specifically the notion of proximity, Gould creates the sensation of depth, how close the subject *appears* to the listener. He achieves these using adjustments in volume and emphasizing certain frequency ranges by equalization (high-pass, low-pass filters). In doing so, Gould positions his interviewees in the sound field where one speaker is closer to the listener than the other. Subsequent to proximity is movement. When the listener perceives movement, that is, the subject appears to move in the sound field, there is, generally, no physical movement. The producer creates the illusion of movement by the *dynamic* application of the aforementioned techniques to approximate the appearance of real, physical movement.

All these technical elements combine to present the illusion of independent voices, but in the scenes with multiple simultaneous voices the listener must rely on aural stream segregation. In other words, the listener must somehow parse the single audio stream from their loudspeaker or headphones into separate voices. The concept of the "cocktail party effect" applies here. The effect is "the human's ability to selectively attend to a single talker or stream of audio among a cacophony of others."[24] Early experiments with this effect grew out of concerns of air traffic controllers in the mid-twentieth century who relied on loud speakers, not sound-isolating headphones, to direct multitudes of planes at take-off or landing. Controllers shifted their attention frequently between active loudspeakers without adjusting volume levels. In the first experiments on this effect with speech, researcher Colin Cherry deduced, "we can listen to one speaker when another is speaking simultaneously. There are acts of recognition and discrimination."[25] When the controllers focus on one voice, they actively reject all the other voices as noise. In *North*, listeners must confront this "effect," to varying degrees of success, during Gould's ambitious polyphonic scenes. In these instances, by manipulation of the volume dials, Gould privileges one voice over another, frustrating the listener's efforts to focus on a voice of their choosing.

Gould expands the monophonic linearity of call-and-response "documentary-style" production. All of the middle five scenes are polyphonic in that they use at least one voice and the train continuo. Four of the seven sections in *North* contain at least some element of three-voice polyphony (two spoken voices and train). The most complex scene contains a three-voice polyphony (two speakers at any given time and one composite continuo—the train and other sounds contextual to a dining car) but with four interviewees. I rely on two scenes to illustrate my discussion of texture. The prologue, which uses three spoken voices, is Gould's so-called experiment in texture rather than an effort to re-create form.[26]

However, choosing to recognize Gould's counterpoint as *music* following Gould's semiotic system requires a serious (re)consideration of the analytical framework to trace his analogies between music and audio production. His semiotic and logic is problematic in that there is no direct connection between his use of "trio sonata" in the context of the prologue, because it does not conform to the conventional characteristics of a trio sonata. *Why* and *how* is the prologue an experiment in texture, and why use a term for form if the scene in question is not about re-creating the form? Similarly, why is the dining car scene like a fugue if it doesn't align with the well-established craft of writing a fugue?

My examination of textural "experimentation" in the prologue relies not on the content but on vocal independence. I focus primarily on timbre, volume, and equalization because they were the primary elements to create the appearance of independence. Lorne Tulk's graph of the prologue illustrates my discussion. He produced this illustration post facto for a print version of Gould's expository essay on contrapuntal radio, "Radio as Music." Tulk plots the progress of voices in volume unit (VU) over time (MIN) irrespective of semantic content. He represents the voices visually by patterned lines that distinguish one from another.

These patterns may as well represent the unique timbre of each voice. Even without adjustments in volume, the voices sound different enough that the listener could identify each speaker without confusing one voice for another. This was Gould's intent.

> Glenn worked very hard on getting people with different timbre in their voices so they didn't even sound alike. That was one very helpful quality and, number two was . . . if there was a distant possibility that they might blend together . . . we would employ a filter. We'd simply employ some equalization on one voice to make it sharper or brighter so it stood out. . . . We used filter to make things more foreground. . . . We rarely did that because most of the time just the timbre in one voice, the voice quality, was different enough that we didn't have to do that.
>
> Glenn wanted to keep people au naturel in terms of the voice quality. We did not want to make people sound better or worse than they were. We wanted them to sound like who they are.[27]

Indeed, the interviewees who appear in the prologue sound distinctly different. Marianne Schroeder's voice is melodic in breadth of contour. Her rounded southern Ontarian diphthongs are inflected with hints of her German origin. Her smooth, poetic cadences contrast Frank Vallee's shotgun staccato that flows in bursts between pauses for breath. Robert Phillips measures his speech evenly with a regular rhythm and confidence befitting his position as an upper-level bureaucrat with Canada's Ministry of Northern Affairs. Each phrase is sufficiently long that he requires a large breath before continuing with the next phrase. The natural means of delineating voices to demonstrate independence is only one approach. Gould's heavy tape manipulation imposes new cadences and pauses to create a more attractive compound rhythm and counterpoint.

Gould's texture experiment in the prologue was about controlling the density of texture. Though he employs three voices through the scene and, in his introduction, four voices, he maintains the appearance of only two voices. Here the listener encounters the issue of the cocktail party effect or, rather, is denied the opportunity to participate in that effect. Concurrently, Gould uses the idea of the composite melody to actualize this experiment in which two voices merge to form a composite voice and become, in effect, a continuo with near unintelligible speech as the "melodic" content.

I divide the prologue into three distinct sections (table 5.5) where Gould plays with the illusion of two-voice polyphony.

The first portion of the prologue, 0:00 to 1:10, is an introduction by Schroeder with Vallee interjecting. I mark the beginning of section 1 at 1:10 when Gould pairs Vallee and Phillips. For a full forty seconds, their voices are distinctly independent because the dynamic adjustments of volume and equalization create the illusion of movement in proximity to and from the listener. That, twinned with their vocal timbre, renders them distinctly different. Here, the two-voice texture *sounds* like two voices.

Gould's experiment begins in section 2 as he reintroduces Schroeder's voice to join the other two. Vallee and Phillips respective voices get grouped at VU-7, effectively pushing them away from the listener. Very little of either voice's speech content is intelligible beyond the occasional word or broken phrase but not just because of the decreased volume. By keeping their voices within the same location in the proximal plane at the same volume level the voices "mask" each other. Subsequently, they appear to merge into one voice, albeit a distracting one. Schroeder's voice, undulating between VU-3 and 0, comes closest to the listener and immediately takes the focus. As regards the cocktail party effect, the listener is denied the opportunity to privilege one voice over another as if they were all equally audible. Instead, Gould actively accepts one voice for focus and rejects the other voices as background. In the only example of a link in the prologue between semantic content and the production technique, at

Table 5.5. Sectional Divisions of Texture in the *North* Prologue

Section	Time	Voices
1	1:10–1:50	Vallee and Phillips (with Schroeder introduction)
2	1:50–3:00	Vallee, Phillips, and Schroeder
3	3:00–4:00	Vallee, Phillips, Schroeder, and Gould

2:55 Schroeder intones, "and I wished it would never end," just as Gould decreases her volume to end section 2.

Section 3 technically falls outside of the three-minute-long prologue but is part of the introductory section, an extension of the prologue. Here, the three interviewees' respective voices are joined together at VU-10 and moved further away from the listener on the proximal plane. Reducing the volume allows Gould to merge all three voices into one background voice no matter their timbral differences. None of their speech, words or incomplete phrases, is intelligible at such a distance from the listener. Gould's introduction, though situated consistently at only VU-3, is sufficiently forefront as to render the compound voice mere background babble. The results of Gould's experiment are extraordinary. He maintains the two-voice texture in each section by *reducing* vocal independence by clustering voices at a similar volume level and situating them at the same distance from the listener on the proximal plane. Significantly, after a minute of Gould's introduction, he subtly removes the compound voice and introduces the train continuo. This establishes that there will never be fewer than two voices through the remainder of the work.

As for his mention of an exercise in texture rather than recreating a form, he did not elaborate further, so this discussion of his experiment can only conjecture at possible semiotic linkages between "trio sonata," "texture," and what actually transpires. Certainly, the terminology downplays the herculean feats of technique required to "compose" and "perform" the prologue. The dynamic adjustments of volume and equalization, in addition to controlling three tape playback machines (one for each voice), were actualized in *real time*. Production required thorough planning, preparation, and choreography to ensure proper timing for starting/stopping the tape players and adjusting the appropriate knobs. The listener does not hear or see the audio engineer, the man pulling the levers behind the curtain, but only hears the result of his work.

The prologue is a complex work of audio engineering involving only three voices. The "dining car," scene 4, is significantly more complex for the sheer number of variables to monitor and control. Gould constructs an intricate four-voice "fugue" with speech and sound effects. No matter Gould's description of this scene, it might also bear the disclaimer: "This fugue is not a fugue." Philosopher Mark Kingwell in his biography of Gould perceives contrapuntal radio technique as something other than traditional counterpoint and brackets the contrapuntal aspects of it: "*Contrapuntal* is not the right word. . . . Despite Gould's claims that the [dining car scene] was constructed on the model of a fugue, it does not . . . offer the satisfaction of resolution to a tonic or even the meta-satisfaction of deliberately dashing the expectation of resolution to the tonic."[28] There is an air of truth to Kingwell's critique. In the strictest sense, the scene is not a fugue, but it is contrapuntal insomuch as it is polyphonic. Discussions of tonic or resolution to a tonic are sufficient in the realm of notated music with pitch-based content. However, it also ignores the atonal composers of the twentieth century who continued writing polyphonic music and even fugues without tonic resolutions. Further, those terms are not adequate in the context of semantic harmony where "tonic" simply does not apply unless coached in terms of agreement and disagreement, tension and release. Gould does not produce a fugue by the standards of common practice but at least adheres to a rudimentary concept of fugue: the subject and countersubject. In other words, the speech is based on a common topic, encounters with "the Eskimo." Each conversation pairing bears its own related topic. The musical semiotic applied to this scene breaks down after "fugue," which leaves me to my own analytical devices.

At one end of the car is Lotz and Phillips, at the other end is Schroeder and Vallee. This is the essence of counterpoint: "conversations" between people. Here, the counterpoint occurs in the form of two simultaneous conversations, though only one takes the focus at any given time. As in a real fugue, some conversations take priority over others. Gould's theatrical premise indicating motion is, more or less, the equivalent of

Figure 5.1. Map of polyphonic texture and vocal pairings in the dining car scene. *Source*: Created by the author.

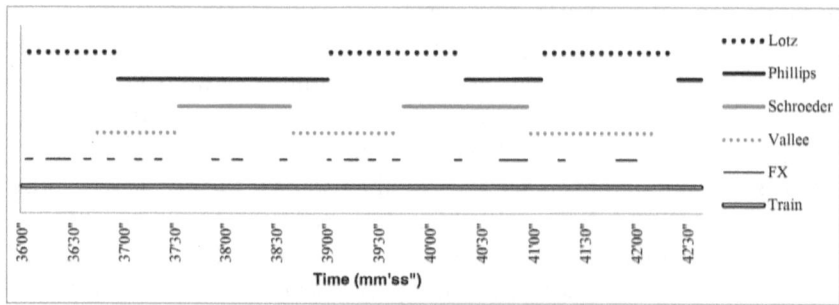

Arnold Schoenberg's *Haupstimme* markers in his scores to indicate the prominent musical line. And, like a performer, as Gould prioritizes one voice, it fades in and out of earshot.

Gould's theatrical nomenclature—in the absence of a viable musical explanation—betrays the complexity of the audio production choreography required to produce this scene (fig. 5.2). The movement was controlled by dynamically adjusting the volume and the respective voices.

Figure 5.2 demonstrates proximal movement of the voices through the scene, representing a way of hearing what Gould's porter hears as he traverses the length of the car. In this form, elements of the production technique emerge. Often, a volume decrease in one conversation corresponds with an equal and opposite increase in the other conversation. This is not unlike the contours indicated by dynamics markings in notational music. The volume changes in this instance create the sensation of depth, space, and the listener's location in that space. To invoke the cocktail party effect, the two conversational pairs inhabit a physical location that is not unlike a cocktail party. Gould as producer, in the guise of the porter, does not allow the listener to privilege one voice over another. He acts as a proxy for the listener to determine what voice takes priority.

The dining car presents another instance of techniques idiomatic to audio production for which there are no analogs in the traditional musical nomenclature. Gould's nod to fugal construction does not lead us toward describing the actuality of this scene's construction. If musical concepts formed the core of Gould's compositional approach to the scene, it is not evident, with perhaps the exception of the *concept*.

Figure 5.2. Map of proximity by character in the "dining car." *Source*: Created by the author.

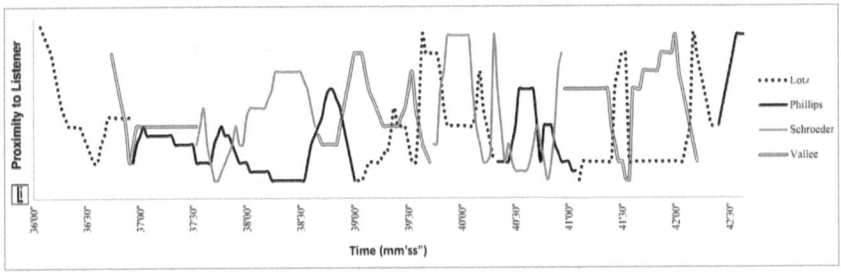

Conclusion

That Gould relied so heavily on theatrical terminology may render moot my original question as to whether or not Gould relied on his musical semiotics to guide composition or to explain *Idea of North* as a composition. The work evinces a clear mixture of influences for the conception and composition of this work. By this point in Gould's career, he had already completed a string quartet and a handful of other short compositions, and he presented regularly on CBC radio and television performances and analyses of musical works from eras spanning hundreds of years. His experience with the Petula Clark documentary no doubt also gave him some practical experience from which to draw for *North*.

The gaps in Gould's musical semiotic are surprising, especially considering his fastidious approach to writing, editing, and revising draft articles and scripted interviews. In his discussion of form in scene 1 he opted for a convoluted mapping of the structure in lieu of a more intuitive, simplified, symmetrical form. Or perhaps he used the more complex structure to underline his point about employing a form that demonstrates the limitations of form. Perhaps it was because he did not have sufficient distance from the work to formulate the simpler analysis.

Alternately, the gaps reveal a keen mind at work, employing analogies from other disciplines when a musical explanation was simply inappropriate. The extended audio production techniques employed in the prologue and dining car scene are without parallels at least in terms of the vocabulary idiomatic to notational music. Had Gould relied solely on traditional musical models for the entirety of *North*'s production he likely would not have realized the compositional potential of radio. The use of theatrical and cinematic analogies gave him the tools to articulate and translate his concepts into practice and, ultimately, the final work. Moreover, it would be unfair to say that Gould failed in creating a robust musical system. By drawing so heavily from many disciplines, Gould's music/theater/drama hybrid allowed him to conceive and actualize something different than his American and European avant-garde contemporaries.

Whereas Gould used musical concepts and other concepts *informed* by musical practice, composers like Stockhausen and Cage bound themselves to using musical systems either wholly or partially notated. Their systems often required somewhat elaborate explanations and symbology to communicate their performance practice. These composers were very much wedded to their image as "composer" and, as such, imposed those compositional strictures. Gould, not so inclined to identify himself as a composer so much as a creator, did not appear bound to any particular system. This complicates any particular mode of analysis, especially when dissecting his later works for radio wherein he relied decreasingly on musical analogies. *The Latecomers* and *Quiet in the Land* with their rich, stereo palette allowed Gould to not so much abandon the musical semiotics of contrapuntal radio, but forefront the dramatic and theatrical elements, underpinned by more advanced audio production techniques.

This again brings to mind the early experimental works of Arnold Schoenberg and Pierre Schaeffer, who relied on terms derived from long-established musical forms. They did so until they developed their craft further and began to use more abstract or generic titles that did not bind their creative endeavors to any expectations as to how the work should unfold formally or harmonically. Schaeffer and later composers Cage and James Tenney produced their works idiomatic to the electronic production methods at their disposal with imaginative titles like *Imaginary Landscapes* and *Collage #1 (Blue Suede)*, respectively.

Similarly with Gould, the musical semiotics was his figurative foot in the door to his radio works. Alternatively, the question may arise as to whether Gould used the musical analogies to justify the work against criticism as a "method to the madness" stance. "Radio as Music" appeared in print a full four years after *North*'s premiere—a significant temporal gap between conception and justification.

The difficult task of debating whether *North* stands as drama, music, or theater may be a simple matter of saying "yes." I endeavored to provide an analysis of the musical elements of the work. This is not such a straightforward task, as many musical elements are dependent on other, extramusical analogies to complete many analyses. In that regard, all three disciplines are not mutually exclusive. It may be a simple point of finally putting the debate to rest to enjoy *North* as an imaginative work of radio art.

Notes

1. Lorne Tulk, email to author, 5 September 2010.
2. There is a significant body of scholarly literature on applying a semiotic approach to music. Among these works: Roland Barthes, *Image-Music-Text* (New York: Hill and Wang, 1977); Jean-Jacques Nattiez, *Music and Discourse: Toward a*

Semiology of Music (Princeton, NJ: Princeton University Press, 1990); Philip Tagg, *Music's Meanings: A Modern Musicology for Non-Musos* (New York: Mass Media Music Scholars' Press, 2012).

3. Glenn Gould, "'The Idea of North': An Introduction," in *The Glenn Gould Reader*, ed. Tim Page (New York: Vintage Books, 1990), 393.

4. Lorne Tulk, email to author, 5 September 2010.

5. Radiodiffusion-Télévision Français (RTF) engineer and announcer Pierre Schaeffer developed and defined *musique concrète* in 1948 while working with the broadcaster's new magnetic tape recorders. Schaeffer assembled the first electronic audio production studio at RTF and equipped it with variable-speed tape recorders, phonographs, microphones, and sound effects records. He called music produced with this equipment *musique concrète* because he worked with "concrete," recorded sounds as opposed to prescriptive notation.

6. The metaphor of tape and splicing is still in use in modern digital audio workstation (DAW) software packages like ProTools and Logic Pro. The digital audio data is represented graphically as ribbons on multiple tracks, not unlike how recorded audio exists on multitrack tape as electromagnetic impulses.

7. Paul Sanden, "Hearing Glenn Gould's Body: Corporeal Liveness in Recorded Music," *Current Musicology* 88 (2009): 7–34. Sanden introduces the concept of corporeality in Gould's piano recordings. In *North*, apart from the introduction, the listener does not hear Gould or Tulk's voices, but, instead, hears the outcome of their actions, their respective bodies, as they manipulate the volume and filter knobs.

8. I do not here consider Gould's inclusion of the Sibelius symphony in the work's epilogue, as it is not an integral element of the work's structure.

9. Kent Kennan, *Counterpoint* (Englewood Cliffs, NJ: Prentice Hall, 1987), 1; Hugo Norden, *Fundamental Counterpoint* (Boston: Crescendo, 1969), 1; Felix Salzer and Carl Schacter, *Counterpoint in Composition: The Study of Voice Leading* (New York: Columbia University Press, 1969), xvii.

10. Norden, *Fundamental Counterpoint*, 1.

11. Gould, "Radio as Music," in *The Glenn Gould Reader*, 383. Gould played the organ as a child and so was amply familiar with the pedal board. He recorded Bach's *Art of the Fugue* on organ in 1964. In his String Quartet, op. 1, the relatively inactive cello part often functions as a continuo to the more active violin and viola parts.

12. Gould, "Radio as Music," 379, 385; Gould, "'The Idea of North': An Introduction," 393; Bruno Monsaingeon, *Gould the Alchemist*, dir. François-Louis Ribadeau, DVD, EMI Classics, 2003.

13. For example, to accompany the lyric "I run along the street," the composer may use a fast, *moto perpetuo*–like figure to imitate the quick steps along the ground.

14. Glenn Gould, *The Idea of North* (1967), in Glenn Gould, *Glenn Gould's Solitude Trilogy: Three Sound Documentaries*, CBC Records, 1992, 23:26–23:29.

15. See Christopher DeLaurenti's chapter in the present volume for detailed discussion of the technicalities of radio transmission at the time of *North*'s first broadcast.

16. Gould, *North*, 33:05–33:17.

17. Gould's discussion of form in "Radio as Music" encompassed two other documentaries *The Latecomers*, the second work in the *Solitude Trilogy*, and *Stokowski: A Portrait for Radio*, which was his first long-form radio work to make extensive use of musical excerpts.

18. Gould, "Radio as Music," 374. Gould invoked McLuhan's parlance about linear media and the end-to-end form of interviewer question and interviewee response.

19. He uses these terms interchangeably or describes a soliloquy in the epilogue.

20. Though he did not identify a ternary form at the macrolevel, this analysis reveals what may have been Gould's conception of the work's narrative structure. The clean division of scenes by semantic content provides grist for my argument to that effect.

21. Gould, "Radio as Music," 374.

22. Gould, "Radio as Music," 382.

23. In notated music, vocal independence creates polyphony and lack of independence creates harmony, even if atonal. Conversely, in contrapuntal radio, a failure to create vocal independence produces cacophony, aural dissonance.

24. Lisa J. Stifelman, "The Cocktail Party Effect in Auditory Interfaces: A Study of Simultaneous Presentation," MIT Media Laboratory Technical Report, 1994, 1.

25. Colin Cherry, "Some Experiments on the Recognition of Speech, with One and with Two Ears," *Journal of the Acoustical Society of America* 25, no. 5 (1953): 975.

26. Gould, "Radio as Music," 379.

27. Lorne Tulk, interview with author, 6 September 2010.

28. Mark Kingwell, *Glenn Gould* (Toronto: Penguin Canada, 2011), 131.

6

North, History, and the Shadow of Hanslick

Glenn Gould's Ideal of Musical North and Northern Listening

MARKUS MANTERE

One could argue that Glenn Gould, despite his insistent statements about the importance of "going north," never went to the *real* north.[1] A few months after he ended his career as a concert pianist in 1964, Gould took a long trip by train, finally reaching the little town of Churchill, Manitoba, on the western shore of the Hudson Bay. This corner of Canada is only the furthest north you can go by train; that's where the railway ends. Beyond Churchill, communities of Canada's Indigenous communities sparsely populate the truly remote expanses of geography. Even though most Canadians never even brave the trip to Churchill, exploring the extreme north has for centuries been a cultural trope in Canada's literature, art, and cultural history. The north, in short, was for both Gould and his fellow Canadians, a place to "dream about, spin tall tales about, and in the end, avoid."[2]

The north's prominence in Canadian national identity has outstripped its actuality, which is why it remains an abstract, indefinable idea.[3] Canadian composer R. Murray Schafer wrote on the matter: "There is (and was) a definite Canadian attitude towards the North. It resulted from Canada being such a vast and unpopulated country.... It was the true myth of Canada. While no one actually went there everyone thought that if things in the South ever turn bad, they potentially could go there and start life again. The North was pure. The North was uncorrupted and temptationless."4 Schafer's testimony portrays the north as a domain of uncorrupted beauty, a place to start fresh if need be. It is the opposite of the "corrupted" civilization of the south. The north is pure and unspoiled, and this quality has, by Schafer's reckoning, a healing and purifying effect on anyone who goes there.

Literary scholar Sherrill Grace, in her book on the subject, reminds us of the ambivalence that Canadians have toward their northern frontiers. "On the one hand," writes Grace, "*we* love *our* North (however carelessly or romantically we define it) and see nordicity as our uniquely defining quality; on the other, we fear and loathe it and reject everything that might remind us (in the land and in our minds) of our inescapable northern latitude, climate, and topography."5 On one hand, north stands for Canada, represents it, but no one is in a position to define it: "In the exciting ongoing debate not only over *where* North is but also over what its history is and *who* can tell it lies the creation of Canada itself, and North is neither synonymous with Canada nor different from it (from southern Canada); it is not either/or but both/and: it is part of the imagined community called Canada and a defining characteristic, a crucial metonymy, for the whole. It is North and north(s) co-existing in interdiscursive dependency."6 Gould's northern destination in 1965, Churchill, is hundreds of kilometers south of the Arctic Circle and just above the fifty-third parallel; it is no further north than Edinburgh in Scotland. By what measure can we say that Churchill is in the "real" north? From my Finnish perspective, Rovaniemi, a town of approximately thirty thousand residents, is not crucially different from Boston or Toronto in terms of climate. The summers in Boston are warmer and there is a wider variety of shopping and entertainment available, but internet, Netflix, Tinder, and the rest of our technologically mediated domains of leisure in our current Western consumer culture, are all equally available in Rovaniemi as in big American cities. You can also play tennis and beach volleyball (indoors during the winter, however), go to a spa, listen to live concerts, and so on, in all of these places. The concert life is admittedly richer in Boston and Toronto, the stores are bigger, and public transportation works better, but *in principle* the latitude makes no difference here. Sometimes the very top of the music world even comes for a live visit. One of the most memorable musical experiences during my visits to this Finnish town on the Arctic Circle was a wonderful piano recital by Aleksei Ljubimov. The week after that he gave a recital with the same program in Carnegie Hall.

But I am being silly and provocative on purpose here. First of all, in spite of the latitude, the climate is much harsher in Churchill than in Rovaniemi, or Edinburgh, for that matter. Churchill is, in all ways that count, a more extreme place than Rovaniemi as well as some other cities further north above the Arctic Circle. Churchill is separated from the rest of Canada by virtue of limited transportation options. With no roads connecting Churchill with the south, travelers reach the town only by a thirty-six-hour train trip, or expensive flights from Winnipeg. In the winter, locals drive as far as Thompson, Manitoba, and ride snowmobiles alongside the train tracks to complete their journey.

But what of Gould? Did he experience the harsh reality of the *extreme* north? Was it a venture he actively sought out? He may have preferred to venture into his daily northern explorations from the coziness of his hotel room in Churchill. We might argue that there really was no "real northern" adventure in his case then. Where is the exploration, sense of danger, and desire to conquer one's fears that originally drew him to be fascinated with the north? We have come, over the centuries of Canadian cultural history, to associate "going north" as a significant venture. Why was Gould so obsessed with the north?

I do not mean to underestimate the extremity and profundity of Gould's northern experience, given his well-known aversion to cold—wearing gloves and scarf in the middle of the summer, for instance. I do not know how much his northern journey actually required endurance and courage. What is important here is that the north is always relative. There is always a more northern place that asks of its visitors and residents alike more hardiness and resolve. Leaving aside the theoretical possibility of looking at the geography from the polar north, one may argue that for any northern place, there is always somewhere that is even more northern, more harsh, and more challenging. The one who describes the north always does so from a specific geographical perspective. North is not a stable location. As the literary scholar Sergei Medvedev puts it:

> The North is more often communicated than experienced, imagined rather than embodied. Talking of the signifier and the signified, Ferdinand de Saussure used the metaphor of the sheet of paper: the *signifié* and the *signifiant* are inextricably linked

> as two sides of the same sheet. In the North, this structuralist link is far less obvious; indeed the North may be a one-sided sheet of paper, a signifier without a signified. The North is the emptiness we are filling with our imagination, narratives and texts; a blank sheet of paper, on which words are written and erased; an empty snow field on which lonely figures emerge, pass, and disappear.[7]

This relativity, vagueness, and indefinable matter of the north are important aspects of its historical appeal. "Going north," an important ideology for Gould, not only related to the physical geography, but it was also a metaphor. This metaphor is ultimately not about going somewhere, or about competition of roughness, extremity, or challenge, but rather about solitude and locating one's own creative resources. Further—and relating to the topography of north—Gould's north is not the Canadian north but rather a philosophical and ethical concept. The posthumous reception of his musicianship as a Canadian cultural icon might have us believe otherwise.

Gould avoided politics, even with issues related to the north and in spite of the patriotic motivation for the commission, which coincided with the Canadian centennial celebrations in 1967. He did not appear to engage with the pertinent questions relating to the geography, history, population, or economy.[8] Rather than focusing on a particular place, Gould's fascination with the north seemed to align solely with the symbolic and metaphorical meanings that the north implied for him. For Gould, the north served as a metaphor for things he regarded as indispensable for his musicmaking:[9] isolation and loneliness, both of which represented a more general idea. For him, true original artistic creation takes place outside institutions, canons, and conventions of the art world.

On many occasions Gould reiterated his stance on the north as a driving, creative force. In his introduction to *North*, Gould wrote of how, over the course of working on his audio documentary, he found himself "writing musical critiques, for instance, in which the north—the idea of the north—began to serve as a foil for other ideas and values that seemed to me depressingly urban oriented and spiritually limited thereby."[10]

Gould's concept of north serves this chapter as a broad aesthetic and musical category, which also carried ethical dimensions. My aim in all this is hermeneutical—an effort to try and understand Gould's thought and exceptional musicianship in a more fundamental way. Through this discussion of Gould's ideas of north and music, I also hope to contribute to the emerging musicological study of performing musicians, an area too long neglected in the academic study of music.[11] Any and all interpretations of music by professional performers are intellectual undertakings that unfold in a cultural, social, ideological, and historical context. One should not value or listen to music solely against the backdrop of performance traditions and canons. Musicians, just like other intellectuals, work in dialogue with values, norms, and ideas. Through this perspective one can achieve a more thorough and contextualized view of a musician's work. It lends the perspective of evaluating his or her art only against the backdrop of established canons, conventions, and traditions of the music world.

Hermeneutics has a long and complex history as a mode of interpretation. The term here is applied loosely, inspired by the philosopher Martin Kusch's equally broad definition of hermeneutics as tackling "the challenge of understanding" any given object of scholarly inquiry.[12] Although that may be overly simplified, phrased differently, this chapter seeks a deep, locally, and historically contextualized understanding of Gould's conception of north. The discourse lacks an understanding that reaches not only to Gould's musicmaking and musical preferences but also to history. In particular, the nineteenth-century aesthetics of music carried aesthetical stereotypes of north and south. Rather than look exclusively at Gould's conception of north that ties him to his time and place—postwar Canada—this chapter locates historical resonances from the European aesthetic discourse of the nineteenth century—a discourse in which the specter of Eduard Hanslick, arguably the most influential music philosopher of the nineteenth century, looms large.

Though this chapter is primarily concerned with Gould's written statements, the discussion at hand centers on historian Quentin Skinner's distinction between a causal and semiotic context of a literary text.[13] The causal context, according to Skinner, refers to a view in which the meanings of a text emerge from the surrounding reality. The analysis of such a text means situating these meanings in a causal relationship with the outside world.

The semiotic context applies here. The fundamental point of departure in this view is an assumption of the web of significance that ties together the text and the world around it—however, one without causal relationships from one to another. The web itself is the starting point for a hermeneutical interpretation—looking at a text, or an individual for that matter, situated in a web of cultural or ideological significance lends itself to a deeper understanding of the subject. Both the intellectual and the text are autonomous entities. The cultural agency is interplay between the creative individual, the ideas, and institutions and cultural patterns.

Against this backdrop, the chapter concerns itself with a general goal: as far as the issue of north is concerned, one can attempt to reconcile Gould's identity as a musician and in what cultural/historical contexts his ideas resonate(d). Within the scope of this exploration, the discussion here weaves together the historical, cultural, and aesthetic-discursive web of the north that implicates the pianist. To grasp this hermeneutical web, one accesses this perspective through a close reading of Gould's texts—published essays, lectures, and correspondence—in parallel with a number of other texts. Expanding on the web metaphor, threads of the web are scattered around Gould's writings, interviews, and musical interpretation. Skinner points out that, fundamentally, the scholar works in a hermeneutic circle. Interpretation of the past can never be exhaustive, but, through careful scrutiny and close reading, it grows deeper. The aim of this chapter is not to seek a "definitive" interpretation of Gould's idea of the concept of the north, but one in which the musical and aesthetic qualities that he associated with the north are viewed as part of a larger horizon of meaning—a horizon within which he made music, wrote, and spoke.

Gould's *North* as Music

Anyssa Neumann, in her article on Gould, proposed that his conception of the idealized north relates to the concept of the sublime. This concept grew out of writings by eighteenth-century philosophers such as Edmund Burke and Immanuel Kant. Using the north as a metaphor, Neumann argues, Gould developed "a conception of the sublime that linked metaphysical philosophy with artistic invention."[14] This contention is justified by what the north and an aesthetic conception of the sublime have in common: the incomprehensibility of the infinite and the preoccupation with the vast unknown.[15]

Neumann's arguments on the sublimity of the north aid the effort to understand Gould's own conception of the north. His north is an aesthetic and moral construction somewhat similar to Burke's and Kant's definition of the sublime. Gould's idealized north also emphasizes an aspect of incomprehensibility, vastness, and multivoiced reality. In this context, it is worth recalling that Jean-François Lyotard, the first philosopher to propose a definition of postmodernity, proposed the sublime as a concept that points to an effort of the subject to base authenticity on something larger.¹⁶ As an aesthetician Gould is neither post-Kantian nor postmodernist à la Lyotard. Kant's theory of beauty (and sublimity) implicates a metaphysical agent that is behind the "purposiveness without a purpose"; this is the essence of artistic beauty and the metaphysical aspect, which Gould, the agnostic, did not seem to publicly ponder.¹⁷

In a scripted interview with the French musician and journalist Bruno Monsaingeon, Gould propagated a philosophy of noncompetition even to the extent of arguing that "competition, rather than money, is the root of all evil."¹⁸ As such, there is nothing extraordinary in this assertion. Based on my personal experiences from many years of music education, I can attest that many musicians dislike the competition system and attempt entry into the music through other means: personal relations, pursuing degrees from institutions, tireless private enterprise, and self-promotion. Some artists succeed in this better than others. Video-sharing sites, social media, and other means of advanced information technology give new tools to avoid direct competition with peers.¹⁹ For Gould, the statement extends beyond practical concerns to an ethical imperative.

In the same interview with Monsaingeon, Gould asserts, "In the concerto we have a perfect musical analogy of the competitive spirit."²⁰ This idea is one of the curious aspects of Gould's musical thought. Gould was certain that musical genres embody ethical and moral meanings within them. In his mind, competition is associated with specifically musical features—and whole musical genres, such as the solo concerto—that Gould associated with the corruption of classical music.

Gould shares this attention to ideological ramifications in the structures of music with the German culture critic Theodor W. Adorno. By Adorno's reckoning, society is mediated through music's material, and thereby ideological aspects of music are made manifest in musical structure.²¹ This process surfaces prominently in Adorno's critique of the "standardization" of popular music: the forms and harmonic structure of popular music and jazz—Adorno writes particularly about the commercial songs of Tin Pan Alley—are standardized such that the listener has come to expect songs to unfold in a particular fashion.²²

Gould's argumentation does not reach—for better or worse—the complexity of Adorno's prose. Adorno's holistic theory of music's social mediation is not something to which Gould aspired. At times Gould's thoughts verge on the "Adornian." Gould argues that a solo concerto is a perfect musical analog to the socially prevalent competition principle.

Following this logic, Gould wanted to dispose of this principle. This effort led to nonconventional results: Gould's 1962 concert recording of Brahms's d-minor concerto comes to mind. In his interpretation of the concerto, Gould disposed of the traditional contrast in tempo between the two main themes of the first movement—the common practice of slowing the tempo of the second theme represented the false temptation of "wooing the upper balcony" (Gould's phrase) through sentimental clichés of piano performance, that is, of making aesthetic choices to appease the audience.

Gould held in contempt the idea of the nineteenth-century piano concerto with its structural contrast between the soloist and the collective.[23] Accordingly, even composers Gould respected, Beethoven and Brahms, were at their worst in concertos. In Gould's mind, the "absurd musical conventions" limit their true abilities as composer. These conventions include the orchestral exposition the function of which is to pave way to the flamboyant entrance of the soloist, thematic redundancy between the orchestra and the soloist, as well as the cadenza as the venue for the soloist's bravura. According to Gould, all this brought about "some of the most embarrassing musical examples of the primeval human need for showing off."[24] In its historical context, the term "concerto" refers to the antagonism of, and competition between, the soloist and the accompanying collective. The etymology of the Latin *concertare* points to "fighting" or "contending," and it is these aspects of music that Gould shunned: display of bravura, aggressive virtuosity, and theatricality.

For Gould, music existed in its ideal state beyond emotion, excitement, and display of virtuosity. Gould biographer Kevin Bazzana highlights musical features that Gould favored over others such as contrapuntal ingenuity, harmonic sophistication, and motivic development. He judged musical works negatively based on the extent to which they emphasized their own pianistic, idiomatic qualities and thus exhibited the performers' virtuosity.[25] In writing about Bach's *Die Kunst der Fuge*, Gould describes the composer as "withdrawing from the pragmatic concerns of music-making into an idealized world of uncompromised invention," and, more generally, about the "magnificent indifference to specific sonority" as indicative of the "universality of Bach."[26] "Universality," for Gould, meant music the aesthetic value of which was purely abstract, independent of any sounding realization; while the lack of idiomatic specificity in Bach's keyboard works could indicate *flexibility*, Gould prefers to see that lack as a promotion of the abstract qualities of the music. "Universality" also entailed music that transcended national or local spheres in his estimation.[27]

Gould's ideal involved detaching the music from any particular instrument and, by extension, the act of performance. Following this, the reader can come to understand how Gould deplored works like Bach's *Chromatic Fantasy* and the toccatas, while simultaneously praising the composer's universality. In works such as *Die Kunst der Fuge*, Bach's "withdrawal from the pragmatic concerns of music-making," which he praises in his essay on the "Art of the Fugue" cited earlier, meant also a withdrawal from the physical and corporeal aspects of music. Thus Gould's "good music" becomes a pure, abstract, and necessarily nonidiomatic entity.

Gould's distinction between music as *sound*—defined as an idiomatic and physical entity—and music as an abstract, nonphysical *structure* was ultimately motivated by ethical considerations. He ridiculed Mozart's "theatricality" and "pretension to self-sufficiency," which he saw as the merely idiomatic, pianistic quality of Mozart's music. While Bach's compositions were full of structural and abstract beauty, Mozart's piano sonatas offered only "tactile pleasure" of running the fingers "up and down the keys, exploiting all those scales and arpeggios."[28]

Gould's preference for polyphonic musical texture is discussed by the cultural critic Edward Said. Said was inspired not only by Gould's recordings but also by the analogy that Gould drew between democracy and polyphony. Said recommended reading cultural archives "not univocally, but *contrapuntally*, with a simultaneous awareness both of the metropolitan history that is narrated and of those other histories against which (and together with which) the dominating discourse acts."[29] Said defines the essence of his cultural critique: consciously open to different angles and awareness of the asymmetrical power relations between the scholar and his object. Said's contrapuntal reading also means epistemologically doing away with the notion of absolute truth as the outcome of any research—any interpretation is always ultimately relative as far as its truth value is concerned.

Just as Said embraced a multitude of perspectives with his "contrapuntal reading," Gould himself never formulated an absolute idea of north, unless *North* was itself such an idea.[30] He enforced multiple perspectives through his carefully layered voices of "contrapuntal radio." Kevin McNeilly, writing particularly about Gould's *North*, argues that there is not a single normative "philosophy of the North." Rather, the work unfolds as a "site at which many voices and 'ideas' coalesce, antagonize, support, subvert, mingle, and separate." Conceptualized this way, "north" emerges as a "name for a certain multiplicitous music, an imaginative zone in which the voices, noises, and ideas of the human community entangle and sound themselves out."[31]

Gould's interest in experimental, polyphonic radio composition sprang from his musical preferences. Homophonic musical texture in which one line is "permitted to become the focus of attention" seems to function as an iconic representation of a "totalitarian ideal" in which one melodic line is promoted at the expense of the others. Gould's quasi-philosophical considerations are the key to understanding the metaphorical meanings of counterpoint, which is the central aesthetic in Gould's audio documentaries. One might argue it is the same approach as his musicmaking in general. Counterpoint lays bare the antagonistic, diverse lines in the musical structure. Counterpoint, through its very mode of unfolding as a musical narrative, leads the listener to dissect the musical discourse.

The important point here is that, for Gould, counterpoint is like the north itself: a multivoiced *utopia*, which, by its nature, is more a way of thinking, a process, than something normatively defined. In a letter to Roy Vogt, an interviewee for his documentary *The Quiet in the Land*,[32] Gould ventures into a philosophical reflection on the nature of counterpoint in music:

> I hope to devise a form for the programme which in musical terms could be called "contrapuntal." I really cannot apologize for that analogy, however, because in my view—and I think this view would be shared by most 20th century, as opposed, perhaps, to 19th century historians—counterpoint is not a dry academic exercise in motivic permutation but rather a method of composition in which, if all goes well, each individual voice lives a life of its own. . . . In musical terms, the more accurate expression of the totalitarian ideal to which you refer in your letter could be found in homophonic music in which one thematic strand—usually the soprano line—is permitted to become the focus of attention and in which all other voices are relegated to accompanimental roles.[33]

Counterpoint, to Gould, implies a democratic, diverse, and multilayered existential and musical presence in which there is no totalizing center of attention. Rather it is a simultaneous multiplicity of perspectives, narratives, and discourses in existence.

What, if any, are the ethical implications of contrapuntal obsession? I return to the "ethics of isolation," which for Gould functions almost as an ethical maxim. The ethics of isolation run parallel to the notion of counterpoint and polyphony as allegories for an ideal condition of human life. As the music scholar Mark Lee Harris argued, Gould's ideal of polyphonic musical texture functions as a metaphor for his ideal of dissociation from the social collective. There is, ideally, an autonomous, independent life and space for each of the melodic lines. Harris calls the elaboration of the fugue, together with the field of ethics, "the Gouldian problematic."[34] The characterization is apt, as Gould's privileging of counterpoint and structure over sonorous color and impressions is imbued with a strong ethical component.

The Shadow of Hanslick and Gould's "Musical Tosspots"

Western musical aesthetics juxtapose the sensual, superficial, and ornamental music of the south, against the organic, structural, and abstract music of the north. We need only recall Friedrich Nietzsche, whose harsh criticism of Wagner was largely based on issues related to this juxtaposition. In Nietzsche's critique he argued that Wagner's Teutonic, pompous, and dramatic music "sweats," "rattles about devotion, loyalty and purity," and is generally too heavy and pompous to be enjoyable. Georges Bizet's music, in turn, "approaches lightly, supply, politely," treats the listener "as intelligent, as if himself a musician," and enables the listener to become a "better human being" and a better musician and listener.[35]

In *Beyond Good and Evil*, Nietzsche famously extends his critique to all of German music. Because "German" in this context is an important epithet, Nietzsche's assertion is worth quoting at some length:

> Against German music I feel all sorts of precautions should be taken. Suppose one loves the south as I love it, as a great school of convalescence, for all the diseases of senses and spirit, as a tremendous abundance of sun and transfiguration by sun, spreading itself over an autonomous existence which believes in itself: well, such a person will learn to be somewhat on guard against German music because, by spoiling his taste again, it will also spoil his health again. Such a southerner, not by descent but by faith, must, if he dreams of the future of music, also dream of the redemption of music from the North and have in his ears the prelude to a deeper, mightier, perhaps wickeder and more mysterious music, a supra-German music

which does not fade, turn yellow, turn pale at the sight of the blue voluptuous sea and the luminous sky of the Mediterranean, as all German music does.[36]

A thorough search of the Glenn Gould fonds at Library and Archives Canada did not reveal any books by Nietzsche, neither did Gould comment or cite any of his works in interviews, essays, or letters. Nonetheless, Gould did not share Nietzsche's anti-German view of music—we already examined his appreciation of Bach's nonidiomatic and abstract music. It is on those qualities that he bases his appreciation of composer Arnold Schoenberg's works. "Mediterranean culture," which is what Nietzsche sought in music, represented everything of which Gould disapproved: competition, virtuosity, sensuality, emotionality, flashing display of musical color, and so on. Music, in his view, was something rational, abstract, and a mental activity, in which the musician prioritizes the relationship with musical structure.

So it would seem that Gould and Nietzsche are polar opposites in terms of their musical views. In one sense, perhaps they are. However, they both participate in the same stereotypes; both associate "south" with spontaneity, musical color, dance, even corporeality associated with music. The musical north represents for Gould and Nietzsche, structure, musical development, seriousness, as well as music's nonidiomatic and abstract quality. Nietzsche, despite his German origin, rejects these values in favor of the southern light enjoyment of music. Gould maintains his musical idealism, but as with the issue of north, without a particular emphasis on nationalism. He appeared to believe in a nordic music that was supranational. Many Germanic works were discounted on the same criteria that led Gould to shun the Mediterranean. Gould had reservations about many of Beethoven's middle-period works, and he did not adopt the German standard repertory of the nineteenth century to the same extent as many of his contemporaries. His complete recording of Mozart's sonatas is an extended, sounding critique of Mozart's entertaining, easily comprehensible musical style. Likewise, many of his recordings of Beethoven's sonatas may be mistaken for musical parody.

Enter Eduard Hanslick. In his book *The Beautiful in Music*, arguably the most influential aesthetic tractate of the nineteenth century, Hanslick wrote the following: "The tyranny of the upper vocal part among the Italians has one main cause in the mental indolence of those people, for whom the sustained penetration with which the northerner likes to follow an ingenious web of harmonic and contrapuntal activity is beyond reach.

So the pleasure is more superficial for hearers whose mental activity is slight, and such musical tosspots are able to consume such quantities of music as make the artistic soul shudder."[37] In this oft-quoted passage, Hanslick excludes Italians from the real, "northern" contemplation of music. Contemplation, for Hanslick, means the "sustained penetration"—the corporeally sensitive deconstruction of this metaphor is best reserved for a later occasion—of harmonic and contrapuntal activity, of which only Germans, as opposed to Italian musical tosspots, are capable. Hanslick's idea of separating music's substance from its sonic aspect was central in German aesthetics of the nineteenth century. It is pertinent to the idea of a musical work as an autonomous object, ontologically independent of its performance. As the German music historian Carl Dahlhaus observed, referring to the writings of E. T. A. Hoffmann and Friedrich Schlegel, two of the pivotal figures of early nineteenth-century music criticism: "To understand music means . . . grasping the structure, the harmonic and thematic logic of a work, so as to be able to fathom its aesthetic meaning, a meaning that remains inaccessible to mere mindless enthusiasm."[38] This kind of physical, corporeal, and instrumental transcendence allowed music to function as a metalanguage by which to approach the absolute, metaphysical reality. These terms also turned the experience of music into an aesthetic contemplation, a devotion to the work, which came to be separated from pure enjoyment. This post-Kantian mode of listening as meaningful structure meant "immersing oneself in the internal workings of a piece of music as though nothing else in the world existed."[39]

So what about Gould? His aversion to live concerts, which he saw as an event similar to bullfights, were marked by a potentially strong adrenaline response, impulsivity, and spontaneity. In his essay "Let's Ban Applause!," Gould associated applause with the spirit of Italian opera, as a manifestation of the "vulgar artistic hostility of those sun-baked societies who have built an operatic tradition in which their primal instinct for gladiatorial combat has found a more gracious but thinly disguised sublimation."[40] Even if Gould's critique was just a bit tongue-in-cheek, he was earnest when he wrote in the same essay that art functions through the "internal combustion it ignites in the hearts of men and not its shallow, externalized, public manifestations." "The purpose of art," Gould continued, "is not the release of a momentary ejection of adrenaline but is, rather, the gradual, life-long construction of a state of wonder and serenity."[41]

In spite of the chronological and geographical distance between Gould and Hanslick, the similarity of their definitions of musical pleasure is striking. The listeners that Gould had in mind, persons for whom music was more about "a momentary ejection of adrenaline," were similar to those who, in Hanslick's formulation, merely "consumed" music. All this took place at the cost of analytical contemplation or structural listening. Gould's "state of wonder and serenity" was to bring to the listener a corollary in what Hanslick regarded as the proper intellectual, noncorporeal enjoyment of music.

Additionally, in the similarities between Gould's and Hanslick's preferred modes of concentrated listening, an acknowledgment must be paid to the "geographical" aspects of their arguments. Hanslick wrote about the "northerner," a northern listener of music as someone capable of "sustained penetration" and intellectual focus on music. Gould wrote somewhat pejoratively of "sun-burned musics" and "sun-baked societies" whose inhabitants' "primal instinct for gladiatorial combat" brought about false modes of listening to music. Gould's "tosspots" are not defined nationally, but the reference to "operatic tradition" brings to mind Italy.[42] However, the "gladiatorial" aspect of music, for Gould, was to be found in liveness and the adrenalin response of the audience and the artist that this liveness causes. This is why he wrote that the audience "is a force of evil."[43]

What is "northern" about Hanslick's ideals? The "tyranny of the upper vocal part" on display in Italian opera is aesthetically removed from the austere, abstract, and nonsensual music of, say, Bach's *Kunst der Fuge*. But why is the latter, contrapuntal music of highest structural integrity and learnedness associated with the north? The north/south dichotomy at issue here is in the historical juxtaposition between Protestantism and Catholicism. This ideological, aesthetic, and theological divide had important consequences not only for the religious life in Europe but also for the centuries-long accumulation of European music history. As Hanslick indicates, this dichotomy is also implicated in the kinds of national stereotypes related to music common in the aesthetics of nineteenth-century music.

Northern listening, for Hanslick and Gould, means an ability to comprehend music as *structure*, as an entity independent of its sonic realization. Contemplating abstract music entails an intellectual undertaking in which emotions, bodily engagement, and sensual pleasure have no part. All these fall in the category of "pathological listening" in Hanslick's treatise. Likewise, Gould's contention that the purpose of music is not to bring about "ejections of adrenaline" points in the same direction. Hanslick's distinction between "northern and southern" listeners betrays the German bias in his aesthetic thought, but Gould did not identify this distinction in primarily national terms. Further, he associated many of the same qualities with this category as did Hanslick. Ultimately there is an argument to be made of Gould's conception that the musical north has its roots in the nineteenth-century, Austro-German aesthetics of absolute music, exemplified here by Eduard Hanslick's treatise.

North as an Aesthetic Category

I contend that Gould's entire musical thought is the unfolding of one central idea. Even if his concept of north is such a prominent and pervasive element of his musical thinking and performance, I believe that he did not, nor did he intend to, leave a consistent musical philosophy. It bears repeating that the intention here is not to exhaust Gould's rich musical mind through a brief exploration of the north, or by excluding other potential approaches to his musicmaking. Perhaps Gould should be, as he indeed has been in several accounts, discussed as first and foremost a Canadian artist, whose ideas and musicmaking should be viewed in a Canadian context. This is where I started my exploration of Gould fifteen years ago.

My extended archival journey through the literary material that Gould left behind did not, however, support my initial hypothesis of Gould as a Canadian nationalist. What emerged from this search was a man of paradoxes: a musician who wanted to communicate but believed in solitude as an ideal condition of human life; a philosopher who was patently suspicious of philosophical systems; a concert pianist who preached the importance of noncompetition, even anonymity, as ideals for musical practice. Gould thought "one's creativity is enhanced primarily by the more-or-less single-minded pursuit of one's own resources without reference to the trends, tastes, fashions, etc. of the world outside."[44] At times he said that audiences are a "force of evil" and that "all the live arts are immoral" because one should not "voyeuristically watch one's fellow human beings in testing situations that do not pragmatically need to be tested."[45]

Isolation was his preferred mode of existence. In one of many letters touching on the topic, Gould wrote of the "blessed isolation" and "wonderful advantages that isolation offers."[46] As to the philosophy of noncompetition, Gould upheld those ideals in his personal and professional life. For the few honors he accepted during his life, he turned down just as many. In 1968, he was approached by Floyd Chalmers, a Canadian editor, publisher, and philanthropist, then acting Officer of the Order of Canada, whether he would be available for a candidacy to receive the prestigious prize. Gould would surely have been an attractive candidate. Gould's response and rejection of the offer was telling. He wrote Chalmers that he was not happy with "the particular kind of stratification implicit in the Order of Canada" and thought that "there is something unnecessarily divisive within that system as it is presently constituted."[47] In later years he grew stricter about his principle. Sometimes it is difficult to distinguish whether Gould's preferred solitude was more an outcome of his aversion for being in public or disdain for competition. In 1975, Gould, upon John Hobday's invitation to be awarded the prestigious Diplome d'honneur by the Canadian Conference of the Arts, responded briefly that he "does not attend public events and suggested his friend John Roberts as proxy."[48]

Gould's concept of north provides a context for his thought and musicmaking on four levels: first, his public image, the public reception of his art, as well as his personal fascination with the north; second, Gould regarded music as an abstract, nonsensual, rational, and structural entity. He emphasized music's nonvirtuosity, counterpoint, and polyphony, which makes music a representation of "democratic" and "antitotalitarian" qualities; third, the north is reflected as an idealization of music as an individual, isolated contemplation. This contemplation, in Gould's mind, unfolds by default outside the social collective; and fourth, through his work and ideas, Gould subscribes to a particular Canadian "discursive formation of the North," whose history in Canadian arts and letters has been traced by Sherrill Grace.[49]

Gould's voice as an individual demands a modicum of attention while his musicianship should be evaluated not so much against the backdrop of tradition, but in the context of his aesthetic and ethical ideals. It is these ideals that resonate with his concept of north. Gould's complex and sometimes controversial ideas about music were thus part and parcel of equally complex intellectual, historical, and cultural webs within which his musicianship finds its meaning.

Notes

1. A shorter and earlier version of this chapter is published in Mantere, *The Gould Variations: Technology, Philosophy and Criticism in Glenn Gould's Musical Thought and Practice* (Frankfurt: Peter Lang, 2012).

2. Glenn Gould, "'The Idea of North': An Introduction," in *The Glenn Gould Reader*, ed. Tim Page (New York: Vintage Books, 1990), 391.

3. See also chapter 7 in the present volume, in which Wetters and Cushing discuss the national(ist) implications of the work's commission.

4. Murray Schafer, letter to Markus Mantere, 11 November 2004.

5. Sherrill E. Grace, *Canada and the Idea of North* (Montreal: McGill-Queen's University Press, 2007), 47, emphasis original.

6. Grace, *Canada and the Idea of North*, 50.

7. Sergei Medvedev, "The_Blank_Space: Glenn Gould, Russia, Finland and the North," *CTheory* 23, no. 2 (June 2000): 2.

8. Given Gould's stature as a public figure in his country, this is actually somewhat surprising. The public discourse concerning the rights of the Indigenous people of Canada was very much in the air in the 1960s. In 1966, the government established a new ministry called Indian and Northern Affairs Canada. Around that time, there was considerable media coverage about this in the Canadian media. Gould did not appear to engage with these issues publicly.

9. Gould took frequent road trips to Wawa, in rural, northern Ontario, to brainstorm on projects and other ideas.

10. Gould, "'The Idea of North': An Introduction," 391.

11. See Nicholas Cook, *Music, Performance, Meaning: Selected Essays* (Aldershot: Ashgate, 2007) for groundbreaking work in this area.

12. Martin Kusch, *Ymmärtämisen haaste* [The Challenge of Understanding] (Oulu: Pohjoinen, 1986).

13. Quentin Skinner, "Hermeneutics and the Role of History," *New Literary History* 7, no. 1 (Autumn 1975): 216.

14. Anyssa Neumann, "Ideas of North: Glenn Gould and the Aesthetic of the Sublime," *voiceXchange* 5, no. 1 (Fall 2011): 35.

15. Neumann, "Ideas of North," 38.

16. Jean-François Lyotard, *Lessons on the Analytic of the Sublime*, trans. Elizabeth Rottenberg (Stanford: Stanford University Press, 1994).

17. Lyotard's conception of the sublime is fundamentally based on Kant's sublime. For the latter, the sublime occurs when our faculties are overwhelmed by manifestations of absolute power and magnitude, and "reason is thrown back upon its own power to conceive Ideas (such as the moral law) which surpass the sensible world. For Lyotard, however, the postmodern sublime occurs when we are affected by a multitude of unpresentables without reference to reason as their unifying origin." See Gary Aylesworth, "Postmodernism," in *Standford Encyclopedia of Philosophy*, https://plato.stanford.edu/entries/postmodernism (accessed 20 June 2017) for more detail.

18. Gould, "Of Mozart and Related Matters: Glenn Gould in Conversation with Bruno Monsaingeon," in *The Glenn Gould Reader*, 41.

19. Many of these new technologies, of course, contain their own "competitive" features like "hit counters" and "likes."

20. Gould, "Of Mozart and Related Matters," 41.

21. Max Paddison, *Adorno's Aesthetics of Music* (Cambridge: Cambridge University Press, 1997), 55.

22. Theodor W. Adorno, "On Popular Music," in *Essays on Music: Theodor W. Adorno*, ed. Richard Leppert (Berkeley: University of California Press, 2002), 441–444.

23. Glenn Gould, "Twenty-Five Years as a Recording Artist: Gould in Conversation with Ulla Colgrass," in *The Art of Glenn Gould*, ed. John P. L. Roberts (Toronto: Malcolm Lester Books, 1999), 348.

24. Gould, "N'aimez vous pas Brahms?," in *The Glenn Gould Reader*, 70–72.

25. Kevin Bazzana, *Glenn Gould: The Performer in the Work* (New York: Oxford University Press, 2003), 33.

26. Gould, "Art of the Fugue," in *The Glenn Gould Reader*, 17, 21.

27. Gould's take on Bach was highly idealized. For national and local influences on Bach's musical idiom, see Christoph Wolff, *Johann Sebastian Bach: The Learned Musician* (New York: W. W. Norton, 2000).

28. Gould, "Of Mozart and Related Matters," 33.

29. Edward Said, *Culture and Imperialism* (New York: Vintage Books, 1994), 51.

30. In the final chapter in this volume, however, Brent Wetters argues that, through careful manipulation of his source interviews, and by giving Wally Maclean a privileged position at the end of the documentary, Gould does approach something like a thesis, even if its conclusions are left open-ended.

31. Kevin McNeilly, "Listening, Nordicity, Community: Glenn Gould's 'The Idea of North,'" *Essays on Canadian Writing* 59 (Fall 1996): 87.

32. *The Quiet in the Land* (1977) is the last work in the so-called *Solitude Trilogy*, a collection of radio documentaries that Gould produced for CBC between 1967 and 1977. Its working title was "Variations of a Theme of Bach," Item 1979-20 23, 33, 2, Glenn Gould fonds, Library and Archives Canada, Ottawa. The second audio documentary in the series is *The Latecomers* (1969).

33. Glenn Gould, *Glenn Gould: Selected Letters*, ed. John P. L. Roberts and Ghyslaine Guertin (Oxford: Oxford University Press, 1992), 150.

34. Mark Lee Harris, "Fugue States: Music, Dissociation, and Ethical Implications," unpublished PhD diss., Concordia University, 2001, 2–3.

35. Friedrich Nietzsche, *The Case of Wagner*, trans. Walter Kaufmann (New York: Vintage, 1967), 157.

36. Friedrich Nietzsche, *Beyond Good and Evil*, compiled from translations by Helen Zimmernin and Walter Kaufmann, http://www.thenietzschechannel.com/works-pub/bge/bge-eng.htm (accessed 29 September 2016).

37. Eduard Hanslick, *The Beautiful in Music*, trans. Geoffrey Payzant (New York: Da Capo Press, 1986), 64.

38. Carl Dahlhaus, *Nineteenth-Century Music* (Berkeley: University of California Press, 1989), 91.

39. Dahlhaus, *Nineteenth-Century Music*, 95.

40. Gould, "Let's Ban Applause!," in *The Glenn Gould Reader*, 247.

41. Gould, "Let's Ban Applause!," 246.

42. Gould indulged occasionally in nationalist stereotyping, musical tastes, and sense of humor, his caricatures of Myron Chianti, Herbert von Hochmeister, and Karl-Heinz Klopweisser notwithstanding. Further, his expression "sun-baked society" is a manifestation of this. There are also many examples of this in the archival material. In a letter to the wife of Cincinnati-based businessman impresario J. Ralph Corbett, Gould suggested, upon hearing of her recent car accident in Mexico, that "it was one of those drowsy, siesta-bound Mexicans and I really feel that for your vacations in the future you must head North to the cool, clear air of Canada."

43. Kevin Bazzana, *Wondrous Strange* (Toronto: McClelland & Stewart, 2003), 179.

44. Glenn Gould to William Clark, 14 February 1973, Item 1979-20 32, 19, 20, Glenn Gould fonds, Library and Archives Canada, Ottawa.

45. Interview with Robert Hurwitz, *New York Times*, 5 January 1975.

46. Letter to principal at Terrace Bay High School, 8 November 1965, MUS 109/24, 31, 28, 18, Glenn Gould fonds, Library and Archives Canada, Ottawa.

47. Letter to Floyd Chalmers, 15 March 1968, Item 1979-20 31, 35, 26, Glenn Gould fonds, Library and Archives Canada, Ottawa.

48. Glenn Gould to John Hobday, 17 December 1975, Item 1979-20 32, 31, 25, Glenn Gould fonds, Library and Archives Canada, Ottawa.

49. See Grace, *Canada and the Idea of North*.

7

The Genius Is in the Genesis

Demythologizing the Idea of Gould as Creative Outsider

Anthony Cushing and Brent Wetters

> In five-score summers! All new eyes,
> New minds, new modes, new fools, new wise;
> New woes to weep, new joys to prize;
>
> With nothing left of me and you
> In that live century's vivid view
> Beyond a pinch of dust or two;
>
> A century which, if not sublime,
> Will show, I doubt not, at its prime,
> A scope above this blinkered time.
>
> —Yet what to me how far above?
> For I would only ask thereof
> That thy worm should be my worm, Love!
>
> —Thomas Hardy, "1967"
> 16 Westbourne Park Villas, 1867

In 1867, Thomas Hardy penned the preceding poem with the title "1967" to speculate what might come to pass in the following century. The first stanza looks forward to all that will be novel and yet couches novelty in a sense that little will change structurally. We will still find a collection of changed fashions, new visionaries, new fools. Those changes will not be insubstantial; the third stanza confirms his faith in progress. He does not, however, predict that any of those changes will be *revolutionary*. Everything that is new will fall into existing categories.

The one hundred years between 1867 and 1967 bore many technological developments that changed society in fundamental ways that Hardy could not have predicted. Many of the seeds of change existed for Hardy, but few recognized their potential. The first daguerreotype camera was already in use by 1839, but it would be almost another hundred years before Walter Benjamin wrote his landmark "The Work of Art in the Age of Mechanical Reproduction," assessing the cultural impact of the invention. Audio recording technology lagged further still, and radio broadcasts were not even in the realm of fantasy.

From the Canadian perspective, 1967 was not an ordinary year, though neither was 1867. The popular historian Pierre Berton called 1967 "the last good year." It was, after all, the centennial, and the nation participated in a year-long celebration of its statehood. Canada was finally on the cusp of greatness, ready to assume a more prominent role on the international stage. At a time when much of the world was embroiled in intractable conflict, Canadian politicians celebrated their military's important role in global peacekeeping and hailed their country as a "land of opportunity."[1] The nationalist optimism engendered by the centennial year and the widely attended Expo 67 in Montreal buoyed the country following the tense early years of the Cold War. Canadians now look back at that moment with nostalgia, and some like Berton with not a little regret. It may not be so much that Canada failed to deliver the change it seemed to promise in 1967, as the promise of change is always more alluring than its actuality, which appears as a series of incremental steps.

Glenn Gould, at the CBC's behest, contributed his *Idea of North* in service of the national celebration. The work, in its own way, addressed the notion of north—the then underrepresented portion of Canada's cultural boundaries—and furthered the cause of a new Canadian national identity.[2]

Gould presents his documentary as something novel, as its own turning point in music history. Critical discussions, including many in the present volume, typically begin with some amount of hand-wringing about the generic category to which the work belongs. Do we prioritize the musical and structural devices and call it a musical composition, or is it simply an unconventional radio documentary? The emphasis, in either case, is placed on its unconventionality. The mythology that enshrines this work, promoted at least partially by Gould himself, suggests that it was wholly unprecedented, but that characterization is squarely at odds with concurrent developments in Europe at electronic music studios in Paris, Cologne, and Milan. The current chapter attempts to problematize the work's creation myths and situate *North* within the musical avant-garde and broader tradition of radio and soundscape works of the 1950s and '60s. More importantly, we aim to destabilize the facile characterizations of *North* that either reduce it to something common (a documentary) or elevate it to something wholly unconventional ("contrapuntal radio").

How did Gould, a virtuoso and controversial pianist, find his way into radio production for the CBC? That he would break established conventions was unsurprising given the trajectory of his career to that point, but few would have predicted a speech-based philosophical exploration of the Canadian north to be his first departure from piano performance. Several years after *North*, by which point he had completed two additional documentaries, Gould sat down with John Jessop, then an audio engineering student at Ryerson Polytechnic Institute, for a scripted interview, "Radio as Music."[3] Jessop and Gould discussed how Gould arrived at what he then called "contrapuntal radio."

Gould traces the roots of his interest in radio documentary to broadcasts he heard as a teenager, in particular the *Sunday Night Stage* radio productions of Andrew Allan. Gould cherished those broadcasts, which ranged from adaptations of Shakespeare to political satire, for successfully eliding the generic distinctions between drama and documentary.[4] His personal interest in such documentaries predated *North* by some ten years. Already at this point Gould felt constrained by the conventions of radio:

> In the late fifties, I began to write scripts for documentaries occasionally, and I was always dissatisfied with the kind of documentaries that radio seemed to decree. You know, they very often came out sounding—not square, because that's not necessarily a pejorative word in my vocabulary, but they came out sounding—okay, I'll borrow Mr. McLuhan's term—linear. They came out sounding "Over to you, now back to our host, and here for the wrap-up is"—in a word, predictable.[5]

What became of those early scripts, if they ever existed at all, is unclear, but he resigned himself to the concession that radio had to be linear until he began work on *North*. He describes to Jessop the two-hour, 1962 documentary about Arnold Schoenberg, admitting that the contrapuntal techniques of *North* might have been difficult to sustain for that length of time.⁶

When Gould broaches the topic of *North*, he places it firmly in the context of his ongoing radio work for the CBC. Gould even goes so far as to deny that he ever had any revolutionary motivations in his conception. According to Gould's recollection, he arrived at "contrapuntal radio" through a completely natural series of practical decisions, which finally ended in something novel. The decision to overlap voices, Gould assures us, was nothing more than a way to pack more material into the one-hour time slot: "That [set of cuts] brought the time down to about one hour, twelve minutes—at least fourteen minutes too long, allowing for Harry Mannis's closing credits—and I thought to myself, 'Look we really could hear some of these people speaking simultaneously—there's no particular reason why not.'"⁷ Jessop responds, "That's a pretty inauspicious birth for 'contrapuntal radio'!" Gould immediately cautions that he exaggerates "ever so slightly," but he denies that it arose from any strong theoretical or aesthetic goals.

He suggests musical ideas as source material for the technological innovations in *North*. Anthony Cushing, in his chapter in the present volume, extensively examines Gould's construction of a musical semiology. For this discussion, it suffices to say that Gould finds musical justifications to account for the aesthetic merit of his recording studio practice. For example, he compares the transition from one speaker to another by way of similar thematic content to the way that Webern used "motives that are similar but not identical . . . for the exchange of instrumental ideas."⁸ Webern's so-called "crossover in continuity" was a contrapuntal technique of eliding motivic material to accomplish a voice exchange. In Gould's case, it was *literally* to exchange spoken voices to shift focus from one to the next. As Cushing argues, the recourse to musical terminology functions by way of analogy, but musical practice may not be the ultimate source of those ideas.

Perhaps most telling is how Gould retrospectively casts his artistic trajectory. He compares *North*'s genesis to the compositional method of Beethoven: "The early outlines of 'North' . . . were intriguing in the way Beethoven's sketchbooks are intriguing—rather naive and only distantly related to the eventual outcome."⁹ The early sketches for *North*, scrawled quickly in Gould's cramped autograph, reveal a very rough structure that does indeed bear only a passing similarity to the final work.¹⁰ Rhetorically, the invocation of Beethoven has the effect of claiming absolute autonomy for Gould's eventual discovery. Gould is only willing to concede two types of influence. Either he applies something from instrumental music, for example the Webernian crossover applied to a new medium, or he uses familiar techniques from his studio practice—but for him, they seem to have compelling artistic or musical meaning. In both cases, Gould claims ownership on the discovery. In the first case, he recognizes and applies some important principles from music, those which no one else had ever thought to apply to radio. In the second case, he "discovers" the artistic merits of something that radio engineers had just been doing because it was convenient. He has not appropriated or borrowed these new ideas from anyone else, except via a circuitous train of thought, and the final product is so removed from the banal sketches—as in the case of Beethoven—that only his "genius" could be responsible for that leap. This, we stress again, is the *mythology* of Gould's discovery of "contrapuntal radio."[11]

When we examine the historical context of Gould's discourse on contrapuntal radio, a murkier picture emerges. For as revealing as "Radio as Music" appears to be, the mythological patina does not hold up to scrutiny. The document is problematic inasmuch as the interview is *not* an interview in any conventional sense of the form. Gould and Jessop (though we can likely infer Gould's voice was decisive) went through three drafts of the interview text to be published in a Canadian trade publication.[12] In this respect, the interview was less an interview and more of a script in interview format. The result is a text that reads as rehearsed, and Jessop's voice sounds remarkably Gouldian—with the same wry humor and classic setup questions crafted to elicit a similarly rehearsed response.

Moreover, Jessop often assumes a curious role in the interview as he offers his own interpretations of the audio production techniques involved in the making of *North*. Jessop could not have had any direct, personal knowledge of those techniques. During the work's birth in the production suite, the primary contributors were Gould and Lorne Tulk. Jessop would have been in his final year of high school or early years of college. Tulk, who did the manual work and was tasked with translating Gould's lofty goals into the practical tape and dial manipulation, was not consulted for the interview.[13] In Jessop's defense, audio production often allows several ways to achieve the same effect. If he conjectured at what actually transpired in the studio, even if his assertions were incorrect, they may have been based on his aural experience of the work and nevertheless rooted in production theory and practice. If Gould fed Jessop the technical material via the early script drafts, then his assertions may have been only partly informed. Gould and Tulk negotiated a common language during production and each learned a great deal about the other's approach to the material. However, as Tulk realized Gould's concepts, the actual techniques may not have been fully articulated to Gould. It is entirely possible that Gould and Jessop developed the technical information in tandem based on very limited knowledge of actual events—an incidence of the proverbial blind leading the blind.

Perhaps the most important detail in "Radio as Music" is patently false, specifically how Gould arrived at the contrapuntal element of contrapuntal radio. He claimed he initially conceived the work as five separate stories, and the other interviewees would occasionally comment on a particular point.[14] Though Gould claims that the contrapuntal composition of *North* was relatively a last-minute decision to fit all his material in the time allotment, his scribbled lists of interview questions, annotations on interview transcripts (the last of which was conducted in late autumn 1967), and sketches of the work's structure indicate contrapuntal intent. Tulk, who worked on the project from the outset, even as the technician for the interviews conducted in the CBC's Toronto studios, claimed that Gould came to the project immediately with the intent of creating vocal polyphony.[15] These issues do not entirely invalidate "Radio as Music"; it is an important document that provides an accessible, if flawed, explanation of Gould's aesthetic goals. "Radio as Music" is an important piece of the puzzle: it gives a very clear picture of the ways Gould wanted to frame his practice *retrospectively*.

Conspicuously absent in Gould and Jessop's portrayal is a recognition that musical works composed with recorded sound on magnetic tape—that is, notated versus nonnotated—were not new circa 1967. Considerable generic confusion might have been avoided had Gould simply aligned his work with the electroacoustic music emerging from European music studios, or even the much-closer-to-home studios in Toronto and New York. To the last point, there is something to be said for what Gould may have known of contemporary popular music production through his travels between Toronto and Columbia Records' New York studios.

Where *North* Fits in the Context of Popular Music

At first blush it may be difficult to tease out a connection between contrapuntal radio and popular music production in the mid- to late 1960s.

In the Petula Clark documentary, Gould disparaged the Beatles for the "ineptitude of the studio production method," no small slight to George Martin.[16] It is unclear how Gould arrived at that conclusion apart from, perhaps, close listening to the Beatles' recordings. Surely, he could not have known of their studio production method, separated as they were by an ocean with no chance of witnessing Martin's ministrations at the mixing board and tape recorder(s). Indeed, Jay Hodgson in his exhaustive volume on music production details an intricate network of recording practice employed by Martin and the Beatles in the service of their more adventurous late work.[17] The detailed use of pan potentiometers, filters, bouncing tracks to optimize the available space on four-track tape, and even harnessing two four-track tape recorders simultaneously speaks to a highly imaginative and creative use of the studio resources available to the band in the Abbey Road studios. The Beatles were not the only innovators in the recording studio. At the same time, Brian Wilson and the Beach Boys forged their own creative path on the West Coast in Los Angeles.[18]

Wilson, much like Gould, deserted concert touring in 1964 to focus on recording and studio production, his own love affair with the microphone, albeit in a different idiom. The Beach Boys' 1966 album *Pet Sounds* also made creative use of the recording studio to produce an early iteration of the concept album. Wilson, in producing *Pet Sounds*, sought to "outdo" the Beatles' 1966 *Rubber Soul* album, itself an innovative album for its use of multitrack recording.[19] Although recorded on a four-track recorder, *Pet Sounds* was mixed down to the final mono product. Gould and Lorne Tulk did not have the luxury of multitracking, rather only five mono tape players fed into a mixing console and distilled into the final mono mix. Although it is likely that Gould would have heard portions of *Pet Sounds* either by personal home listening or via the radio, it is highly unlikely that he was privy to Wilson's production method in Los Angeles, from his perch in Toronto. If Gould did not have firsthand knowledge of what transpired in the recording studios of popular music artists, then perhaps the audio technicians at the CBC may have had some knowledge thereof.

Many CBC technicians completed their education in audio production at Ryerson Polytechnic Institute before finding their way to the public broadcaster. Lorne Tulk, Gould's production copartner for *North*, was largely self-taught, having apprenticed in his father's home recording studio and working with Canadian sports broadcasting luminary Foster Hewitt. Tulk's work at the CBC was primarily in service of *Ideas*, the predominantly documentary-focused radio show that did not require much in the way of popular music production or multitracking, which was simply unavailable in the CBC studios. As noted elsewhere in this volume, Gould and Tulk spent dozens of hours finding a common language to actualize the pianist's lofty artistic goals with the resources available at the CBC. Had Tulk the experience of working in a popular music context, the time required to produce even the *North* prologue may have been greatly reduced. Instead, a more productive avenue of exploration lies in what Gould knew or may have known of his European contemporaries and their work with tape composition and studio production method.

Where *North* Fits in the European Context

The roots of the modern era of tape music are usually credited to French composer Pierre Schaeffer, who, like Gould, had a particular affinity for the recording booth. In fact, we stress that Schaeffer was a broadcast engineer first, and only after he began a collaboration with the musician Pierre Henry in 1949 was he taken seriously as a musician himself.[20] Having worked as a recording engineer and acoustician during World War II, he conducted a series of "musical" experiments at the Radiodiffusion-Télévision Française (RTF), culminating in the seminal work *Étude aux chemins de fer* (Study with Trains). The work is composed from a collection of prerecorded train sounds, manipulated in the recording studio. Schaeffer cut and spliced pieces of magnetic tape until he arrived at the work's final three-minute form. The title "study" indicates the extent to which this work was experimental; Schaeffer makes little claim to the musicality of the new art form. And yet, the possibilities inherent in the medium were immediately apparent to others in the European avant-garde.

Schaeffer would go on to deliver a lecture, entitled "La musique concrète," at the Darmstadt Summer Courses in 1951.[21] This new method proved attractive to the European avant-garde, because it allowed them to engage directly with their musical material. The French term given to this new genre of music was *musique concrète* in recognition of the fact that composers were working with tangible "sound objects"—bits of magnetic tape—rather than musical ideas that could only be realized later by a performer.

By the time Schaeffer founded the Groupe de Recherches Musicales in Paris in 1958, many of those colleagues from Darmstadt had already established or affiliated themselves with electronic music studios in their own countries. Karlheinz Stockhausen and Gottfried-Michael König found a supportive community at the state-sponsored Westdeutscher Rundfunk (WDR) in Cologne.[22] In stark contrast to the developments in Paris, the composers in Cologne were definitively not interested in recording naturally occurring sound; instead, they focused on electronically generated sounds and tones.[23] In the United States, the Columbia-Princeton Electronic Music Studio was set up to more closely follow Cologne's model.

At Radiotelevisione Italiana (RAI) in Milan, composers Bruno Maderna and Luciano Berio set up the third of the major European electronic music studios in 1954. The RAI studio struck a kind of balance between the synthesized music of Cologne and the natural sounds of *musique concrète*. From the beginning, composers sought to focus on speech and phonetics, as was clear from the studio's full name, the Studio di Fonologia Musicale di Milano della RAI. In addition to works like Maderna's *Invensione su una voce*, an abstract work using a set of phonemes written by German poet Hans G. Helms, other works were more documentarian in form.[24] The very first work of the RAI studio was a collaboration between Maderna and Berio titled *Ritratto di Città*. The work is a cityscape of Milan, paired with a text composed and read by Roberto Leydi. Subsequent works by Maderna and Berio relied on speech but also developed new techniques for its assemblage. While these works use techniques that seem derived from more standard radio practice—voice-overs, illustrative sound effects—they also borrow elements of musical structure and experimentalism. Berio's *Thema (Omaggio a Joyce)* was one such work. Berio described his intent as follows: "I tried to interpret musically a reading of Joyce's text, developing the polyphonic intent that characterizes the eleventh chapter of *Ulysses* (entitled "Sirens" and dedicated to music), whose narrative technique was suggested to the author by a common procedure of polyphonic music: the *fuga per canonem*. . . . In Thema I was interested in obtaining a new kind of unity between speech and music, developing the possibilities of a continuous metamorphosis of one into the other."[25] Here we see Berio at pains to justify his studio techniques in musical terms, in part it would seem, so the works will fit neatly into his existing artistic output. It is easier for a composer to call an unconventional work a "musical composition" rather than expect to be taken seriously in an entirely new artistic discipline.

Maderna's *Ritratto di Erasmo*, completed two years after *North* in 1969, was in many respects a standard radio documentary. It gives a robust account of Erasmus and his role in the Protestant Reformation. In addition to a subtext for the documentary that appears to express Maderna's personal frustrations about the European music scene, the final fifteen minutes departs from documentary conventions and combines the voice of Calvin with a swirling text describing a set of demons and electronic sounds.[26] A feature of both this work and Berio's *Thema*, which seems to arrive without much fanfare in both cases, is the overlapping of distinct fragments of speech.

While Gould never references these works specifically in relation to his own radio works, there is also reason to believe that he would have encountered many of them during the fifties and sixties. David Jaeger, a composer of electronic music who would go on to collaborate closely with Gould at the CBC, believes that Gould would have heard and been interested in these sorts of compositions. In Jaeger's estimation, even if physical recordings may have been hard to come by, the composers were well enough known that Gould would have at least known them by reputation.[27]

Finally, there was in Europe—primarily Germany—a radio genre with the potential to subsume most of these stylistic differences: the *Hörspiel*. Translating literally to "hear-play" but usually translated as "radio-play," the term had been primarily applied to radio productions of a narrative nature. By 1950, most countries had their own such works and, before the widespread adoption of television, these represented some of the most popular radio fare. (Orson Welles's *War of the Worlds* from 1938 is often cited as one of the first such works.) Outside of Germany, however, these broadcasts tended to be conventional and aimed at a mass audience. At the WDR, perhaps because of the proximity to the electronic music studio and perhaps because of the productive ambiguity inherent in the category, the *Hörspiel* became a site for experimentation and innovation. By the time Mauricio Kagel, a Darmstadt participant and member of the circle at the WDR studio, produced his first *Hörspiel* in 1969, many abstract and experimental works had already been produced at the many radio institutions in Germany. Importantly, from at least the end of World War II, there is not an apparent disciplinary boundary around the genre. Although many of the first *Hörspiele* were scripted by writers such as Max Frisch and Ingeborg Bachmann who inevitably receive top billing,[28] musicians and composers were also given prominent roles. A Bachmann *Hörspiel* from 1954, *Die Zikaden*, included music by Hans Werner Henze, a onetime member of the avant-garde.[29] Because the *Hörspiel* was a genre where everyone was equally not-at-home, no single discipline could claim it as their own.

For someone like Kagel, who had long been interested in bringing theatrical elements into his compositions, the *Hörspiel* was an ideal medium. As Björn Heile suggests, the main practical distinction between *Hörspeile* and *musique concrète* was one of distribution: "Both [*Hörspiele* and *musique concrète*] are stored on tape and played through speakers; electroacoustic music can involve text and elements of a narrative nature, while, conversely, radio plays can be abstract and sonically complex. Where they differ is in the primary means of distribution: electroacoustic music is played back in concerts or sold as records or CDs, whereas radio plays are broadcast."[30] Heile goes on to suggest that other differences were decisive for attracting Kagel to the genre. First, the *Hörspiel* tends to focus on "content" rather than what Kagel began to see as the "fetishized" technical procedures of the electronic music studio. Where Kagel may have made the genre his own was in his reluctance to compose by way of "producing a script." Instead, Kagel preferred to regard "the technical production as an important part of the creative process."[31]

Interestingly, the German magazine *Der Spiegel* referred to Gould's radio works unproblematically as *Hörspiele* when they published a short article on his recent activities in May 1968.[32] The veracity of the article is suspect given that in the same sentence it mentions Gould's current participation in *Jazzmusiken* and indicates he had then just finished his String Quartet, op. 1, when in fact it had been written some thirteen years prior. Nevertheless, the article was intriguing enough to European audiences that Klaus Mehrländer of the WDR wrote to Gould to inquire about rebroadcasting the works in Germany:

> Last week there was a very interesting article about you and your work in the magazine "Der Spiegel" (Jargh. 22/Nr. 19). We read it with great pleasure. In this very article it was said, that the famous pianist Glenn Gould has also written some radio-plays. We apologise to you this way to get in contact. We—the section for radio-drama of Radio Cologne, the greatest radio-station in Western Germany—would like to get to know one of the other of your plays to look for a possibility to produce and to broadcast one of them.[33]

When Mehrländer refers to the works as "radio-plays," the standard English translation of *Hörspiel*, we can assume he means *Hörspiel*. All of this suggests that even if Gould was not consciously aware of the

European context for *North*, it was not the unprecedented work it might have seemed to Canadian audiences.

Gould's Influences

Gould's influences remained largely unnamed in print sources and interviews. In "Radio as Music" he cites a musical influence (Webern), a theatrical influence (Andrew Allan and *Sunday Night Stage*), but conspicuously absent is the cinematic influence, which is curious because, according to Lorne Tulk's recollections, Gould frequently relied on cinematic analogies to illustrate his arguments. Lorne Tulk recalled Gould citing a 1965 Stanley Kramer film as a key influence: "For 'North' he frequently made reference to *The Ship of Fools* (a movie he adored), because it, though in a far less complicated [way], it sort of conceptualized visually what *He* [original emphasis] was trying to do aurally."[34] The movie, based on Katherine Porter's novel of the same title, transpired on a ship from Vera Cruz, Mexico, to Bremerhaven, Germany, in summer 1931.[35] Shot in black and white, the film included a sizable cast with several narrative threads with several crossovers between characters and scenarios. The movie itself was reviewed mostly in the popular press, but even then reviews were short and largely superficial, remarking on the size of the cast and Vivien Leigh's performance. Conversely, Porter's novel received little in the way of insightful commentary in the popular press but appeared prominently in the literary criticism journals.

The similarities between Porter's book and *North* are striking even with only a superficial reading of both works. Smith Kirkpatrick's review of the novel points to several characteristics shared by both Gould and Porter's respective works. In both, there is no identifiable protagonist or antagonist.[36] However, in *North*, Maclean appears more prominently as a commentator if only because he appears first in scene 1 and in the epilogue. Porter employs a similar narrator in the role of Karl Glocken, who establishes the scenario on the boat and then closes the story as all the characters disembark in Bremerhaven.

Curiously, Porter inserts herself into the story via Glocken after a brief introduction, "I am a passenger on that ship." Gould, too, imposes his own voice in *North*, not so much through Maclean but, literally, his own voice after the prologue. If Gould created *North* as a composition, his choice of personal introduction after the prologue is unusual insomuch that it interrupts the flow of the work and does not allow it the opportunity to stand on its own. Perhaps he fashioned the prologue as a kind of overture, followed by his introduction to serve as notice that he only observed the goings-on in the train during the trip from Winnipeg to Churchill. In both cases of *North* and *Ship of Fools*, after a brief introduction that establishes the subtext, the works choose a clearly defined venue for their respective stories. This seems to contrast with more usual storytelling techniques, which first establish location allowing the subtext to emerge over the course of the narrative. Literary critic M. M. Liberman's analysis suggests, "Miss Porter's method is to dramatize the theme in a microcosmic setting (the ship) with a cast of contemporary types, on a traditional, mythic quest (the journey home)."[37] Porter chose a ship on a transatlantic voyage though it could have transpired on a plane or a train if she set the story during a transcontinental voyage. Liberman's "mythic quest" resonates with Gould's choice of a train, voyaging into the mythic north, the great white unknown.[38] Porter and Gould's choices of transit were arbitrary and serve only as a theatrical backdrop rather than any narrative function.

In terms of the narrative construction, Gould employs the theatrical delimiters of scenes with a prologue and epilogue, each with its own theme. In that respect, *North* may be regarded as several monologues on a common theme, at least in the scenes with voices following end-to-end rather than overlapped. Liberman levels a similar criticism at Porter: "*Ship of Fools* has been faulted in many ways as a bad novel, and likened to a single badly attenuated short story, or beheld as a tedious, directionless aggregate of many short stories in a single setting with a common cast of characters."[39] It is difficult to deny the similarities between the two works, especially given Gould's private admission of pervasive cinematic influence through *North*'s genesis.

Following the example of the Petula Clark essay, Gould reveals small hints of his knowledge of the avant-garde in a previous essay, "The Prospects of Recording," arguably his first significant foray into media theory. Brief mentions of technologies and repertoire indicate more than a passing familiarity with his contemporaries. Early in the essay he discusses technological advances in music at the University of Toronto's (U of T) music department, specifically a "computer-controlled phonographic information system."[40] By 1966, the university built one of the premiere electronic music studios in North America, led by pioneering composer and inventor Hugh Le Caine. It would have been impossible to know about one development in the U of T music lab without knowledge of related technological developments or the subsequent creative output.

While musical developments in Gould's native Toronto would have provided a significant outlook on the world of the electronic avant-garde, global distribution channels provided access to international print and audio media. Periodicals provided insight into the global music scenes. In particular, Gould cites an interview with Claudio Arrau that he read in the English journal *Records and Recordings*. Clearly, Gould had access to print materials to keep him attuned to contemporary composition. In Toronto, it was possible to purchase recordings of both American and European modernist music by the early 1960s.[41] This significantly widens the probability of Gould's exposure to the sort of electronic music repertoire that could have influenced, however unconsciously, the conception and production of *North*. In "Prospects," Gould discusses new music in a modernist bent and gives a passing nod to a French contemporary: "The most accessible scores are those that superimpose conventional instrumental or vocal textures upon electronically produced sound sources—such works as Henri Pousseur's superb ballet score *Electre*."[42] Pousseur's score features a Webernian pointillism that runs parallel to Gould's admiration for Webern's skeletal brand of polyphony. However, the score also makes use of a much wider timbral palette with the use of electronics and tape manipulation.[43] This new work is distinctly unlike the modern notation-based works that Gould championed in the recording studio, but it reveals a shade of Gould known to his close acquaintances if not his audiences.[44]

Gould also mentions the Italians and Germans in a few contexts. By 1974, he was clearly very familiar with the work of Boulez, Stockhausen, and Berio. In a review of Henry-Louis de La Grange's then recently published biography of Gustav Mahler, Gould speculates as to why Mahler's music was of such interest to the European modernists:

> But the advocacy of such self-proclaimed radicals as Boulez, Berio, and Stockhausen could not have been predicted by even the most optimistic Mahler booster as recently as twenty years ago. . . . One might venture a guess that to Boulez, the attraction would be to Mahler's pointillistic handling of the orchestra; to Stockhausen, his attempt to synopsize and transcend all experience through art ("Waves, rainbows, polyphonic composition, must all be approached in the same way," Mahler wrote in

1900); while to Berio, Mahler's mania for montage, his delight in mingling the ridiculous with the sublime, would be key.⁴⁵

Gould must have known of Berio earlier, because he mentions Cathy Berberian in the documentary on Petula Clark, deriding the supposed "high-art" cachet she brought to her 1967 collaboration with the Beatles. Unsurprisingly, Gould did not mention Maderna as an adherent of Mahler, even though few advocated for Mahler's continued relevance as strongly as Maderna during that period.⁴⁶ He did rate Maderna very highly as a conductor, naming his "luminous" 1962 recording of Schoenberg's op. 24 serenade as one of his "desert island discs."⁴⁷

We can assume that the European avant-garde knew considerably less about Gould, and especially his compositional and radio studio activities. Composers who maintained an active interest in the musical canon would certainly have been familiar with his recordings of Bach and his unconventional and controversial performance style. Moreover, his recordings and advocacy for works of the New Viennese School were justly famous. The previously mentioned article in *Der Spiegel* and subsequent correspondence from the WDR shows that there was interest in Gould's radio works, but it is highly unlikely that a work like *North* would have been "influential" even if composers found affinities therein.

It would seem that we are no closer to a definitive answer as to the source of Gould's interest in radio composition, nor to answering the question of how much of the European electronic music scene he was familiar with and what he may have absorbed. Two options seem implicit in the accumulation of evidence presented thus far. In the first option, Gould was unaware of the European context, or at the very least never saw it as applicable to his own radio endeavors. In the second option, Gould was aware of the European context but sought to minimize it for his own ends, claiming ownership over the methods to present himself as a "genius." But there might be a third option. Perhaps he was aware of the European electronic music scene, and even recognized some of his own work therein, but a combination of pragmatism and humility kept him from referencing it explicitly. Pragmatically, if he tried to present *North* as a work of *musique concrète* or *Hörspiel*, he might have immediately alienated a large potential audience. As a thought experiment, imagine if the CBC prefaced *North* with "tonight we're presenting a new *Hörspiel* by Glenn Gould." This would have required a substantial explanation of the term and genre *Hörspiel*. The same would be true for *musique concréte*. Such explanations would also reek of pretension, likely putting off the CBC's relatively mainstream audience. In considering Gould's humility with respect to this third option, claiming a direct relationship with the European scene would invite direct comparisons of himself as a "composer" writ large. Despite outward appearances of confidence and ease, he may not have felt qualified to present himself on the same compositional plane as Stockhausen or Berio. We could speculate that claiming that kind of affinity might have colored him as arrogant.

Finally, a close reading of Gould's and Maderna's respective writings on and practical activity in the recording studio reveals some subtle but important differences. Specifically, the way Gould proposed a unique conception of the prospects of the recording booth. Brent Wetters has noted the philosophical approach of composers like Cage and Maderna; they continually looked for new ways of composing by reevaluating traditional methods. The traditional model was one where the composer wrote music on paper, followed by an infinitely variable performance. This form of composition, while common, grew anachronistic in various ways. The newfound philosophical approach to composition fostered in places like Darmstadt fed into the degradation of this traditional model.[48] The electronic music studio offered a tangible opportunity for composers to rethink their methods; it was simply not possible to realize compositions following the notational model. It may be worth noting that in some of the earliest electronic works, the old model persisted because composers lacked the technical means to operate the equipment. As a result, composers often told studio technicians the results they wanted, who in turn became "performers by instruction." As composers became proficient with the technology, the fact that the compositional production happened at a temporal, and geographic, remove from the concert meant that composers could exercise greater control over the final product. Gone were the days of imperfect, prescriptive notation and subjective, interpretive performance.

In 1952, after only a few years of activity in the electronic music studio, Maderna delivered a lecture at Darmstadt titled "Compositional Experiences in Electronic Music." He begins by stating that the studio "caused a real revolution in [his] relationship with the materials of music" and that he "had to completely reorganize [his] intellectual metabolism as a composer."[49] This change is chiefly one of linearity. In composing by traditional means, the composer works from start to finish. In the studio, composers contend with the time-space of composition as a field or canvas waiting for the sonic brushstrokes. Components of a work can be manipulated, reordered, and even discarded until the moment of a work's completion. Maderna suggests that listeners should also not expect musical material to develop traditionally over the course of a composition, but allow the "sound images" to work in ways that "can no longer be represented by a one-dimensional logic."[50]

Maderna says, "It is not necessary to ask whether it was the electronic experience which provoked such a renewal or whether this experience is itself the result of a development in this direction which was already present in recent music." But his evasive stance illustrates a key distinction between the way Gould and his European counterparts used the studio. Gould *never* seemed to see music as a fundamentally linear art form, and this is why, as a performer, he shunned composers like Chopin who embraced an ephemeral, sensual, and transitory concept of music. His preference instead favored more abstract composers like Bach, Schoenberg, and Webern. Gould's view of music might be productively likened to architecture; while one experiences an architectural design as a temporal activity—walking from room to room, circling a building—the object itself is fundamentally static. Music on record or tape is much the same. A listener always hears a given recording as a linear succession of sounds, but the recording and the content is fixed and invariable. Gould's 1981 rerecording of Bach's *Goldberg Variations* is a case in point. He conceives of the recording not as a series of pieces but as a set of abstract metrical interrelations. The tempi for each variation are strictly choreographed so that each is rationally related to the tempo of the "Aria." The precision of these metrical relationships could only be realized with the mechanical aid of the studio, and yet one senses that recording is not bound to that practice; the concept predated the technology. In contrast to the composers, Gould did not find freedom in his first attempts at radio work, but was instead frustrated by what he experienced as an artificial linearity to radio documentary. Therefore, we may surmise that Gould's unique perspective on music as architecture may have finally allowed him a pretext for arriving at "contrapuntal radio," even if composers had been arriving at the same realization via another route.

If it has not already become clear, this chapter offers no definitive answers to most of the questions it poses. We are no closer to a determination of what genre, category, or even word we can use to identify *North*—we have so far accumulated "radio documentary," "radio play," *Hörspiel, musique concréte,* "electroacoustic composition," and "contrapuntal radio." Instead, we offer an opportunity to forgo all such labels and to argue, forcefully I hope, against those who have been too quick to pigeonhole *North* as just one thing. A favorite, but perhaps simpler, example of what we are trying to do is the answer to a question like "What is Gustav Mahler's nationality?" Calling him Austrian is wrong, calling him Czech is wrong, calling him Jewish is wrong, and calling him German is also wrong. The only way that question is meaningful or interesting is if the answer to the question is a conversation. The set of contradictory and confusing circumstances and motivations surrounding Gould's work *is* the answer to the question of what genre or artistic tradition *North* falls into.

Notes

1. John Nicholson, quoted by Pierre Berton in *1967: The Last Good Year* (Toronto: Doubleday, 1997), 17.

2. See Brent Wetters's discussion of the north's role in Canadian identity in chapter 9 in the present volume.

3. Glenn Gould, "Radio as Music: Glenn Gould in Conversation with John Jessop," in *The Glenn Gould Reader*, ed. Tim Page (New York: Vintage Books, 1990), 374–388. Jessop later joined CBC Radio in the role of audio technician, where he worked with Gould on subsequent projects.

4. Gould, "Radio as Music," 374.

5. Gould, "Radio as Music," 374.

6. "Arnold Schoenberg, the Man Who Changed Music," aired on 8 August 1962 on the program *CBC Wednesday Night*. Among Gould's papers at Library and Archives Canada are several incomplete script drafts. A complete transcript of the program is available in Box 22, the John Roberts Collection, University of Calgary Special Collections.

7. Gould, "Radio as Music," 376.

8. Gould, "Radio as Music," 379.

9. Gould, "Radio as Music," 375.

10. Glenn Gould, "Idea of North sketches," 1967, Item 1979-20 4, 99 2a, Glenn Gould fonds, Library and Archives Canada, Ottawa.

11. It might be notable, as well, that Arnold Schoenberg followed a similarly tortured argument to claim that his twelve-tone method was both novel (and his discovery) and a historical inevitability.

12. Glenn Gould, "Radio as Music/Draft 3," 1971, Item 1979-20 8 12, Glenn Gould fonds, Library and Archives Canada, Ottawa. This draft is annotated and marked "final," indicating that there were some minor changes but no further drafts were required. This is consistent with other "final drafts" of articles and scripts in Gould's papers.

13. Lorne Tulk, interview with Anthony Cushing, 6 September 2010.
14. Gould, "Radio as Music," 375.
15. Tulk interview with Cushing, 6 September 2010.
16. Gould, "The Search for Petula Clark," in *The Glenn Gould Reader*, 304.
17. Jay Hodgson, *Understanding Records: A Field Guide to Recording Practice* (New York: Continuum, 2010).
18. Virgil Moorefield, "Chapter 1: From Mirror to Beacon," in *The Producer as Composer: Shaping the Sounds of Popular Music* (Cambridge, MA: MIT Press, 2010), 16–21.
19. M. Leaf, *The Making of* Pet Sounds, Capital Records, 1966, 109.
20. Francis Dhomont, "Schaeffer, Pierre," in *Grove Music Online, Oxford Music Online*, Oxford University Press, http://www.oxfordmusiconline.com/subscriber/article/grove/music/24734 (accessed 2 July 2015).
21. Gianmario Borio and Hermann Danuser, *Im Zenit der Moderne: die Internationalen Ferienkurse für Neue Musik Darmstadt, 1946–1966*, vol. 3 (Freiburg im Breisgau: Rombach, 1997), 551.
22. The Cologne studio was set up following a series of theoretical exercises and explorations of the idea of *elektronische Musik* by Werner Meyer-Eppler, Robert Beyer, and Herbert Eimert. The radio station in Cologne was called the Nordwestdeutcher Rundfunk at the time, but it split into NDR and WDR in 1956. See Thomas Holmes, *Electronic and Experimental Music: Technology, Music, and Culture*, 4th ed. (New York: Routledge, 2012), 61.
23. Holmes, *Electronic and Experimental Music*, 61–62. The distinction between the two approaches was far from amicable. German composer Konrad Boehmer would even recall it having been a "cold war." The German approach, summarized hastily, derived from serial music and used the technical precision inherent in the studio to more rigorously organize the musical structures and therefore used electronically generated tones as their primary musical material.
24. Brent Wetters, "Idea and Actualization: Bruno Maderna's Adaptation of Friedrich Hölderlin's *Hyperion*," *19th Century Music* 36, no. 2 (Fall 2012): 172–190.
25. Luciano Berio, "*Thema (Omaggio a Joyce)*—Author's Note," Centro di Studi Luciano Berio, http://www.lucianoberio.org/node/1503?948448529=1.
26. Brent Wetters, "Allegorical Erasmus: Bruno Maderna's *Ritratto di Erasmo*," *Cambridge Opera Journal* 24, no. 2 (2012): 159–176.
27. David Jaeger, interview with Brent Wetters and Anthony Cushing, 15 June 2015.
28. Bernhard Siegert, "Das Hörspiel als Vergangenheitsbewältigung," in *Diskursgeschichte der Medien nach 1945*, ed. Irmela Schneider and Peter M. Spangenberg (Wiesbaden: Westdeutscher Verlag, 2002), 87.
29. Hans Werner Henze attended Darmstadt in its early years but became disillusioned by what he saw as serial orthodoxy. See Hans Werner Henze, *Music and Politics: Collected Writings, 1953–81*, trans. Peter Labanyi (Ithaca, NY: Cornell University Press, 1982), 43. His break from the musical avant-garde culminated

in a very public dispute with the composer Helmut Lachenmann. See Helmut Lachenmann and Jeffrey Stadelman, "Open Letter to Hans Werner Henze," *Perspectives of New Music* 35, no. 2 (Summer 1997): 189–200.

30. Björn Heile, *The Music of Mauricio Kagel* (Aldershot, UK: Ashgate, 2006), 88.

31. Heile, *The Music of Mauricio Kagel*, 88.

32. "Eskimo am Flügel," *Der Spiegel*, 6 May 1968, 180, http://www.spiegel.de/spiegel/print/d-46039937.html (accessed 13 April 2015). "Er löste bald alle Engagements und zog sich in sein Haus am kanadischen Lake Simcoe zurück, wo er Jazzmusiken, ein Streichquartett Opus 1 sowie Hörspiele und Funk-Features niederschrieb und sich fast nur noch per Telephon mit der Außenwelt unterhielt." Translation included in the appendix to this volume.

33. Klaus Mehrländer to Glenn Gould, 14 May 1968, Item 1979-20 34 25 16, Glenn Gould fonds, Library and Archives Canada, Ottawa.

34. Lorne Tulk, email to Anthony Cushing, 5 September 2010.

35. Gould owned a copy of Porter's novel, which is among his papers in the Glenn Gould archives. Katherine Porter, *Ship of Fools*, 1962, Item B99, Glenn Gould fonds, Library and Archives Canada, Ottawa. The choice of Vera Cruz ("true cross") and Bremerhaven ("broken heaven") is interesting given the book's narrative teleology. The influence of *Ship of Fools* is, however, noted in Kevin Bazzana, *Wondrous Strange: The Life and Art of Glenn Gould* (Toronto: Oxford University Press, 2004), 297.

36. Smith Kirkpatrick, "Review: *Ship of Fools*," *Sewanee Review* 71, no. 1 (Winter 1963): 94.

37. M. M. Liberman, "The Short Story as Chapter in 'Ship of Fools,'" *Criticism* 10, no. 1 (1968): 68.

38. Similarly, Gould could have chosen a plane since, in reality, Schroeder, Lotz, and Vallee all arrived at their northern destinations by plane.

39. Liberman, "The Short Story as Chapter in 'Ship of Fools,'" 65.

40. Gould, "Prospects," 332.

41. It is unlikely that Gould would have had much opportunity to hear tape compositions by the Darmstadt cohort live in concert, because of differences in recording standards and the cost of transporting tape masters between Europe and America. But as Gould was well known to prefer the private listening experience, the fact that he could not see them in a concert setting would likely not have been a barrier. The Gould archives, however, show no record of his having owned any such recordings at the time of his death.

42. Gould, "The Prospects of Recording," in *The Glenn Gould Reader*, 345.

43. Henri Pousseur, *Electre*, Universal Edition, UE 13.500, vinyl record, 1961. The score calls for tape recorder and spoken text, instruments and electronics. Most notable about Pousseur was his association with the Darmstadt school of composers, including Luciano Berio, Bruno Maderna, and Luigi Nono.

44. David Jaeger, personal interview, 15 April 2015. The former CBC music producer and close friend asserts that Gould was aware and cognizant of developments in contemporary art music and likely knew more than he acknowledged.

45. Gould, "Data Bank on the Upward-Scuttling Mahler," in *The Glenn Gould Reader*, 81–82.

46. Maderna, in a conversation broadcast on WEFM in Chicago in 1970, said, "In [Mahler's] symphonies—and particularly the 7th—I think there is a man in all his complexity, with all his mistakes and his darker sides, also, but illuminated by an inner tension which is always the greatest, like a bow stretched towards the Whole and towards the Absolute. I now feel Mahler as though he is present, I feel that he is just the poet, the ideal as I imagine it." Raymond Fearn, *Bruno Maderna* (Chur, CH: Harwood Academic, 1990), 311.

47. Gould, "A Desert Island Discography," in *The Glenn Gould Reader*, 437.

48. Brent Wetters, "Darmstadt and the Philosophical Turn," PhD diss., Brown University, 2012.

49. Fearn, *Bruno Maderna*, 294–295.

50. Fearn, *Bruno Maderna*, 295.

8

De-Northing *North*

Thematic Continuity in Glenn Gould's *Solitude Trilogy*

PAUL SANDEN

In an interview with Eric Till and Vincent Tovell for CBC TV, Glenn Gould's longtime friend and CBC executive John Roberts reflected that "every time Glenn did a documentary, it not only dealt with the subject, it also dealt with Glenn. More of Glenn was revealed in each documentary that he did."[1] To anyone who has listened to even one of Gould's radio documentaries and has a passing familiarity with his written work, this is not likely to be a particularly earth-shattering revelation. One quickly gets the impression with Gould's documentaries that he is indeed investing something of himself in the messages being conveyed, due in large part to the ways in which those messages resonate with one another—not only across multiple documentaries but also between the documentaries and much of what we know about Gould himself through his interviews, television appearances, and written work. That is to say, even in the documentary format, Gould goes well beyond the role of passively documenting and relaying information; rather, he shapes these ideas into a unique expression of his own voice, much as he did in his writing and in his piano playing.

If we are to adopt Roberts's perspective, then (and I believe we should), the questions arise: What aspects of Glenn Gould were in fact revealed in these documentaries? What was *he* trying to tell us through the voices of his documentary subjects, by way of his extensive shaping of the materials? It is this line of questioning that informs the present chapter, along with an interest in beginning to track what we might call a network of themes that connects many of Gould's different documentaries, essays, and other projects together. In other words, Gould (like many of us) had a number of ideas that he was particularly drawn to, and I argue here that he was inclined to revisit these ideas throughout the body of his work. As such, an attempt to interpret the content of *The Idea of North* with this in mind is also an attempt to understand how Gould may have been trying to communicate on a broader level, not just in this particular documentary, but across multiple projects. In this chapter, I will focus primarily on connections between the three documentaries that make up the *Solitude Trilogy* (*The Idea of North*, *The Latecomers*, and *The Quiet in the Land*), but I will also refer to a few other Gould projects where appropriate.

In adopting the perspective that we can better understand Gould's overall creative output if we consider the network of ideas that runs between multiple projects (rather than just considering each project on its own merits), I am indebted to the work of both Edward Said and Markus Mantere, and their arguments are worth visiting here briefly before I proceed any further. In "Glenn Gould, the Virtuoso as Intellectual," Said observes in Gould's work (as a somewhat tangential point to his main argument) what he calls a "polyphonic web . . . that radiates outwards in several voices."[2] He is referring here to connections that he identifies between Gould's rather Adornian reading of J. S. Bach's music and elements of Gould's personality, written output, and performing choices. He is arguing, then, at least in passing, for an understanding of Gould's artistry that recognizes a continuity between all of these different elements, in this case connected by a particular interpretation of Bach's music (which constituted the centerpiece of Gould's pianistic output). What Said identifies as Gould's "intellectual virtuosity" is characterized by this kind of extension of his musical ideas beyond the confines of the concert stage (which Gould abandoned early in his career, in 1964) and into parallel manifestations in his writing, interviews, and even the views that governed his behavior.

In a similar rhetorical move, Mantere has argued for an understanding of Gould's entire output as a manifestation of his (Gould's) own concept of the north as an abstract aesthetic category. Mantere writes, "The North, in his aesthetic thought, served from the very beginning as a metaphor for things Gould regarded as indispensable to his music-making: isolation, loneliness, and the ideal of artistic creation as an activity taking place outside institutions, canons and conventions of the art-world."[3] From this perspective, Mantere encourages us to identify elements throughout Gould's body of work that resonate with what this particular metaphor of "the north" implies, especially the characteristics of isolation and non-conformism that have long been associated with Gould and his work.

I am more drawn to Said's metaphor of a "polyphonic web" than to Mantere's specific use of the northern metaphor as an intellectual tool for helping us to understand Gould's work, however. First, I believe trying to capture all of the complexities of Gould's work (however repetitive some of it may be) with a single thematic metaphor, even one as abstract as what Mantere proposes, oversimplifies the matter somewhat. For instance, I believe there are more recurring themes to be found in Gould's work than can convincingly be associated with this northern idea, such as Gould's intense championing of the benefits of audio technologies, to choose a prominent example. Second, I think that placing a geographic signifier on this idea runs the risk of essentializing it all; of associating Gould's idiosyncrasies, ideas, and ideals, too easily with his "Canadianness," which would do a disservice not only to Gould but also to the many people worldwide who find in his work something more universal and unrelated to place, even in an abstract sense.[4] While I do not believe this to be Mantere's intention, the risk remains nonetheless.

With Said's metaphor of the polyphonic web, on the other hand, we are presented with the concept of a potentially vaster (and perhaps undefinable) collection of ideas, concepts, arguments, themes, and so forth, all of which connect in various ways through many of Gould's projects. Finding meaning in one documentary or another, in one essay or another, can then be a task of comparative reading and hearing, a reciprocal dance between Gould's many artistic offerings, rewarding the attentive reader and listener in ways that would not be possible if only considering one project in isolation. Taken together, the themes that emerge tell us about Glenn Gould's overall artistry, his ethical concerns, his aspirations, his musical and humanitarian values—all of the things that laced their way through his often very convoluted prose in an effort to better explain why he did what he did. The task for the remainder of this chapter, then, is to identify a few of these themes, taking as our starting point *North* and branching out into the network from there.

The background and overall description of *North* have been well rehearsed by many who have come to this topic before me, and so anything more than a brief summary here would be both inappropriate and unnecessary. Nevertheless, a few basic details are worth reviewing, if only to provide the appropriate context for my own arguments. Prior to *North*, Gould had forayed into the medium of the radio documentary a few times, but never to the same extent. His first documentary, produced in 1962, was *Schoenberg: The Man Who Changed Music*. Gould claimed to be unsatisfied with the results of this project, however, particularly with what he considered to be the conventional way in which he approached its overall structure. He would produce a couple of other minor radio projects between then and 1967, when he claimed to have really found his voice with *North*. The most significant breakthrough, Gould felt, was his decision to adopt a few musically derived techniques—not only the concept of multiple voices speaking against one another in counterpoint but also thinking of formal sections of his documentaries in musical terms.[5] Over the remainder of his life and career, Gould would continue to engage in earnest with productions for CBC Radio (many of which were subsequently picked up by other radio stations in the United States and elsewhere). In addition to several less extensive projects, and two lengthy series of weekly broadcasts both called *The Art of Glenn Gould* (13 November 1966 to 30 April 1967; 18 May 1969 to 5 October 1969), Gould produced eight major documentaries (as listed in the introduction to this volume).

In an interview with *Rolling Stone* writer Jonathan Cott, Gould stated that all of his major documentaries—not just those of the *Solitude Trilogy*—had been about isolation in one way or another, insofar as those that were ostensibly about individual musicians were about musicians who chose to work outside the conventional norms of their times (something that Gould admired greatly).[6] I would like to probe this idea a bit more deeply. Isolation, after all, is a rather broad concept with which to work.

First, I would argue that if *North* is *about* anything, it is not really about solitude or isolation; rather, solitude emerges as a recurring and varied motif, as a kind of supporting idea, from the broader issue of reflecting on a journey to a foreign place. As Gould points out in liner notes that he wrote to accompany the CBC's initial commercial release of the documentary (and as has already been discussed in reference to Mantere's arguments), for him north was a bit of an abstract concept, one used in this documentary as "an excuse—an opportunity to examine the condition of solitude which is neither exclusive to the north nor the prerogative of those who go north but which does perhaps appear, with all its ramifications, a bit more clearly to those who have made, if only in their imagination, the journey north."[7] And the *journey* is an essential element of what emerges repeatedly throughout *North*: all of Gould's interviewees for this documentary were, like Gould himself, "outsiders" with respect to the Canadian arctic region. All of them *journeyed* north, and each of them, several times over, talks about people who *go* north. While the Indigenous population of Canada's northern territories are discussed at different times and perspectives, they never emerge as major players in whatever drama is unfolding. The reflections we are offered are *all* from the point of view of people for whom the north was previously unknown, for whom the north was a destination, and for whom the north remained, even after their time there, *another place*.

The *journey*, then, and the reflections on that journey, become the focus of the documentary. In this respect, any discussion of isolation or solitude is not a reflection on the isolation of the native northern communities from the rest of Canada, nor the social isolation resulting from the perception of racial differences between Indigenous and nonindigenous Canadians; these topics seem not to have interested Gould, or perhaps they never presented themselves clearly enough in the testimonies of his interviewees to be pursued. The reflections on solitude all emerge from the personal experiences of Gould's outsiders, and as such reflect only their own isolation (or lack thereof), either from the communities they had left behind, or in relation to other people who had also journeyed to live in the north.

The outsider perspective is reinforced by a theme of being irrevocably *changed* by an experience of the north, particularly in the way this topic is broached both in the documentary itself and in Gould's commentary on it. For instance, just over one minute into the opening prologue, Robert Phillips speaks about how he "can't conceive of anyone being in close touch with the north . . . being really untouched by the north for the rest of his life."[8] In his liner notes to the recording, Gould makes this statement even more strongly (from his "expert" position of having interviewed five such people): "Something really does happen to most people who go into the north—they become at least aware of the creative opportunity which the physical fact of the country represents and—quite often, I think—come to measure their own work and life against that rather staggering creative possibility: they become, in effect, philosophers."[9] The northern experience, then, is implicitly contrasted with that of anything further south, but only from the perspective of people who originated in those southern regions.

A similar reflection emerges in *The Latecomers*, in a brief passage during which the speakers reflect on the experience of visiting the northern areas of Labrador (Gould's interviewees for this documentary were from the Port-aux-Basques region of Newfoundland, in the southwest corner of that province). We hear a very clear parallel with Gould's previously quoted words about the effect of the arctic region on travelers there, when one of his speakers says, "People who go to Labrador, quite regularly get entrapped by the country. And this seems ridiculous, because Labrador, and other parts of the Canadian north, are extremely harsh. Very very difficult country to live in, really. But, something happens to people who go there."[10] What strikes me in particular about this passage, aside from its similarity to Robert Phillips's reflections in *North*, is the extent to which it seems somewhat out of place in *The Latecomers*. Gould places this brief reflection on the effect of Labrador (once again on people who *go* there) in the midst of a longer section full of comparisons between Newfoundland and other parts of the world—essentially, various reflections on the extent to which Newfoundland is cut off from mainstream society. Yet aside from this one brief passage, the question of northernness is entirely absent. Gould seems to have been unable to resist exploring this parallel between the two documentaries, however brief and out of place it may have been.

Another parallel emerges, considerably more prominently, between *North* and Gould's third *Solitude* documentary, *The Quiet in the Land*, which offers us, perhaps, the clearest perspective on just what kind of solitude Gould was most interested in exploring. About one third of the way through *North*, Gould establishes a bit of a duet between Robert Phillips and Marianne Schroeder, as they reflect on a similar theme:

> RP: When you're living in a big city in the south you can always retreat when you fail in your relations with society. You can just go away and nobody really knows the difference. You can't go away when you're in a little village and a thousand miles from nowhere and a couple of weeks from the next plane, high in the Arctic.
>
> MS: You can only live with the knowledge of many other people. You can't say I'll take the weekend off and I'll go to the next motel and I'm not going to be disturbed. This is impossible.

RP: There's all sorts of curious things that happen. In some ways you may have gone to the north to get away from society and you find yourself far closer to it than you've ever been in your life. You know your neighbors intimately. You know each walk they take down that little 500-yard road. Uh, you know what their problems are because they're bound to talk to you about them. If they don't, they'll go nuts, just as you'll go nuts when you don't talk.[11]

A particularly dichotomous relationship is explored here, between the forced social quality of life in an isolated community and the ability to be anonymous in a highly populated city.

In many ways, *The Quiet in the Land* constitutes a large-scale extrapolation of this particular dynamic of solitude. The final installment of Gould's trilogy, this documentary is perhaps the most consistent in its exploration of a single theme, and the richest of the three in terms of contrasting viewpoints (which Gould clearly delighted in setting against one another contrapuntally). At many points throughout the documentary, Gould's speakers reflect on the common Christian teaching to be *in* the world, but not *of* the world. In a Mennonite context, this idea inspires for some of Gould's interviewees a reflection on how they might maintain their Christian identity (i.e., their relative solitude), even while participating fully in the mainstream trends of modern North American life (i.e., being part of the larger community). One speaker also reflects on how Mennonites create a very strong sense of community among themselves, even though they are isolated in many ways from mainstream society. In highlighting these discussions as he does, Gould creates a very strong sense of continuity between the two documentaries.

The Quiet in the Land is also, I think, the documentary that presents the best actual *discussion* on the topic of solitude, primarily as a result of how deftly Gould handles the opposing viewpoints of his interviewees. On this point, I think it is worth briefly visiting Otto Friedrich's assessment of the trilogy as a whole. He writes that "the most important weakness in 'The Idea of North'—and by implication in the whole 'solitude trilogy' . . . is that Gould never really told us what he thought about solitude."[12] "In the way Gould presented 'The Idea of North,'" he continues a bit later, "he made it seem that these were his own ideas, his own creation. And yet he never signed the check. After Gould's brief opening statement, the listener never again hears him express any opinions whatever, never even hears him ask any questions. . . . He remained offstage, the marionette-master, the magician."[13] There is in this assessment an unwillingness to accept the role that Gould designed for himself in this project, perhaps even a suspicion of that role's validity and worth. At another point, Friedrich dismisses the documentaries of the *Solitude Trilogy* rather curtly as mere editing jobs, claiming that Gould had succumbed to the common editor's delusion that they were his own original creations and that "these are neither abstract sounds being organized according to Gould's aesthetic plan nor are they Gould's words expressing Gould's ideas."[14] Indeed, Gould was quite excited by the possibilities afforded the editor not only in the production of his radio documentaries but also in the process of making his commercial piano recordings, as he wrote about elsewhere.[15] The point, then, for Gould, was that this kind of editing—of shaping some kind of new creation from previously recorded material (be it recorded music, recorded speech, or both)—was in fact a kind of creative practice.

In his unfavorable assessment of (as he sees it) Gould's lack of direct authoritative voice within his radio documentaries—of Gould's desire to rearrange the ideas and arguments of others rather than to share directly his own ideas and arguments—Friedrich is betraying, perhaps, the same bias against extensive editing that Gould often encountered when discussing his piano recording practice. One of the clearest examples of this bias is demonstrated at times throughout Gould's seminal essay on technology in music, "The Prospects of Recording," in which Gould quotes several prominent musicians and recording industry executives that both support and counter the arguments that Gould puts forward himself in the essay. The quotations appear at strategic points in the margins of the pages to provide the appropriate foils for whatever Gould himself is arguing on a particular page. One common point of contention among these quotations is a skepticism about the relative inauthenticity represented by a recording of classical music compared to a live musical experience, especially if any "tampering" had been done in the recording process.

These examples also demonstrate a parallel, in print, to Gould's "contrapuntal" approach to the overall narrative of many segments of his radio documentaries, which ultimately constitutes a key factor in understanding what Gould may have been trying to say—and, perhaps most importantly, what he was happy *not* saying—with many of his projects. This key factor is, essentially, a willingness to present multiple perspectives to an argument or topic, without being overly concerned about clearly identifying and supporting a singular definitive argument from within such a counterpoint. To extend the (perhaps overused) fugal metaphor: the subject is likely to be clearly stated at some point, but Gould is just as happy reveling in multiple countersubjects, which may have the effect of obscuring somewhat the subject itself. In "The Prospects of Recording," one such example unfolds on the very first page.

Gould opens his essay by introducing his conviction that the conventional live concert will, in the relatively near future, essentially cease to exist, and its place of primacy will be taken up by the recording. This rather (deliberately) contentious point sets up the central topic of the essay—a thorough exploration of the relative merits of recordings over the traditional live musical experience—around which Gould is happy to present a multitude of perspectives. Alongside his opening remarks about the impending demise of the live concert, for instance, we see the following range of opinions by Gould's contemporaries in the margins, some seemingly sympathetic to Gould's point of view, and others rather strongly opposed:

> The concert is an antique form as it now stands. Most towns cannot afford the best concert artists and I don't see the advantage of seeing a second-rate artist over hearing a superb one [on a recording].—Lieberson

> With all the progress that we have made in the reproduction of sound, I have yet to hear on record what I hear in the concert hall or what I hear in my mind when I read a score.—Marek

> In a recording an artist can be encouraged to give a more immediately intense performance than he could under concert or theatre conditions.—Culshaw

> For me, the most important thing is the element of chance that is built into a live performance. The very great drawback of recorded sound is the fact that it is always the same. No matter how wonderful a recording is, I know that I couldn't live with it—even of my own music—with the same nuances forever.—Copland

> I can't believe that people really prefer to go to the concert hall under intellectually trying, socially trying, physically trying conditions, unable to repeat something they have missed, when they can sit home under the most comfortable and stimulating circumstances and hear it as they want to hear it. I can't imagine what would happen to literature today if one were obliged to congregate in an unpleasant hall and read novels projected on a screen.—Babbitt

> Many people have come to the concert hall expecting to hear glowing, glossy, beautiful performances they have heard on records only to be shocked by the natural acoustics. The Dvořák Cello Concerto on a recording can easily have the soloist as the absolute protagonist, with great presence, whereas he is often drowned out by the orchestra in the concert hall. But—I also think that many more will feel that the adventure, the accidental excitement of a live performance is much more stimulating and satisfying than just listening constantly to a record.—Chapin[16]

In the climactic segment of *The Quiet in the Land*, Gould exploits the ability of the recorded medium to present multiple simultaneous recorded tracks, to realize the same kind of argumentative counterpoint in a way not possible in print. Of this segment, Friedrich writes:

> It is a most impressive scene, about ten minutes long, and almost completely incomprehensible. At one point, for example, while one character says, "The Catholic Church takes a hard teaching like 'You shall not kill,'" a second character simultaneously says, "To me Christianity means unselfishness," and a third says, "When I am threatened as an individual, maybe then we had better re-examine how we have been doing things." Precisely because each of these speakers is saying something that requires concentration and reflection, the simultaneity of their words contradicts their purpose. . . . The voices of two or three Christians speaking seriously at cross-purposes is itself almost a *burla*, indeed almost diabolical in its reduction of spiritual statements into spiritual babble.[17]

I would argue for a different interpretation, albeit one that perhaps takes less offense at what *kind* of discussion (i.e., one about interpreting the nuances of Christianity) Gould is manipulating and focuses instead on exactly what he is accomplishing, and how, in more objective terms. Gould's usual technique in these kinds of scenes (we hear the same contrapuntal approach, for instance, at several points throughout *North* and *The Latecomers*, and also at one point in *Casals*) is to organize the multiple threads of dialogue by his many different speakers along thematic lines, so that the listener is offered multiple (sometimes conflicting) reflections on the same general idea. At the beginning of the scene in question in *The Quiet in the Land*, the primary talking point is the differences that arise between different generations of Mennonites in interpreting their role as Christians in a broader Western society. Gould is able to emphasize these differences of opinion by setting different sentiments against one another simultaneously, and also by linking successive statements through common key words and key ideas. In effect, he constructs a debate on the issue between his interviewees, out of material gleaned from conversations that he had with each of them independently. Moreover, unlike with some of his other more pointed arguments (throughout his various projects), here Gould in fact does not seem to betray any particular bias toward any one side of this debate. Rather, he seems quite satisfied to simply revel in the polyphonic consideration of the many perspectives he has presented.

Over the course of approximately three minutes, Gould presents us with the thoughts of six individuals (four women and two men), two of whom speak only once, and the others of whom have their fairly continuous thread of dialogue split up into multiple segments depending on how it might work alongside the words of one of the others. The entries are staggered, but on the whole Gould maintains a continuous two-voice texture—one on either side of the stereo spectrum—with each speaker being replaced by another with a linking thought or phrase in their general area of the stereo spectrum when their segment has been concluded (see fig. 8.1).[18]

By way of some concluding thoughts, I would like to recall an interview that Gould recorded with John McClure in 1968, in which he argued that unlike a concertizing musician who revisits the same piece of music night after night for years on end, as a recording artist he enjoyed working with a piece of music once (to get it recorded) and then never revisiting it again. In the same interview, he also argued that one should not even record a piece of music at all that many others had recorded unless one had something new to say about it.[19] However, one should not assume from this that Gould was necessarily *against* having something new to say with one's own interpretation, thus necessitating a rerecording of a

Figure 8.1. Transcription from *The Quiet in the Land*, 33:42–36:21. *Source*: Created by the author.

Left Region of Stereo Spectrum	Right Region of Stereo Spectrum
Woman 1 *33:53–34:17* We are not really dictated to from a hierarchy. And I think this makes for, probably, a great divergence of opinion among Mennonites. I think by and large, Mennonites believe that God has given man free will. And that everyone can interpret scripture, or life, in their own way. **Woman 3** *34:20–34:42* The scripture won't change. But, our understanding of it needs enlightenment, and more enlightenment. And, at no point dare we say, I think, that we've got absolutely all the light there is. We constantly have to humble ourselves and say that maybe our knowledge still needs more enlightenment. **Man 2** *34:42–35:34* And there are always people in the church who would like to impose some kind of hierarchical system. There's no conference. No outside body which can tell us [inaudible], this is what you have to believe. We get together every three years to decide on actions we want to take and we admonish each other but I think essentially we're quite free with our open congregation to decide what we are going to do and what we are going to believe. I still think, however, that some things that we carry with it are useful, and some elements of the puritan, I think that time is an important thing. If you go to a party, you don't have to stay up till 4 o'clock, you know, leave when it's good. And I wouldn't tell my children don't go to a dance, don't go to a party. But I think I would tell them look, the rest of them think it's the modern thing to stay up all night and have breakfast together in the morning. If you have things to do next morning by all means get to bed early as you can. **Woman 4** *35:34–36:08* I had a father who was a minister in the Mennonite Church, who was a very staunch evangelical. He was a very strict father; a very concerned father about his family, we weren't always very happy with some of the things we had to conform to. Today, we feel that, when we're with Father, some of the things that we believe, and that have changed in our way of life, we just don't talk about, because the last thing in the world we would do is hurt him.	**Man 1** *33:42–34:15* The ideas of many young people are different from those ideas which were before. New ideas among the young people... Free love... That's a very – how to call it – not desirable fact. It shouldn't be. It wasn't before. But it is now, and we fear these trends among the young people. **Woman 2** *34:16–34:46* I do think the pressure nowadays is making things more difficult for the children than it did when we were youngsters. Our whole world has changed so dramatically, no matter how you bring children up nowadays when they get out into the world, the standards, or lack of standards, are really very difficult for young people. I think we can teach them not to just be taken over by all the bluff, in plain words, that's around, but pick and choose and don't be apologetic for what you have and what you are. **Man 1** *34:47–35:10* We call ourselves a Christian country. And we can't understand how it can [inaudible] among young people. How it's possible but it is. And, we have to control our young people, and keep them, as much as possible, separated. **Woman 2** *35:10–35:54* I think too though, where there has been an overly narrow home situation, the rebellion is the greater there. And perhaps this is where we have to be careful. If there's joy in living, and joy in Christianity for the years that we have, young people are going to realize that there *is* something to this. That it isn't just some old lost custom. That we have something that we should treasure and keep and that we don't have to just go overboard for everything else that is coming our way. Of course, there is rebellion even where there has been a very loose homelife. You just see rebellion period, I think people rebel just for the sake of rebelling nowadays. And if they bang that drum and give you all the rock-sock in your ears well that's one way of doing it. And making money. **Man 1** *35:55–36:21* They are under the control of the church, and they are responsible. The church is making them responsible, and they have to answer this question: "Are you willing to follow these rules, which we have read to you, which you've heard?" And they answer, "Yes," and so they are responsible to the church, for, for their life.

particular work. Gould rather famously did so himself, of course, in one very dramatic instance: the final commercial recording released during his lifetime witnessed Gould providing an entirely new interpretation of J. S. Bach's *Goldberg Variations*—the same work with which he had launched his recording career in 1956.[20] In his written work, Gould practiced this process of reinterpretation again and again, by constantly coming back to a theme that he had already explored and offering up a fresh take. And if Gould's own subsequent explorations of an idea fell a bit short of an entirely *new* interpretation (to the extent that his two *Goldberg* recordings truly achieved this particular goal), he would often—especially through the multiple simultaneous perspectives afforded him through the mechanism of an interview—rely on other people to express such differing viewpoints, and in some of the more intriguing examples, offer them up side by side for his readers and listeners to contemplate together in all of their contrapuntal richness.

To return then, finally, to Friedrich's criticism of Gould's *Solitude Trilogy*: that Gould preferred to manipulate the ideas of others rather than share his own clear arguments on any of these topics. I think this criticism misses the mark, and rather misses the defining characteristic of Gould's argumentative style within these documentaries—a style, I argue here, that is reflective of a much broader approach Gould took to work that he did throughout his wide range of projects and throughout his career. Where Friedrich wanted Gould to provide a direct and authoritative meditation on the topic of solitude, Gould preferred to revisit such themes in various projects, repeatedly, from multiple perspectives. If he did favor a particular opinion, sometimes he was even content to obscure it within a complex texture of other contrasting opinions. The *interrogation* of a question from these multiple perspectives was, in and of itself, seemingly often the point. A broader picture than what Friedrich sought, perhaps, is painted by this approach, but only from within the complex counterpoint of this network can one begin to see Gould's own perspectives truly emerge.

Notes

1. John P. L. Roberts, Vincent Tovell, and Eric Till, Interview part 1 (video recording), 8 August 1984, Canadian Broadcasting Corporation Fonds, Item 393405, Library and Archives Canada, Ottawa.
2. Edward W. Said, "Glenn Gould, the Virtuoso as Intellectual," *Raritan* 20, no. 1 (Summer 2000): 9.
3. Markus Mantere, "Northern Ways to Think About Music: Glenn Gould's *Idea of North* as an Aesthetic Category," *Intersections* 25, no. 1–2 (2005): 86. See also Mantere's chapter in the present volume.
4. On the flip side of this coin, one can imagine plenty of "northerners" who find nothing whatsoever in Gould's work with which they can relate. What

signified "north" to him may be entirely foreign to their understanding of that same concept.

    5. Glenn Gould, "Radio as Music: Glenn Gould in Conversation with John Jessop," in *The Glenn Gould Reader*, ed. Tim Page (New York: Vintage Books, 1990), 375–380.

    6. Jonathan Cott, *Conversations with Glenn Gould* (Chicago: University of Chicago Press, 1997), 99.

    7. Gould, "'The Idea of North': An Introduction," in *The Glenn Gould Reader*, 393–394.

    8. Gould, *North*, 1:22–1:37.

    9. Gould, "'The Idea of North': An Introduction," 392.

    10. Gould, *North*, 26:15–26:33.

    11. Gould, *North*, 19:35–20:30.

    12. Otto Friedrich, *Glenn Gould: A Life and Variations* (New York: Vintage Books, 1989), 204.

    13. Friedrich, *Glenn Gould*, 206.

    14. Friedrich, *Glenn Gould*, 184.

    15. See, for instance, Glenn Gould, "Forgery and Imitation in the Creative Process," in *The Art of Glenn Gould: Reflections of a Musical Genius*, ed. John P. L. Roberts (Toronto: Malcolm Lester Books, 1999), 219.

    16. Glenn Gould, "The Prospects of Recording," *High Fidelity Magazine* (April 1966): 47. This essay has been reproduced more recently (see Gould, "The Prospects of Recording," in *The Glenn Gould Reader*, 331–353) but without the marginal quotations that appear in the original *High Fidelity* printing. Unfortunately, without these quotations this very important element of Gould's argumentative strategy, at least as demonstrated in this essay and in several of his documentaries, is lost. The individuals quoted in this excerpt were: Goddard Lieberson, president of Columbia Records; George R. Marek, vice president and general manager of RCA Victor Record Division; John Culshaw, manager of classical recordings for Decca/London; American composer Aaron Copland; American composer Milton Babbitt; and Schuyler G. Chapin, vice president in charge of programming at Lincoln Center for the Performing Arts.

    17. Friedrich, *Glenn Gould*, 198.

    18. Glenn Gould, *The Quiet in the Land*, CD3 in *Glenn Gould's Solitude Trilogy*, PSCD 2003-3, CBC Records, 1992. I offer a somewhat simplified representation of the opening and closing seconds of this segment in my transcription. At the beginning there are two other voices (not transcribed here) that can be heard for the first portion of the opening statement by Man 1; at the end I have left out a few more seconds of dialogue from the end of the statement by Woman 4, and the beginnings of a new statement by another speaker. I have included these slight edits to better focus on the thematic content of the material that is transcribed in figure 8.1.

19. Glenn Gould and John McClure, *Glenn Gould: Concert Dropout, in Conversation with John McClure*, Columbia Masterworks BS 15, 1968, LP. Printed in *Glenn Gould* 7, no. 2 (Fall 2001): 46–60.

20. Glenn Gould, *Bach: The Goldberg Variations*, Columbia Masterworks ML 5060, 1956, LP; Glenn Gould, *Goldberg Variations: BWV 988*, CBS Masterworks IM 37779, 1982, LP.

9

Monstrous North

BRENT WETTERS

As the eighteenth century drew to a close, a fictional Dr. Victor Frankenstein found himself close to death in the cabin of a ship originally bound for the glories of northern discovery. Frankenstein was not on the ship because of an exploratory impulse, but because he was in pursuit of the monster he created from a cadaver in the name of scientific discovery; the monster, spurned by society for a lack of humanity, sought to destroy Frankenstein, whom it held responsible for its misery. It did so not by murdering its master, but by maiming and destroying all that its master loved—a destruction for which Frankenstein in turn felt responsible. Frankenstein, thus obligated to rid the world of his evil creation, pursued it to the extreme northern regions to which it fled. He failed before he could achieve his goal, finally dying of exhaustion aboard the northbound ship.

The ship's captain found the monster examining Frankenstein's corpse in that cabin. Its master now gone, it lost its only link with humanity and resolved to leave the boat on one final quest. It would search out the North Pole—"the most northern extremity of the globe"—where it resolved to burn itself on a funeral pyre.[1] The choice of location was not accidental. The north, covered in darkness for almost half of the year, bears associations with all that is antithetical to mankind—cold, isolation, death—and there could be no spot more fitting for the final conflagration of this monster.

Shelley's narrative assumes that such a journey to the pole will present little difficulty to the monster. The ship's captain, on the other hand, having been trapped in ice floes for the preceding several weeks, just resolved to return to England after failing in the attempt to reach his goal. For humans, traveling north is *hard*, and at the time it was insurmountable. It would be another hundred years before a nonfictional human reached the pole, and the polar seas are littered with shipwrecks like the one described in Shelley's *Frankenstein*.[2] But the monster seems to traverse the north without incident. It is unhindered by cold and needs no special preparation: a monster is at home in the north.

Shelley's characterization, however, is not the only way we are accustomed to thinking about the northern portions of the globe. Positive associations with the north are equally pervasive. For anyone living above of the equator, the word "north" most often connotes simplicity and isolation. In the eastern United States, the north promises pine forests, brisk nights, lobster boils, and a generally slower pace of life. A trip from southern New England up Interstate 95 to Maine, for example, presents the traveler with a series of anachronisms. Cellular communication becomes more and more unreliable, restaurants and shops often appear as if they haven't changed in fifty years, and many of the ubiquitous commercial entities of the south have yet to penetrate large swaths of the north; it can be refreshingly difficult to find a McDonald's.

However, as has been stated repeatedly in this volume, north is relative and is contingent on the place of origin. For a resident of Alabama, it might mean only crossing the Mason-Dixon Line and may be associated with urban cosmopolitanism rather than isolation. But even in this case, popular imagination still holds a land beyond those urban centers where society becomes scarce again. For the confirmed Torontonian Glenn Gould, the north was only as far as Churchill, Manitoba, the northern end of the train line originating in Winnipeg. But for researchers studying northern habitats, Churchill represents the south; to achieve a feeling of north, such researchers need to travel to Baffin Island or the northern sections of Nunavut, places still only sparsely inhabited by small native communities.[3] Those Aboriginal inhabitants of northern communities who do not travel north by choice often find southern depictions and obsessions with "northernness" silly (see Jeffrey van den Scott's contribution in the present volume, for example).

Whether fair or not, Europe and America's domination in all things cultural ensures that "south" does not have similar resonances, in part because most of the literature and history that created this sense of north was written in the northern hemisphere. The physical terrain also plays a role. Though the southern hemisphere has its own extreme in the form of Antarctica, there is no southern equivalent to the large arctic and subarctic inhabited lands of Canada, Siberia, and Scandinavia. In the south, those spaces are almost all covered in water, and as a result, one does not have the same associations with "going south" that people of the north do with "going north." To call this "nordocentric" is to miss the point. I am not so much interested in the north itself as I am in the various ways that the concept of north is constructed and used in the Western context. And as such, Glenn Gould's *Idea of North*, which is overtly less concerned with the north as an actual space than as a cultural construct, is the ideal starting point.

In his work, Gould investigates what it was about the north that provides such endless fascination. Is it the isolation? Gould leads us to believe so, if only because it became the first part of his so-called *Solitude Trilogy*. Gould may have shifted the focus toward isolation after the completion of subsequent radio programs.[4] The north's capacity for isolation notably forms only a small topic in the overall scheme of the documentary. However, if isolation is the primary topic, as Lorne Tulk asserts, then Gould's exploration is mostly figurative.[5] His participants cover a variety of issues from the environmental to the sociological to the philosophical, but one of the most compelling and persistent claims is that the north represents a kind of utopian potential space. Because the north is largely uninhabited but open to future development, observers can imagine development happening according to idealized schemes. Paradoxically, the utopian character of such spaces is founded on their potential, and to consider such development simultaneously conjures the opposite: dystopia.

Gould is hardly alone in regarding the north—or any space where humanity feels itself not-quite-in-control—as a kind of utopia, or at least a place where change is possible. His uniqueness lies in his ability to hold the positive and negative aspects of the north in a kind of perpetual balance. The listener is never quite sure whether Gould's north is a utopia or dystopia. I argue that a shadow of the monstrous haunts Gould's north, and that with a close listening, we may find that the shadows in *North* may speak louder than any of its participants.

∽

I approach this study from an impression that the final moments of Gould's *North* have a troubling character that belies the triumphant ending.[6] It ends on what seems an optimistic note; paired with the finale to Sibelius's Fifth Symphony, the narrator Wally Maclean compares the north to the idea of a "moral equivalent of war," an idea he borrows from William James. James argued that meaningful and universal peace could only be attained by uniting humanity against a common enemy. Maclean (and by extension, Gould) believes that the north represents precisely this "moral equivalent of war," and we would do well to retrace the steps by which he reaches this conclusion.

In the documentary's final nine minutes, the contrapuntal layering of voices ends, the train basso continuo suddenly fades out to introduce the finale of Sibelius's Fifth Symphony.[7] The only voice heard in the remainder is Maclean's. He casts his soliloquy as a conversation between himself and a fellow traveler on his first trip to the north—a Harvard-educated scientist introduced in scene 1, studying the northern lights. We previously heard the motivations for this young man's trip, but now Maclean is asked to "answer in kind": Why is he on a trip north and what attracts him to these remote regions? He begins by struggling—what can he, someone for whom the north is anything but "new," say to someone who embarks on this monumental journey for the first time? He recognizes that the person who goes north will have unique motivations and hopes for such a journey, and that he should not be overly forceful in his opinions. Moreover, he is altogether skeptical of any such hopes—he is a disillusioned northerner. He is not, however, prepared to give up entirely on his own "idea of north," and as such tries to temper his response.

In a backhanded critique of the whole enterprise, Maclean denies that there is any challenge to going north. His interlocutor, who found the first half of his thirty-six-hour train trip rather challenging, resists; he had gone so far as to compare the trip to Sisyphus pushing his rock up a mountain.[8] In response, Maclean cannot help but equivocate. At Gould's bidding, or through Gould's editing, he proceeds by way of ever-deepening parenthetical statements, mimicking Gould's own style of communication. He asks whether the question has anything to do with the actual north, "Most of us have a built-in sense of direction . . . this need have nothing to do with north."[9] He frames the entire question as an existential crisis for "inner purpose." The train ride north, however, is a manifestation of this sense of purpose, a journey from the "known, securely to the unknown."[10] He points to an earlier time—"certainly in human memory"—when this journey presented a "challenge."[11] He likely refers to the period of polar exploration when reaching the pole at all was largely impossible. The only viable routes to the north were by sea, and most of those ended in failure, many disastrously. Before Maclean mentions any specifics, he halts again and tries to define exactly what he means when he says that the north is a "challenge." He now introduces James and the "moral equivalent of war" to support his claim.

James proposed that some other unifying project, what he called a "war against war," was needed to take the place of military conflicts with other nations.[12] James begins by extolling the virtues of war in its capacity to unite communities, and its importance in constructing history and our current view of ourselves. Who, he asks, would choose to expunge "those ancestors, those efforts, those memories and legends"?[13] Who, in short, would change history to eliminate war from our collective past? He posits that only a very few "eccentrics" might willingly accept such a reversal.[14] On the other hand, when he poses the opposite question of who would willingly accept the bloodshed and destruction as the means to acquire that same cultural capital (Who would wage war for the sole purpose of creating good stories?), he assumes that very few would answer *that* question in the affirmative.[15] With the passage of time, humans enjoy the spectacle of war even if we reject its reality. War, James continues, organizes and disciplines society, creating hierarchies and structure without which societies would dissolve.[16] Only when it replaces war with something that provides the same functions could humanity hope to move into a peaceful phase. To banish it altogether would simply not do. In this sense, James was a pragmatist who opposed the more altruistic pacifists with whom he nevertheless sympathized.

But Maclean's soliloquy and invocation of James is based on a misreading of the latter's essay; or more charitably, Maclean offers his reading of James without the benefit of having the text in front of him. Instead, Maclean speaks informally based on his recollections of having read the text some years prior. He understandably does not always remember the exact formulations of James's arguments. Nevertheless, there are differences between Maclean's gloss and James's text that prove instructive. Maclean goes on to argue that humanity could find a "moral equivalent of war" in the form of Mother Nature, and that there was "a cleanness" to pitting oneself against nature, but he does so problematically as if James had not suggested precisely this solution. Maclean broaches this entire topic by attributing to James not a call *for* a "moral equivalent of war," but a claim that "there *is no* moral equivalent of war,"[17] despite the fact that James proposes "*Nature*" (capitalized and in italics in his original) as the enemy with which our "moral" armies must do battle.[18] Rather than conscription to an army, James says, young people would be called to the "immemorial human warfare against nature," naming among other tasks the creation of "coal and iron mines," "skyscrapers," and "road-building and tunnel-making."[19]

Maclean states that this moral equivalent of war must be something against which humans can fight, stating, "We can all be fellow men, when we know what we're against."[20] Even though Maclean also settles on Mother Nature as that moral equivalent of war, he immediately questions whether nature can function in the way it did previously. Whereas James assured his reader that nature was a legitimate combatant for humanity, Maclean's suggestion elicits a pregnant pause and confusion from his imagined companion. This doubt for Maclean and the lack of such doubt in James stems from the vast difference in nature's standing relative to humanity that appeared in the first half of the twentieth century. By 1960, at the height of the Cold War, humanity showed itself capable of complete planetary destruction, and certainly no one would have then counted "coal mines" among humanity's great works. Other humans, as it happens, were the greatest perceived threat to mankind when Gould produced his documentary. Having now passed the fiftieth anniversary of *North*, nuclear anxiety has lessened somewhat in favor of fears of societal and environmental collapse. While temptation might draw one to see the challenge of climate change as a uniting force among countries, as yet there is little cause for optimism.[21] These challenges, however, are still primarily man-made.

Maclean equivocates once more but now inserts his own voice, confirming that humanity, not nature, is the greater threat: "My patience—my patience, perhaps with myself—runs out. And I say, 'ah yes, but that's, as I say, the North that was.' No longer do humans combine to defy, or to measure, or to read, or to understand, or to live with this thing we call Mother Nature. Our number one enemy instead of being Mother Nature, is of course: Human Nature."[22] Gould choreographs this moment to coincide with a modulation to the minor key in the musical accompaniment and introduces a moment of conflict, resolved in the remaining two minutes. There are thus two simultaneous dissonances, one musical and one dramatic. Sibelius concludes his symphony with a convincing cadence in E-flat major, but the rhetorical dissonance is left unresolved.

Gould forces a kind of dramatic resolution to coincide with the conclusion of the symphony, but it seems to contradict what preceded it. *North* ends with a reassertion that "the moral equivalent of war" is "going north": "This William James . . . I suppose he meant really, not war, the moral equivalent for us is going north."[23] This conclusion occurs, however, even though what precedes this moment is an equally forceful assertion that we are not, in fact, up against Mother Nature at all, but human nature. And if human nature, then the conclusion is singularly unsatisfying—how can we possibly engage in a war against human nature, and what, ultimately, does that have to do with the north? The blame or credit for this contradiction lies entirely with Gould. The original interview transcripts indicate that Maclean made that last statement at the outset of his discussion of James.[24] Maclean's argument progressed naturally in the interview transcripts; he began by saying that the north was the moral equivalent of war, then explained that the moral equivalent was nature, and finally concluded that human nature was the ultimate challenge because it failed to respect Mother Nature. Gould's intervention in the editing booth changed the order of his statements and introduced confusion.

The conclusion that human nature is the final impediment to lasting peace is yet another instance where Maclean unwittingly passes off something stated definitively by James as his own. James writes, "That mankind was nursed in pain and fear, and that the transition to a 'pleasure-economy' may be fatal to a being wielding no powers of defense against its disintegrative influences. If we speak of the *fear of emancipation from the fear-regime* [emphasis in original], we put the whole situation into a single phrase; fear regarding ourselves now taking the place of the ancient fear of the enemy."[25] Having progressed technologically to the point where nature no longer offers this sense of challenge, humanity now contends with its own lack of boundary as its new foundational threat. How is it, then, that Gould can suggest that the north, as the "moral equivalent of war," is simultaneously a manifestation of nature's power over humanity and also a symbol of our subjugation of that nature?

Gould through Maclean, at this moment, struggled to give a conclusive answer to the question that formed the pretext for the documentary: Why are we fascinated by the north? Why, as Gould states in the introduction, do we find the north such a compelling place to "dream about" and "tell tall tales about"?[26] But these questions are not ones that lend themselves to definitive answers. The reasons why people are fascinated by the north are elusive and diverse. The documentary answers the question by offering many—at times contradictory—answers, but aesthetic concerns led Gould to desire a conclusive ending. He could have ended with cacophony to emphasize the divergence of responses to the north, as Mark Laurie did in his *Pilgrimage to Solitude* (see Laurie's chapter in this volume), but a dramatic conclusion required a unified resolution. Gould chose James's "moral equivalent of war" in spite of the obvious contradictions in Maclean's presentation, because in it he seemed to find something suitably climactic. It did not answer the questions posed at the outset. However, in spite of Gould's best efforts, the conclusion ran in two directions at the same time. The contradictions in the final two sentences introduces a doubt that makes the triumph of Sibelius's symphony ring hollow, showing the north both as a force for good and a force that reveals a fundamental darkness in humanity—perhaps a kind of darkness that lurks inside humanity's greatest triumphs.

This troubling moment, however, works despite and *because of* its obvious defects. The unresolved tension allows something else to emerge from that moment of finality—the conclusion is also a site of rupture, and thus Gould emphasizes the documentary's inconclusiveness. It is unable to decide whether the north is a site of monstrosity or sublime goodness, just as it is unable to decide what humanity's role should be vis-à-vis the north. What conclusion does Gould suggest in his reversal of Maclean's conclusion about human nature and Mother Nature? As a preliminary corrective, I emphasize that Gould, in rearranging Maclean's words, says that "going north," not the north itself, is the moral equivalent of war.

Neither Gould nor Maclean hid that they struggled to conclude the documentary. At one point, Maclean even begins, "I'm just guessing, now, this is hard to get at . . ."[27] Gould, in fact, had painstakingly removed "ums," "ahs," and other markers of indecision from the recordings of his other participants, but he leaves them in place for Maclean's soliloquy. The invocation of James seems arbitrary, although the finale unquestionably aims high. The triumphant ending projects the appearance of conventionality to an otherwise unconventional work; the grandiosity is at odds with the circuitous and nuanced route by which it travels. One possible explanation is the patriotic intent of the commission. It is unclear whether Gould himself had any strong nationalist motivations for composing the work. However, it fit neatly with broad themes that emerged from the Canadian centennial celebrations of 1967. The CBC commissioned Gould, himself seen as something of a national treasure, for a work providing his unique image of Canada. As a result, anything but a rousing conclusion would have been subversive to those nationalist agendas.

Canada's status as a "northern country" was, to varying degrees, useful in asserting a national identity that it seemed to lack on other fronts. A 1967 *Globe and Mail* article about a BBC program on Canadian identity opened with "Canada still lacks national identity but deserves respect for avoiding the ways of chauvinism."[28] Canada never had a strong nationalist sentiment—at least if by nationalist we understand "chauvinist" and exceptionalist rhetoric of the United States. In practical terms, "north" as a marker of Canadian identity often has little to do with the nostalgic and romantic portrayals found in the documentary. Instead, "north" functions to delineate the political and cultural boundary between Canada and its southern neighbor. To assert that Canada is "northern" is to say that it is not the United States, a claim that was especially important during the 1960s. At the time, the United States was embroiled in a deeply unpopular war in Vietnam, and for young citizens of the United States "going north" meant dodging the draft and engaging in peaceful abstention. In this sense, "north" was often little more than a pragmatic category. The documentary, and other nationalist endeavors, thus romanticizes and adds emotional layers to that pragmatism.

One such emotion is fear. When Maclean invokes the challenge of "human nature" the resulting emotion is an undeniable anxiety. The exact nature of that anxiety is less clear, but I identify at least three fears that emerge in the course of the documentary. First, American influence is seen as a corrupting political and cultural influence. Cold War nuclear scares featured prominently in 1960s Canada. Given that the north was a no-man's land between the West and the Soviet Union, Americans feared an airstrike launched over the pole and sought to deploy missiles to the northern regions, thinking that the Canadian government would be unable to contest the USA's political clout. Canadians who opposed nuclear proliferation viewed this move skeptically. The issue amounted to a crisis in the early 1960s when the conservative government rejected the installation of American BOMARC missiles in North Bay, Ontario;[29] the next liberal government reversed the decision when they took power in 1963.[30] A second fear that still resonates is the ever-increasing threat from industrialization and development of the pristine northern environment. Finally, *North* expresses a fear that Canada will become indistinguishable from the United States through the combination of these anxieties.

While anxiety resulting from Maclean's statement that "the enemy is of course human nature" remains ambiguous in the radio documentary, a version made for television in 1970 pairs the speech with images that solidify its meaning. Gould accompanied the slightly altered documentary with images and a rough narrative; he follows a young man on his first trip north aboard the train to Churchill and his encounter with an older traveler whom we are led to assume is Maclean. When Maclean condemns human nature, the images invoke the industrialized and commercialized south: huge factories billow smoke and a sign flashes "Coca-Cola." In this brief moment, Gould encapsulated visually all that Canada feared would happen if it failed to assert itself internationally, on its own terms.[31]

The documentary only alludes to the north as the antithesis of the United States. Instead, Gould presents the vast empty north as distinctively Canadian because it is the feature that accounts for why Canada is "a kind of civilization that does not conform to the rest of North America"[32]—but the standard to which Canada refuses to conform is the United States. To refer to Canada as a "northern" country is somewhat problematic, given that most of its population straddles the southern border, and Toronto lies south of large American cities like Seattle and Minneapolis. The actual north offers a convenient pretext for Canadians to deny that their national identity is rooted in opposition to their southern neighbor, because it suggests a potential for Canada to *become* a northern country.[33] The north is a space that points to the future, and a hope (and fear) that it will not always be as it is now. The developed spaces of the south are in a state of perpetual decay, preservation, and revival, but we do not customarily think of those spaces as "developing" in significant ways. In Canada, the north represents a frontier in the same way the "west" did for nineteenth-century America.

Phillips articulates this most succinctly: "There is a wonderful cliché, which I hope I may be forgiven for mentioning once more, that a nation is great only as long as it has a frontier. Now we've got that frontier, other people are nostalgically having to dip back a hundred years to find their frontier and vicariously become part of it."[34] A frontier is a space residing within national boundaries, but which is also at its edge and thus escapes inclusion. As such it defines a limit to a nation-state and represents its future. In Phillips's terms, we can think of the "greatness" thus defined by its prospects for future development and expansion. In a country whose borders are already filled, such expansion only comes at the expense and conquest of other nations. In the north, Canada can assert its future potential without problematic colonial aggression; it does so, of course, only by denying or minimizing the presence of Indigenous populations, and by assuming an implicit right to those northernmost portions of the Arctic around the pole.[35]

But what does it mean to call Canada's northern edge a frontier, and what does it mean for those native communities? Phillips mentions, though not forcefully, that Canada has often behaved less than admirably to its Indigenous populations residing in that "potential space."[36] In contrast to Indigenous populations in the American west of the nineteenth century, the Inuit do not appear in popular discourse as "aggressive savages," and they remain marginal to Canadian society. They do provide a pretext, symbolically, for asserting Canadian uniqueness, but only as a romanticized vision of arctic life. The popular depiction of life in the high arctic customarily ignores the realities of such life. As Phillips points out, "The Igloo is not a part of Canadian life, because the life expectancy of twenty-seven years isn't part of Canadian life."[37] Any frontier operates both as a zone of exclusion and inclusion, literally and figuratively marginalizing its inhabitants.

Jim Lotz, described by Gould in the introduction as a "geographer and anthropologist," articulates insightfully the north's role in Canadian identity. He is also the most compassionate of the five toward the Inuit.[38] Gould lays out Lotz's testimony in a more disjunct fashion than that of Maclean, whom Gould allows the space to present and develop arguments. Gould presents Lotz, by contrast, in a series of vignettes. Though they lack the grandiosity of Maclean's final soliloquy, Lotz's statements form a compelling counternarrative to the idea of frontier and the moral equivalent of war. One comment in particular, though insightful in the context of the documentary, is even more pertinent to the current discussion when augmented by Lotz's writing in his book *Northern Realities*: "In the North we are witnessing the final playing out of those two great dreams of man: Eldorado and Utopia."[39] In the documentary, he appears to consider Eldorado and Utopia as equivalent, whereas his book proposes the two concepts as opposing paradigms by which a nation relates to its frontier; both of them are at play in the Canadian north.

For Lotz, the utopian paradigm is characterized by the American west and "manifest destiny." People left the comforts of the known for an uncertain frontier in search of a "better life." The unknown on the other side of the frontier was thus an ideal and idealized potential—a place where things might be better, a place where Utopia could either be found or created. The Eldorado paradigm, by contrast, was associated primarily with Spanish conquistadors in South America, where the interior was regarded as a land of wealth and resource. They sought those resources not as a utopian place to live, but a site from which to plunder.[40] The "treasures" claimed during those excursions to the "savage" frontier (the "interior" in the South American context) were to be brought back to the "civilized" exterior. Lotz argues that both impulses have been proposed and enacted in the Canadian north; there have been oil and gold rushes, but those, like Phillips, who see the north as frontier believe Canadians will eventually settle and develop those regions.

In this sense, the frontier is itself just another manifestation of James's "moral equivalent of war," which posits that humans under some form of uncontrollable oppression will unite against that oppression. If humans are justified in opposing that force—as in fighting for survival—then we do not speak of right and wrong actions.[41] In the north, nature presents such an ever-present sovereign force, and daily activity is arranged to accommodate such survival.[42] Cutting down a tree is permissible for someone who needs shelter from the elements. It is not merely a question of preparing for, say, a snap of bitter cold, or helping the fellow residents of the north when they find themselves in difficulty.

In what may be the clearest example of a constructed dialogue in the documentary, Schroeder and Phillips describe the ways that the north enforces a kind ethics among the communities of the north. Schroeder believes that cultivating these communal relationships happens "naturally"; we treat our fellow humans well because there is something special about the north. She describes an almost idyllic situation where her neighbors have profound, intimate investment in each other's lives: "I didn't have to go to somebody in Coral [Harbour] and say I'm lonesome or I'm depressed. I just had to go and visit them . . . and right away there was a sense of sharing this life. One could realize the value of another human being."[43] Phillips, playing the role of skeptic, responds: "And probably what you'll never know, and what nobody else will ever know, is whether you're kidding yourself or not. Have you really made your peace with these other people or have you made a peace because the only alternative to the peace is a kind of crack-up."[44] This moment is followed by an extended respite from the speech, leaving the listener to contemplate the train sounds. Rhetorically, this moment appears to be a natural lull in the "conversation"; the listener is placed in the role of a fellow passenger overhearing the conversation, who then turns to look out the window at the passing scenery. The pause makes space for Lotz to enter with an interior reflection on the preceding conversation. His response seems to synthesize the divergent opinions of Phillips and Schroeder, expressing both the ways that the north imposes itself on its inhabitants ("it's so big . . . it cares so little") but also the ways that inhabitants recognize their own strength in the mere fact of their survival in such an environment ("My God, I am here . . . I live, I breathe, I laugh, I walk, I have companions").[45]

All these responses suggest that the physical environment is a determining factor in ethical behavior, and that there is arbitrariness to other ethical decrees not derived from nature. It is often suggested of the biblical book of Leviticus, for example, that the prohibitions against eating pork arose entirely from practical health concerns of the time. A place where nature presents legitimate danger to its inhabitants prioritizes those ethical guidelines that relate to basic physical needs. Anthropologists know this phenomenon as "lifeboat ethics."[46] Phillips writes in a telling passage from the introduction of his book, *Canada's North*: "When men live in the North, their values change. They build new civilizations on a mud flat in the Klondike. They live a lifetime alone and die when they emerge. They become citizens of a different country, a country where nature is overwhelmingly stronger than man."[47] These northern ethics are universal (and therefore also utopian), because they are precultural, implicitly suggesting that a member of any culture transported to the north would behave the same.

Lifeboat ethics, however, are not the same as universal ethics. In fact, though lifeboat ethics may presume a universal set of rules to be adhered to under ideal circumstances, it also proposes that all ethics are, in the end, situational. Even cannibalism is sanctioned on a shipwreck as a matter of last resort. The search for an ethical substance in the north may lead therefore not to utopia, but to dystopia. Even the search for pristine nature—the creation and preservation of a space free from humanity and human intervention—brings us uncomfortably close to the "*völkloser Raum*" ("peopleless space") that Hitler sought to create in Eastern Europe.[48] And the concentration camp founds, in its own perverse way, its own ethical system that banishes external consideration. As Giorgio Agamben has argued, the camp is a space where everything is possible, a place of pure potentiality.[49] Likewise the north, as is stated repeatedly in *North*, is "the land of the possible"; these possibilities include not only humanity's salvation but also its capacity for monstrosity.

I stress again what I hinted earlier: what is at stake is not the north itself, nor even, as Gould emphasizes with his title, the *idea* or concept of north, but the *journey* north—the winter's journey. The trip north represents this search for universality; is it any wonder that it inevitably leads to shipwrecks and monsters? The monsters, however, like the one in Shelley's *Frankenstein*, are not "naturally" monstrous—they become monstrous through humanity's intervention and cultivation. Again, we are confronted by opposing manifestations of the north. On the one hand, the north is one of Canada's defining geographies, what makes the country special, or even "great." It is a frontier where humanity might finally come to live at peace and build an ideal society, but it is also—at the *same time*—a justification for all manner of reprehensible behavior and environmental destruction.

Even though both Gould and Maclean avoid saying so directly, what is at stake in "the moral equivalent of war" is no less than a universal system of ethics, possibly even a replacement for the God of the Old Testament. By proposing an explanation of the allure of the north that is so far-reaching and yet neglects to fully explore its consequences, Gould reaps the dramatic benefits of that idea without concerning himself with the darker implications. The north offers an ethical purity to those who live and travel there. It may be a place where we can all be fellow humans. The north, in short, is a utopia where people get along with each other not by official decree but because they know intuitively that their actions are right. Nature is the God that gives laws and dictates behavior.

The north as frontier, and frontier as ethical substance, however, also acts as *justification* for basic human action—for the very fact of human existence. Setting nature as something apart from humanity and simultaneously the source of ethics makes all ethics a form of tautology. Nature as something separate from humanity is the phantom; any attempt to actualize it and deploy it in service of ethics or justification will inevitably be self-serving. The need for such justifications—the need for ethics—may ultimately be the rotten core at the center of humanity.

And this perhaps is why *The Idea of North* succeeds in the end. The north functions not as a potential space, as many of the participants would have us believe, but as a mirror. It shows humanity both its highest aspirations and most monstrous impulses; it does not, however, distinguish between the two. Another journey away from mankind—a different sort of northern journey—Franz Schubert's *Winterreise*, may prove instructive. The work recounts a solitary journey from the comforts and community of mankind into isolation and death. Near the end cycle, in the song "Mut!," the lonely traveler turns away from mankind into the snow and wind. He ends this thought with the declaration, "If there's no God on earth, / We're gods ourselves!"[50]

To return to our initial question about the "moral equivalent of war" and the opposition of Mother Nature and human nature: I would like to substitute Mother Nature for God in Schubert's song. This is to say, perhaps, that the God who imposes ethics reveals herself to be none other than Mother Nature, and that Mother Nature, as sovereign, exerts a controlling and unifying force on humans. The oft-quoted words of Nietzsche, "God is dead," would mean that nature no longer has any hold over humans. "Going north"—again, as opposed to the north itself—is an act of encounter. We are forced, as Lotz says, to recognize ourselves at both our "greatest and most grotesque."[51] Our challenge is to differentiate between the two.

Notes

1. Mary Shelley, *Frankenstein* (New York: Penguin Classics, 2007), 225.

2. See Fergus Flemming, *90 Degrees North: The Quest for the North Pole* (New York: Grove Press, 2001). Interest in the North Pole began in earnest during the beginning of the nineteenth century, with the first serious expeditions leaving Europe around the middle of the century. At the time Shelley published *Frankenstein* (1818), many still held that the poles, when found, would be temperate and filled with open water. Shelley's conception was thus much more rational than many of a more scientific persuasion. Robert Edwin Peary, after many failed attempts, believed that he reached the pole by crossing the ice pack from Ellesmere Island in 1908, but his claim was later proved false. In 1926, Roald Amundsen, Lincoln Ellsworth, and Umberto Nobile crossed the pole in an airship, and in 1948 a Russian team successfully landed on the pole (xix–xxi). The catalogue of failures is much more extensive.

3. Michael Goodyear, then director of the Churchill Northern Studies Centre, personal communication with author, 2001.

4. It was only after the completion of *The Latecomers* and *The Quiet in the Land* that the three works became known collectively as *The Solitude Trilogy*.

5. See Mark Laurie's chapter in the present volume: "It had nothing to do with north . . . what it had to do with was solitude" (103).

6. Indeed, the whole of the *North* has something of its own monstrous quality. I have always heard it in the context of my longtime interest in soundscape, experimental radio, and Gould's artistic endeavors as a pianist. However, there is ample reason to hear the work as "unhinged" in its construction and lack of focus. Having taught this work in several music appreciation courses to inexperienced listeners, I have considerable anecdotal evidence to support this mode of listening.

Within the work itself, as a student recently pointed out, there is the inherent irony of a cacophonous collection of voices—all speaking at once—about *solitude*.

7. The transition, however, is not as abrupt as I have just characterized it. Gould must have chosen this particular work of Sibelius in part because driving *tremoli* in the string parts are a close approximation for the clickety-clack of the train sounds.

8. Gould, *North*, 11:10.

9. Gould, *North*, 51:20.

10. Gould, *North*, 52:15.

11. Gould, *North*, 52:55.

12. William James, "The Moral Equivalent of War," in *Writings, 1902–1910* (New York: Library of America, 1987), 1281.

13. James, "The Moral Equivalent of War," 1281.

14. His argument would have seemed more plausible at the time of writing because he was writing a mere five years before the onset of World War I. In the immediate aftermath of that war—which would come to be called the "war to end all wars"—he probably would have found many more hypothetical citizens ready to question the value of war as a creator of culture. Well into the twenty-first century, more than one hundred years since writing, we may assume that World War I has again assumed that same mythological status.

15. James, "The Moral Equivalent of War," 1281.

16. James concedes that without the war apparatus peaceful nations and societies will always be at the mercy of the more aggressive or a new opportunistic "Caesar" (1286).

17. Gould, *North*, 53:38, emphasis added.

18. James, "The Moral Equivalent of War," 1291.

19. James, "The Moral Equivalent of War," 1291. The desire to replace wars with other nations with some other external challenge was not lost on twentieth-century politics, from John F. Kennedy's New Frontier and space exploration to Ronald Reagan's vain hope for an alien invasion that would unite the people of the world. These two examples, in turn, suggest greatly divergent motivations. The first, in line with James's proposal, suggests a positive challenge, which could unite humanity to overcome challenge in the name of scientific discovery, whereas Reagan's proposal would have maintained all of the negative aspects of war—bloodshed, destruction—but simply replaced human enemies with an enemy with which we would not need to empathize.

20. Gould, *North*, 54:27.

21. James's principle might apply if climate change were an external challenge with which humans could battle in order to protect a status quo. If, for example, a specific insect caused climate change, we might quickly unite in support of its eradication. As it stands, however, climate change is an internal challenge. To fight it humanity needs to *challenge* the status quo by changing our behavior and not our environment, and that is precisely what humanity seems unwilling to do.

22. Gould, *North*, 57:11.

23. Gould, *North*, 58:30.

24. Glenn Gould, Interview transcript with Wally Maclean, Reel One, 1967, Item 1979-20 4, 95, 9, Glenn Gould fonds, Library and Archives Canada, Ottawa.

25. James, "The Moral Equivalent of War," 1287.

26. Gould, *North*, 3:30.

27. Gould, *North*, 51:15.

28. "Size the Enemy: BBC Reports Canada Lacks National Identity," *Globe and Mail* (1936–Current), 23 December 1967, ProQuest Historical Newspapers: *The Globe and Mail*, 2.

29. "Ban the A-Bomarc," *Globe and Mail* (1936–Current), 4 May 1961, ProQuest Historical Newspapers: *The Globe and Mail*, 6.

30. "Expect 1963 Delivery of First A-Warheads," *Globe and Mail* (1936–Current), 17 August 1963, ProQuest Historical Newspapers: *The Globe and Mail*, 1.

31. Glenn Gould, *Glenn Gould on Television: The Complete CBC Broadcasts, 1954–1977*, "DVD 8:1970," New York, Sony Classics, 2011, 55:07.

32. Gould, *North*, 24:54.

33. It could be said that the geographic placement of population is not determinative of a country's status as "northern," but other geographically northern countries like Ireland are not customarily thought of as "northern," in part because they do not have a northern frontier. Because the mostly southern population of Canada turns toward a northern expanse, the north is the site of its future development.

34. Gould, *North*, 24:12.

35. See the chapter by Jeffrey van den Scott in the present volume. Recent Canadian politics, in part provoked by a diminishing ice shelf, has revealed new colonial conflicts as well. The Arctic Ocean and its potential resources are increasingly the site of conflicts between the major countries with claims to the Pole. Shortly after becoming prime minister in 2006, Stephen Harper gave a speech tellingly titled "Securing Canadian Sovereignty in the Arctic," where he asserted Canada's territorial claims in the face of competing moves from, most notably, Russia. Stephen Harper, "Securing Canadian Sovereignty in the Arctic," official statement, 12 August 2006, http://www.pm.gc.ca/eng/news/2006/08/12/securing-canadian-sovereignty-arctic (accessed 2 June 2015).

36. Gould, *North*, 30:15.

37. Gould, *North*, 40:56.

38. Gould, *North*, 3:46.

39. Gould, *North*, 34:37.

40. Jim Lotz, *Northern Realities* (Chicago: Follet, 1971), 7. "In South America, the frontier was a land to be endured, looted, then left. In the United States, people travelled west in hope of a better life."

41. And if a society can convince itself that other humans residing at the edge of a frontier are in some way savages or "not human," then it justifies their opposition and even destruction.

42. The Inuit do not present a "savage" threat, but neither are they accorded the respect they deserve as Canadian citizens.

43. Gould, *North*, 22:03.

44. Gould, *North*, 22:23.

45. Gould, *North*, 23:15.

46. Nancy Scheper-Hughes, *Death Without Weeping* (Berkeley: University of California Press, 1992). Nancy Scheper-Hughes's *Death Without Weeping*, for example, explores the ethical compromises made by the women of the Nordeste in Brazil as they confront oppressive living conditions on plantations. How, she asks, can they take such a detached and uncaring attitude to something as devastating as the loss of a child? Precisely because forces beyond their control make such events inevitable, the detachment appears to be a coping mechanism necessary for survival in such conditions. What would be seen as neglect in more affluent societies cannot be judged ethically in this instance. On the other hand, Scheper-Hughes does judge—and judge harshly—the powerful forces that are responsible for the suffering of the people she studies.

47. Robert Phillips, *Canada's North* (Toronto: Macmillan of Canada, 1967), xi–xii.

48. Hannah Arendt, *Eichmann in Jerusalem: A Report on the Banality of Evil* (New York: Penguin Classics, 2010), 217.

49. Giorgio Agamben, *Homo Sacer: Sovereign Power and Bare Life*, trans. Daniel Heller-Roazen (Stanford: Stanford University Press, 1998): "Only because the camps constitute a space of exception in the sense we have examined—in which not only is law completely suspended but fact and law are completely confused—is everything in the camps truly possible. . . . Insomuch as its inhabitants were stripped of every political status and wholly reduced to bare life, the camp was also the most absolute biopolitical space ever to have been realized, in which power confronts nothing but bare life, without mediation" (85–86).

50. Ian Bostridge, *Schubert's Winter Journey: Anatomy of an Obsession* (New York: Knopf, 2015), 428–429.

51. Gould *North*, 9:34.

Appendix

1. Letter from Jim Lotz Accepting Gould's Interview Request
(7 September 1967)

We include this letter from Jim Lotz accepting Gould's invitation to participate in *North* as a prelude to Lotz's interview transcript. His thoughts on liminality, Eldorado, and Utopia figure prominently in the interview.
Credit: The Estate of Pat and Jim Lotz

∽

The Canadian Research Centre for Anthropologie
223 Main, Ottawa 1, Canada
Sept. 7/1967
Glenn Gould, Esq,
110 St. Clair Avenue West,
Toronto, 7 Ont.

∽

Dear Mr. Gould,
    Thank you for your letter of September 1st.
    I am delighted to hear about the proposed programme. I am in the course of writing a book on the north, and part of the reason for writing it is an attempt to determine exactly what the North is all about.
    Some random thoughts are as follows:

People up north talk about "Outside"—where is "Outside"? And if there is an outside, then the people must be "inside." The most recent large government building to be put up in Whitehorse is a prison—you will have people "inside" inside the North. A double incarceration.

Marshall McLuhan's ideas were derived in part from those of Harold Innis, who did field work in the North.

When the "outside" comes to the "inside," and northerners feel part of Canada—shall we then have a northern nation?

The North as Canada's white elephant. In India, I think, when a petty princeling got out of line, he would be presented with an elephant. It took all his time, money and effort to feed the beast and to clean up after it. Is this going to be the story of Canada's North—it is not going to go away, and we don't know what to do with it.

The north as the place to find Eldorado or Utopia—those two myths of western man. People go north to get rich quick or to find solitude and silence.

I shall be delighted to take part in the programme. We have a research Associate, Miss Hilary White, who is doing a study up in the Yukon on the adaptation of white to northern living. She should be back south soon—perhaps you could use her. I am to lecture in Toronto on October 10th, at the Royal Ontario Museum. Perhaps we could set up the interview for the 11th, in the morning, before I return to Ottawa. Save you travelling, though I should be delighted to see you in Ottawa. If October 11th is not convenient, then any time this month or next will be fine. I have specific appointments and commitments (Wednesday nights I lecture), but can arrange matters at short notice to do the interview.

With best wishes,
Sincerely,
Jim Lotz (Professor and Res. Dir.)
P.S. Is this steam radio or TV.

2. Gould's Interview Questions for Jim Lotz

We include the first page of questions and notes Gould used in his interview with Jim Lotz. The interview was conducted in September or October 1967 at the CBC Radio studio in Ottawa's Chateau Laurier hotel. Though some notes are legible, they do not correspond one for one with the questions and answers in Lotz's interview transcript.

Appendix | 223

Figure A.1. Gould's questions for Jim Lotz. *Source*: Library and Archives Canada and Primary Wave Music I. Used with permission.

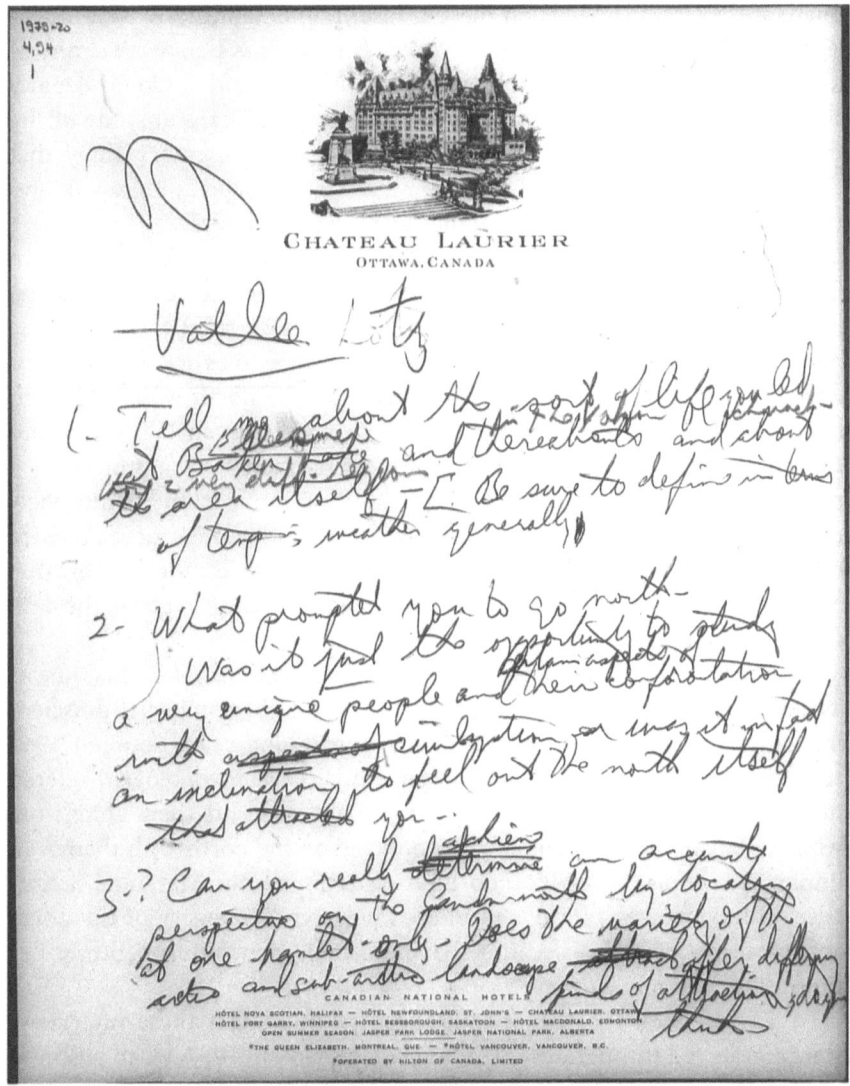

3. Introduction to Transcripts

We include all five interview transcripts from Library and Archives Canada, which show the original shape of the documentary participants' answers to Gould's questions. Gould used these production transcripts to make edits on paper and note remarks of particular interest for his "exclusions," the quotes he would ultimately edit together to form the documentary. There are several markings on these transcriptions to indicate what material Gould would use in the final work. Pending one's perspective, one of the most interesting (or troubling) aspects of *North* is that Gould departs significantly from objective documentary practice. A careful study of the transcripts with their final composition in the documentary show that Gould treated the interviews as source material to shape as he saw fit and was less concerned with the original meaning and intent.

The original transcripts purposefully exclude Gould's questions in favor of short cues likely to jog his memory during the editing process. For the purposes of this volume, the participants' responses present the more interesting material and reflect their respective roles and relationships with the north. Wally Maclean's experience in the north was dominated largely by his time on the train plying its way between Winnipeg and Churchill, Manitoba. He served as a de facto narrator for the project. As a result, Gould's task in constructing a kind of narrative from his interview responses was more difficult than it was with other interviews. Where other respondents could be cut up and pasted in an erratic fashion that often makes for a kind of pastiche, Maclean's material is given the task of creating a thread that runs from beginning to end.

Robert Phillips's recollections and prognostications reflect his time as a senior bureaucrat in Ottawa and have proven to be somewhat prescient in how the north has developed in the intervening years between 1967 and the current day. Frank Vallee, an academic anthropologist, offered in-depth observations about northern inhabitants and their goings-on, while Lotz, another academic, philosophized on the north with themes of liminality, Utopia, and Eldorado figuring prominently. Marianne Schroeder's interview was shorter but offered more vivid imagery of the north and more personal insight into the Indigenous population befitting her profession as a nurse.

To that end, the reader must keep in mind that these interviews were conducted throughout Canada's centennial year, 1967, when attitudes toward the north and its Indigenous population, the Inuit, were a great deal more paternalistic. Phillips acknowledges this attitude and is perhaps the more "progressive" of the participants in his responses, while Vallee, befitting his role as an anthropologist, highlights the *us* versus *them* dichotomy. Most notably, as discussed in this volume's introduction, the documentary is missing an Indigenous voice among those interviewed and the now-offensive term "Eskimo" is used frequently, reflecting the contemporary cultural discourse.

Editorial Notes

Every effort has been made to be faithful to the transcripts; however, "ums, ahs, you know, sort of, of course," stutters, and repetitions, which were included in the original transcripts, have been excised by the editors of this volume for clarity.

Punctuation was used erratically throughout the transcripts with commas serving for every kind of pause. The editors of this volume have edited the punctuation to be more intuitive without altering the meaning of the interview content.

In Lotz's transcript he refers several times to people by their initials. The editors of this volume were able to locate some of those referenced in his book about his time in the north.[1]

There are several editorial remarks in the original transcripts; these were made by the original transcriber, likely at Gould's behest. Any editorial remarks made by the editors of this volume are placed in [square brackets].

Credit: All transcripts are used here courtesy of CBC Licensing.

4. Jim Lotz Interview Transcript

Q. "Fellini's"[2]

A. Oh, yes, definitely yes, no not really, I suppose, could be, no, I just don't think that's at all possible. I think this, that's a bit outlandish even for the north—yes, yes—no not particularly—some circumstances, perhaps.

Q. "Biographer"

Well, like I think quite a large number of people who end up in the north, I got there by mistake. I strayed in there. I think my first attempt to go north was when I—during a summer vacation at University of England—I thought about going to Iceland. I am not too sure why and instead, because I made a mistake about the fare, I ended up in Morocco. I am a geographer by training and I have this belief that geographers are people who have no sense of direction, just as sociologists are people who don't like society, and economists are people who can't really manage their own money. Though some evidence in the north indicates they have a pretty good time with the public purse.

I came to Canada after I had been in West Africa for a year. I came to Canada, again like so many immigrants, because I couldn't get a job in England. I came to Ottawa to place my services at the disposal of the federal government and the federal government had other ideas. So, after working in a few dead-end jobs in Ottawa, writing advertising copy of all things, I applied to McGill and was encouraged to go north with McGill, and McGill is one of the English Universities in Canada and has a good reputation for sending people north.

One of the reasons they sent me north was the fact that they couldn't find enough Canadians—native born Canadians—to man the McGill sub-arctic research station, which, at the time, was and still is in Schefferville in the center of Labrador and which is not very far north. It is about 55 north and round about and not too very much further north than my own home town of Liverpool. So I went up to the McGill subarctic research laboratory and spent a summer there as a weather observer. In typical graduate student fashion, I was paid enough money by the university to enable me to turn around and pay them my fees.

And I spent a year, the winter, in Montreal and went up to McGill's subarctic research laboratory again. This was the summer of 1957. This time I went in to do some field work for a thesis. The thesis was on soils and agricultural possibilities in the Knob Lake area of Quebec. There is not a great deal of soil and, as far as I can make out, there is no agricultural possibilities. This is what is known as negative evidence in science. But out of this, I attempted to plant eight bean pods in a row, I tried to grow some grass, some kind, type of vegetables. The whole thing was a complete disaster not from a scientific viewpoint, but from the agricultural viewpoint, everything was killed by a killing frost about the middle of July or something like that. And I began to get the impression—this is an impression that has been increasingly impressed on me—is that the north is a land of very narrow, very thin margins.

Man is a biological improbability at the best of times. If you wanted to design something that could live on this earth you would not design a man and, in the north, in many respects we are at our greatest and most grotesque.

Just about the time I was finishing for my thesis on Knob Lake, the phone rang and Dr. Svenn Orvig, then with the Department of Geography at McGill, asked me if I would like to go north on an arctic expedition, and being English, I said yes.

There are several traditions of Arctic expedition, the English traditions where everyone puts £50 in the pot and hires husky dogs from Greenland

and lives on Bovril and Ovaltine. And then there is the American tradition where you have a massive before-operations report and a massive after-operations report but very little in the middle. I was to undergo an American Arctic expedition, and I use the term "undergo" as of an operation advisedly.

So, Dr. Svenn Orvig phoned me up and asked me if I wanted to go on an Arctic expedition and I said, "Well certainly," and I was even tickled to death to find out they were going to pay me for this. So I went to Ellesmere Island with the International Geophysical Year, an expedition mounted by the Defense Research Board and lead by Dr. [Geoff] Hattersley-Smith of the Defense Research Board. Now I was there in the summer of '57 and in the summer of '58. One problem with the north and flitting about in the north is that time and space get kind of mixed up. What happened on this particular expedition, I just had a wonderful time.

We were all, to some extent, specialists, i.e., these are beginners who are not afraid to admit they are beginners. We lived on an ice glacier. We transported around all over the place. Here we drove dogs, we drove snow toboggans. We lived on dried food and we really had a wonderful time. There was a certain isolation and yet of community in the group of people I was with. This is—memory tends to cast a pall over all our worst and best experiences but looking back on this, this is one of the experiences of my life. A group of men isolated, each trusting the other, and each respecting the other. A small community in isolation and it's just not touch of the old nostalgia, it is a feeling of having participated in something very meaningful both personally and professionally.

One of the things we did on this glacier, in this particular International Geophysical Year, in a sense we scratched the surface of knowledge, we didn't scratch it very deeply. I think many of the things which came out of the expedition of '57 and '58, many of the conclusions we had to think about again when additional evidence came about again.

This addition of the north as a place where you can test things out, where you can probe at nature, where you can extend the limits of your knowledge while admitting the limits of your ignorance. This is the north to me, as a scientific environment more than anything. This is what I look to the north as.

Now in '59 I quit the north. However, so often it is like the drunkard. His wine, you keep shaking it, you keep going back. And I took a job selling advertising for the *Montrealer*. I had some vague ideas about breaking into the newspaper business or writing. And the day before I was due to start I went skiing in Montreal, a few miles north of Montreal,

Vale David. And I broke my leg. This was the only real serious injury I have experienced among the ice and the snow; this was north of Montreal. And what happened was, I went back to the north simply because a man with a broken leg doesn't have many opportunities, especially if he is a geographer, which is looked on in many respects as an unskilled trade. This has all the advantages of professionalism without any of the disadvantages. I went back to the north with an American expedition to northern Ellesmere Island. This was to the ice shelf of northern Ellesmere Island, even further north than I had been in '57 or '58.

Now, this was a fairly ghastly experience. I always remember that on the Canadian expedition we had eaten dried meat and that sort of thing and we enjoyed ourselves. Somebody says, "Well, you know, when you go on these Arctic expeditions don't you start missing women?" Well, after about the first month then you start talking about food. Well, what happened on this one, they kept on, they had loads of equipment, we had three or four vehicles, which took you, no which kept breaking down. Now, the [blank line] with dogs, which we had on operation Hazen, which is, I suppose as the last resort, you can eat them but they don't, in a sense, break down. And these mechanical marvels we had with the Americans kept breaking down and they had to fly over with terribly expensive aircraft to drop very small parts or tracks or something like this.

I remember once I had an American P.F.Q. with me as an assistant, at least I think he was working for me, and the—they dropped one of the tracks and also very kindly dropped us some lettuce and tomatoes and I said, "My goodness, look at these fresh vegetables," and he said, "Um, um, no salad dressing."

Well, there was also a rather bad personal experience in relation to a good friend of mine who died on that expedition. Anyhow, the whole thing was, in a word, a shambles and a mess. Scientifically, results were minimal, the whole experience was rather frustrating and disagreeable. It may have been me. I expect this about the north. One always worries about whether it is you or whether it is the counter, the other people.

Then, and in '60 I went back with Dr. Hattersley-Smith to Ellesmere Island for a month and we just about got off the glacier. That year we had expected about a month before the water started to melt on the glacier and the water, the glacier started to melt about a month earlier. So the plane came in to get us. This was the Royal Canadian Air Force who did a magnificent job and we just got off the glacier. We were airborne 40 knots with jet-assisted take-off, which I understand from aviation people, is a rather slow speed to get into the air with.

Then I had always wanted to work with people in the north and in '60 I transferred to the Department of Northern Affairs and Natural Resources as a community planning officer. Now again, the characteristics of the frontier is that they are always short of labor. Always short of hands, you don't really have to be properly qualified to get a job. Well, this was precisely my experience in '60. There had been a vacancy for a community planning officer and I was the closest thing they had within range at that salary for about a year. I seemed to know where the north was, I seemed to have some sketchy idea of its main outline and I seemed to be enthusiastic about going north and these qualifications secured me the post.

The first thing I asked to undertake was a study of the squatters of Whitehorse. These were a group of people who ultimately, at least in my own work, turned out to be key to the way the north is viewed in Canada. [*Word corrected by hand but not legible*] the north can and may have developed. These people had a tremendously bad reputation. I was told by old northern hands that when I went up to Whitehorse they would drive me out of town on a rail, they would throw me into the Yukon river, and the Yukon river never gives up its dead. All these hairy stories about the wicked squatters, and I found these were a bunch of people who were trying to do the best they could in an area where their economic future was uncertain. They didn't want to invest in nice, tidy middle-class houses on nice, tidy middle class lots served with nice, tidy convenient sewers and water. They lived as well as they could. I know it is kind of a cliché but some of my best friends in the north—and one of my best friends in the north, and a man who has been an enormous help to me, provided me with a great deal of information—have been squatters.

Well, I did this study and I came back alive, shattering the myth of the wicked squatters. They would not talk to anybody in Ottawa and they hated Ottawa in the north, they just loathe Ottawa.[3] And I came back alive, and brought back the list of the people. And from that time I was entitled to call myself a northern expert. [*Blank line*] check about the word expert having derived from two things, 'ex' meaning formerly, 'pert' meaning a drip under pressure, is by no means inappropriate for the north. Really, it's a matter of fact. You can't talk about the north until you have got out of it, so the definition is not at all that incorrect.

Well then, I did a series of quick and dirty studies. I was up in Inuvik and I wrote a long report with a very large number of recommendations and, again, this is par for the course in the north. You come from Ottawa, you go in the north, you write your report, you make the list of recommendations, you take it back to Ottawa, and nobody pays any attention to it.

I was up in Whitehorse helping the planners to look at the center—to look at the Whitehorse metropolis area for planning—another magic word. You can try and plan the north, you write a report, nobody pays any attention to the recommendation.

Then, in '62 I broke loose from the Northern Administration branch of the Department of Northern Affairs and Natural Resources and I went to work with the NC and Research Centre. Fortunately in NC and Research Centre there were two men, now at Carlton [University] and still with the department who gave me the opportunity and the support that I needed to do what I think is some slightly more significant work in the north than was the case when I was working with an administrative organization. I know the people in the north don't like Ottawa but it seems that northern crises always occur in Ottawa on a Friday at about 5 in the afternoon when a short letter bearing a tag "URGENT" comes down and everybody has to stay on the weekend.

In '62 to '63, with the exception of the year I was at the University of British Columbia endeavoring to further my learning, I spent the summers in the north. I spent the summers in the Yukon, I mounted a Yukon research project. Now, I was quite selfish in this, I was intrigued by the squatters. They worried about the future of Whitehorse. I started wondering about the future of Whitehorse and started looking at the future of the Yukon and then from there the future of the north, the future of northern Administration and then the future of the world. I kind of stopped there. This brought me [*blank line*], O blessed man, in contact with BF and vicariously with a number of people like BG, DB, and MM, who have worked on this whole concept of, first of all, what a world we are in and certainly what a world we are moving into.

I carried out a study of Dawson [Yukon], did a redevelopment report on Dawson, which no attention was paid. I enjoyed myself, I don't now particularly care for the north because for one thing the north has changed and the north changed rapidly and it doesn't take long in the north to become an authority—an expert—and this can be quite terrifying, especially since the north is a kind of place that leads people, in a sense, to see visions.

Since '66, since I have been at St. Paul University, the Canadian Research Centre for Anthropology, run by the Oblates of Mary Immaculate, a missionary order with a very fine reputation in the Canadian north. Most of them or many of them are Europeans, they had the same trouble: They could not find Canadians to go north.

Since '66 I have not been back, I was in Alaska this last summer and in [blank line] and I spent the off week or two there. I have not really spent an extended time in the north since about the summer of '65 when all these bits and pieces about the north that I had been collecting, all these impressions—I had been over the Chilkoot Pass, I got lost going over the Chilkoot Pass and I had been rolled in a car in a ditch in the Yukon. I am not quite a northerner, I am not quite a sourdough, but on the other hand I am not quite a chikatto.[4] I have commuted between Ottawa and the Yukon and I have seen the difficulties at both ends. There is a feeling in the north, there is some great [blank line] against them, the paranoid style this has been obvious in a place like Alaska that Ottawa is apt to do so well. One of the phrases I use "There are no devils in development." I think there are some very, very serious problems in the Canadian north, that is a real cliché.

And what does the north mean to me and what is the future of the north? Well, first of all, it seems to me that in the north, we are seeing one of the final playings out of those two great dreams of man: Eldorado or Utopia. Both Eldorado or Utopia were both located in parts unknown. I mean, it is very difficult to think of Utopia down in Toronto for instance, with all due deference to Toronto. We know too much about it, we have too much understanding of the reality, but north of 60 it is still empty, it is still in many ways the land of the possible and so we have the story of: a) the rich north, the vast treasure house of literature which, you know, like making me in Dorothy Parker's terms, thrown-up, or b) the vast, great, empty useless desert. To me the north is so Canadian, A.S. mentioned this about a window on the future, a future he was writing in 1937, well before most Canadians woke up to the reality of the north.

My feeling is that the north is not going to go away. The Federal north is 40 per cent of the country, it is populated by a very small number of people and—we keep getting—we have this lovely idea that the department of Indian Affairs and National Defense is pursuing, that all the wagons are going to line up along the 60th parallel and we are going to have a land rush. You know, all of a sudden the people are going to rush in. We have had two films made recently, you know, by the propaganda arm of the government, the National Film Board, on the accessible north, which shows stores, supermarkets, nightclubs, and hospitals just to show us that it is like the rest of Canada. Well, my feeling is, if it is like the rest of Canada, why should anybody go there? The thing about the north is that it is more truly Canadian than anywhere else. The things that impress you as being Canadian or, you know, at least impress me, and remember I am speaking as a new Canadian, in many respects I am Canadian, more nationalistic. I have seen the shape of a possible future in the north and, quite frankly, it scares the hell out of me. I have seen an [*blank line*] which demands a scientific approach and science, to me, demands the open society where people go. I have seen this in a very real sense bureaucratized. I have seen whatever the old support of the north has been resolving itself in a rather dreary routine. [*Blank line*] that a booster support that would put an American developer of the nineteenth century trying to sell a chunk of sand to shame. I have—I have the feeling about the north, this is the land of the possible. If we can't create Eldorado or Utopia we can create some reasonable compromise.

You see, the north demands a very high level of science and technology, it demands you be careful, it demands that you work with the land, not against it, and that you work with the people, the Eskimos and Indians, for instance. The Eskimos a long time ago understood what a task force was all about. I mean, we had to invent these things during the second world war in order to hunt our fellow man, which the Eskimos and the Indians, they had task forces when they went out to hunt. They selected the best hunters, they didn't select one individual and say, "well he is a powerful politician or he will be able to sign the vouchers for us." They didn't. They got up in the morning, they looked out, they read the signs of the land. You know, I think this is what McLuhan is talking about in many ways. They read all these signs through all of their senses, they were not trapped by the book, they were not pinned down on the printed page, and when the signs were right, the wind was right, the weather was right, the time was right, they formed a small group and went out to hunt. Now in the present time we expect them to sit down and send a memo to three or four other people saying "further to your what's-a-name of such-and-such a time," by this time the caribou season is over and they have to get welfare. It seems to me there is some wisdom in this approach, the task force—what we call systems analysis—an integrated approach to reality. The Eskimo and the Indian had this a long time ago. The Eskimo invited and constructed out of his own substances of the land, the igloo. Well, this is the maximum space involved, enclosed in the minimum volume. The maximum volume with the minimum outside space, in other words, the best shape for the north. You know when we finally put these things up here, up in the north, they were on the dew line, they were geodesic domes. The Eskimo had the geodesic dome a long time ago, but he didn't get a patent on it.

And it seems to me that up in the north there is a [blank line], it is a hit in Canadians' teeth and a way in which we can test ourselves. We are being tested in the north. In the good old days when the British Empire was—you know, the sun never sets on the British Empire—there were all sorts of ghastly mistakes made in Africa and in India, you know the Charge of the Light Brigade and all this thing, and all but the glorious bits were suppressed. But we are in the era of electronic media now and every time we fall over on our faces in the north, and we have been falling over on our faces in the north, it is all over the electronic media, it is all over the front page, etc. And if you look at Alaska, they have a phrase about the Bureau of Indian Affairs and they talk about atrocity stories, which are the mistakes of which the Bureau of Indian Affairs has made.

And in a sense, the north is stretching, the north is, in a very real sense, calling us and saying "Now look, you know, let us forget," let's first of all define development but, secondly, how do you control this vast area and how do you control it in the interests of the people who are there and who are going to be there. And the idea that there is going to be a great big rush into the north is, I think, false. I think the population of there may decline. We have some lovely ideas for boosting up the figures of the northern populations by saying that in such-and-such a year the census showed 40,000 people. Well, this is a peak summer population and it can be dropped by about a third. People don't and will not go into the north unless there is something specific for them to do in the future of the north. People will go to do specific things for specific lengths of time.

The north is a truncated society, you go only so far in the north. I mean, if you are the biggest, best mill superintendent in copper mine [blank line] only be the superintendent of a very small operation.

The future of the north relies on getting young, healthy, intelligent people into the north and this means most of them will be married, or they should be married, because the north is no place for the single man, and they should have kids. The north is a glorious place for kids. They can see, they can touch reality, they can have a real sense of being, of being alive. This is provided they don't lock them up in the classrooms as they do in the north as well as in the south. They can get total sensory immersion, which is so very important to have. The future of the north is going to depend on attracting young, highly skilled, highly trained specialists, and the north is one of the worst places you can send these people.

The north, at the present time, is not particularly a happy place. It is run like a colonial appendage. I know this is a cliché, but it is very real to the people who live up there. It is important for development that people have a say in the decisions that affect their future and, regrettably, this is just not the case in the Yukon with which I am most familiar. As a matter of fact, in the Yukon a kind of autonomy movement has started. I think we just have to answer the question and I am trying to answer it in this book I am writing. I think I am writing it or it's writing me, it's a bit difficult to say. What use is the north, what do we do with the north? Now these are questions that I think should clear away all this 'hoo haa' and get to the facts. What use is the north? What can be done in the north?

Q. Inner resource versus technology

A. There is a very interesting photo in north which showed children in Alaska looking at a TV set for the first time and what they were seeing on the TV set were themselves. They had a closed circuit rigged up. I suppose in Einstein's terms, if space is curved and we ever get our eyesight up, or our missiles up, I suppose we will be seeing the back of our heads. I think this is part of the north like with the gold seekers. I remember an old Swede who probably hadn't even read Robert Service and he spread some gold out for me. They kept their little nuggets and he said, "Take some gold," and I said, "I can't take your gold." He says, "No," he says "it's not the gold, it's the finding the gold." And I think the north is process—the north is finding—no, not so much finding as seeking. My experience with the north has enriched immeasurably. I have enjoyed it, I've liked it, I have done some very foolish things there, you know like sticking a knife in my mouth in below zero temperatures, and losing bits of flesh. The north is a challenge, it is adventure, but mostly in a very real sense it is a kind of looking glass, you see yourself in it. You can't escape yourself in the north. The north is the last place to go to escape. So whatever I've got out of the north and, again, I can't talk about it in tangible senses, I suppose I have been initiated into the north. The north will always carry with me, the north I shall always have. And curiously enough, out of this northern experience it has made me much more strongly Canadian. In a very real sense, I couldn't really have become a Canadian if I hadn't have gone north.

Because life in a place like Ottawa or Toronto or Vancouver would be really so much like life in England or the states. But being in the north, experiencing the north, living in the north, I think it is a thing that people should go through. Maybe one of the uses of the north would be kind of a compression chambre, the opposite of a decompression chambre where, you know people aren't up there for a couple of years to become Canadians. It is amazing how consciously you do become Canadian. North of 60 you stop worrying about French Canadians and English Canadians, German Canadian or anything like that. You are all Canadians. You shrug off all provincial, local, parochial responsibilities. I always remember a friend of mine who was a very French Canadian separatist nationalist. Well, when he got lost in the north, one of his rescue notes was written in English.

Q. "Do you or did you while in the north or indeed at any other time in your life think of yourself as a solitary?"

A. Well, I think—I know it is fashionable to talk about alienation. I think, essentially, man's condition is a solitary one. I was in many respects solitary but in a strange way the north has made me more gregarious. Because the north does show you how much you rely on your fellow man and what a sense of community means. The sense of community in the north, unlike in the south, is a matter of life and death. I can't imagine the things that happen in New York where Kitty Genovese was stabbed before 36 people, I can't—people fall down and people walk over them—I can't see this happening in the north. There is a very real sense of community. The thing about the north in personal terms is that you feel it is so big, it is so vast, it is so immense, it cares so little and this diminishes you, and then you think, "My God, I am here. I've got here, I live here, I live, I breathe, I laugh, I walk, I have companions." And somehow it has this feeling of pushing you down and bringing you up at the same time, which I think is essential to all meaningful human experience. Now, I think it is difficult to say whether one is solitary or not in the north and I think the north tends to make one, in a sense, more of a private person and also more of a public person.

Q. Conversational camouflage and habit of James Lotz, Inc.

A. No, I think in the north it is very difficult to be a private person. It is very difficult to be a private person. It is very difficult in a sense to live one's own life. One never does live one's own life but in the north you become very much aware of this. The other thing about the north is that it is an oral society. There is a great stress laid on messages passed by people, by mouth, and by ear is the right way to describe it. In a very real sense, the north opens, enfolds you, and puts you out again. And you see, you can't really be the same person even if you come back and submerge yourself in the city. It is impossible to escape this business of the north calling, the north being part of you.

Q. Time lag and fashion making via mass media

A. I remember on the Ellesmere Island we could regularly get the Radio Moscow broadcasts and I remember one very detailed description in English of a football match, I am not too sure why. One of the things about the media in the north is that it is a selection. The messages come in and, as far as the published material is concerned, the written material, books, magazines, etc. in the Yukon they come in pretty quickly, they come in the remoter areas in a series of bundles and also for the traditional peoples they give a very curious idea of how we work. One of the most bizarre magazines is *Vogue*. Can you imagine *Vogue* dropping into a place like Snow Drift. I mean, these people would say, "If this is civilization, let's leave it," but the other thing is bush telegraph and this is no myth—messages do, important messages do—the only thing about the north is you have to sort out the important messages from the trivia very quickly. You cannot afford to ignore an important message in the north. The government with its memos generate such enormous numbers of messages but how few of these are really relevant? You have to think of the flow in the other direction of what messages come out of the north. One of the really serious problems we have in Canada since Canada's north is the federal government's responsibility, therefore the federal government is working on behalf of all Canadians is the messages [that] are relayed from the north to the south. What accurate estimate can you get of what is going on in the north? Somebody said last year's expert just left and this year's expert hasn't arrived yet. The important thing about the north is I would like to see some sort of northern dialogue, a real discussion of what is going on up there. What is really truly happening? One of the major problems is when you have one government department so dominant and has such a vested interest in doing what they call developing the north, they can generate all sorts of messages. George Rogers mentioned, for instance, in Alaska, the visiting firemen are taken to Juneau, Anchorage, Fairbanks, Point Barrow, and Nome and this is about as much as they see. In the case of the trips around the north where do they go? They go to Pine Point, they go to Inuvik, they go to New Imperial in the Yukon, the projected Anvil Dynasty property, United Keno Hill, etc. So what we do, or what these people do for us, the news makers, they select certain little bits out of the whole context and it is like, in many cases, a diamond on a dung heap. And this is one of the major difficulties. I think I have some ideas of how the north could be represented in totality. I think there is so much garbage in our schoolbooks and on the market, to me, the reality of the north, especially doing scientific research there and finding out about things.

The reality of the north is so much more wonderful and so much more staggering than any false impressions we could conjure up. The major problem is, and I would like to see something done on this, the problem in the north [is] you have research done which shelved the whole thing for a couple of years but I would like to see some analysis of what messages pass backwards and forwards between the north and the south or the south to the north because we have this idea we are developing the north but the north is developing us too. It is testing us, it is seeing how good we are, in a sense, as to how we are able to control this great area.

Q. The Developing Eskimo.

A. Well, there is a fascinating book called *Prospero and Caliban: the Psychology of Colonization* by Octave Mannoni who worked in Malagasy Republic of Madagascar and brings up this idea of Prospero and *The Tempest*, [that] could only be Prospero simply because we had Caliban to do all the dirty work, and he points out a kind of symbiosis in these colonial situations where we think we're helping the Eskimo, we're doing things for the Eskimo, and he should be grateful to us, and we feel we are in a sense manipulating him. We don't seem to realize there is another end to this that he is manipulating us. We have some detail of this in George River that, because we say, "Oh, you know the wonderful Eskimos, the fine hunter, etc.," he will play the role that we assign to him and he will play this only so far as they will keep us happy. I think there is something fairly insidious about this, but on the other hand, we have only been in the north for 10 or 13 years and the Eskimos have weathered worse things than civil servants and bureaucrats, and the invasion of white foreigners. And remember, the northern development since '54 is only the last in a sense and the most important in a number of ways. The whalers and people like that, the Eskimo is no stranger to the white man. We had a good press image and I am inclined to think that, from the Eskimo, from this ability, we admire the Eskimo not as a stereotype but as someone who is able to live and survive.

Eskimo lived, hunted, and raised children in a place where 140 of Britain's best—the Franklin expedition members [who] died—we admire the Eskimo for clinging to the earth by the skin of his teeth but he does it. Life expectancy before the white man came in force was very low. I am inclined to think if we would only look at the Eskimo as a quaint, funny little hunter or as an artist—these ghastly clichés that clutter up literature—if we could only look at him as a human being and adapt some of his ways of doing things, his culture, his values for instance in child rearing, permissiveness rather than authoritativeness, a sense of community rather than a sense of individualism. I quoted in a paper I wrote the reactions of two men to the north. One was that the winter was the good time, the food was in, we could have games, etc.

The story of the Eskimo in the MacKenzie district at the mouth of the MacKenzie [river], there was that isolation, that terrible threatening horror that hangs around you, which was [Charles] Rivett-Carnac's book on *Pursuit in the Wilderness.* He was talking about the north. It makes sense to me to send the Eskimos to the moon if we have to go to the moon simply because they are accustomed to living in isolation, they are accustomed to living in enclosed [spaces] for extended periods of time. If you look at the records of what happened in Antarctica stations where we had aggressive, individualistic white men huddled up together for a winter there is some pretty grizzly things came out of that. I think the Eskimo, if we don't wear him down and render him into a stereotype image; I think there is promise here.

I would like to see Eskimos employed in our school system, telling our school kids exactly what it was like. I remember I watched my small daughter's Christmas play—or whatever it was. You know these things you're never quite sure what they are in schools—and the kids were portraying Eskimos and "Oh, I am a great artist and hunter," etc. Well for most of the Eskimos it is, "I do jobs that no white man will do," because they are either too low to their status or too dirty. I would like to see the Eskimos into the school systems teaching our kids how it really was, exposing them to the north as it really was in the past and how it has changed rather than this secondhand Gutenberg gibberish of the printed page, which was out of date at the time it was written.

Q. Future

A. What you are asking me for, in effect, is my personal vision and nobody need apologize for being visionary about the north. The north is the land of the possible. In the year 2000, I would expect something like the following: There will be a small number of settlements located around mines or transport centers, they will be all year-round settlements, they will be linked together by very specific type of communications media where information will be related backwards and forwards instantaneously and backwards and forwards to Ottawa. In the summer, when the land opens up, I would think these towns, these communities would be built for the north and not for the suburbs of Toronto as most of the communities in the north are at the present time—most of the houses.

The north, Alaska, Northwest Territories, and the Yukon lie between three densely populated areas: North America (United States and southern Canada), China and Japan, and northwest Europe, and right in the middle—plump is this vast outdoor recreation area, you know, the things we took for granted like clean air, and clean water. Somebody once said we would have to keep smallpox virus alive because the doctors won't know how to deal with them if we ever get smallpox. Clean air and clean water and the chance to look a long distance, these sorts of things. It may be that this is what the north will have to be. This will be a place where the people can actually come and enjoy this. This is recreation, the chance to be alone, to be quiet in the north, which we desperately need in this urban civilization, though I am a town man, I'm afraid. The chance to be alone and be quiet with one's friends and one's family, this may be the use of the north, the other use of the north I would see—I would see us sending our school kids every year in the summer up there to learn about—the north shows you everything under a microscope. This dichotomy is so big and yet you can see the processes. You can see a flower growing beside a glacier. I can see our school kids going up there in the jumbo jet and learning biology by looking at things, walking around, learning botany through the soles of their feet. I am a geographer; this strikes a responsive chord.

Learning history firsthand from the people who made it, from the people who changed an empty area into not a developed area, not a controller area, but a Canadian area. I would like to see this, I would see the north—is where no Canadian would be a Canadian unless he had spent some time there, perhaps even three months getting the feel, getting the size of the country. As far as other things are concerned like resources, water, mines, and things like that, oil and gas, we are not short of minerals in the world today. I think so much of this quest for Eldorado sets my teeth on edge, it's so phony, it's so unreal, so anti-northern. The north is universal it is a universal environment. So many of the problems that we have in the north, things like cultural contact, social exchange, these are world problems and I think the north could be a kind of laboratory. If you are doing anything with people you have to be very careful, for no matter what you say about computers and things like that, you know people are the most human things we got and with the Eskimos, they are a people-oriented society. We're such a machine-oriented society. You can tell this if you see the air-conditioning break down in an office, it is fixed in five minutes. But if it breaks down where there are people working it isn't fixed for a week, "Oh, well you have to wait your turn chum," that sort of thing. The north could become a kind of laboratory where, we could, because we are an affluent society, take our time and involve people in solving these very complex problems of social change.

Many of the problems of the underdeveloped world, for instance how to bring a very high level of science and technology into what we are pleased to call primitive areas among primitive people, and how to do it in such a way as not to harm or hurt people, this is very important in this day and age. I would like to see the north as a great outdoor laboratory. In a sense one could study and examine these processes and we could take our time and we could care about it. I think in this way, Canada's north would become part of a—would be—because it is a universal environment, would have its role in solving many of these big problems.

I was talking to the Vista Director of Alaska and he said [he] worked in the slums of Guayaquil and had half a million people there. He says "how can you tell whether you're making any progress?" He says, "What I find satisfying with the people up here in Vista, Alaska in a year," he says, "you see some change. It may be change for the better, it may be change for the worse, but at least you see." And this is so terribly important. The ultimate output of the north, which nobody seems to pay much attention to, is the ultimate basis of civilization, and that's information and knowledge and we have got this opportunity to get a marvelous output of information and knowledge and trained people who have dealt with a real world. A world that is as broad as the horizon and isn't limited by a six-by-six experimental room.

This to me is what I would see the north as being, as a vast outdoor laboratory where we can experiment and, in the social sciences, we can take our time, we can be careful, and if we read the message correctly we can avoid harm and hurt. I think this is very important in relation to Canada's role in the world today. Because when we talk of the north, we are talking about an underdeveloped area and so many of the problems are so similar to the problems elsewhere. We should use this place to train our people and get knowledge and information on the right way to do things. And when I say "the right way to do things," I mean the scientific and humane way to do things, and when I say this I mean when

I'm talking to a Russian or if I'm talking to a Dane or an American. And I'm talking about the north, I'm talking about common problems, I'm not talking about what happens in Vladivostok or what happens in Fairbanks or what happens in Inuvik. I'm talking about common problems and I'm admitting that we know so very little about this spaceship earth, and in the north we can find out so much and we can do it in a relatively short space of time with a relatively small sum of money. Again, these are important considerations.

5. Walter "Wally" Maclean Interview Transcript

Maclean: Common sense? I saw that there is no absolute when it comes to the north as it is. I, perhaps I can agree that the north as it was has relevance, has use, has something, but how about the north that is—Well, I just can't go along with that, I can't buy that at all. It is no part of my past, no part of my present, and let's hope it is no part of my future. Alright, I could say definitely, not only definitely but actually further it a little bit. I could say that programs answer a need, not only for the north, but for all of us. South, north, anywhere—Oh, I would say absolutely definitely not, not a chance—Now to this I can't help but agree. I agree perhaps on second thought, not on my first premise. Yes, certainly, yes indeed, no not at all, no, no.

Q. Biographer

A. Well, the only way I see this happening is in an extended ride north. When I say that I mean a long terrible, trying trip, perhaps to Churchill by the way of Thompson, going and coming, pass Ilford and Gillam, this long, almost trans-Siberian experience that we now sort of face, and for those who face it for perhaps the first, second, and third time, it is almost a traumatic experience they feel.

This is going to become impossible; it may not be now but it is going to become and yet they are able to do little or nothing about it. What, finally do you ask is done about it? Well, here's my guess. What really happens is this: That the train is about to leave the Pas, say a specific point and 500 miles away north and east is going to be Churchill and a day later, and what does a person do while leaving the Pas? Do you know what happens, he sits there in the day coach. The newsy is just ahead of him and these people, the conductor, the brakeman and so forth who are accustomed to this are making nothing of it. He sits there wondering, "Oh, this is going to be forever. It has already been one day, now it is going to be another one, and what about this one?" He sits there and wonders until the wretched train gets in motion. I am going to be uneasy, I am uneasy but why? Because unless the confounded train moves out of here my mind is trapped. I'm caught, somehow I have to face myself. What a horrible thought.

Well, is this a surprise, well this is the person who makes the trip often. No, it is no surprise at all. The person who makes the trip more often is going to realize that before long he is going to be up against himself, not up against his fellow travelers. Not so much but he is going to have to be up against his own sad self. Well, in order to overcome this he has a continuing novel that he has already started. He is sitting there away from the madding crowd that's stampeding up and down the aisles, peeling oranges and what not, and actually he is trying to sort of isolate himself because in fact shortly he will be isolated for a long period of time in the lonely north let's say. So he is with this book that has already dropped his interest. He's already two thirds of the way through it, he knows the next chapter will prove, well, at least readable if not enchanting. So he mentally says, "I am going to shut myself off from the hysteria." What hysteria? Well, the hysteria of not being in motion because as long as the train of course itself does not move, then of course, his mind races on to endless conclusions mostly about himself, putting him on the spot in a way that perhaps he wouldn't understand if he hadn't made the trip.

Now he is isolated and what he comes up against is this: Before long he is going to have to perhaps say hello and pass the off word to his fellow man. Now, to whom is this going to be, who is the object of his affect in this particular sort of place, this particular situation, only until he gets along with himself part of the trip up perhaps as far as Thompson—Isn't it funny that when I say Thompson of course this is going to be 200 miles up and the funny thing is that the train itself, by reason of nickel to be found, has to go those 30 odd miles in and 30 miles back in a sort of a reminder that all of us are faced with, what do we call it, an endless task. You know, one fellow told me who was taking, I forget what he was taking, probably philosophy. He said this was the myth of Sisyphus. As a matter of fact he lisped but I didn't and the fact is that he had quite a time with it, and here was some wretched, was it a king? Yes, a kind of Greece, Corinth, and here he was rolling this confounded rock up to the top of this precipice for some reason or other, then gravity took over and it hit the bottom and then he did the same thing again.

No doubt with a larger rock. Well, somehow the sameness of the trip in and the trip out from a place, a necessary place in the nickel north, like Thompson, is part of this analysis sort of feeling, this myth, this business for having to do things for no apparent reason.

Fine, it's on the trip back then, to what do you call it, the main line, yes, it is on the trip back to the main line you say to yourself, "Well, which of these people I'm seeing now for the last 230 or 240 miles, am I going to say hello to?" Well, it isn't as though you've lasted that long, you've said hello to half-dozen, maybe fifteen but you had no intention to establish, or what do you call it, rapport with anyone in particular. Now you find it necessary. Isn't that funny, you find it necessary, why in fact. Well, this gets hard to find out the reasons who was it that said that the how of it is relatively easy, but the why is almost impossible. You are up against now not the how but almost the ultimate why. Why must I say something? Why must I express myself? Why must I be myself in this endless trip? Oh, yes, put it this way, umm, how late are you? Well, you know three or four hours, it doesn't matter, this part of it doesn't matter except that you somehow beat yourself with this business of being late. "Oh, it's late, I'll never get there." What does your arrival mean, if anything? Supposing it is Churchill, the end of the line, at 7 odd in the morning. Ah, little of nothing, all you can do then is perhaps have breakfast, take a look 'round at the confounded sweep of the northern winds and hunch yourself up much further into your parka than you ever expected to, no matter the season.

So, not to anticipate here we are, we're riding towards the mile 200 on the Hudson Bay railway and indeed we're saying hello to somebody. It isn't long before we've heard what he had to say why for the first time he is going to Churchill—with what, with the army, with the navy, with the air force, with these initials that he always throws at you DPW, what's that? Oh, Department of Public Works. DRNL, what's that? What is—Defense, Research Northern Laboratories, what's that? Well, you're studying the northern lights then, now you can listen for a while because what do any of us know about the northern lights and this is the days that were, this is the Churchill that, in a sense, has sort of passed some of our interests, some of the future ones, that have to do with different kinds of research. Of course, are still what I call the rocket racket, you know this is PAN AM now, whether it still will be I don't know. How in the name of all that's holy are they, 15 miles away from this place called Churchill, shooting rockets, Canadian ones mark you, Alouette, and Black Brant and what all, into the night sky to find out how far they go and what they do and catch some atmosphere and where they go no doubt and to get tape—somehow they get, this all goes on those whirling things in a place called Digis on tape. I don't know how they do it and, in any case, this man has just told me this is what he is about to do. Now, I have to answer in kind, surely I have to tell him how I came to get stuffed away up there. Oh, this is a little harder isn't it because here is a man, you must be tender, to here is a man who has got to live with himself over the next 18 months. I think they let him, you know, get a free pass or some sort of transportation in that time, but you must treat him tenderly. You can't let him have the north all in one barrel so to speak. So what do you say? Well, umm, what do you say? I suppose you sort of try and become truthful with yourself. This is tough. It is so nearly impossible that it takes all these miles and all this understanding, and perhaps a need for human company to perhaps make it possible when you're making a trip over the same track that you came in on two hours and a half ago. I'm just guessing now, this is part to get at. So, you begin by saying, "Oh well, we did, at least some of us, thought that this was a challenge a while back." He looks at you sort of—Well, surely it is a challenge now. I mean, this is the first time he has been on these rails that run north and incidentally east to get to Churchill.

Oh, yes, you say, but the challenge was different then. Well, you know he has got to listen. He's a captive audience; incidentally you've been one up to now because you know he's got to tell somebody this business about his research and his hopes, he is a young fellow and so on—You don't want to, oh, you know, smash his dreams before it becomes a sort of—has dimensions. So what do you say? You just say "alright." A few years back certainly in human memory, people thought that this, well what we call our north, well it's just northern Manitoba, it's not the great beyond, it's not the Arctic Circle. This is not the North Pole you say. These things, indeed, even in northern Manitoba presented a real challenge. Now what form did it take? what form, as if everything must have somehow a form that you can sort of put in words. This is hard, this is hard on you. He must notice that you're struggling a bit. But what you're really saying is something like this: That the north that was, is certainly never the north that is and will hardly recognize that the north that is yet to be. Surely there is a stretch in there that he is able perhaps to reach for. What is it the chap said, what is it? Your reach should exceed your grasp somehow, or what is a heaven for. Well, of course you don't try and tell him, but you try and indicate this by the fact that there was a time when the challenge was understandable.

What challenge, then? Oh, well here you have to take it easy, you have to put it somehow in your own words, you have to say this is a challenge. Alright, let's get at it. A certain William James, then, perhaps up to the turn of this twentieth century said that there was no moral equivalent of war. Well, I read that. There is no moral equivalent, said William James; no moral equivalent of war. That is, that there is nothing like war for providing something for you to be against. Apparently, in this north or in this south or in this east, or in this west, very few of us can be, can afford to be "for" something. Apparently all of us can be against something. Alright then, so I can tell this chap, this Defense research chap heading for Churchill, that we can all be fellow men when we know what we're against. We never seem to know what we are for, right enough, but what are we against in this situation where we are rolling north, the endless miles of steel, clickety-clack of the rails, the punctuated monotony of the telegraph wires outside of the day coach window. Now, this and that which make us at least fellow humans. Well, we're, I'm almost, I find it impossible to get this over except to say to this chap who is bound to listen because the miles are bound to stretch out and the night is going to fall endlessly it seems.

There is going to be a little place called Pikwitonei at mile 214 and he will wonder why the train is standing this long at this lonely spot and the darkness of night is going to surround him and then we're going to back up and he is going to be twice as perplexed and in order to answer this perplexity I'm going to say this: William James who wrote in Harvard this many years ago, whatever he did, I suppose he meant really not war, the moral equivalent for us I guess is going north. Oh, he says for us, he's willing now to be a fellow traveler in my, of my imagination. So we are going north and we are fighting against a common enemy of both of us, be it now or yesterday, or forever. I suppose this common enemy is Mother Nature. When I say that, of course, I suppose I'm explaining it to this man I'm up against it because he's got one of these social-scientific minds. I feel embarrassed telling him or suggesting to him that there is something more than figures and quantitative things and measurable things that enter into the whole picture of how you get along with yourself, or if you get along with yourself. He's a young—he's a nice fellow, you know, I don't want to destroy his dream, also I don't want to smash my own, which is paper thin at times. So I go on to say that the north is the, is the war, that you can afford to be against Mother Nature if only humans make it possible. Well, he asks, "what's wrong with that, what's good about that or bad about that?" Well, I said, there was a time believe me in living memory again when humans used to combine against Mother Nature not only because they had to, but because in a sense there was a cleanliness, a sureness, a definiteness about coming up with Mother Nature that is lacking in our stony hearted sidewalks, in our rootless pavements, in our big city anonymity. You—he shrinks from this, he has got to listen though, remember, the train is barely pulling out. There's almost, you know, how many hours are left in his mind, I have no idea, but perhaps he hasn't any idea either.

So, we are up against this William James bit, the moral equivalent of war. The equivalent of this war now is the north. We are willing to fight it because as humans we make not an inroad on Mother Nature but we come to an understanding with ourselves when we face nature aided by our fellow men. Well, now, of course I get into a complaining mood shortly after this; he looks at me questioningly and my patience, my patience perhaps with myself runs out. And I say yes, that's as I saw the north that was. No longer do humans combine to defy, to measure, or to read, or to understand, or to live with this thing we call Mother Nature. But somehow now the human nature business is taking over. Our number one enemy is now of course human nature. It's crept stealthy from the south not necessarily by steel, all these long and endless miles we sort of passed. And now is it infecting, it's infecting the north with a contagion that's, I know whatever it is. I don't dare tell this person that it's that bad, I just indicate it. Well, he is not, he is willing to listen, remember captive audiences being what they are. He has to go along with it.

Q. The latitudinal factor

A. Well, regionally, why would a person, say, like the northern part of Manitoba. What is there to attract; well of course, one thing that does attract is minerals. Surely we don't have to be magnetically inclined to understand there is nickel in quantity in and around Thompson, which will soon surpass Sudbury; however, this is not necessarily the end of—the reason why a region attracts. Even as perhaps as my father did before, going to Labrador for some obscure reason, possibly to do with the forestry, possibility to do with something else. I found the north had a certain attractiveness, which somehow isn't answered by Robert W. Service. I thought the north had a certain attractiveness that wasn't really answered by the *Songs of a Sourdough* the sort of Robert W. Service business, in fact I found that in going north from Winnipeg. Oh, it is almost worth getting something out of this, I went north from Winnipeg because of a certain challenge. But why did I come to Winnipeg from Toronto? Well, in those days I had the feeling that Toronto, although it was a big town, had something of a small mind. You know, I thought of it as a small-minded big town, you may not want to believe this. Now in coming to Winnipeg I thought I was coming from a small-minded big town, and where do you think I was arriving? At Portage and Main, at the wind-swept center of a big-minded small town. Thank you. And thus it is with the north.

It somehow challenged me without this structure, without this business of being able to praise it. Not simply because of its future in terms of dollars and no doubt common sense, but in other terms that I couldn't define for myself. So, I suppose this, as much as anything else, was the challenge and my response to it was another thing indeed.

Q. Book-lined box car

A. Well, when you say book-lined box car it is more like a box car with a number on it that is stuffed with books. Actually, it is a bunk car. When you say it is a box car that reduces it to one of, say, a hundred thousand such red cars that a certain publicly owned railway operates from coast-to-coast and, indeed, in [Newfoundland] if we must get specific.

So, this bunk car that was stuffed full of paperback books, because, of course, they take less space, was one of the things I forced myself to do. It is as simple as this: I would never have read them unless I got them somehow, I had them with me when there was nothing else to read but tomato cans. So I get stuffed in a lonely siding, only me and the wolves, or whatever, and I find myself reading into the endless night, these confounded books. And then, of course, once reading them, I challenge my fellow bunk mates and people like that. Oh, why didn't you get it—There is something here for you. Of course, I would be the department of useless information north of 53. Of course that's the answer there.

Q. Mass media

A. Oh, well, there is no question about this. In a remote area, I am, of course, a radio person. And, well, you like to be a choosy radio person even at that don't you? Here is where the rub comes into it, because unless you can sort of isolate yourself by an earplug business into a transistor set and listen to your own program, of course you are subject to the many various noises that come from three of four separate transistors in a single enclosed bunk car, now this is something else again. Rather than put up with the noise, that I suppose exists and I would prefer to almost get myself into another car or another location in order to listen to what I wanted to hear, however this is one of those big problems as far as I am concerned, not a small one. I claim that those of us who must be creatures of radio, of must be listeners, I think the title of that British publication, that is actually called the *Listener*, comes out every Thursday. I am indeed a northern listener, and the pity of it all is that I am not always able to select what I want to hear. I hear what other people inflict upon me, you know the noise. And sometimes what it is, the noise of civilization and its discontents. Wow, just think of that. You are not isolated in this sense from, what did I call it before? The big city and its blues and the enormous sounds and sights, and things that are. What is it, things are in the saddle, somebody said a hundred years ago, and ride mankind.

Well, indeed they ride us. Now when they creeped into our bunk car through various transistor radios and blare at us as well, this is something, isn't it? So no matter what we do to try and escape them, unless we select and understand and use what we hear, we are lost indeed. Just not lost listeners but indeed lost people.

Q. The synthesizing approach

A. Well, I put it this way: Mass media is getting at us, through only two senses surely. The eye and the ear. We are not going to say we have the smellies or the feelies as yet. Alright, I do believe that being able to select, I do believe being able to reflect on that selection, makes you more than the mere analyst that most of us claim we are. You see, I think the world is riddled with analysts, I think it is haggard with self-appointed people who cut society apart and say, this part is worthless and this part is something else, and very little of it is community, certainly in spirit. So I say, that in detaching and in reflecting and in listening, I suppose I am able to not make a synopsis of, but to synthesize, to have this, sort of different rails meet in the infinity, which is our conscious hope. And very often then I am able to put more of a structure on this thing we call mass media than our fellow man. I hate to say it this way, but I am not other directed. I'm only to a small degree inner directed, but now I get to it. In fact, I am in part Riesman corrected, in any case, people like Erich Fromm and David Riesman are the people, that in a sense help with the mass media structuring if there is such a thing.

Q. Solitary

A. Well, now a solitary or a hermit? Yes I do. But there is such a thing as being a hermit by choice rather than being a hermit by, certainly, by a necessity. Now, it all depends whether you think you are in part answering a challenge, or escaping from yourself. Are you, in fact, escaping in any real way by retreating north or by retreating perhaps in any direction? This is very hard to answer. I am a solitary in some respects, I can reach peoples' minds by not interfering with the common squabbles of here and now. I am able, perhaps, to contemplate but then perhaps this is one of those terms. I am able to meditate without perhaps intending to do. You know, I like to think of myself as part of Shakespeare's, what was that, "Sweet are the uses of adversity"? I like to think that when I'm stuffed away up north in some forlorn place where there's not a section house or there's not a, perhaps not only an odd wolf or dog team within a long distance—I like to think that I'm getting along with myself. Not only that I'm getting along with myself but that I understand the problems that are, not the problems that I create. You see, I think we all create our own problems and if we haven't got some to discuss, that we would sooner be kicked than remain unnoticed. And so, in a way, it isn't retreating as hermit like a thing as I sometimes think it is.

Q. Perspective

A. No, does solitude enhance—Well, there is always, always this tendency when you lead what amounts to, when you lead this sort of life. You sort of make up for it when you first re-enter civilization do you do something like, you bubble over, you tell people the last five or 10 things that are on your mind and they get the feeling that somebody is absolutely charged with *aurora borealis* or some other confounded thing that comes out of the north they can't understand, so in this way you feel you have something to offer that is not particularly structured. That is, you have something to—well—thought. You reach certainly peoples' mind, whether it is the printed word or whether it is listening—special programs of one kind or another, and you are surprised at times having selected something which you want to listen to. To find out it has a great deal to say that you have already thought, say, more than have these thoughts and you are able to articulate. This is the nice part, you're able to say something further along those lines, you're able to project it as it were into its next stage and when you can do this you feel so pleased with yourself that the only tragedy of it is that you're not immediately able to tell some poor listener that you know how interesting this next step is about to become.

Q. Type of solitary and environmental feature

A. Well, what appeals to a person in order to have him get along with himself, that is really what we are thinking about. My claim, of course, is that when you have a physical challenge, that, answering it brings you a physical glow. It is not a very far step for you to round out your evening, let's say, by having not an intellectual glow or not a mental sort of feeling of euphoria but something special that comes with having a rounded existence you are physically, well, because of your fight against blasts and temperatures and the actual outdoors. Mark you, this must be outdoors or this thing is not relevant. To sit in a cooped up tiny cubicle of an office, punching away at this typewriter, you are almost part of the typewriter whether you are north, south, or anywhere. But if, in fact, you are measuring the stony features of Mother Nature herself, there is something, I don't say refreshing, there is something that is so physically challenged that you are willing to accept a mental challenge the same evening. Indeed you are and this makes these two—the physical and perhaps the other, and when you say the other you can throw in all these things you may want to do. I don't like to analyze too far like I say the world is full of analysts and the world is trying to synthesize these threads of sense or these structural things into something that has a wholeness or a realness about it.

Q. The romantic north and disillusionment

A. Well, the north is dillusioning [sic]. I sometimes think that the north to me—you could almost make it the same as a Christmas tree in your early days. Long ago and far away a Christmas tree used to be the height of something. It used to have—with its very breakable ornaments close to the ground, these of course are the illusions of your ideas of the north. These soon break, they soon destroy, the dog doesn't have to chase the cat very long to have these baubles, these colorful things, these illusions of the north destroyed and smashed. Now, what is left of the north that is still unbroken, I wonder. Sometimes we think very little, sometimes we think the very green of the lovely evergreen tree, which is our Christmas, that is our home, has become a sort of a grey. Whether these flashing lights, the star above and what not still exist for us as would-be northerners, is open, ah, is not only open to questions, it is seriously a matter for us to deplore, perhaps, because our illusions have been shattered in many cases. And perhaps the only thing that remains, the single star at the top of this tree.

Q. The technological invasion

A. Well, now when we sort of parallel what has been the national anthem and speak about the true north as opposed to the pseudo north, the north above the Arctic Circle, as opposed to any other degree of north, I don't believe by that perhaps by just retreating further against more, well, against fearful odds is perhaps the answer. With others it may be. There is no real answer in simply appealing to a direction in your own mind. Now, most of us have got a built-in sense of direction that is physical, that is to say north, south, east, west. We all have a gyro compass that gives us inner direction or a sense of possible purpose, certainly a sense of awareness that we don't properly understand ourselves. Now, this gyro compass I talk about is directional in this way that it points us to a direction but it rarely recognizes the landmarks. Very often we travel in two ways. We travel either by pinpointing at some point in our journey, something we can say we know this place; we go from the known securely to the unknown. But this gyro compass of ourselves, our inner self if you like, has got a direction that has nothing to do with the physical north or perhaps any other direction. So I don't pretend that the answer to one retreat, if indeed it is a retreat from reality to the pseudo north, can be answered by a further retreat, sitting on top of the North Pole itself.

Q. Road and rail building.

A. Well, when we discuss and think of road and rail building, we are of course trying to get at surface transportation. When we do that we are up against these little—what are these little strange devices that we see that are able to move when we talk about surface transportation we are simply projecting our ideas of road building, of rail enterprise, and building beyond where it now exists. Now we've seen maps, Northern Affairs, have had them out for years where the north and beyond to the Arctic Circle has sort of been reached by rail and indeed it is in Russia. It is also equally important to think that the roads whether two resources or otherwise are vital if there are people to be serviced by them. Now some people say, but a road to resources must, in fact, have a resource to reach before it becomes, well, feasible, possibly useful. I would say that this is only partly true. I don't think that we should, as has been claimed by Eric Nicol simply build railroads for the joy of building railroads. Nor do I think that our sort of vision of the new north is simply to be answered by roads that run off in all directions something like Stephen Leacock's horse, if you remember the one. I therefore feel that the other means of transportation are now the ones that become of equal or greater importance. I mean things that will travel on the level, strange, perhaps, devices that will go over Muskeg a few feet above with jets to support them. These new ways of transportation as well as our ways of communication, incidentally, it always gives me a shock to think that communication is simply the transfer of messages whereas transportation is also the transfer of things, so the two are really the same thing; the two. No, just whatever we can say about the possibilities of road building further north, the possibilities of a rail endeavor in those parts, which is great because it's virtually desert, there is very little snow, this is a thing that people don't realize about the barren land which we are not discussing. Just short of Churchill, for example, there is very little snowfall. We all think of it of course otherwise and we're wrong, so railways are in fact feasible but they are no longer the same thing they were in the development of this, our country, from east to west. Granted, we would like to see lines of steel from north to south, to break this monotony of having a country that is held together only by the other sort of direction. But I say by-and-large the other means of transportation and possibly other means of communication, in fact, are part of the answer to the north as it beckons.

Q. More Fellinis

A. Well, yes—yes—ah, yes—certainly—well about that, of course yes . . . . Oh oh yes . . . about that whole field I would say yes . . . no, no, I'd say YES . . . AH, yes, ah yes . . . Well now perhaps . . . perhaps . . . perhaps not though. I'd say maybe . . . maybe . . . why not . . . there's a chance only a chance that this is true, above all though I have to qualify that or I won't get along with myself . . . oh granted . . . I'll give you that . . . mark you.

Q. Technological invasion—inner direction

A. Well, now if we, each of us as individuals have this gyro compass built in, how come I think that perhaps a sense of direction not necessarily normal is far more important than today's landmarks? The things of here and now which seem to be with us. Well, I get the feeling that we all have our own guiding systems long before ballistic missiles and what not sort of filled the air. So the compass belongs to the individual and if you can switch, why not switch here and say our own inner compass has to do with the proper study. Who was it said the proper study of mankind is man then who followed up by saying man's inhumanity to man? Oh, ya, man's inhumanity to man makes countless thousands mourn. I always forget that latter part by Robert Burns of a couple centuries back. What then, considering all this guidance business have we got today? We seem to have man's indifference to his real self. I don't know whether you would say his proper self because that gives it a scuffy [sic] overtone. Man's indifference to his inner or the self that is going to save him perhaps, although I don't want salvation to be the need of the individual as such what prevents this business of man listening to himself. Does he listen with his inner ear? Has he got an inner psychic ear somewhere? How does he listen? We know, perhaps, why he listens because of the pressures of here and now are perhaps increasing can he listen to himself without distortion. If it is amplified what happens to the little message, the little the message—the still small voice, of calm not of conscious maybe, in other words, I suppose what I'm getting at, what price serenity? We used to say what price glory, what price this and that. Now what price serenity.

What do you wind up with when you listen to yourself? None do these days. We inflict ourselves with noise and we are told, at least those who are electronically geared, tell us that we need something that is called a negative feedback, ever since, what was it, 1927 can correct ourselves whether as individuals or as a society. Well isn't that nice. A person like what's that name from MIT? Norbert Wiener, with a book called *Cybernetics*, the human use of human beings, wanted us somehow to accept the stimuli as he, I guess he calls, the impulses, the messages to steer ourselves toward a useful common goal. Well, I wonder if he had any idea of trying to build this sort of self-steering device on the background of what Russia gave us; Pavlov he was the man who had something to do with reflex but a special kind, ah, wait a minute, when the doctor hits you on the knee you hit him in the teeth, conditioned reflex you see. Now, if Mr. Pavlov was right in 1930 odd and Mr. Norbert Wiener, if Norbert Wiener in his idea of steering society is right and if in fact Ivan Pavlov, this strange Russian is correct in his conditioned reflex action idea, surely there is quite a case for building by special stimuli our responses as individuals so that society can get along with itself as well as with the individual. Will this make an individual lose what little is left of his personality? Hmm, that is a question isn't it? How much can you afford to lose of yourself in order to get along with the rest of us all? Perhaps precious little in these days of howling individualism.

Q. Sub insert to transportation question

A. Well, now everybody has a whack at the future of transportation. In fact everybody has a whack at the future of communication as well with knowing just as little about it perhaps. When I see that Canada has—well—50,000 miles of steel, that's the railway and when I see the U.S. of recent date has perhaps 250,000 miles of the same steel, that's two tracks incidentally, then we get a sort of an idea that Canada with one tenth of the population has of course, almost a quarter of the actual rail to carry itself across from east to west, presumably increasingly from north to south or south to north, as the Pine Point Rail line recently built would indicate.

Now, let us not forget that the old and established railroad, the roads to resources are important and well remain so to uncover those resources, but basically the railway of course must be for base metals for heavy roads. It's not for specialized things that can be lifted or transported in other ways. For this we turn to the hovercraft, it's worth mentioning (here begins extended anecdote re: Port Manager Churchill)—————

[*Item in parentheses was not transcribed. The text appears as it did in the transcript with many long dashes and interview text truncated.*]

No, I'd say the standard methods of rail and road with human resources as well as the natural ones of nickel and of other base metals are the predominant ones. I think the fringe benefits only are to be met by these strange and unusual two-seater hovercraft this or that special equipment. I do not think that they are the generalized answer.

Q. Sub insert to solitary

A. All of us perhaps then would sooner be kicked than remain unnoticed. It seems to me that ah, that a man by the name of Pascal, years back, said that most of mankind's troubles would be over with or done away with if he would stay in his own room. At the time I thought this was such a self-evident, banal, a sort of, well, silly thing to say that I gave it little thought. But then I, on looking back, perhaps after a few decades, I thought to myself how indeed true this is. Can a man get along with himself usually in this solitary life of the hermit north or the solitary life of any place where he secludes himself, where he, in a sense, I guess what he really does is to, what is the word, when you insulate yourself, yes. You insulate yourself against isolation in various ways. To do this, of course, you must have something called inner resource. Now this is such a field that we won't, there's no use running at it, is there, inner resources and your own little self, usually when you are faced with yourself alone, and what the existential people call nothingness, the sort of yawning gap of just you and no one to talk to. Ah, it does drive you into a sort of non-acceptance perhaps of yourself and it is easier actually to be a little bit concerned about society and critical of it because you are so self-critical you don't want to face it. You don't want to have anything to do with this nasty person that is you, of course.

Q. Sub question anthropology excerpts only

A. Well, anthropology, as such, eh, surely it is a studying of different cultures, the cultures of both the present and the past. What can we learn from the mores, the customs, the ways of life of those in different climates, different centuries, with different traditions. What can be gained if we stress the similarities of these civilizations as, perhaps, who was it, Toynbee—If we look at the overlap of cause and effect, the unaccountable by-products of conflict or conquest. What is added if we note the difference in cultures, the tribal customs—(Mead, etc.)—What adjectives can you use when you're describing anthropology. Well, you can call it social anthropology, etc.— —(social versus cultural—applied and physical anthropology)—(Voltaire and adjectives, etc.)— —You know there are far too many people that, when they discuss anthropology it is almost an apology for anthropology if you'll excuse me saying so.

Q. Sociology

A. I think sociology is separate enough. They usually say that it's one of those social sciences and I object to the word "social" in front of the word "scientist." A scientist then broadly disciplined in social competence. Well, does that mean he can pass trays or accept drinks, or what does it mean, eh? Then sociology based on an attempt to somehow evaluate and analyze man's behavior, well as an individual, then you have to compare it with his mass behavior and then you have to say a little bit qualifying that it is basically in our own society, once again you are very careful to say society, you rarely say community unless you mean it. A little later we find that society breaks outwards. I think you call it centrifugal force whereas community has a way of being centripetal, it works inwards towards a core that we have in common. There are two great German words for it and I can't pronounce either. One's *Gesellschaft* and one's *Gereinschfant*, and the former is society and the latter is community, however.

— — —La foule etc.— —Hitler etc.— —Riesman's etc.— —Instincts of the Herd in Peace and War— —This man, this real sociologist is engaged in structuring society, very little of this structure is applicable; it just doesn't sort of fit on the face of society as it's not composed or possibly decomposed, so the basic society we went on to say, the basic difference between society and community is the tendency for one to fly outwards. That is society where we are competitive and a tendency for us to cohere in a community when we have a common purpose. Fine, this is of course an actual upgrading of social effort [that] can be felt in things like, well, continuing education, what is it, adult education. A discussion that makes a community possible in an otherwise fragmented segment of society. Always present is this increasing anomie— —alienation etc.— —This person that gets out of touch is me, this person that is out of touch at times is you. Of course, I don't like the word anomie that well, social disorganization it is apt to be called by sociologists, I'd sooner, I would sooner call it social entropy. I'm trying to use a thermodynamic term there because I think there is a tendency towards destruction that is inherent in our very makeup because it is a way of being transcendent. You can either create or equally you can destroy, and we rarely think of both as being opposite sides of the same coin of reality.

Q. Social work

A. In the north that lies ahead of us, in the north of the future, we can see the great shape of tourism coming up, in all its glory, not just from the south and east and west, but all us it appears want to distribute ourselves over, say, northern Manitoba hinterlands, and this works almost directly as what we come to know as welfare. On the one hand we are trying to look after races and people that have long been the first Canadians perhaps but they're the last Canadians who have benefitted from our common sort of citizenship. What I'm saying is that these two work so directly against each other. That we are, in a sense, becoming a tourist paradise but it's hell for the Indian put in that way. Of course, etc.— —nickel etc.— —Whether the new north, the north of the future, is the true north, is open to doubt. And here of course, one of the greatest things we come to doubt about it what we know as social work.— —(cup in hand charity, etc.)— —always re something etc.— —

6. Frank Vallee Interview Transcript

Q. Biographer

A. I went to Baker Lake in 1959 for the summer. I was teaching at McMaster University and was approached by people in Northern Affairs to try my hand at doing a little community study up in the, somewhere in the north and it was felt that this particular area, Baker Lake, which is the inland as you know, the stomping ground of the Caribou Eskimo, so called. There was less known about this group of Eskimos than there was known about other Eskimos in the coastal regions and new settlements such as Frobisher Bay. So, I went up there a complete greenhorn, having had a bit of experience in doing community studies, that experience having been with the Gaelic speaking Hebrideans off the west coast of Scotland, but never having in my life seen an Eskimo.

I found that the expectations I had, the images that I had built about the place had to be revised after I had been there about five minutes. The people that I met, the ones that approached me when I got off the plane and who quote "took me in," and were very nice to me were the people who were very much like the people whom I had left down south. They were kabloona, as the Eskimos call the white man and most of them were civil servants. One of them was a policeman, most of them were, shall I say, bureaucratically oriented. That is, they had belonged to institutions of one kind of another, whether the RCMP or the Department of Transport or the Northern Affairs Department for quite a long time. And I could see right away we talked the same language, because I had been a member of such large organizations for a long time too. I found that I was, in a sense, screened by people like this from meeting initially. The people I had come to look at primarily, although I should point out I wasn't there only to study the Eskimos, the white, or kabloona, or whatever you call them, interacting with one another. It wasn't a piece of Eskimology but nevertheless I had counted on mixing in very quickly with the Eskimos and I found I was taken in by the white. They didn't do this deliberately, it's just quite a natural thing when another white person arrives for the first time. The people on the ground want to know what he's about, they want to "protect him" from the unknown things that might happen to him, unknown from his point of view.

It took me quite a while to establish any kind of links with the Eskimos, and of course in order to do this I had to do it with, I should say through Eskimo people who spoke English, and the only ones who spoke English at that time in Baker Lake were young people, young kids. So, I found myself very much in the company of younger people and initially seeing the world through their eyes as well as through the eyes of the whites. As I said, the images that I had brought with me into the place were not shattered, they had to be changed quickly. It wasn't until I got out of the settlement into what they call the land—that's the term they use to denote those places where people live outside of settlements—I got out to a land camp and I began to feel that I really was with people from another culture or even another time. Unfortunately, my first visit out to the land occurred during a flu epidemic when the small camp I visited was completely ravaged by flu. The people there mistake me for a doctor because my luggage had arrived in Baker Lake with my name Dr. Frank Vallee stamped all over it, and of course they thought I was "luchtak," which means a medical doctor in Eskimo, and I wasn't, so I had quite a time in this camp, dispensing medicine, which I picked up at the nursing station, at the same time trying to assure everyone I wasn't a doctor. Of course, I couldn't speak any Eskimo and the only one that could speak English was my interpreter whose grasp of English at that time wasn't very good. Well, I did after a few weeks in that camp come to feel that there was another way of life, sputtering with faint life somewhere in the vicinity, and that this was the kind of thing which those people who profess to be north men, this is the kind of thing that they profess to want to go out and live on the land with people, out in the open air and all that kind of stuff.

That was the first time I'd tasted that and even that after a while got to pale on me because I found that the wide-open spaces concept, the concept that when you get out there in the wide-open spaces, it isn't quite what it's cracked up to be, at least for me it wasn't. And this perhaps because I was brought up in a city, and in a large city for that matter, and had not been oriented to the open spaces. I found that I felt cooped in in the wide-open spaces because I was so afraid to get lost—that the environment around me, while being vast in the physical sense, one could see theoretically for a thousand miles because there's nothing in the way to block your view. No habitation in between where you were and the place you're looking at. Theoretically, you could have felt that you were in a great void with no boundaries around you but realistically I felt that I was surrounded on each side by dangers, dangers for instance of getting lost. This was to me the biggest danger of all so that whenever I went out on dog sled trips, for instance, I would find that if I would want to wander away from the camp for a certain purpose, you don't have to be explicit about the purpose, I would be terrified. Well, I was terrified on one occasion I remember, when I wandered about 100 yards away and then couldn't find the camp, couldn't find the snow house, came back, and it was then that it struck me that the wide-open spaces do not have the connotation, which they have to romanticize in the south where you feel free and you feel, they say, rattling around in a void. Rather, I felt as if I had real walls around me. There weren't any out there, the walls were those of my own making.

Now this was one of the things I hadn't expected to feel up there. In other words, I felt more restricted than I feel, say, in the east end of Montreal. This was another thing that I picked up quite early in the game in my visits to Baker Lake. I went back there again in the summer of 1960 when, at that time, I wasn't able to get a year off. I hadn't been at the university long enough to warrant a leave of absence and so it wasn't until 1962 that I was able to take a whole year and spend the winter and spring, fall as well as the summer in the Arctic. In the second summer I moved around a bit more and saw Rankin Inlet, which, at the time, was quite a, well, it was a place to where Eskimos were moving. I don't know whether you're familiar with it, moving to work in the mines. There were a few hundred working in the mines and there was a great deal of dispute going on as to whether this was a wise thing to do, that is, was it wise to encourage the Eskimos to do this? It was said it wasn't in their nature to work in mines, it wasn't in their nature to observe the time schedules that we have, and so on.

So, I found it fascinating to actually live in that community for three or four weeks, while it was the center of controversy among these people who engage in the debates in what I call the art of northmanship. The debate that is about how the soul and culture of the Eskimos are going to be saved. Baker Lake, I revisited after, let me see, five years, in 19—, no after six years. I had the opportunity of going back for a very brief visit and found it completely changed physically, when I had gone there at first the hovels that the people were living in contrasted with the comfortable homes of the whites. It was something that would bother anyone's conscience, I would think. When I went back, the hovels had been replaced by small houses that were at least neat and roomier than the other ones, the people had abandoned most of their dogs apparently and were driving Skidoos on trapping trips. Superficially, things looked quite different but after poking around for a few hours and seeing some of my old friends and talking to them I gathered the relationships among people hadn't changed very much. That the, it was still pretty much a segregated social system in the place and that the Eskimos had a world of their own and the whites had a world of their own, and these two worlds overlapped at some points, but there wasn't very much intense mixing and seeing eye-to-eye going on. That is about all I can think of offhand.

Q. The degrees of north

A. I don't think, well, yes—————I don't think it was the north itself, I think, like every Canadian, I grew up with this notion that this is a northern nation and that one should want to go north and all that kind of thing and it perhaps, in that respect, I wasn't unique except I must say there aren't very many people who take advantage of the opportunity to go north because one of the other things that I discovered up there is that a higher proportion of the people who were not born there, the people that is, the whites who come from outside, a higher proportion of the people up there are not Canadians, than are people who live in the provinces so that one finds among the nurses for instance, a large proportion of girls from Australia, Scotland, and places like that. The doctors are mostly, I think, I haven't done a careful statistical check on this, but my impression is that the doctors are mostly of European origin. The Hudson Bay Co. of course, the bulk of the men in the Hudson Bay Co. were from Scotland and secondarily from Newfoundland. I think the RCMP perhaps had the highest proportion of people who had been born in Canada. The missionaries were—most of them, the ones that I met, from Belgium in the case of the Catholics, Belgium, Holland, France. Or, in the case of the Anglican church from England so that, again, when I went up there, I thought perhaps I'm satisfying some urge that's part of the culture. I'm part of the culture too so this is one reason I'm going up there, to be like other Canadians. When I got there, I found there weren't very many Canadians around, unless you want to count the Eskimos as Canadians.

But it was primarily a matter of my having this kind of vague or latent interest in the north. Secondly, my interest in people who live in small groups, who live in small group societies, shall we say, who are under the gun of change, technological change, and so on. I was interested in these, for instance when I was in Scotland I lived in the Hebrides of Scotland where they were putting up rocket bases and this kind of thing and here was this almost a classic small group of society being invaded by the technological age and the industrial society. Then I found myself, I shouldn't say "found myself," I can't remember how I got into it, but the next thing I know I'm studying the tinkers and gypsies and moving around with them on the mainland of Scotland. Again, a small, the kind of people who live in small groups, upon whom there is this pressure from the massive surrounding society, I also had this kind of interest, which, as far as I'm concerned, made the northern country a fitting place to satisfy these kinds of interests. Thirdly, perhaps most important, there were people working in Northern Affairs at the time trying to organize research programs who knew I had these kinds of interests in technological change among small group people and who persuaded me to take advantage of the contracts they would offer and go up there. So, I'm afraid it is not very romantic, you know, my wanting to go up there to find myself or to lose myself for all these various reasons that people give for going to the north. Frankly, I think that most of these for the bulk of people, most of these are rationalizations, these reasons that people give. You find that most of the people that are up there now are members of some kind of bureaucracy, one bureaucracy or another. Hudson's Bay Co. is a bureaucracy; the clergy, the Catholic clergy, the Anglican clergy, this is a bureaucracy or these are bureaucracies, I should say. The school system, the administrators, all these people belong to bureaucracies and it's part of their job to go up to places like this and to play some kind of a role in developing the north, but [it] is also part of the motivation having to do with their own moving through the system. The fact that they're north gives them some extra kudos. I guess they feel, "What a sacrifice I'm making for Canada up here," but perhaps I'm a bit cynical. I don't go for this kind of stuff.

Q. The deromanticizing north

A. I don't know, I think it's something like marriage. I guess if you, a person who romanticizes or idolizes his girlfriend, and refuses to quote "see reality" as his parents said, well, look, her teeth are falling out. Well, a person refuses to see this and insists on marrying the girl. He discovers after a while that the parents were right perhaps and so he gets disenchanted, right? Now, the reasons for his disenchantment are primarily those of over idolizing, having a wrong image of what he's getting linked up with, but then what he does about it is another matter. It's just not self-evident what persons do about their disenchantment. I think the north is something like that. I've met many people who have gone up there as teachers, for instance, and they refuse to believe you when you tell them before they go up there. Look, you're going to run into what are regarded as quite ugly situations in towns; the segregation, the people who aren't too cheerful, but they cling to this fantasy that they're going to be pinching the cheeks of those nice, fat children and they're going to be helping the parents to adjust and all this kind of stuff. When they get up there, they find, well if they're dealing with the sort of baby classes, the young kids, sure enough they do pinch the cheeks and squeeze the kids, because they are very squeezable little round kids, but then they find they're not getting through very much to the parents. They find they are in a very routinized job; they find that the message that they're carrying isn't being bought by the people. And so you get this process of disenchantment. With such people, again, if they have an over-romanticized picture of what they're going to run into when they get there. What they do about their disenchantment is another matter. One can simply withdraw as I've seen people do. Incidentally, I have just used the example with teachers. This applies to social workers and all kinds of people up there, not just the teachers. I've used them as an example but I've seen people who are disenchanted with the north simply withdraw and concentrate on some activity like fixing, cleaning guns, and collecting guns and stuff like that, or stamps or whatever, and sort of withdrawing into a cocoon and just going through the motions in almost a ritual way of carrying out their jobs. I've seen other people who have turned against their employers or against the government, for instance, and say "if it weren't for them everything would be alright" and to hit out at Ottawa. Other people turn against those that they came to help and with "these stupid Eskimos, they're still in the stone age." You get this variety of reactions and the most common one of course is simply to take off. Well, I think I'll try Africa or some other place where the people need me.

Q. Technological invasion

A. Yes, well perhaps I have the wrong impression. Anthropologists tend to look for people who have been relatively untouched by influences from outside their own culture and their justification for this is that they are trying to find cultures that are as much different as possible from our own, and which are in danger of disappearing, to record them while they're still alive and that kind of thing you see. So, they do tend to press against the frontiers and to look for the more and more remote people and to look with some scorn and disdain. Those people say it is the case of the Eskimos who are being swallowed up by the surrounding society. But I don't have that approach. To me, any human group is worth looking at and what I mean is worth giving yourself to, entering into a composition or something like that and you work your way through it. You might like one kind of music better than another kind of music but nevertheless there's at a certain level, it doesn't matter what kind of music. You're giving yourself and getting feedback from it. Well, I find that in just about any human group with which I've mixed. I have this approach which is perhaps the measure of the kind of detachment I try to maintain. I didn't know I've never analyzed myself. There are other people like the Honigmanns, for instance, are like this; John Honigmann, Irma Honigmann from North Carolina. They're anthropologists and one would expect if they are acting according to the stereotype that they would go off to Axel Heiberg or some place and find people who haven't been touched but no, they chose to go to Frobisher Bay and did an excellent study of Frobisher Bay and they did it much more realistically, I think, than the reports that I've seen on the parts of other people who are supposed to know a lot about Frobisher Bay. No, in my case, I think the, I don't go, let me say this again, I don't go for this northmanship bit at all. I don't knock these people who do claim that they want to go farther and farther north and so on but I see it as a kind of game, this northmanship bit. People say, well, you know,

"Were you ever up at the north pole? You know, hell, I did a dog sled trip in 22 days," and the other fellow says, "Well I did one of 30 days." You know, it's very childish. It goes on like this as though there's some special merit, some virtue to being in the north or some special virtue in having been with primitive people. You know, what special virtue is there in that? And so, I think that I'd be more interested in Baker Lake right now if, indeed, it is changing significantly, which I doubt very much, if it is changing. It's changing but I doubt if it is changing that significantly. More interested in that than I think I would be in going way up to, well I can't think of any place left outside of Pelly Bay and a few places like that, which are still markedly primitive in the sense that they don't have much in the way of technological accoutrements and stuff like that.

Q. Solitary

A. Ya, I think the latter is true. I was too preoccupied with one thing about the north that, apart from the few people who have hermit-like inclinations, most people who go there enter into more intensive mixing with other people than they do in the south. You go into a community like Resolute Bay for instance. I should perhaps not call it a community, it's—I'm not talking about the Eskimo community, I'm talking about the white one, you know, which I call the yellow submarine; they live in these buildings which are all sort of joined together and painted an orange color, which reminds me of the Beatles song "we all live in a yellow submarine," and there you're constantly in touch with other people. You even sleep in a bunk hou—no, not bunk houses in these rooms with four or five other guys. You're working with other people, you're in a lounge, you eat together in a huge dining room, the interaction with other people is very intense and because you're cut off from your environment because you're afraid to go out any more than five miles from the camp lest you get lost. Again, you're thrown more onto other people so that the illusion of isolation, at least social isolation, well, let me put it this way, social isolation in the north is an illusion except for those people who deliberately take off from the settlement and go out and spend a couple of weeks at a time on the trail. Now, physical, geographical isolation is something you do feel. You're missing the Grey Cup, you're missing this and whatever is going on and that you would like to take off and see another community where the buildings don't all look the same. And so there is something in that feeling of physical isolation but that's—I would distinguish that from social isolation, and I would say that the people in the north on the whole are less socially isolated from one another, from networks of friendship and all that, than those in the south who are more isolated than, say, one of those fellows selling pencils with no legs, sitting against a wall of a department store in Times Square, trying to sell his pencils and, regarded as part of the street furniture by others. He's the most isolated guy in the world, yet there are millions of people passing him all over the place. That sort of isolation is not common in the north. People don't like it except, again, I come back to some people who claim they do, like trappers, white trappers specifically, they do like to get out on their own. Well, these are rare people. I haven't met many people like that in the north. Most people are ready to relate to others and indeed they find it hard to resist relating to others, the pressure is on you to join in and be part of the group and all that kind of thing in the north.

<u>Note GG interrupts</u>——————those white people who choose to go against the norms or rules of the community will feel the pressure very, very much. The—it's a highly conformist society, it's almost Victorian at times except backstage. You know, when the Eskimos can't see you it's a kind of backstage situation, maybe having parties in a remote, remote in a sense that people can't hear you from outside and so on, you might get a bit, well—sort of suburban like parties, that kind of thing goes on but otherwise there is a high degree of conformity among the outsiders there.

Q. Mass media

A. That's an interesting question I hadn't really thought of that. I think that, perhaps they see in, they would see themselves as more skeptical than others than those people who are outside. This term "inside" and "outside," "up here," and "outside," more skeptical about the offerings of the mass media, taking a stand that the world outside is too complex and complicated and so on. The mass media, which incidentally, don't reach very far into the far north, but where they do reach, I think the people tend to go for the more homey kind of things. For instance, the programs that seem to be the most popular from Frobisher Bay and from Yellowknife and these places tend to be the more homey kind of chatty things, personal messages sent to people, "I am in the hospital but will be getting out soon" kind of thing. With western music, church music, and morality plays, up in Frobisher now the Eskimo segment or element or whatever you call it in the broadcasting field puts on these morality plays where the man is in a drama, acted out on the radio. The man is made out to hammer his children when he is drunk. The message being "you shouldn't get drunk, drinking is a bad thing" and all that kind of stuff. They really go for this kind of thing in a big way. Now, the mass media, as we know it, when we think of the messages coming from "the center" whether it's "Big Brother" or whatever it is, the mass media haven't really reached into the far north with these kinds of messages. Of course, I think you can expect though that when the mass media do reach in there they will not have to compete too much with the printed word, as they have had to do to some extent in the south.

The printed word, newspapers and so on aren't of the same importance. The printed words, I should say, aren't of the same importance there as they are here. Although another interesting thing that is happening in the north is the burgeoning of the newspaper fields——small newspaper field. There are at least five small newspapers in the Northwest Territories but these are really not gossip sheets, exactly. That wouldn't be doing them justice. Some of them provide excellent editorials, but again, they're oriented very much to the local scene. You see, they're not oriented to the big picture as the mass media tend to be in the south. How the people would respond, I just can't see right now except to say that perhaps they would be a bit more skeptical about the kinds of messages they would get because they are supposed to be more grassroots like people who depend on face-to-face interaction and don't listen to some guy telling you who's thousands of miles away. This might be a selective factor making them a bit different in their response to the mass media.

Q. Discrimination and time lag

A. Yes, I think that, here you would have to distinguish between the generations. I think that the wee bits of evidence that we have from those urban places such as Frobisher Bay and Inuvik indicates the young people quickly pick up the styles that are current in the south. They would have more difficulty with miniskirts and that sort of thing, with the weather conditions if nothing else, but the rock and roll, the haircuts and these kinds of things, the way the girls dress.

Q. Conversational camouflage

A. No, I didn't notice it with respect to conversational style so much with respect to front perhaps in general. The conversational style is only one part of front and with respect to front, inevitably you're cast in a situation unless you really are a fantastic individualist and you have such a strong ego that you know, you can only act in one way with everyone in. I've never met such a person in my life but nevertheless it's a theoretical possibility unless you're like that. You find yourself adopting stances, which would of course improve the kind of conversational style you adopt vis-a-vis other people, like for instance, the Eskimos. Well, for one thing you have the language barrier and this calls for stereotyping, a stylizing of behavior with the other where you are different. It's something like one's confrontation with, say, a deaf person. Now, no doubt it's the same to the Eskimo looking at us. I'm not just talking now from my point of view, so that you do find yourself taking on, well, almost naked behavior. So you have a kind of masked persona, which you put on there, but with the others no, the interesting thing is with quote "your kind" unquote, the whites and so on, you find that to some extent you have to drop some of the specific fronts that you have, and if you're an RCMP there is a certain kind of style, I guess, when you're acting in office that you adopt and you're mixing in a place like that, with a Hudson's Bay Co. manager, with the manager of the Department of Transport radio station, with the teachers and so on. And because you're thrown together so much with these people you tend to become, to let your own person show through much more, your own inside, your ego show through more. This would be in contrast with the front that you adopt with the Eskimos, you see. I found that going on would affect the image, the conversation style, the conversational style becoming more ritualized, stylized if you will with the——in the case of the Eskimos and less so in the case of the others with whom you interact, provided of course you're on good terms with them, and this is a very important factor up there, being on good terms with people.

But you do get a deliberate building up of a kind of cult of personality, yet lots of people attempting to create a style of their own to be known as characters and this is wonderful, I'm all for it. Well, of course some people say it's hypocritical, well, to heck with that, this is good. People should have style. You get a lot of these old-timers, especially, well, I mind the time when I was forty days without food. And the idea that nothing can shake you is quite strong with some people up there, to this becomes part of the front, the stance, that nothing can shake us, that we are down to earth people. It's a cup of tea in your hand the minute you stick your head in the door and if I had a bottle, the last bottle, no plane coming in for, say, six months I'd still split this bottle with you because that's the way up north. There's a lot of that going on. That is to some extent stereotyped, although like most stereotypes, people get to believe it that this is the way they are even if that's not the way they were when they first went in. They come to believe this Pirandello and others point out that you come to believe in your own role.

Note GG interrupts

Q. The evolving Eskimo

A. Yes, I would say they would. They would be more individualistic. This doesn't mean that they don't appreciate being, that they're not gregarious, they don't appreciate being with other people, but they do value being for lengthy periods with—on their own, and when I say on their own, I don't mean in solitude, I mean with one's family, a group of relatives in one's band and their, this is very difficult to put this point that I want to make. The land people, as they're called in Nunamiut, is what I call the people who live on the land, tend to resist the kinds of situation where they become dependent on someone in the settlement. They're friendly with people in the settlement but they don't want to get themselves locked into dependency situations with them. It's almost as if they fear to lose something they have, some inner core of selfhood or something would be lost through too much interaction with people of the settlements, too much giving of one's self. It's like playing a role in the settlement. I know many Eskimos who live in the land and they come into a settlement there is nothing they like better to do than to go to a church service, to sing, and holler, and go to dances, to hang around the trading post, to do stuff like that. But as to playing a concrete role which ties you in the settlement, now that's a different matter, then you get identified with the networks in the settlements and, to the extent you do that so much of your selfhood, is given to the life there. Now, there are Eskimos who have been born and grown up in settlements and I'm talking about adult ones, not kids and they are many of them experts on the land. They like to go out too, hunting and stuff like that. But to them the trips, hunting, trapping, and fishing trips are really sidelights to a career which they have in a settlement, either as a Hudson's Bay assistant or a special constable with the RCMP. These people have roles in the settlement and often quite valuable ones; very often they are catechists that perform some kind of meaningful function although I must say many of them perform functions which we, from the outside, consider degrading, like honey bucket carriers.[5] I suppose you could put it this way: there are similarities between the people who live in settlements and who are committed to settlement living primarily, and those who are committed primarily to land camp living, there are similarities between them. It is still something to be proud of, a good traveler, and also that you're a good hunter and trapper.

Travelling is the secret of life up there; however, the land man depends primarily on this, the person in the settlement depends secondarily or tertiarily, or whatever you call it, but they do share the liking for that kind of life. What they don't share are roles in the community, in the settlement, the settlement people are committed to networks of kinship, networks of friendship, the networks of economics, the economic kind in a settlement were as the land camp people aren't, but of course this is becoming an academic question because there are so few land people left. There are some in the central Arctic, in the high Arctic, the distinction between being settlement or land is becoming meaningless.

Q. The Eskimo as aide de camp

A. They are not so much guiding the kabloona as they are advising and getting themselves into key positions. The people who have committed themselves to settlement living and particularly those who have received more than a let's say a grade five education is equivalent almost to a university degree in the Arctic right now. These people are becoming, they are keys in the networks of communication in the north. The outsider has to sort of pass through the screen of these people to get at the others and these are the people who are becoming conscious of being not only members of a settlement or members of a given band, but are conscious of being Eskimo as contrasted with white and these are the people who are becoming the closest thing that the Eskimos have to nationalists. The small signs that there are of the pan-Eskimo movement indicated that it's among people like this, that the movement will spread. That is among people who are primarily oriented to settlements who've received some education and who get along well with the whites and act as interpreters, mediators, and the like. So that the power of these people is increasing, relatively to, say, what it was a generation ago when the equivalent persons would have been, let us say, Hudson's Bay assistants, clerks, that kind of thing, special constables for the RCMP and catechists for the missionaries, that was the equivalent some time ago. Now you have community health workers, radio announcers, people who translate and edit Eskimo publications, sponsored by whites, of course, in some cases administrators, working for the civil services, teaching assistants, nurse's aides.

There is a whole category of person here of a kind of white-collar type, if you will, which is getting more and more influence but they're still not so influential that they have a determining say in what happens. They are still, I hesitate to use the word "second-class citizens," they are not that, they are still used by the whites to get messages across to their fellow Eskimos, but they in turn are coming to have more and more influence in calling the tune and writing the script for what happens.

Q. Projections

A. I would say that it should reach its peak with the development of organizations like the co-operatives for instance, which are quite strong in the north. I mean, there aren't many single co-operatives like in given communities, which are very, very strong, but the movement is strong, the movement as a whole. You can get ten or twelve fairly weak co-operatives but when they start getting together, the movement itself takes on a kind of life of its own and there are signs that this is happening in the Arctic. Now I see these kinds of links that are established between co-operatives, let's say. I'm just using these as one kind of example, providing a kind of vehicle for the expression of pan-Eskimo sentiments. I see these co-operatives as an opportunity for people to flex their muscles as Eskimos say, "Well, we can do it, the whites did it in Saskatchewan" and so on, we can do it and to the extent that this movement grows and other movements such as the Indian/Eskimo Association, and whenever you get an equivalent to the National Indian Council among the Eskimos, much depends on this. In other words, much depends on organization to the extent that these people get organized then they will quite quickly play a prominent part in the big picture. But it is very hard to predict just how strong these organizations are going to be, say, ten years from now or something like that because these co-ops could fold overnight with a withdrawal of support and the movement would be killed. But this is where I would look, look also into the educational system, to put it very crudely, of people from the upper reaches of the educational system, excluding universities, that's not feasible for large numbers of Eskimos now. I'd look there, and I'd look in the organizational, I'd look at the organizational picture as it's developing, I should say, in order to make some predictions about how strong this pan-Eskimo movement will be and what kind of influence the Eskimo spokesman will have.

Q. Prophecy—the future

A. I find it hard to visualize what will happen to the people of the north as distinct from what will happen to the things of the north. Let me clarify that if I may. I can visualize enormous freight submarines coming up through the ice and putting in at some port to take on freight or oil or whatever it is and then going down under the ice again and emerging in New York or some place, right. I can visualize monorails going from the west side of Hudson's Bay up to Copper Mine or someplace. I can see mines opening up in C Lake district and so on. I can see these little planned towns like Pine Point being set up with the help of professional planners and the like. My visual image of the things that happen is pretty clear, the development going on, I'm not as optimistic as perhaps some spokesmen for the government are about the speed of this development but nevertheless I see it happening.

But what I find difficult to envisage is the future relationship among the people. There is, certain processes get started, which is very difficult to break through, for instance the process that started with the separation of the Indians from most of the rest of society when they were encouraged to go onto reserves. Here, a process started, which we now have to live with apparently and which we find it extremely difficult to do anything about, but it's like a spiral you can't reverse, that is you can't reverse the direction of it or [it's] very difficult to reverse it and you find it very difficult to break through the spiral and to break into it, I should say, and to change the flow right. And so, what we're getting is a deplorable situation as everyone knows among the Indians, which I am rather pessimistic about to tell you the truth.

Now, to come to the Eskimo situation there, well we have a better chance there. We can learn from what has happened in the past and if we can bring the Eskimos quickly into the emerging economy, the emerging society up there, then I think that the vicious spiral in which we are now sort of spinning around, with reference to the Indians, this will have been prevented. But it is just so difficult to say though, because I find in some places the attitudes of the whites is one of "look, I'm here and I'm only going to be here for another five years so it doesn't behoove me to do anything special. I want to—let me live my own life and I'll respect the Eskimos but let them keep to themselves, and so on. I respect the Eskimos so much that I don't want them to lose their culture. Therefore, let's leave them alone, let's do a minimum amount of formal education." The attitude, this had consequences which a person who is preaching the doctrine won't have to face up to because he'll be out of the north 25 years from now, he'll be dead probably. It is this kind of thing that puzzles me in a sense that I can't foresee, because I don't know enough about the human situation and its development. I don't know enough whether to be able to foretell whether we'll get ourselves into one of these vicious spirals. I hate to use the term over and over again, that [what] we've got ourselves into with the Indians if that can be avoided then I can see the Eskimos taking part the way they do in Russia, right, Siberia, the way they're doing in Greenland, and to a lesser extent, although to a greater extent than in Canada, in Alaska, a kind of melting in with the emerging industrial societies. One thing I should point out though is that we're moving ourself. If you look at the larger picture, we're moving into what we call the post-industrial society and many of the values held by the people going in and sort of helping the Eskimos were the values of their grandparents who lived in a time when the big problem of the society was production, and so they, the idea of people getting money without working physically for it is so abhorrent to these people. What they're doing is preaching a kind of doctrine, which is already a generation out of step and which another generation from now will be about three generations out of step.

This is a factor which is difficult to take into account. The extent to which a post-industrial society, the kind of people who are required to keep it going, the kinds of problems of consumption and distribution rather than the production. How this will affect the people of the north that's again, I'm reluctant to rub my crystal ball and have a clear look into it. And I won't say even that I'm optimistic or pessimistic about this. I just don't know enough about the situation and I'm myself quite bewildered by it, and I wish—25 years from now if you asked me the same question, I would be able to commit myself to some more clear prediction.

7. Robert Phillips Interview Transcript

Q. Biographer

A. I guess my love affair with the north went back oh, fifteen years. I was in the east block then, as a young officer in the Department of External Affairs, back from my stint of about three years in Moscow, a year in the National Defense College and was then concerned with Canada-U.S. defense relations and that of course, included the north, it included defense bases there and negotiations with the Americans. And in the course of my work in External Affairs it gradually sort of bore into me that Canadians were, well if not throwing away their north for a mess of pottage at least being supremely oblivious to the responsibilities we had to the people there and I supposed oblivious to the kind of resources, the wealth that we could get from it. We just don't care about the north, there was a great sort of *terra nullius*.

I got kind of frustrated about this, became more and more fascinated with the north, wanted to get up there, I couldn't find any very good way to do [that] so I volunteered to take some leave and ship as unskilled labor as a freight handler on an Arctic weather station re-supply mission. Well, that was, I suppose about 14 years ago now and that was tremendous fun. Went up into the Queen Elizabeth Islands, saw a bit of the country, one of the, it was really one of the cook's tours in a way. I wasn't there for only about a week but that's enough of an inoculation as just about all visitors to the north find. So, I became keener and keener and naturally more and more anxious that we in the Government should do something about our responsibilities in the north. So, I kept bombarding my unwilling superiors with my views on the subject and well, eventually it turned out sometime later to skip over the not so interesting details of my own career that I found myself in the Privy Council Office just about the time the Government decided to do something pretty dramatic about the north. That is to introduce a new law into parliament, the Northern Affairs and National Resources Act. Well, that for the first time set up a department whose really prime concern was the north, it was a recognition that there was this great area and that we weren't doing anything about it and in fact the Prime Minister at the time speaking at the second reading of the bill said apparently, we have administered these vast territories in an almost continuous state of absence of mind. Well, that was a pretty fantastic——that was a pretty fantastic admission for a Prime Minister of a government, of a party that had then been in power for, well, well almost 20 years, but it was the sort of honest and frank approach to the fact that neither that government nor any other government had really done much thinking, much action, about well at least the northern third of our country.

Well, the end of 1953 was the beginning of the sort of administrative revolution in the north. Now not everything started from then, a lot of things had started before, and a lot of things were far from starting for years to come. But at least there was the focus of the department and when it was decided to set this up, to give a new focus, and make a new investment in the north, to take it seriously. The new deputy minister asked me if I would join him in the new department, it wasn't an easy decision. I had been very happy trying to do what I could in the cause of world peace, and External Affairs which was and, I am sure, always will be a tremendous sort of career but eventually I decided I would sit for a competition for a job in Northern Affairs on the sort of conviction that one small person could probably do a little more for Canada by working in the north where there were so very few concerned than in the broad field of international relations. And therefore, in 1954 on April Fool's day if the truth were known, I moved over, changed my life and you might say and then did something serious about the love affair with the north. And then for another eleven years I served the north in various capacities.

Q. The north as life-conditioner

A. Ya, the north is, sure the north has changed my life. I can't conceive anyone being in close touch with the north whether they live there all the time or simply travel it month after month and year after year, I can't conceive of such a person as really being untouched by the north for the rest of his life. When I left in 1965, at least left the job there, it wasn't because of being tired of the north, the feeling that it had no more interest or anything of the sort. I was as keen as ever. I left because I am a public servant, I was asked to do another job which was related to fighting the war against poverty and I suppose the main reason I was asked to because the experience that I had got in the north and fighting some of the worst kind of poverty that this country has ever experienced. Well, since that time I have, of course, not had the same close contact with the northern third of the country. In fact, I've not been up there since, but it's, or it, the north will always remain something as a cross between a hobby and a profession, I'm sure this will always be so.

Q. Deromanticizing the north

A. I suppose that any perceptive person who wanders the north and gets to know the northerners a little bit is bound to have some of his old illusions shattered, if his illusions are based on the kind of romantic approach that we traditionally got from the books and the school room or from even the traditional kind of newspaper story, books and so on. The stories I mean, about the lovely Eskimos in their gleaming white igloos and how life is simple and unspoiled and unchanged and so on. Well that kind of life is really ugly, ugly, ugly. And you can't have all your illusions about the charming old life when you go up and see the tuberculosis and when you see the wretched health conditions, the wretched living conditions and the unspeakable sanitation. When you see the racial distinctions between a sort of white master race and the lesser breeds that have always been kept just a little outside the law. I'm not blaming anybody for this, unless I blame us all collectively but there's a lot in that romantic tradition that was, in my mind, pretty ugly judged by today's standard.

Now, of course, it is pretty unfair morally to judge the past by today and the sort of way we treated the Eskimos, the northern Indians, Metis, 25, 50, 100, or 200 years ago was according to the mores of those days. We weren't any nastier to native peoples there than we were to the rest of the world, but for today it is not good enough to treat native peoples as natives with that kind of snarl in our voice or that kind of paternalism in our voice either. These are Canadian citizens, and let's face it the igloo is not a part of Canadian life, because the life expectancy of 27 years isn't a part of Canadian life. The illiteracy isn't a part of what we think of as Canadian Life. Wretched bronchial disease—ah—a horizon that sees no kind of occupation except the dwindling trap line, none of these are part of Canadian life so they aren't part of Canada in the far Arctic either.

Well, you begin to see this when you go north. If you don't begin to see it you get identified with that old romantic idea, then God help you because you are swimming against the current, you're trying to preserve to keep the north in a sort of cold storage, it simply won't work. You're trying to preserve it the way Captain Lyons saw it, more than a century ago, but time moved on since then. It's moved on in ugly ways; I'm not suggesting that everything about the new life in the north is good; heaven knows, there are ugly problems, alcoholism is talked about a lot, it's probably talked about more as a disease than a symptom and it should be talked about as a symptom of the contradictions in societies. Alcoholism has a lot to do with the sort of protest, the articulate protest of those whose voices were once silent about their place in life—that's ugly. There are still very ugly living conditions in the north, the lack of access to meaningful education is still something we can't be very proud of in this country. However, we are moving forward. When I was first associated with the administration of the north, it—one of our heartbreaking tasks was to add up how many Canadian citizens had starved to death in that season. And we used to almost keep a chart on the wall of the starvation and hope to heaven that the curve would go down. Well, thank heaven, with all the ugliness that there is in the north today, let's remember that chart, is that line is showing a downward curve, in fact I think it is some years since we've had out and outright starvation in the north. We do have malnutrition, we do have bad health, but there's been a revolution in the personal living standard of so many northerners in these past dozen or two dozen years.

The trouble is when you go north today if you go as a one-time tourist, or even if you go often to stay for a year or two, you start taking mental snap shots of the world around you, you never see the north as a kind of movie film, you don't realize quite how it's changed. You fall into that fallacy of thinking ha, ha, the north's being opened up, it opened up the day before yesterday, that's just the day before I came and there it all is suddenly. Are we right to open it up, but the real truth about the north is that it opened a very long time ago. It opened up when the first white man with his supreme confidence towards the rest of the world first ventured into the north and either consciously or unconsciously changed the life up there. That sort of change, whether it is good or bad, is certainly inevitable but I think it is demonstrable that almost on any grounds that changes in recent years have been for the good. The combination of a certain national-social conscience and the extraordinarily devoted and efficient work of the medial progression for example has wrought enormous changes in health standards amongst the Eskimos and other northern people. This is one of the stories we tend to forget.

When we go into a shack in the north and think how awful that Canadians live this way. And it is one of the stories we tend to forget when we perhaps go into a beerhall on a Saturday night in the north and say, "My God, why, isn't it awful that these people are allowed alcohol?" Well, I don't think it is particularly awful, I'm as unhappy as anyone else that there are problems of alcohol but I wonder if it is better for us to have a racial problem than a liquor problem. Is it better to try, for example, as we once did, either overtly or quietly, to keep these people as a sort of separate race, a race that must be treated as children, for some indefinite period in the future. In these recent years we've seen the terrible growing pains in the north in human terms and we're going to see it for some time to come. I think that what we forgot on the positive side because it isn't that visible is that we also see the emergence of people as adult human beings. Facing problems, sometimes being drowned in problems, but at least trying to live as human beings and as adult members of the community. They are no longer cute little Eskimos, they're no longer children, they're no longer the kind of people to whom we throw candies and pennies and things and think how charming the way they come and thank us. I think the end of that kind of era pretty quickly, is one of the great triumphs of the north. And I am kind of pleased that we have achieved this much there though naturally our minds, or eyes, our ears, and our noises are much more dominated by what's immediately around in terms of the filthy honey buckets, the kids who can't read and write, the hacking coughs, and so on.

Q. The evolving Eskimo

A. I think one lesson that very few of us have learned about the north, very few of us who have loved it and known it have learned and that's the lesson of patience. We have such a terrible emotional feeling about the people there and how we've let them down over the centuries and we also have our excitement about the enormous wealth of the rocks and the sort of thing that can be made out of this country, this million and a half square miles of nothing. But we want it to be done tomorrow or the very latest the day after tomorrow and, of course, this can never be. And we get impatient that the mines, the oil wells [that] we predict, because we know the stuff is there, take a long time to come and we, at times sort of overlook some of the difficulties of attracting capital from more salubrious climates into this pretty unknown, pretty cold north. Well, if we're impatient there I think we're even more impatient on the human side of the north, we want to see a revolution, well in health, in the place of Eskimos, Indians, northerners generally. We want to see them be real citizens, no longer just a kind of well, a practical ward, although theoretically they have full rights of citizenship. We used to say in the early days of the new administration that our work would, in effect, show signs of success when for the first time an Eskimo stood up and said no. And it was really extraordinarily difficult to achieve this. We brought, really on a massive scale, health services to the north, we brought classrooms to the north and we brought co-operatives, we brought various kinds of local industries, and we were lucky in a few mines that came to the north, and so on. This certainly had its physical impact on the people up there. But the really toughest thing to do was to sort of transfer from our hands into theirs to break down the old tradition that the white man is the master race, that the white man is the occupier of the house, the white house, up on the hill.

One of the really tough things was the whole process of what's conventionally called community development. All sorts of approaches were tried to get the people of the village to set up some kind of local council to take decision making into their hands and out of the hands of the bureaucracy. The people in the administration were very conscious of their size, of their pervasiveness, and I suppose ultimately their power and this is a kind of scary thing. You really aren't going to do any permanent service for the human being of the north unless you get, persuade, those people that they can be human beings and start making their own decisions, start, if not taking over from the administration immediately at least being a countervailing force to it. Well, these things take a long time, sometimes these community councils worked, they had their own ideas, they started protesting occasionally about what the government was doing and this was one of the real triumphs. This was the beginning of the emergence of an articulate soul in the north. I'm not suggesting that the soul ever disappeared but the articulate soul disappeared when the days when the white man was boss and no one talked back to him.

Well, in our impatience and the "our" here I think, is the people of Canada, of the people of Canada who have some interest in the north anyway. I think we have often tended to do a disservice to northerners by putting them in places where they shouldn't quite be, that is, putting them in places they haven't earned themselves, putting them in places we hope they will earn themselves. There's a tendency at times to show one's respectability anywhere on this continent by having on your board of directors the tame negro or the tame female or the tame Indian and this sort of mood has not been entirely absent in the north, it comes from the noblest of motives, the very absence of racial prejudice but there is behind it a sort of paternalism and we tend to say, "Look we're terribly good fellows and broadminded, we whites, and we do want to turn things over to you Eskimos so come and sit on our boards so to speak." I don't literally mean a board of course. And then there is such a tendency for the Eskimo, the northern Indian to be a kind of showpiece, a doll, a puppet, and this doesn't do anybody any good, because those who are sitting quietly back on the rock watching all this say, you see, ya see, those fellows never know anything. How can they discuss a budget, heavens, they're not understanding anything at all, they're just serving as the sort of stooges for you whites who have all the power. Well, that's one of the dilemmas of changing power over from a master race, if you like, to a minority race. It's one of the dilemmas that changing power from a pretty all-pervasive set of power elites that is government, traders, churches, into the hands of fairly small local people who don't have any huge institutions behind them.

Q. The future look and its influences

A. Let's not kid ourselves. The north is going to be made up in future years of gigantic plastic bubbles surrounding Arctic villages with the cloak of warm air. And it isn't going to be modeled on at least what's represented as pretty highly scientific rational northern towns of the Soviet Union. It isn't going to have the sort of flow of economic life of an Alaska which is so largely based on a defense industry. I think the north in the future is going to look appallingly like the rest of Canada and that's great as far as I'm concerned. It's going to look like suburbia and with all the things that we deplore about suburbia; the silly western ranch style split level bungalows that are absolutely unfitted to the climate of Toronto, Montreal, and Ottawa are absolutely unfitted to the climate of

Frobisher Bay or Iglulik and that's where we're going to go on building them. This is the Canadian way; we're not going to do really dramatic things like spending a hundred million dollars for a whole new approach to community living up in Resolute Bay. We're not going to build a kind of Arctic version of Habitat around Tuktoyaktuk; we're not going to do so because that isn't quite the Canadian way as well as for the very practical reason that the first government that suggests such a 500 million dollar expenditure is going to find that the treasury board removes it from its next year's estimates on the first cut.

No, the general process of Canadian development I think is going to carry on in the north. We're going to do things that are dramatic in a way; we've already done things that are dramatic in the sense that we've had oil wells being drilled in the most inconceivable of places virtually in the shadow of the pole, that's dramatic alright, how many Canadians know about it? How many Canadians even know about such a dramatic story as running a telegraph line down the whole Mackenzie River done in practically silence while we're still looking at sixth-run movies about how they did it in the American west. Yee, Gods, we've done things in the north. But what we're not going to do in the north is things which in the Canadian context are a bit phony. We're going to live our irrational lives, we're not going to go together, for example, in high rise apartments in tremendous propinquity because generally Canadians don't like doing that except in the larger cities. We'll live in our urban sprawl and waste money on our sewers—that way we'll waste money on our heat and so on. Because that's the way we tend to be happy and because that's the way we can go on living without committing enormous resources of our future to a, something no one's ever done before.

Q. The Canadianism of isolated life

A. There's a wonderful cliché which I hope—I may be forgiven for mentioning once more. That a nation is great only as long as it has a frontier. Now we've got that frontier, other people are nostalgic, other people are nostalgically having to dip back a hundred years to find their frontier and vicariously become part of it. We've got it and we have a very, very small percentage of our population who really take advantage of it in the specific physical way but for a lot of the rest it is a sort of a frontier in much more than a physical sense. Now this does something to the Canadian character, it means to put it into simple terms that for some million and a half or more square miles we've got a kind of civilization that does not conform to the rest of North America. There's a lot of living space up there to do curious things and we've been doing curious things in the north. We did the most curious-est of all things I think probably in the era of 1898 during the Dawson City gold rush. Now that's an era of Canadian history well-worth studying because it illustrated something about, oh, the kind of goals that people may be looking for in society or at least the kind of society they are trying to escape from. And it shows what they can really do when all the sort of fetters are off and they have the chance to make their Brave New World. Now that was done in a very dramatic way in a very colorful way in a little town on the mud flat in the very far corner of the back of beyond. But in a somewhat less dramatic way, less visible way we've been doing the same thing ever since throughout the Yukon and Northwest Territories.

Some years ago, a large employer in the north decided to employ consultants to find out what kind of people they should be looking for amongst their employees and the answer came back the kind of person who goes to the north is rather odd and really that is true of your employers now and if you're smart, you'll go on looking for this kind of odd person and so the employers concerned did do. Well, this is kind of a commentary too, on Canadian life. I think it is a commentary on the strength of the north, and the strength of Canada. That here is a sort of place that nonconformists really can find a sort of haven. Now no matter how the north develops, it's not going to develop quite as southern Canada, you're not going to have the gradual roll of civilization across the homesteads into the next little railway junction then gradually peopling the places between. You're going to have little spots where there are derricks where there are head frames for mines and then you're going to have a very great deal of inexpensive real estate between. A very great deal of real estate where the nonconformist can live and flourish and I don't think that all the changes in the north are going to change that fundamental character of our frontier, our permanent frontier.

Q. Isolation

A. I think it takes a strong person to live in the north, and really to be a part of it and to find satisfaction there. When you're living in a big city in the south you can always retreat when you fail in your relations with society, you can just go away and nobody really knows the difference. You can't go away when you're in a little village a thousand miles from nowhere and a couple of weeks from the next plane, high in the Arctic. So all sorts of curious things happen, in some ways you may have gone to the north to get away from society and you find yourself in one dimension far closer to it than you've ever been in your life, you know your neighbors intimately, you know each walk they take down that little 500 yard road, you know what their problems are because they are bound to talk about them and if they don't, they'll go nuts just as you'll go nuts when you don't talk.

And yet the kind of people you have chosen as your friends and associates in that particular village, in that sort of desert island of the north, if you like, are not people that you have really chosen at all. They're there by accident. The only thing in common is that they did have enough sort of get up and go to try something violently new and different by going to the ends of the earth.

Sometimes you'll find yourself rather pathetically perhaps persuading yourself that this is great and you'll sit on a Saturday night on that kind of couch that you'll see in every village of the north from Baffin Island to the Mackenzie Delta. They are all identical in the government houses. And you'll get in a singsong with a trader and his wife and the priest and the other missionary, the policeman, and so on, and you'll sing the same sort of song whether in Baffin Island or the Mackenzie Delta, and you'll exchange the same sort of gossip about so and so; who has just moved from this store to that or Dr. So and So, who is probably coming through on the next flight in ten days and so on. And you convince yourself that this is really the life, that there is a kind of precious intimacy about all this, you're excluding the rest of the world that will never understand and you've made your own world with these other people. And probably what you'll never know and what nobody else will ever know is whether you're kidding yourself or not; have you really made your peace with these other people or have you made a peace because the only alternative to the peace is a kind of crackup?

If you don't make—if you don't become partners with the rest of society in this extraordinarily removed and self-centered little village then you have to live entirely on your own. You may think you're strong enough to live on your own and if you lived in an igloo really a 1000 miles from nowhere you might live on your own but you can't live on your own with 20 neighbors.

Q. The informed solitary

A. It is probably about now to make the sort of qualification one should make very early in a conversation, in the middle of it and towards the end and that is a terrible mistake to generalize about the north and it is a terrible mistake to generalize about the people in the north. For a lot of people in the north, and here I am going to generalize, sure there is the opportunity for a kind of synoptic stance towards the rest of the world. But I would venture to suggest that a fairly high percentage of people who live in the north find as one of its satisfactions the ability to withdraw from the man-made problems of the rest of society. The foreign news does not figure largely in the northerner's life. Now there's been a good deal of pressure from time to time in communities to get better mail service and to get better newspaper service, and this has gradually been improved. But I don't think it is really so much because people want to keep in touch with the problems of the world whether it is Vietnam or hunger in India or budgetary problems in Canada and so on. I think it is a comfortable feeling that you do have this link with the world outside, but once having established the fact that it's there, do you really want it? I think for most people in the north— —no, and it is perhaps significant that even the most world shaking of events outside the north don't really get much of a mention in the pretty numerous northern newspapers. No, I think that you can perhaps safely generalize that in the north there is less concern, there is less sense of involvement in the foreign world than any other part of Canada. And I don't think this is accidental and I don't think that it's because of problems of communication. And when people go in the north, I don't think it's entirely so that they can look at the world through more detached lenses. I think it's that they would rather build their own world with the problems they can grasp and solve and perhaps quite happily seize the opportunity to turn their back on the problems of the rest of the world that they can't do much about anyway.

Q. Opting out

A. I guess the question of opting out is a matter of degree rather than kind; in the total scale of world opting outs, Canada has been, I think, among the more opting out of affluent nations. We don't seem to have taken our responsibilities to the more unfortunate peoples of the world that seriously in Canada. If you look at the pages of our daily newspapers you will find a great deal more about the trivia of North America or the home town that you'll find about the global issues. This is, I suppose, a phase of growing out. Now if you project it back for 50 years, it is true of the United States. The U.S. has got its role in the world and now it's had to opt in. Maybe someday Canada as a whole will have to opt in more and I think probably the north will have to opt in a great deal more but there'll be a lag, let's say between the north and the rest of Canada about the sense of responsibility and involvement in the world outside. I don't think you can say in a sort of black and white way that the north has opted out but I think there is a great deal less sense of identity between northerners and people outside the Canadian border.

Q. The translative factor

A. I don't want to claim to be any authority on the kind of personality and profile of an arctic village because I have never lived there. I've travelled a very great deal but I can never be anything but an outsider. But I have had the feeling that the approach to understanding what's really going on in minds and hearts in those villages is probably the small town in southern Ontario, perhaps the small town 50 years ago would be a little more appropriate than today because it probably finds itself in a superhighway, television station and all the rest of the bit. And therefore, you get a kind of an intensification of relationships, you feel you are part of the member of the club in that community whether in effect, whether in fact your emotions allow you to be or not. Now sometimes people get terribly close knit in a community and that relationship is strong enough to persist outside when they've both gone outside later and I suppose that's the real test. I wonder, however, if it isn't much commoner that the relationship doesn't really stand the test outside. There is a certain tradition that when you see another northerner, at least so an outsider observer would seem to find, you greet him extremely affably because you're both members of some sort of fraternal organization, you've got to recognize that it's expected of you. But you're really grateful that you don't see one another before breakfast every morning.

There have been a lot of cases in the north of severely strained relationships in these tiny communities just as there have been in the small communities in the earlier days in the south. Some of the interesting stories I think of people who, for example, living 50 yards apart will go a year without speaking to one another, there have been some classic feuds like this. They don't say a word until they sort of meet in a bar in a hotel down in Winnipeg on the way out and then they turn to one another and they resume volubly, affably, and without hesitation a conversation that began 15 months before. It is O.K. to have a relationship now because you know there are limits to the demands that your neighbor will make on you and if you don't like his demands you can go off into the next street or escape, but up in the north you always have that sort of feeling that you've got to be a little careful of the relationships with your neighbor because you've simply got to live with him, you've got to establish patterns that you can accept. In other words, maybe there can't be the sort of relaxation in relationships that is commonly assumed in people who are very close neighbors and assumed to be very close friends.

Q. Transportation

A. Maybe just because I'm getting to be a tired old man, I'm looking at the world a little conservatively but I don't quite see the argosies of magic sail in the north. I think that certain types of vehicles are going to be very useful and, in some places, technology is really going to come to our rescue in the north; the hovercraft does seem to be a northern natural, but if we were to project how we're going to get around the north in the next 20 or 30 years I would like to get an answer first to how we're going to get around in the south. One thing we must bear in mind is that with all this so-called hidden wealth, the north is economically not a very large part of Canada. In population terms it is an extraordinarily small part, therefore it is not the kind of place we're likely to invest massive sums in the development of revolutionary new methods of building, moving about, and so on. We're going to have to adapt from what has been developed for the rest of North America or for the rest of the world. No, these adaptations are often quite considerable but with the kind of attention that the north's had now for the past 20 years, say the sort of planes you find up there, the sort of trains, the sort of vehicles and so on are extraordinarily like the south. The adaptation for example that is made in vehicles is probably a piece of corrugated cardboard upside, up the front of the radiator. Now that isn't a great technological breakthrough, you know, people in Toronto are known to do that. The sort of planes you get there that might have been predicted in a kind of Buck Rogers sense 20 years ago turn out to be the kind of planes that are no longer economical to run in the south. It is all the north can afford so that's what they get. I wonder if things are really going to change that much in the future. After all, the decisions on what kind of transportation we get in the north in 20 or 30 years aren't going to be made by the scientists alone, alas. They're going to be made by the economist, they are going to be made by the taxpayers. Consequently, I think we will see adaptations, but they are basically going to be adaptations of what the rest of the world has.

Q. Housing

A. I think if you ask me what kind of house, what kind of building we're going to have in the north in 20 or 30 years I have to ask you what the cost is going to be. Now Habitat would be just swell in the north and I'm sure lots of northerners would like to see it in Frobisher Bay, but are you really going to put a 25 million [dollar] apartment block there? Of course you're not. We are going to be government by the cash, nexus in the north far more than the south even because so much of the north is financed by public funds, which are scrutinized by Parliament, public funds, which are in strong competition with funds for things far nearer home; the local subway, the nearest freeway and so on. This alone is a strong factor dictating toward conservatism in approach, in design. Now whenever an architect draws something that's really imaginative, bright, and so on this doesn't really necessarily bring us much closer to a new approach in the north. What really counts is not the architect's comment, it is the politician's comment, the administrator's comment, above all it's the taxpayer's comment.

Q. Supplement: What Canadians should do about the north

A. Well, it is pretty hard to say what Canadians should do about the north. If you happen to have ten million dollars burning a hole in your pocket, I hope you'll think seriously about investing it in perhaps an oil field in a promising mineral formation in the north. If you are perhaps a young person at heart as they say as well as physically, if you have a profession like nursing or medicine or teaching and so on I'd hope you would feel a sufficient sense of involvement to go up to the north, and to give some of your talents to the people up there who so badly need them. I think that the educational process can be a pretty mutual one. But for most Canadians, the other 99 percent, there isn't much question of huge investment, there isn't question of going. There is something pretty important though, and that is a sense of national engagement in the north. We shouldn't think of this great land as just a place, which is rather an exotic background for a lot of Eskimos; we shouldn't just think, well, that's nice, we've got a frontier and the Americans haven't. That's a kind of interesting story about that chap who survived on a plane and so on.

By damn, this is Canada and we have a real responsibility for it, not just for the few tens of thousands of people who live there but because this can have an impact not just on the economy but on the whole character of Canada. How the northerner suffered badly, the northerners suffered badly and Canada suffered very badly through the long, long years of indifference. When the north was a place where you didn't spend money, the north was a place to economize, when the north was a very, very distant land whose pains couldn't be heard because the voices were very quiet and very distant. That must never, never happen again; we've got to fulfill our responsibilities to the people in the north, we've got to get rid of housing conditions, which in terms of climate are the most ghastly and scandalous in the world. We've got to get rid of the scourge of illiteracy and be able to point to ourselves with some modicum of pride and say that this wealthy country is at least able to give every one of its citizens some decent kind of schooling. And we've got to think of the sort of challenge if I may use a cliché that faces us by helping these people of the north, bring themselves into the maelstrom of the 20th century with all its difficulties as well as with its benefits. Now this isn't going to be done in isolation with a few pipe smoking tweed jacket enthusiasts, it is going to be done if there is a sense of identity of 20 million Canadians. This is our problem and this is our national village, to paraphrase Mr. McLuhan. We have as much concern morally for the distant reaches of the north as for the distant reaches of the Atlantic provinces. I'm not suggesting we concern ourselves only with the problems with the most ghastly poverty in our country with conditions of living that would still shock most of us. I think, too, we have to concern ourselves about the possibilities as the potential of the north, because even though we have to be patient, and even through a lot of these resources aren't going to mean much to us, but will mean a great deal more to our children or even our grandchildren. It's high time we did start realizing that action is required from now on, really to accept the responsibility we have. I wonder if we can't get some sort of perspective about the north, by, if you like looking at the rest of the world, looking at the density of our population for example. Do we really have the right to go and bury our talents in the way that we have in the Canadian north, and sort of say the rest of the world can go and starve, the rest of the world can go and live on top of one another while we just sit and spend our money in a callous way in the comfortable cities of the south and don't do a damn thing to invest in the resources of the north, for Canada or for the rest of the world? This just isn't good enough in the late 20th century. All of Canadians should regard the north as a very large domestic problem, a very large domestic opportunity and I think they should think of it as part of our role in the rest of the world. We should be doing something about [it] and we shouldn't simply be clucking about the problems of the rest of the world. We shouldn't be rather supercilious about the terrible things that are happening to people outside our borders; they are happening inside as well, and they're happening because of the continuing indifference of so many Canadians to that northern third of their country.

 Q. Fellinis

 A. Yes, of course——yes—oh, I should think so—no, I wouldn't put it exactly that way——um, yes, with some qualifications——mmm, not exactly——no, no, not at all.

8. Marianne Schroeder Interview Transcript

Q. Why you wanted to go

A. To be included in exclusions (pertains to necessary training and advice she received). (Includes words such as "challenging, humanitarian ideas, adventure") 4 minutes 35 seconds.

Q. Time sense and other things which necessitated a modification of conception

A. Contains words such as "adopt, adjust, environment, preconceived ideas, resentment and hostility, help them")

1 minute and 50 seconds

Q. Fellini's

A. I think so, yes, that would be possible, no, definitely not. I don't agree with this statement. I really don't know what I would have to be there in order to make a valid statement, no, I wouldn't think so.

Q. Feel of the place

A. I was greatly fascinated by the country as such. I flew north, by that I mean from Churchill to Coral Harbour, which is located on Southampton Island at the end of September 1964. Snow had begun to fall and the country was partially covered by it. Some of the lakes were partially frozen, especially around the edges but towards the center part of the lake you could still see the clear, clear water. And flying over the country you could look down and see various shades of green in the water and you could see the bottom of the lakes and it was a most fascinating experience. (pause) I remember I was up in the cockpit with the pilot and I was forever looking out, left and right and I could see ice flows over Hudson's Bay and I was always looking for a polar bear or some seals that I could spot but unfortunately there were none in sight. And as we flew along the east coast of Hudson's Bay as I said before this flat, flat country and it frightened me a little because it just seemed endless, we seemed to be going into nowhere. And the further north we went the more monotonous it became. There was nothing but snow and to our right, or right below us, were the waters of Hudson's Bay. Now, this was my impression during the winter. But I also flew over the country during the spring and summer time and this I found intriguing. Because then I could see the outlines of the lakes and the rivers and it just looked like children's toys when you have sort of a landmark, a big map you give the children to show, and you could see the rivers going into the lakes and they were brown or green in color and then on the tundra there were huge spots of moss or rock. And it is most difficult to describe because there is hardly any vegetation that one can spot from the air. And yet there is a fascination about the country.

Q. Factor of barrenness

A. In a way I did. It was extreme isolation, this is very true, and I knew very well I could not go anywhere except for, say, a mile or two of walking, in walking distance within the settlement. Yet I had a feeling of freedom, openness. The country was just so vast. It has, it has a fascination as far as I can see, which is very difficult to describe. In, when thinking about this I always think of the long summer nights when the snow had melted, the lakes were open, and the geese and ducks had started to fly north. During that time the sun would set but when— —there was still the sun, the last shimmer of the sun set in the sky, then I would walk out to one of those lakes— —lakes and watch those ducks and geese just flying around peacefully or sitting on the water. And I felt that I was almost part of the country, part of that peaceful surrounding and it was just so peaceful that I wished that it would never end.

Sub insert

The lakes

NB end of non-recorded material refers to "prison without bars"

Q. Re: Vallee and the notion of void also romantic north

A. Yes, it did seem like a very romantic place to me and this was one of the reasons why I wanted to go north, because I think considering a place romantic means that one doesn't know too much about the place and it, a great deal had been written about it, and I had read a great deal about it, and it sounded very, very romantic to me and I suppose in a way I was influenced by this. And when I went north and, so actually the day I arrived it was a cold September day. It was snowing in Coral Harbour on my arrival and there was absolutely no one there to meet me. I stepped off the plane and there were a number of rugged looking men with beards wearing heavy parkas and boots and here was I, this frail little girl from Winnipeg who came to the north to help the Eskimos. And at that time, I think I was more in need of help than anyone else. I felt absolutely lost.

Then after a short time a friend who had gone to Coral Harbour about a month before I did, she arrived then and it was a great feeling of relief to see a familiar face. But then when the plane left I stood there and watched and thought, now am I really doing the right thing? I must be out of my mind to come to this place. What will I do here, what is my purpose—and I was a little shaken just for a minute and I seriously contemplated going back onto the plane and flying south. I think in that particular instance I was somewhat frightened by the bleakness of the country and the vastness of it. There was just nothing around and that, in a way, probably it shattered my romantic illusions of the north.

Q. Media

A. Yes, in a way it did. This was especially true for me as a nurse because of the fact that whenever I spoke to a person, to a patient for instance, in that case it had to go through an interpreter and in the Eskimo language there are no names or expressions that we use in the nursing field or in the medical field for that matter, too. So, at times I felt that I was just not getting through or that our interpreter just did not understand what I was trying to explain and this was extremely frustrating at times because it was so important to get that message through to the person in order to initiate proper treatment. So, I did feel and did establish a certain way of communicating with them. The simplest expressions that I could think of sometimes. Illustrations such as pictures were used or even making various diagrams on a piece of paper in order that they would understand. And then it also depends on the intelligence of the individual like in any other society, of how much you can communicate, and how well you can communicate with a person. As far as the white people were concerned, I also felt that there was a difference in communicating with them. As you know and as had been said before, you get a conglomeration of white people in the north and you don't choose to live with them. You go there and you find them or they come and find you and it is such a small place, such a small, confined area that whether you like it or not, you are attempting or you should at least attempt to associate with these people because one really depends on the others in the north.

But then again, there are great differences. You probably have a mechanic or a storekeeper who may have a certain level of formal education but then you find another person coming who has maybe one or two university degrees and there are certainly different topics that you can discuss with a person like that. This is not meant in a negative way, as you know, but there are just certain possibilities that exist with the other group and I felt this was causing a problem occasionally. Certain people tended to stick together because of their common background and the others felt left out. And yet when everyone was together there was just sometimes a complete lack of communication because one group was just not interested in the interests of the other group.

Q. Translative factor

A. Yes, this is very true and a similar situation in the south would allow you to just discontinue contact with that type of a person. Whereas in an isolated area, in a small settlement, it is absolutely impossible and one has to try and make compromises in order to get along with those people. And it is not that there is a certain resentment toward the other person as such; this is not the case. But there is just not enough in common to establish a real good relationship. And there is another thing. I don't know whether it is relevant at this time or not but a single woman in the north has a special status. Any white woman who goes north has a very specific status. Usually, she is married to a man who is assigned or willingly goes north for a special purpose either with the Department of National Health and Welfare, the Department of Northern Affairs or the Department of Public Works. Whatever it may be, the desirable thing for many of these is to be married and take their families with them. So, the wife, the woman, accompanies her husband, probably has small children and her purpose of going there is to be with her family. None of these women are officially employed and the only women I have ever encountered in the north [who are employed] were either teachers or nurses. Now, this causes some difficulties as you can probably imagine. There are 20 or 25 white people in the settlement and all of them are married except, say, two nurses. The difficult part I think, maybe I'm wrong, but this was certainly my impression—that these two nurses would hold a position of authority—they had a say—I mean, not in any decision making as far as they, the government of the settlement were concerned. But as far as health was concerned, they were the people who were responsible and carried authority in that area. And I felt sometimes that this was rejected and viewed with hostility by other people who had to stay in the background and who could not do the same thing in a way, it was, how should I describe it, a position of authority, responsibility, which carried a certain glamour with it. Yet this was seen by others, not so much the hard work that was behind it all. And this idea did not of course fit in at all with the Eskimo society because the Eskimo society is definitely a patriarchal one. The man is definitely the head of the household, and the head of the society. A woman is only a woman. She has to stay in the background and never do you find a woman in that particular, under those circumstances under a position of authority. So this was extremely difficult for an Eskimo man to accept—a woman in authority. We had an Eskimo employee who was sometimes rather resentful. We didn't order him around but we asked him to do things for us and we were the boss, the big wheel as he kept staying. Now this was very, very difficult for an Eskimo man to accept and at first, I couldn't understand their reasoning, then I thought about it more and I also discussed this situation with one of the missionaries who was of great, great help to me.

NB some lines deleted——suffragette etc.

I couldn't really understand his attitude. But one day it came home to me very clearly when this was still so prevalent among the Eskimos. One woman had made arrangements with another woman who was expecting a child that she would take that particular baby after it was born, she would adopt the baby with the consent of her husband of course. And they all very much hoped for a boy. Anyway, the woman came to the nursing station to have her baby and it turned out to be a girl, to the disappointment of the whole group and family, and everyone else. The frightening part or the shocking part to me was the fact they named the girl Kurmalo, which means a parasite or worm, because of the simple fact that she was a girl. And after that I could very easily understand why there was some hostility towards authority, towards a woman holding authority among the Eskimos because we have

NB lines deleted

Q. Reaction to Ottawa

A. NB lines deleted

As far as I was concerned, I sometimes felt that Ottawa was just too far removed and that some of the people who were there had never lived in the North and that it was extremely difficult for them to conceive what one would encounter—what the problems would be of living up there even though I'm sure many of those people had travelled extensively in the North. But it is never the same to living in a place for one or two years consecutively. Just to travel through, to go through, for an even a month-long trip, I would think is more a pleasure than anything else.

Q. The memo approach

A. NB some lines deleted—these supplement above answer

Sometimes I did get the impression that people just came north and saw the country as tourists—formed their impressions and ideas and thought they knew what the north was all about. But I don't think this is possible. When I went there, I too had definite ideas of what people were like, of what to expect, and more or less they were clear cut, but the longer I was there the clearer I saw that it wasn't that simple. It was very involved and one would, could not get to know the country and its people within a matter of even a year. I think it would need much, much longer of living there—not only travelling but living there to really get to know the people and the surrounding areas. And why they act as they do. Also, why a white man changes when going North. I think I have changed greatly because of living up there.

Q. The changes

A. Well, I definitely think I have become more tolerant of people, that I now am or hope to accept people as they are without trying to impose my values on them. What right do I have of saying I think you should do this in that particular way or manner because how do I know that my way is the correct way? And if another person achieves that same goal by another method, I don't see any reason why he should change. I don't think I would ever have realized this without having lived among the Eskimos.

NB lines deleted

I feel I came to know myself a little better

NB lines deleted

The question is, had I simply discovered new possibilities or was I mainly developing the ones that were originally there? I would think that I developed the ones that were originally there. I don't think I discovered any new ones—new ideas or character traits. And I also came to love isolation in a way, not as an escape because the north is not a place where one goes to escape. I found this out very shortly after my arrival. There is nowhere to escape once you are in a settlement, you have to stay there and you cannot leave secretly. You can only leave with the knowledge of many other people. It just isn't possible to escape from gossip, for instance. I like the phrase "moccasin telegraph." We at Coral Harbour knew what was going on at Baker Lake or at Eskimo Point or Rankin Inlet not by official communication but because it all came more or less by the grapevine of the north we call the moccasin telegraph. It was absolutely impossible to keep anything from anybody. Even if we had a party, they knew it down in Winnipeg and I remember one, well this was I must admit, it was a smashing party, but it was a way of letting off steam. This was, it was absolutely necessary for us.

Lines deleted

There's nowhere to go. You can't say I'll take the weekend off and I'll go to the next motel and I'm not to be disturbed. This is impossible. You are in that station and when somebody knocks at the door you go and answer it regardless of what time it is. This of course was one of the frustrating things, because the Eskimos just didn't seem to have any conception of time.

NB lines deleted re: late night visits etc.

Q. Fashion

A. a (corrected) deleted

NB time answer re exclusions

Q. Family attitudes

A. Deleted NB time re exclusions 1 min. 5 secs.
Q. Eccentricity of the northern urge
A. (corrected)

Well, I didn't think it was an eccentric thing to go north. Many other people who knew me thought it was. They couldn't see my point at all. They didn't think it was a country for a woman, it wasn't a place especially for a single woman to go because they thought about the social life there and thought that when a woman reaches a certain age, she should be far more concerned with trying to trap a man than with making a career for herself or with trying to face the world herself. But I was convinced that this [was] the thing I wanted to do, and so I went there.

Q. Could you go back
A. (corrected)

When I came south, I felt that I'd had it. I'd been at Coral Harbour for many months without a break and this was just too much for me. I felt that I wasn't about to work effectively anymore and my only concern was getting south. I'd had enough. I just didn't want any part of the north any longer.

But now looking back on it I think I would like to go north again, because although there are many disadvantages, people mean something there. You're just not one of so many who walk on the street as in a big city. Sometimes I've been lonelier in a city than I ever was in the north. I didn't have to go to somebody in Coral [Harbour] and say I'm lonesome or I feel depressed. I just had to go and visit them—play a game of cribbage or chess, whatever they wanted to do, and right away there was a sense of sharing this life. One could realize the value of another human being (and the companionship of them).

As far as I can see, this is one of the great attractions of the north. Another attraction for me was working with the Eskimo. I became greatly attached to them and I felt I was accepted by them to a certain degree. And that I was able to help them better their condition.

Q. Reaction to changes in the future
A. (corrected)

Well, I don't think the north can remain the untouched, romantized [sic] country it was many years ago. It has been touched and that contact has not always been favorable.

NB line deleted
re integration the Eskimo.

Appendix | 293

9. Gould's Preliminary Sketch of Form

Gould's rough sketch of *North*'s form was likely drawn late in the production process as a means of getting the main points on paper. For each scene he provides a very brief explanation of the scene's purpose (e.g., scene 2 "Solitude and Isolation"; scene 3, "Disillusionment and Deromanticizing the North," etc.). Of note is how he treats the contrapuntal portions of each scene with the interviewees enclosed in boxes, notably scene 4, the ambitious "Dining Car" scene, which transpires as two simultaneous "conversations."

Figure A.2. Handwritten rough sketch of form in *North*. Source: Library and Archives Canada and Primary Wave Music I. Used with permission.

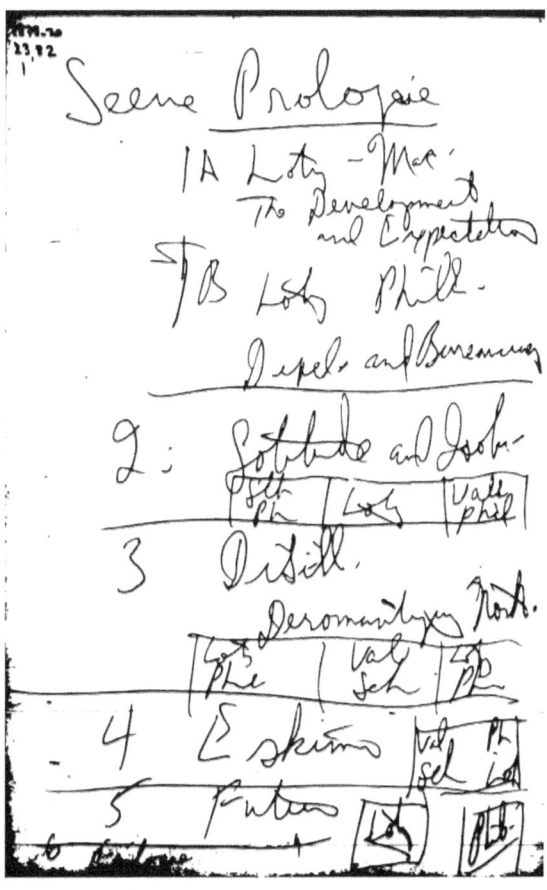

10. Janet Somerville's CBC Publicity Memo (15 November 1967)

Ideas producer Janet Somerville sent this memo to the CBC's publicity department a scant month and a half before *North*'s radio premiere on 28 December 1967. Even at this late stage she refers to two one-hour broadcasts as opposed to the final length of under an hour. She employs colorful prose and engages in mythmaking to historicize the work even before the work premiered, though this is likely to grab the attention of the corporation's publicists. Interestingly, Somerville calls *North* "a Finlandia for Canada without a note played," which evokes the nationalist themes associated with Sibelius's work and, more notably, equates the documentary with music.

Credit: CBC Licensing

∽

Internal Memo
Subject / Objet: IDEAS CENTENNIAL PROJECT
From / De:
Janet Somerville
Producer, "IDEAS"
Public Affairs.
To / A:
Rob Solloway,
Writer Editor,
Press Publicity,
Gerrard Street.

FIVE COPIES of it, so he can give it out to his colleagues who think about on-air promos, about print publicity, about press releases, about cross-promotion, about saturating the public mind with prospects of upcoming delights.

and a cc to:
Eric Koch,
Supervisor,
Arts & Sciences,
Public Affairs

Text: The incomparable Glenn Gould, who is not only The Musician but also one of The Articulators, The Wits, and The Creative Myth-makers in our fragile nation which hasn't got a lot of such types to go around, is breaking new and exotic (though frozen) ground in IDEAS' second (and last, thank God) centennial project. He is doing two one-hour dream documentaries called "The Idea of North;" and they are going to be the impression formed by Canada's most metropolitan man (him) of the kind of humanity, the flavor of human life being drifted into snowy shape by our very own Vast Frozen Spaces. They are going to be verbal music, those programs; a Finlandia for Canada without a note played; an icy crystal of the imagination, formed at leisure and in downtown warmth, which is, after all, where our national mythos must needs be fabricated . . . or at least promulgated. The two hours are going to be delightfully low on information and incredibly potent in insight, in mood, in nostalgia for the unknown, the not-yet-born, the too-late, and the irreducibly personal. If you insist on labelling them, I suppose they're interviews, but they will no doubt come out as stream-of-consciousness, as seduction for the private ear, as utterly contemporary (and therefore ageless) unashamed nature worship. They will juxtapose the most incompatible stereotypes that Canadians have fixed in their minds (like, for example, their stereotype of Glenn Gould himself with the bristly ice-hackers . . . an awful lot of whom have PhDs . . . he has chosen to talk to) so insinuatingly that we will all realize with a jolt that our whole national life, down to the dreams we dream about north and south, are made up of delicious incompatibilities that can't resist each other and thornily embrace. They will . . . oh, hell, I'm exhausted (besides, it is 5:30 a.m.) . . . be broadcast on DECEMBER 28 and 29 (how's *that* for just under the Centennial wire?) . . .

and they NEED PUBLICITY. I hope those programs will create a myth of our north; a beautiful, binding, action-directing, future-creating human myth. Well, we need to create a mythos about the shows before they are heard. PLEASE HELP. Tell me what to do and I'll do it. Maybe even Glenn will too; he's very generous about facing problems like publicity. (Well, don't *tell* him; *ask* him if maybe, etc. Whatever.)

Inspirations, anyone?
Janet Somerville.
Toronto
November 15th, 1967.

11. Scene-by-Scene Analysis

SCENE 1

Synopsis: The beginnings of the characters' "northern experience"
Cast: Maclean, Lotz, and Phillips

Table A.1. Scene 1 of *North*

Section	Voice	Time	Summary
A	Maclean	5:14	Discusses time on the train, being captive audience for chatter.
B	Lotz	7:51	Relates his experience of when he went north. As a geographer he experienced a "land of thin margins."
A	Maclean	9:37	Refers again to the gentleman going north for the first time. Infer a link with Lotz (?)
B	Lotz	9:52	Continues story of going/being north. He went for work on a "scientific expedition."
A	Maclean	11:11	Paraphrases myth of Sisyphus.
B	Lotz	11:52	While on his third trip to the northern ice shelf, talk turned to food. They had a drop of fresh vegetables.
A	Maclean	12:54	Speaks generally about people going north, he's "up against his own sad self."
B	Lotz	13:19	First work task: study of squatters in Whitehorse.
C	Maclean and Lotz	13:50–14:42	Both speak.
D	Phillips	14:43	Explains his "love affair with the North." How he came to like the north and his frustration with Canadians' ignorance of what goes on there.
B	Lotz	15:30	One can't talk about the north until one is out of it. Best related upon reflection.
D	Phillips	15:54	1954—Beginning of administrative revolution in Canadian government's dealings in Northern Affairs.
B	Lotz	16:14	Most government work in the north is "quick and dirty" studies. Make a report, recommendations, send to office and are summarily ignored.
D	Phillips	16:31	Decided he would apply for a position with Northern Affairs.
B	Lotz	16:51	He spent summers in the Yukon.
C	Maclean and Lotz	17:17–1800	Maclean ruminates on a young man in search of himself. Again, implicates Lotz in the narrative.
A	Maclean	18:01	Being in the north is about getting along with oneself. Question is: Can a man get along with himself?
		18:51–18:57	Train sounds.

Appendix | 297

SCENE 2

Synopsis: First experiences of living in the north. Reflections on emotional, community connections
Cast: Schroeder and Phillips

Table A.2. Scene 2 of *North*

Section	Voice	Time	Summary
A	Schroeder	19:02	Told that the north is no place for a single woman. Settling down and childbearing is preferred occupation.
B	Phillips	19:27	It takes a strong person to go to the north. You can escape life and go to the north, but when you're in an isolated village in the north there is no escape.
A	Schroeder	19:56	You live with many people.
B	Phillips	20:06	You get to know each other intimately.
A	Schroeder	20:32	Everyone knows everything, not by official news but by the grapevine. It was impossible to keep anything from anybody.
B	Phillips	20:48	The friends you choose are not really a choice.
A	Schroeder	21:03	It's a conglomeration. You don't choose to live with them [community members]. You find them or they find you.
B	Phillips	21:09	Decries the uniformity of the northern experience. And common tropes of living spaces and communal activities. You convince yourself that it's "the life."
A	Schroeder	22:04	If you're depressed you can just visit someone. There's an intimate sense that you're sharing something.
B	Phillips	22:19	Excluding yourself from the world that will never understand. You make a new life with these people and ask if you've made peace with yourself.

Scene 3

Synopsis: The reality of north and deromanticizing the north
Cast: Lotz, Phillips, Maclean, Schroeder, and Vallee

Table A.3. Scene 3 of *North*

Section	Voice	Time	Summary
A	Lotz	22:53	On reflection, one realizes how reliant one has become on each other and on northern living. Its vastness diminishes you.
B	Vallee	23:44	The wide-open space is deceiving. It's open but surrounded by dangers.
C	Phillips	24:13	A nation is great as long as it has a frontier. Canada still has that. Canadians have a civilization that doesn't conform to North American ideas.
B	Vallee	25:13	He didn't have a romantic reason to go north. Warns about building a cult of personality, by living the stereotypes of northern living.
D	Maclean	26:34	One becomes a hermit by choice or necessity. Are you escaping by going north (or any direction)? Evokes Shakespeare, "Sweet are the uses of adversity."
	Silence	28:01–28:12	Break in the scene.
A	Lotz	28:13	Anecdote about Inuit children who see themselves on television for the first time by CCTV setup.
C	Phillips	29:15	His illusions of the north were shattered by his experiences. Can't maintain illusions when one sees disease, filth, and discrimination. "Romantic condition is ugly by today's standards."
E	Schroeder	30:31	Was enticed by the romance but felt lost when first arrived.
B	Vallee	31:18	It's like marriage. When the honeymoon period has passed, time reveals all.
E	Schroeder	31:51	"What is my purpose?" One questions oneself and one's motives.
B	Vallee	32:01	People get disenchanted.
E	Schroeder	32:46	By the time she left, she didn't want any part of the north anymore. Now she thinks she would like to go back.

Scene 4, "Dining Car"*

Synopsis: Conversation centers around "Eskimos" and colonial attitudes
Cast: Phillips, Lotz, Vallee, and Schroeder
*Contrapuntal construction does not lend itself to a linear formal analysis.

Scene 5

Synopsis: Contemplations on the future of the north
Cast: Maclean, Phillips, and Lotz
*Linear formal analysis is difficult. It is free counterpoint.

Table A.4. Scene 5 of *North*

Section	Voice	Time	Summary
A	Maclean	42:50	Talks of the noise of civilization. Paradoxically, you cannot escape it until you accept it. Being able to select the noise you want/need to hear makes you a good analyst.
B	Phillips	44:09	The north won't be made up of miracle developments. It won't be as economically rich as Alaska, but it may look like the rest of suburban Canada.
C	Lotz	44:56–46:14	These towns will be built for the north, not like in the rest of Canada. In summer, the north will become a vast, open playground. The north is sandwiched between three major geographical areas and is "plump" open space for enjoyment.
B	Phillips		Many things that won't happen in the north because it's not what Canada does. But it will do dramatic things, but not necessarily good, oil wells as an example. It will not do "phony" things.
A	Lotz	47:42	Thinks future should hold a look at the problems of social change in the north. He talks about the "phoniness" in the north (antithetical to Phillips's prognostication).

Epilogue: Maclean's "Soliloquy"

Synopsis: Philosophy on what the north means and will mean to Canada.
Cast: Maclean, Sibelius's Fifth Symphony, third movement.

Table A.5. *North* Epilogue, Maclean's Soliloquy

	Voice	Time	Summary
	Maclean	49:58–58:54	Philosophizes on what the north means and will mean to Canada.

12. "Eskimo at the Piano" ["Eskimo am Flügel"]

Der Spiegel 19 (1968), 6 May 1968. Translated into English by Brent Wetters.
    https://www.spiegel.de/kultur/eskimo-am-fluegel-a-c3d45882-0002-0001-0000-000046039937

The article, which appeared in *Der Spiegel* on 6 May 1968, is an important piece of documentary evidence showing something of Gould's reception in Europe. It addresses the familiar topic of Gould's many eccentricities but also details some of his activities that distinguished him from his fellow pianists. Some of those suggestions are outright false, as in the claim that Gould was involved in jazz; in another case, the article misattributes the string quartet of his youth to his retirement. For the present book and especially chapter 7, however, the salient comment is the genre used to describe Gould's work in radio broadcasting, presumably including *North*, though it is not named specifically: where Gould was at pains to invent a genre for this work, *Der Spiegel* fits it neatly into the existent genre of *Hörspiel*, or "radio-play." Gould may or may not have been aware of similar developments in the electronic music studios in places like Cologne's WDR (see chapter 7 in this volume for extended discussion) but the connections to a current practice were not lost to those looking at Gould from the European perspective.

"Today's concert life will soon be dead anyway," he prophesied four years ago when he stepped down from the podium, never to return.

Since then, the Canadian pianist Glenn Gould from Toronto, 35, has enjoyed the best and most acclaimed years of his life.

Because even though he no longer plays nightly to audiences of highbrowed patrons ["Gala-Gästen"] with "their almost sadistic greed" (Gould: "they only wait for the horn to frack or the strings to smear"), he still provides the record industry with a true Gould-ecstasy as "the most ingenious warlock of the piano" (*Newsweek*), as "a pianist of divine grace" (*New York Herald Tribune*) and "of breathless intelligence and musicality" (*Life*).

The American CBS now awaits the newest artworks by the piano man from the north: the great Gould will serve up five long-playing records with Bach's *Well-Tempered Clavier*, five Mozart sonatas, the complete piano works of Arnold Schoenberg, Franz Liszt's piano reduction of Beethoven's *Fifth Symphony*, as well as a stereo reissue of his twelve-year-old bestseller (over 100,000), Bach's complicated *Goldberg Variations*. And Gould also releases something else: on a sixth record, Gould complains and ruminates about music and musicians, modern music management, and calendar careers ["Terminkalender-Karrieren"]. "When television keeps people from the concert hall," he says, "it is a blessing for music."

Mozart, he says, is "by far the most overrated composer": "He was at his best in his teenage music, but later the fire went out, naturally with a few exceptions." Conclusion: "Mozart died too late rather than too soon."

And he confesses, "I will never again perform for the same reason I will never fly again—the chances of survival are too low." Or: "The life of an acclaimed piano virtuoso is simply disgusting."

For Gould, who also admires the "wonderfully simple art" of the popstar Petula Clark and the "Babadubaba"-Bach of the Swingle Singers, is not only a great but also an unorthodox and eccentric artist, as he proved often enough in his acclaimed virtuoso life—as during a Schoenberg night in Florence when he was, to his delight, booed for the first time. Gould: "The more I bowed, the more they booed, and the more they booed, the more I bowed."

When the "best pianist of any age" (*Washington Post*), who feared bacteria as much as air conditioning, appeared before an audience with long, uncombed hair, he seemed like a displaced Eskimo: even in the heat of summer, he presented himself in winter coat, sweater, jacket, with thick mittens, and thick woolen scarves—only his feet were naked.

Gould was even more extravagant when he sat on the piano—the interpreter self-consciously rejected Bach's and Beethoven's directives, playing wild lentos or dragging prestos, brooding allegros, or lively adagios. "Music," Gould said, "must always sound like you've never heard it before."

Conductor Leonard Bernstein admittedly felt differently years ago: at a Gould concert in New York's Carnegie Hall, the maestro announced that he could not agree with Gould on the tempo and would only accompany him with his Philharmonic because he was a "sportsman."

The pianist was tired of the concert existence. He soon dissolved all of his engagements and retired to his house on the Canadian Lake Simcoe, where he wrote jazz music ["Jazzmuisken"],[6] a string quartet, opus 1,[7] as well as radio-plays ["Hörspiele"] and radio features ["Funk-Features"]. He contacted the outside world almost exclusively with the telephone.

At Lake Simcoe, where he still lives, Gould has now designed an outboard engine that drives his boat, the *Arnold Schoenberg*; there he is also constantly working on his 75-year-old "Chickering" piano, in order to change its playing and attack mechanics. "Finally," says Gould, "a piano must not necessarily sound like a piano."

Only once per month does the eccentric Gould leave "Chickering" and "Arnold Schoenberg" in the Canadian wilderness. He then drives to New York's CBS studio, which must be heated to 25 degrees for him. He bathes his hands for half an hour in hot water, because "you can think more clearly with warm hands," and sits himself in front of the piano in a fur-lined coat.

His recorded playing is as extravagant as it once was in the concert hall, enriched by many strange sounds: Gould's old piano chair squeaks on both stereo channels, constant breathing, humming, and buzzing from his virtuoso mouth turns into classical sounds. "I simply play much worse," Gould says, "when I do not make a few tones"—*such is live*.[8]

And those aren't the only things with which Gould's foes find fault. Many of their criticisms are printed on the cover of Gould's latest Liszt recording. A psychiatrist from North Dakota complains that "the pianist assumes the authority of a conductor." The Hungarian musicologist Zoltan Mostanyi protests that Gould "makes an entire orchestra unemployed just because a characterless pianist has sold his soul to the mighty dollar." And Sir Humphrey Price-Davies sneered, "Mr. Gould has been away from England's podium for years, and that's damn good." About such critics and criticisms—he himself invented them.

13. Anthony Cushing in Conversation with Marianne Schroeder

This interview transpired at Schroeder's home in Hamilton, Ontario, on 22 March 2014.

AC: Your family came to Canada in the fifties?

MS: Yes, we were displaced people, German people displaced by [Josip Broz] Tito at the end of World War II and then we went—because we were displaced, we were looking for a new home and we ended up going to Austria. And when we went to Austria, from Hungary, we went from Yugoslavia where I am not going into all detail, great details on the stories, from what is today northern Serbia to Hungary, and I guess my parents were planning on staying in Hungary, they spoke the language. And then the Hungarian government said we can't guarantee your safety, maybe you better go back where your ancestors came from. So, the little money that my parents had they paid somebody to smuggle us across the border from Hungary into Austria with the intent of going on to Germany.

But Austria at that time was divided into four zones. The Russian, the English, the American, and the French, and we thought they were all allies. And once we were in there and we had no passport of course. So, we went on a train to just go north, go to Germany. And then they checked, they came and asked for a passport at the border for Russia and into the English or American zone. And we didn't have a passport, so they took us off the train, the whole family, and put us in jail. My parents and five of my siblings, there was a total of six of us, and not all were there at that time, I think one was missing. And then by the time all this was done, they took us in a truck, in an old truck, in the back of a truck into the capital city called Steyr. And my father was—they told him not to leave the country for three months. So, we stayed for three months and that turned into seven years. It was a lovely old city, *is* a lovely old city.

So, we stayed there, but we were still too close for my father's liking to the Russians. He said just away from the Russians, just go, so we ended up coming to Canada in 1955. My sister came first and to give us a—she came in 1953 because she was of working age. Whereas my parents [who] were in their midfifties by then, believe it or not, were considered too old for the workforce and my brother and I were considered too young. So, she had to come and find someone to guarantee for us, that we wouldn't be a burden to anyone.

And so, then she found those people and we came in October 1955 to Canada. They went down to Windsor. Actually, I lived in Windsor until I went to Winnipeg. So, the background is German. And just the name itself shows. Father's name is Schroeder and mother's name is Hartman.

AC: Settling in Windsor that must have been quite the shock.

MS: It was, it was. It was like going into the desert or something. I was very homesick for the first several years. My sister then—she and I went back to Europe, particularly Austria in 1960, and I realized in five years some of my friends had gotten married or they had moved away or that it wasn't the same as it was when I left and that was another pain, an emotional pain saying, I have lost contact with these people basically. But then life in Windsor, I just didn't like it there. The adjustment—and I didn't speak English and all that. But my life started again when I went to Winnipeg in 1961. I couldn't have done anything better than that. In 1961, I went to Winnipeg and the reason I went there is because Ontario did not accept my education from Austria. I had to do this and I had to do that and do the other thing and Winnipeg accepted me the way I was. And so, I am going to Winnipeg, which was pretty cold, but it was a very good time for me in that training. It was secure. There was a structure. I was where I wanted to be. I relate for some reason; I decided I wanted to be a nurse and that's where I became a nurse.

AC: Just out of the blue? Was there any specific event where you said, yeah, because of that I want to be a nurse?

MS: Well, no, it had been percolating for some time. I remember when we were in Hungary, I used to visit a young [nun]. She had tuberculosis, she was dying of TB. I didn't know at that time I could get it too, but somehow I had real compassion for her and things like that, experiences like that, I thought maybe I would like to help take care of those people.

And then coming here and not in Windsor, doing this and that and the other job and trying to speak, to learn the language and then I thought, well, this may be the time to try do that. So, I did.

AC: In Winnipeg? It's really a transformational time.

MS: It was, yeah. I had started to take private lessons in Windsor for English and I think about three or four days after we arrived my sister took me to English, to evening classes for English. And the teacher said one word also, but that's "also"—I understood, I thought I understood. He was explaining and he said, and also, also. He said, this is that and also that and I thought oh, I recognize a word, but it means something different in German. Anyway, my English is still not American English, particularly not the way I'd want it to be, but you can't do everything in life.

AC: In '61, when you went to Winnipeg, was that when you started nursing school at Misericordia?

MS: Yes, it was a three-year program at the Misericordia Hospital. In those days, the schools of nursing were all operated by the hospitals. That was the case here as well. It only came in the last twenty years or so that they moved into the community colleges. So, we lived in residence and we had to sign out when we went out and sign in when we came in and there were certain rules, especially with nuns. There had to be order and they had to behave according to your calling. In those days, nursing was almost considered like a semi-religious thing because initially many of the nurses were nuns or religious people. And so, just the whole dress and everything, but then that has all changed since then. But there is still the real commitment to the profession and to each other.

AC: You went through school and you finished in '65.

MS: Sixty-four. And while we were in our last year, our third year, we had people coming from different kinds of nursing. Like there was hospital nursing and there is public health nursing and this and that and one woman came, she worked with national health and welfare and she told us about outpost nursing. And well, by the time she was done, a classmate and I went up there and said we want to go. So, that's how I ended up going into the Arctic and that was—I graduated in May of '64 and in the fall of, say in October, I went to the Arctic. And I said to her afterwards when she came I said, you should never have accepted me, I was far too inexperienced just after graduation. She said, well, look at it this way. If you weren't there, there wouldn't have been anybody. So, that is why I realized then that how much I still needed to learn because we were it, there were two of us and it was a newly established nursing station there in Coral Harbour. And the nearest doctor was down in Churchill.

AC: Quite a ways away!

MS: It's not just—and then plane service was every three weeks, weather permitting, or [if] they are able and willing to fly. And there was telephone connection sometimes with a doctor in Churchill, but other than that we were alone and we had to take x-rays of people. And I thought that's why I decided to do—service initially, I asked for permission from Health and Welfare to go one year and then when I got there and they were saying, a diploma doesn't do much for you these days, you have to have at least a [Bachelor of Science in Nursing] and so I just stayed for three years instead of one. But then I was committed to National Health and Welfare for a couple years after that, which was reasonable.

AC: You were in Coral Harbour for two years?

MS: I was, well, I did three years basic nurses training and three years at post-basic Bachelor of Science in Nursing at [University of Toronto], three years, post-basic at U of T.

AC: How big was Coral Harbour, in terms of population?

MS: Two hundred and forty people including the whites.

AC: Just roughly what was the proportion of whites to Inuit . . . ?

MS: Oh, well, whites were, I would say maybe 10 percent were white and then maybe between 10 and 15 percent were nurses, teachers, administrator, two churches; the Anglican Church was there, the Catholic Church was there. So, we were all white and the rest was . . . .the majority was 85 percent to 90 percent [Inu].

I went online and [Coral Harbour] has developed as—they have a tourist center and there are guiding people in the area, it has lots of birds in that area during the summer and so on. I thought it was very fascinating; this woman was talking about during the summer, the sun never sets, which is true. And the nurses and the people go out and take their tents and they just camp out the way they always used to do and they live on the land rather than those prefab houses. And the nurse just follows them and she has a black bag with everything she needs and she puts it on a rock and she does the immunization, it is something that's so romantic. But then in December, the sun rises and two hours later the sun sets.

AC: Blink and you miss it.

MS: That's right. And I said, next time I go up there, I will ask the government to put a glass ceiling on the house so I can lie in my bed at night and watch northern sky, the northern lights and all that. You are really not as free as you think you are because I was warned never to go outside and get far away from the settlement all by myself because of the dogs. Sometimes there are stray dogs and they travel in packs. And they said, when they surround you there is no help. And I didn't have a skidoo or neither did my friend. The travel from the airport was about a couple of miles away from the nursing station at the DOT, Department of Transport, and there was a Bombardier, we used to call the Bombardier and then they would take us to the nursing station or you would travel back and forth and later even when we were still there some Eskimos got skidoos.

But still we didn't go far away, mind you, I did a very exciting thing once. A number of people went from Coral Harbour across part of the Hudson's Bay over to northern Quebec. They had relatives or somebody there in a boat called *Peter Head*. That's a Scottish fishing boat. And we just have the front that is covered. And I asked if I could go with them and they said I could. Our woman, our interpreter and housekeeper, she went and so I went with them. I can't believe it. They would go over there and then they were hunting, the men, at one time for polar bear. And I watched them and I actually filmed it. They spotted the bear and the boat was taken over too so they could get on land and then a couple of them followed and then they brought the shot bear and pulled it up. They all pulled and brought it to an ice flow. That is a sick thing.

AC: They are pretty big.

MS: Oh, they are huge. But [the Inuit] don't waste anything. What they cannot use, they feed to the dogs; the dogs need to be fed.

And when I came back, my classmate said, don't come any further, go back there, I will heat the water, have a bath first. I said, okay. But that was really an interesting trip. Just to be out there and see the ice flows and how they actually live and so on. And then we ate the fresh liver from the bear. And they did it one way and of course I knew how they do it better so I had some flour. They put in flour and fried a bit in fat and we all ate the liver.[9]

AC: Wow! How was it relative to cow liver? Same?

MS: It is an animal, organic.

AC: How many people can say they've actually had polar bear liver?

MS: Good question, yes. But the isolation eventually is living with the same people all the time and there's little this and that. Also things were starting to happen with the native people, stuff was coming in that wasn't really good for them and they started to buy canned food at Hudson's Bay rather than just eating their own [food] and I am not sure and that was also the time when the children were literally rounded up and taken to boarding school in Churchill whether they wanted to go or not, they had to go and it caused a lot of difficulties when they came back with the families. They ate different food down there and different schedule and the language and everything. It caused a lot of difficulty for the people.

AC: Very disruptive and that's like a whole generation that I suppose, in the long term, would cause a big disruption in the community.

MS: The consequences, well, yes. Well, see I don't know. I was only there for two years, I left, I was there only for two years. I just felt that was enough. I needed to get out. But I also know the introduction of alcohol. And that caused problems. People didn't always appreciate the power of alcohol and then they did things afterwards that they wouldn't have done had they not been drinking. But I went online just last year, I think to check out and they are saying alcohol is not allowed on Coral Harbour.

That I was very pleased to hear. So, they have learned and they are—people in the north, you hear many negative things, but they are a proud people and they do some of their carvings and their artwork and so on and so forth that I respect them.

AC: Yeah. There has been a lot of work done to reclaim that heritage, that way of life. Maybe not reclaim if they never really had it, but reappropriating something that their ancestors had and incorporating that into their life so it doesn't die, keeping it alive somehow. So, how did you deal with the isolation of being up there? Because it makes some people crack like even in the city if they can't go for more than a couple of days without being around people.

MS: Well, of course as nurses we had people coming to the nursing station for colds and this and that and the other thing and they also came sometimes to have their babies. They are at the nursing stations so we did that. And then we would make some visits to various homes of some people we thought needed, older people in a wheelchair and they got foot and hand care and stuff like that. So, that was busy and the other thing is there were sometimes get-togethers among the white people and sometimes with the native people. Then there were people from DOT sometimes, some of the men from DOT were invited to come over for meals and we sometimes did some cooking and entertaining.

And then there was a record listening to music and of course writing letters; in those days to communicate with people would be writing letters.

AC: Then you had a contract to be up in Coral Harbour?

MS: I was an employee with National Health and Welfare. Not really a contract, I was hired by them to go out there and whenever I wished I could resign. But then I ended up after I owed them more than a year because I stayed three years. So, I didn't go back to Coral Harbour. They had offered me Frobisher Bay and I said I will take it and then because somebody else who was there said, no, I am not leaving, I'm staying, so I ended up going to Fort Smith, which is on the border of Alberta and the Northwest Territory. It's located under Great Slave River.

Yeah, and so I ended up there at the request of National Health and Welfare, started a program for nursing assistants. There was a hospital in

Fort Smith and then they could use some people with some knowledge and so on. So, I did that. But for some reason, I don't know there were some, I don't even know what happened; there was a lot of turnover and that only lasted for about a year. And that was pretty well my end as far as working in the north is concerned. And before I went to Fort Smith, they sent me to Whitehorse to see what they were doing there in that particular school. And while I was at Whitehorse I took the train over to Skagway, Alaska, along the Gold Rush Road, that was fascinating. There was a train running still at that time, I don't think it's running anymore.

AC: They probably have highways.

MS: The government paid for my flight too and my stay for Whitehorse. Yeah, so I have really been in the Arctic—in spite of the fact of loneliness and one that I still have a fascination for the Arctic. In '75, I went with a group of people on a ten-day hike on Baffin Island, but that was a private thing. And that was really my last trip in the Arctic. So, it was sort of '64 to '75, yeah. I didn't make it up to Ellesmere Island or the North Pole. And I had been to Inuvik so, that's quite far north and the west.

[*I asked Schroeder more directly about her experience with Gould, being interviewed for* The Idea of North.]

MS: I came in rather at the end. Very late really,[10] when you consider I think it was '66 when he interviewed me and this had to be ready for '67. I think it was '66 or late '65, it had to be '66 because that is when I came back from the Arctic and when I came from the Arctic to go to [University of Toronto] for a post basic Bachelor of Science in Nursing and that is when Glenn contacted me because of these people.

AC: And you were staying at Victoria College.

MS: At that time yeah, I am pretty sure I was at Victoria—yes I was. Next to Victoria College is a small building, there is now a museum of ceramic china or something like that. Between the museum and the main building of Victoria College is a small building where the nurses lived. That is where I lived and it is still there. And Glenn Gould came there to meet me at a certain time and took me over to the studio on Jarvis Street.

Yes, and when Lorne [Tulk] drove by there last week and he says that's the CBC building? I said yes, that is where Glenn took me. And he said, he did? And I said, yes, we went up the stairs and I was in a room, it looked like a telephone booth. And he said, oh yeah, you were in Room C.

I think when we drove by he showed me, he pointed out another building. It's a taller building, a gray building on another street and he said that's where I worked, that's where we did all the work—whatever that means I don't know. See, I don't know that much because I came in, in the end, which is—I did what I was asked to do or invited to do.

AC: And you were introduced to [Gould] through Joan Maxwell?

MS: Yes, actually that's right. When I was in Winnipeg, in the school of nursing, Misericordia Hospital School of Nursing. And while I was there, I was one of the older students. The Director of Nursing was a sister at St. Adeline, they were the Sisters of Misericordia who owned and operated that hospital. She called me into the office and I thought oh, I didn't know anything at all. So, I went there and she said there is this young couple and they have a child. I think he was about two years old if that and they would like someone who is responsible to babysit this boy. Would I go, now what do you say?

You said, you go. And so, I did go and I became part of their family. They kept inviting me back into family events and I had gone to some of the recitals and concerts wherever Joan sang.

AC: And then they relocated to Toronto?

MS: Yes, they relocated to Toronto. And then Joan ended up with severe back problems and she had to give up singing and she became a voice coach. And they had gone, they had moved to Ottawa and then eventually back to Toronto. So, somehow through that I guess Glenn was telling them what he was planning on doing and that he was looking for somebody and so and so and so that's then how he contacted me; he being Glenn Gould.

AC: And that's it!

MS: That's it.

MS: This is a good picture of him [*shows me a photo of Gould in his overcoat, gloves, and hat*], but he was sort of—I don't know what, but he was always with this big overcoat and hunched over and shoes and laces undone, and gloves in the middle of a summer like that. People will probably say who is this? Who is picking up Marianne today?

With Glenn Gould there was, I think it was only one [interview], but we had to break it up because I was so nervous. He told me what he was looking for and I had to have earphones I think and I had to be in that cubicle and he said Marianne, I think you're nervous come on we'll have a coffee and so he was understanding of that and then we talked a bit and then went back in, but I think it was just in one session.

That's why sometimes I think I had no idea at that time that this would be so far reaching. I had no idea that someday we would be sitting here and talking about it and then somebody from Italy and then that film and that—he wanted to talk with me because I was in the north and that's what I lived, you know.

Well, I guess I was kind of settling down then after a little while. And I was just thinking when we did the filming, I don't think Glenn Gould was involved and not when I was there—the filming was done. I had been at the Nightingale School of Nursing at one time; one year I lived at Nightingale and one year at, what's that college again, and then one year in South Rosedale. So, while I was there in three different places.

By the time of the film version, I had gone back north, I was in Fort Smith. So, I was contacted and I came south for the filming and Judith Pearlman said to me, well, you know we were thinking of getting somebody else for the filming, an actress or someone. She says, but you're a natural, we'll keep you, which is okay. I mean there isn't that much of me shown.

AC: You're the only woman that Mr. Gould interviewed, which is interesting. Because also the other four people were there in very detached roles, two academics, so Mr. Lotz, Mr. Vallee, with the PhDs, and then Robert Phillips, who is a bureaucrat, and Wally Maclean. I think almost from the roles as men would have had almost prescribed [roles]. I won't say detached, but I think that's the only word I can come up with now. So, in your role as a nurse there and certainly you say you were the first nurses in Coral Harbour.

MS: Yes, we were. Yes.

AC: You would have many more personal interactions with the community members just by the virtue of, I mean healthcare is a very personal thing. How would you say that your experience in that respect as being a female up there, as a nurse and having personal contact, would that shape your own impressions in your experiences there as opposed to being one of the men with kind of this coming at it as an outsider, very much keeping an us-versus-them kind of professional context?

MS: That's an interesting question. I have not looked at it that way. As a nurse, like I said there were two of us, there was a classmate of mine and I, myself. I really wanted to be in contact with the people, personal contact that's what we do. Like you can only get to know people when you interact with them. We were allowed—they welcomed us into their homes if we needed to go in and the children were just delightful and they were curious about us too. We were the first nurses there. We were just so busy, there was just a steady stream of people coming. The women with the baby in the back and so on. And that kind of established a rapport and the fact that the woman who worked, she worked in the house as a translator, she was Inuit, and we got along well with her and we also had a local man who did the cutting of the ice and bringing the ice and the melting and did some of the heavier work.

So, I think because we had much more interaction with the local people than anybody else, maybe I will say not even the teachers have as much interaction with the families themselves as we did.

And I think that gives me a very different view on the north. And I'm more familiar with the people of that particular settlement of Coral Harbour. The geology and all this of the area, I know what it was like, what I saw, but I'm not an expert in any of that. But my focus was on working with the people and getting to know the people and I think did reasonably well with that. I think they liked us and actually one of the guys said to me one time Marianne stay here, marry one of us. So, you stay with us. I thought well . . .

AC: That comes across in the documentary, just the kinds of responses. You really do get the impression that there was a much more personal connection as opposed to, well, you know this is what I did in the north without really any hint that there was a connection with the people.

Now, in scene 4, the dining car scene, at the very beginning, okay there's the train here, the dining, the equipment, the plates. What you hear first is ice clinking in a scotch glass and they're talking about the "Eskimos" and alcoholism. And it's very brief, it's maybe three or four minutes, maybe not even that long which apparently was the only hint that there was going to be a whole scene about Eskimos. In that scene later on, you talked about the delivery of a new baby girl and someone has assigned a name that translated to worm or parasite. None of these men would have had that or could have had that [experience].

MS: No, they couldn't have. No. Well, that's interesting that you said that. I never—because I didn't meet the men, I know what they are. Yeah, they went there as scientists I guess, I went there as a nurse. And when you talked about alcoholism and who brought the alcohol up to the Arctic.

There was another time that there was this little girl, they brought her into the nursing station. She had a cold, yeah, I guess it must have been the mother and maybe the grandmother and we said, well leave her here, we'll take care of her overnight, and we don't know what had happened, if it was a pneumonia or whatever, the child died. And we were trying to do the mouth-to-mouth resuscitation everything and then we had to go and say look. And the child's father had been away fishing.

And when he came back, the child was gone. She was buried. They had burial above ground because they couldn't dig. So, they put rocks over. And he came and said what happened to our child? And we said, we don't really know. We tried our best. But that's a connection with the family, with families that you get and that was a poor connect—we had a very painful connection, but you don't get that when you go up there as a technician, whatever. We did have intimate relationships, contact I should say, with the local people.

AC: Yeah. That one—the worm and parasite, that really sticks out in that scene, it's very noticeable. And then there was another part where, I'm probably paraphrasing, you said something about women are seen and not heard or women don't have a voice in the family or some such. And as soon as you say that [Lorne] Tulk turns down the volume and you just kind of faded into the background. That's really interesting. It took me a little while to hear that.

You said something in [a previous] interview about the *Idea of North* being operatic.

MS: Operatic, did I say that?

AC: And that struck me. I remember that very clearly because in this article that he wrote in 1970, he talked about contrapuntal radio and all the voices at the same time. He said, no one questions Verdi and the fugue at the end of *Falstaff*. When there is, I think it's eight people singing at the same time, no one complained about Verdi and not being able to understand the words, it's about the texture, it's about the music. And so it was the prologue or the introduction to *The Idea of North* and then scene 4, it's supposed to take place in a dining car, which is his personal favorite.

You can see how Tulk was—where the tapes would have connected, one voice to another and then how he would have been manipulating the volume dials on the console. It moves one voice down or another voice goes up and I mean it's very clear stopping one tape player and starting another, really neat.

There's no other way to describe what it really is. It's operatic.

MS: See that was a special inspiration I had.

AC: What were your thoughts when you first heard it?

MS: Oh, this is a real mix up. And I have my parents down in Windsor watch as well and listen to it as well and they said, well we couldn't understand what was being said. There were too many voices at the same time. You know, they didn't know Glenn Gould and well I didn't really know him either. I just knew who he was but, I listen to it every once in a while, and now I think differently about it than at that time.

I didn't quite know how he was going to put it all together. I don't recall him explaining that it would be contrapuntal and all this kind of stuff, which I wouldn't have known what it meant. So, it was a little bit of a surprise but then there is also kind of—there was a flow to it and Wally Maclean is kind of the background and keeps the train moving.

And the other people—well, I thought it was quite interesting really, although like he says you don't understand everything in an opera either, you sure don't and I didn't get everything but certainly I enjoyed listening to it.

AC: Lorne [Tulk] mentioned actually most of the reactions that listeners had were from the US, in communities that were close to the Canadian relays so they could hear across the border and most of the letters that they got were from Americans saying, what was this? What are you Canadians doing up there? And that's when they had the vinyl [release] pressed and there are several letters where Gould says thank you for your interest, I'm enclosing this album, you might be interested in it. So, people would have a chance to get a better listening experience on their hi-fi.

MS: Yes, that's right. The technology was so much different when it was first heard on the radio. But periodically you can still hear it. I've just had a friend here not too long ago and she said I heard you on radio. I said, oh, did you? But then this has happened a couple of times that somebody said, yes, I did and without me asking they just said, were you in a program this and this and yes. Well, yes I thought it was your voice. And then people I know.

[*Returning to her reminiscences on her time in the North.*]

AC: Your experience of the north has kind of stayed with you all this time.

MS: Oh, it has. It has. Like you see this book, for instance, I go somewhere and I see something and immediately it draws me—there is something, I think it's probably the grandeur of the land, the beauty of the land, the silence. And that's probably a lot of it. It's so clean, so pristine. And I think that's probably a lot of what it is and I'm drawn into silence anyway. I belong to a meditation group and there's a lot of silence in there. That's one of the major things of Zen, and at least the Zen that I belong to is trying to live in the moment. That's all you have right now, trying to live and being sidetracked, doing two or three things and one is multitasking things and all that kind of stuff.

AC: So, apart from joining the Zen group, that love for silence, how has your time in the north manifested itself in life since then?

MS: That's pretty hard to answer. It's so much part of my life. I'm so fascinated by it and whatever we experienced it affects us.

Whether we're aware of it or not, I can't really say anything specific how it affected me but it obviously has affected me. There's no doubt about that. Maybe the fact that I'm involved in Zen and I'm always part of it, drawn into the silence. And the way we do it, it's on a regular basis. At least every day I spend about twenty-five minutes in total silence. No radio, nothing, no talking, no other people.

It's not, you know—people say, well I don't know who I am, my name, I was born here, I was there. But as a person, who I am, really that's one of the things.

AC: That is a tough one to answer. Do you miss the north? Would you go back if you have a chance?

MS: To the Arctic? I think I would like to see Coral Harbour again to see what it's like, to see if any of the people that are there or still there or some of the children are obviously now grown-up people.

I was thinking, actually like I say I went online and there are phones, I contacted the mission up there, the white people and see, I might do that yet. Whether or not I'll make it is a different story. But I do think about wanting to go back to Coral Harbour to see that.

AC: Do you think that if things had changed too much in a way like when you went back to visit Europe after you were in Windsor. Do you think that there might be a similar reaction if you went back to Coral Harbour now?

MS: Possible. I'm sure it is very different after fifty years, but it's almost fifty, if I were to go back it would be fifty years later and much more commercialized, touristy, not the same. It could very well be a disappointment rather than, well, I don't know. It depends, you know, I would be delighted if there were still some people there like the Inuit, the local people that I could talk with. I haven't even thought of—I have a number of pictures of them, make a copy, and send this out and say, I remember so and so is still around and take a picture. Send the picture, a copy of me and my friend and saying, do you remember us, we're the first nurses up there. They'd probably have iPhones and whatnot, iPads, they could answer. I don't know.

AC: So, even though it's more developed now, I think solitude and isolation isn't too far away. But even as the south intrudes, if there had been more southern—a lot of the telecommunications and all that stuff intruding in Coral Harbour in that kind of the pristine solitude. Do you think that would have impacted your personal experience of being there or how might it have impacted your experience of being there?

MS: You mean all these technologies today.

AC: If these technologies had been there, if you had an iPhone, if you had the internet and all these kinds of things, the satellite television, would you still have had to confront that isolation and would you have to confront the question of what am I really? Where am I really?

MS: I don't think I would have liked it. I preferred it the way it was. I mean you were . . . I knew when I was going up there that I would be isolated. And I think many of these things are just distractions and we can live quite nicely without them. I think that they're great to have, sometimes it would have been good to be able to get the people quicker that we needed like the doctors to get some help quicker, and to have better communication with the hospital in Churchill. We sent somebody down with, we had an idea what the problem was with the person, but the situation was, people were treated and sent back and we didn't get any reports from the hospital, we didn't know what the follow-up would be. So, it would have been nice to have a functioning telephone and say like look, what are we doing, what kind of aftercare does this person need?

In that sense it would have been welcomed. But I think personally I don't think it was so much the isolation; what it was, was partially the close knit—you were tied closely to the people in the area and there was no escape from the people. And you would learn to know the idiosyncrasies of the various people and depending on one's maturity or lack thereof, it can create problems.

AC: So, they don't deal with those problems?

MS: Well, you don't have to deal with them, but I don't even watch much television now. It's a personal thing. And if I do listen to tapes and I do watch some TV, it's not that I never do. But I don't really quite know what to say to that.

AC: I've heard similar questions asked of people who lived in other parts of the world that were at one point very isolated now are very heavily developed. And it seems increasingly, it's very difficult to go anywhere and have a kind of isolation out there was thirty, forty, fifty years ago. And that the kind of process of self-discovery because of isolation is going away and is it even possible to have that anymore if you are living in places with so many distractions and you don't have to be confronted with the situation where you have to think about that, which is why . . . ?

MS: Well, okay, you are confronted with it. It was more than down here now. And it's also very magic. Not everybody looks at it that way.

Notes

1. Jim Lotz, *The Best Journey in the World: Adventures in Canada's High Arctic* (Lawrencetown Beach, NS: Pottersfield Press, 2006).

2. In preparation of the manuscript for this book, the editors looked through Gould's questions for both Maclean and Lotz and could not find a reference to "Fellini." It is as much a mystery to the editors as it will be to readers.

3. Lotz refers to the bureaucrats of the Canadian federal civil service, based in Ottawa, rather than the city itself.

4. Like Gould's reference to "Fellini," Lotz's reference to "chikatto" is cryptic.

5. "Honey bucket" is the term used for a bucket toilet or a container to carry human excrement. It came into common use in the 1930s.

6. The source for *Der Spiegel*'s contention that Gould wrote jazz music is unclear. No other documentary evidence exists to suggest Gould ever did anything that could be remotely classified as "jazz."

7. Contrary to what is written here, Gould wrote the opus 1 string quartet in the early 1950s, thus well before he retired from the concert stage. The first commercial recording by the Symphonia Quartet also dates to 1960, thus several years before his retirement.

8. The phrase "such is live" is written in English in the original article.

9. A quick Google search on the term "polar bear liver" reveals that polar bear liver is considered to be quite dangerous. Its high levels of vitamin A can cause a condition called Hypervitaminosis A, which can be fatal.

10. A letter from Jim Lotz to Gould on 7 September 1967 indicates that Gould was still conducting interviews until approximately three and a half months from the documentary premiere date. It is possible that Schroeder misremembered the year in which she was interviewed.

Bibliography

Adorno, Theodor W. "On Popular Music." In *Essays on Music: Theodor W. Adorno*, edited by Richard Leppert. Berkeley: University of California Press, 2002.
Agamben, Giorgio. *Homo Sacer: Sovereign Power and Bare Life*. Translated by Daniel Heller-Roazen. Stanford: Stanford University Press, 1998.
Allan, Andrew. *Andrew Allan: A Self-Portrait*. Toronto: Macmillan Canada, 1974.
Alten, Stanley R. *Audio in Media*. 10th ed. Boston: Wadsworth, 2014.
Anderson, Tim J. *Making Easy Listening: Material Culture and Postwar American Recording*. Minneapolis: University of Minnesota Press, 2006.
Arendt, Hannah. *Eichmann in Jerusalem: A Report on the Banality of Evil*. New York: Penguin Classics, 2010.
Augaitis, Diana, and Dan Lander, eds. *Radio Rethink: Art, Sound, and Transmission*. Banff: Walter Phillips Gallery, 1994.
Baldwin, Carryl L. *Auditory Cognition*. Boca Raton: CRC Press, 2012.
Barry, Eric. "Mono in the Stereo Age." In *Living Stereo: Histories and Cultures of Multichannel Sound*, edited by Paul Théberge, Kyle Devine, and Paul Everrett, 125–146. New York: Bloomsbury, 2015.
Bazzana, Kevin. *Glenn Gould: The Performer in the Work*. New York: Oxford University Press, 1997.
———. *Wondrous Strange: The Life and Art of Glenn Gould*. Toronto: Oxford University Press, 2004.
Bennett, John, and Susan Rowley, eds. *Uqalurait*. Montreal: McGill-Queen's University Press, 2004.
Bergman, Rhona. *The Idea of Gould*. Philadelphia: Lev, 1999.
Bester, Alfred. "The Zany Genius of Glenn Gould." *Holiday*, April 1964, 149–154, 156.
Borio, Gianmario, and Hermann Danuser. *Im Zenit Der Moderne: Die Internationalen Ferienkurse Für Neue Musik Darmstadt 1946–1966: Geschichte Und Dokumentation in Vier Bänden*. Freiburg im Breisgau: Rombach, 1997.
Bostridge, Ian. *Schubert's Winter Journey: Anatomy of an Obsession*. New York: Knopf, 2015.

Breitsameter, Sabine. "Ways of Listening, Figures of Thought." In *Ways of Listening, Figures of Thought*, edited by Sabine Breitsameter and Eric Leonardson, 17–36. Darmstadt: Hochschule Darmstadt, 2013.

Canning, Nancy. *A Glenn Gould Catalog*. Westport, CT: Greenwood Press, 1992.

Capeless, Richard. "How They Heard It: Blue Note Records and the Transition from Mono to Stereo." *LondonJazzCollector* [sic]. https://londonjazzcollector.wordpress.com/2014/07/24/guest-post-how-they-heard-it-blue-note-records-and-the-transition-from-mono-to-stereo/ 23 October 2014 (revision of 24 July 2014 blog post). Accessed 27 December 2023.

Cavell, Richard. *McLuhan in Space: A Cultural Geography*. Toronto: University of Toronto Press, 2002.

Carlyle, Angus. *Autumn Leaves*. Paris: Double Entendre, 2007.

Carroll, Jock. *Glenn Gould: Some Portraits of the Artist as a Young Man*. Toronto: Stoddart, 1995.

Cherry, Colin. "Some Experiments on the Recognition of Speech, with One and with Two Ears." *Journal of the Acoustical Society of America* 25, no. 5 (1953): 975–979.

Cirauqui, Manuel. "Thanatophonics: From White Noise to Forensic Radio." *PAJ: A Journal of Performance and Art* 104 (2013): 20–25.

Coates, Peter A. "The Strange Stillness of the Past: Toward an Environmental History of Sound and Noise." *Environmental History* 10, no. 4 (October 2005): 649.

Cott, Jonathan. *Conversations with Glenn Gould*. Chicago: University of Chicago Press, 1997.

Cook, Nicholas. *Music, Performance, Meaning: Selected Essays*. Aldershot: Ashgate, 2007.

Csampai, Attila. *Glenn Gould: Photographische Suiten*. Munich: Schirmer/Mosel, 1995.

Cushing, Anthony. "Glenn Gould and 'Opus 2': An Outline for a Musical Understanding of Contrapuntal Radio with Respect to *The Idea of North*." *Circuit: Musiques contemporaines* 22, no. 2 (2012): 21–35.

Dahlhaus, Carl. *Nineteenth-Century Music*. Berkeley: University of California Press, 1989.

Davidson, Peter. *The Idea of North*. London: Reaktion Books, 2004.

Der, Lawrence. "Frequency Modulation (FM) Tutorial." Austin: Silicon Laboratories. 2008. http://www.silabs.com/support%20documents/technicaldocs/fmtutorial.pdf. Accessed 10 October 2016.

Despoix, Phillipe. "Radio as Music: A Video Document by (and with) Glenn Gould." *Intermédialités: histoire et théorie des arts, des lettres et des techniques* 19 (2012): 177–180.

Dorrough, Michael. "The VU Meter." Paper presentation 1794, 69th Audio Engineering Society Convention. May 1981. http://www.aes.org/e-lib/browse.cfm?elib=11960&rndx=242582 and http://www.aes.org/e-lib/browse.cfm?elib=11960. Accessed 5 December 2016.

Fearn, Raymond. *Bruno Maderna*. Chur, CH: Harwood Academic, 1990.
Fink, Howard. "Glenn Gould's Idea of North: The Arctic Archetype and the Creation of a Syncretic Genre." *Glenn Gould* 3, no. 2 (Fall 1997): 35–42.
———. "On the Trail of Radio Drama: Organizing a Study of North American and European Practices." *Journal of Radio Studies* 6, no. 1 (1999): 121–133.
Flemming, Fergus. *90 Degrees North: The Quest for the North Pole*. New York: Grove Press, 2001.
Friedrich, Otto. *Glenn Gould: A Life and Variations*. New York: Random House, 1989.
Fulford, Robert. *Accidental City: The Transformation of Toronto*. Toronto: Macfarlane Walter & Ross, 1995.
———. "Glenn Gould in the Age of Radio." *Glenn Gould* 6, no. 1 (Spring 2000): 17–23.
Girard, François, dir. *Thirty Two Short Films About Glenn Gould*. Columbia TriStar Home Video, 1993.
Gould, Glenn. *Acoustic Orchestrations: Works by Scriabin and Sibelius*. B008L8OFJU, Sony Music, 2013.
———. *The Art of Glenn Gould*. "On Records and Recording," radio broadcast. November 13, 1966. AIN 661113-6. CBC Radio Archive.
———. "Forgery and Imitation in the Creative Process." In *The Art of Glenn Gould: Reflections of a Musical Genius*, edited by John P. L. Roberts, 205–221. Toronto: Malcolm Lester Books, 1999.
———. *Glenn Gould: Concert Dropout, in Conversation with John McClure*. Recorded interview. Columbia Masterworks BS 15, 1968. LP. Printed in *Glenn Gould* 7, no. 2 (Fall 2001): 46–60.
———. *The Glenn Gould Reader*. Edited by Tim Page. New York: Vintage Books, 1990.
———. *Glenn Gould's Solitude Trilogy: Three Sound Documentaries*. PSCD 2003-3, CBC Records, 1992.
———. *Glenn Gould: The Radio Artist*. Five compact discs, PSCD 20315, CBC Records, 2007.
———. *Goldberg Variations: BWV 988*. CBS Masterworks IM 37779, 1982. LP.
———. Interview with Robert Hurwitz. *New York Times*, 5 January 1975.
———. "The Prospects of Recording." *High Fidelity Magazine*, April 1966: 46–63.
———. "Twenty-Five Years as a Recording Artist: Gould in Conversation with Ulla Colgrass." In *The Art of Glenn Gould*, edited by John P. L. Roberts. Toronto: Malcolm Lester Books, 1999.
Grace, Sherrill E. *Canada and the Idea of North*. Montreal: McGill-Queen's University Press, 2001.
Grimley, Daniel. *Carl Nielsen and the Idea of Modernism*. Woodbridge, UK: Boydell Press, 2010.
———. *Grieg: Music, Landscape and Norwegian Identity*. Woodbridge, UK: Boydell Press, 2005.

Hall, Margaret Ann. "Radio After Radio: Redefining Radio Art in the Light of New Media Technology Through Expanded Practice." PhD thesis. University of the Arts, London, 2015.

Hancox, Rick. "Film—Is There a Future in Our Past? (The Afterlife of Latent Images)." Keynote speech at Is Film Dead? A Symposium on the State of Celluloid, Atlantic Filmmakers Cooperative, Halifax, 23 March 2007.

Hanslick, Eduard. *The Beautiful in Music*. Translated by Geoffrey Payzant. New York: Da Capo Press, 1986.

Hardy, Thomas. *The Complete Poems of Thomas Hardy*. Edited by James Gibson. New York: Collier Books, 1982.

Harris, Mark Lee. "Fugue States: Music, Dissociation, and Ethical Implications." Unpublished PhD thesis, Concordia University, 2001.

Heble, Ajay. "New Contexts of Canadian Criticism: Democracy, Counterpoint, Responsibility." In *New Contexts of Canadian Criticism*, edited by Ajay Heble, Donna Palmateer Pennee, and J. R. Struthers, 78–97. Peterborough, ON: Broadview Press, 1997.

Heile, Björn. *The Music of Mauricio Kagel*. Aldershot, UK: Ashgate, 2006.

Higgins, Dick. "A Taxonomy of Sound Poetry." http://www.ubu.com/papers/higgins_sound.html 1980. Accessed 23 December 2023.

Hjartarson, Paul. "Inward Journeys and Interior Landscapes: Glenn Gould, Lawren Harris, and 'The Idea of North.'" *Essays on Canadian Writing* 59 (Fall 1996): 65–86.

Hoeverler, Diane Long, and Jeffrey Cass, eds. *Interrogating Orientalism: Contextual Approaches and Pedagogical Practices*. Columbus, OH: Ohio State University Press, 2006.

Hogarth, David. *Documentary Television in Canada: From National Public Service to Global Marketplace*. Montreal: McGill-Queen's University Press, 2002.

Hozer, Michèle, and Peter Raymont, dirs. *The Genius Within: The Inner Life of Glenn Gould*. Lorber Films, 2011.

Hui, Yuk. "What Is a Digital Object?" *Metaphilosophy* 43, no. 4 (July 2012): 380–395.

Ingold, Tim. "Against Soundscape." In *Autumn Leaves*, 10–13. Paris: Double Entendre. 2007.

Jackson, David C. "Militant Sound Investigation." Conference paper read at Circuits of Struggle, Ontario, 2 May 2015.

James, William. *Writings, 1902–1910*. New York: Library of America, 1987.

Johnson, Penny. "Stories Untold: An Interview with *The Idea of North* editor, Peter Shewchuk." Glenn Gould Foundation, 12 April 2010. https://web.archive.org/web/20160429212033/http://www.glenngould.ca/stories-untold-an-interview-with-the-idea-of-north-editor-peter-shewchuk/http://www.glenngould.ca/stories-untold-an-interview-with-the-idea-of-north-editor-peter-shewchuk. Accessed 22 December 2023.

Jones-Imhotep, Edward. "Malleability and Machines: Glenn Gould and the Technological Self." *Technology and Culture* 57, no. 2 (April 2016): 287–321.
Kazdin, Andrew. *Glenn Gould at Work: Creative Lying*. New York: E. P. Dutton, 1989.
Keightley, Keir. " 'Turn It Down!' She Shrieked: Gender, Domestic Space, and High Fidelity, 1948–59." *Popular Music* 15, no. 2 (May 1996): 149–177.
Keithahn, Edward L. *Eskimo Adventure: Another Little Journey into the Primitive*. New York: Bonanza Books, 1963.
Kelman, Ari Y. "Rethinking the Soundscape." *Sense and Society* 5, no. 2 (2010): 212–234.
Kennan, Kent. *Counterpoint*. 4th ed. Englewood Cliffs, NJ: Prentice-Hall, 1999.
Kingwell, Mark. *Glenn Gould*. Toronto: Penguin Canada, 2011.
Kirkpatrick, Smith. "Review: *Ship of Fools*." *Sewanee Review* 71, no. 1 (Winter 1963): 94–98.
Kostelanetz, Richard. "Glenn Gould as Radio Composer." *Massachusetts Review* 29, no. 3 (Fall 1988): 557–570.
———. *The New Poetries and Some Old*. Carbondale: Southern Illinois University Press, 1991.
———. "Text Sound Art: A Survey." In *Text-Sound Texts*, 14–24. New York: William Morrow, 1980.
Kostelanetz, Richard, and Oriana Leckert, eds. *Three Canadian Geniuses*. Toronto: Colombo, 1999.
Kusch, Martin. *Ymmärtämisen haaste* [The Challenge for Understanding]. Oulu: Pohjoinen, 1986.
Lane, Cathy. "Voices from the Past: Compositional Approaches to Using Recorded Speech." *Organized Sound* 11, no. 1 (2006): 3–11.
Lanzmann, Claude, dir. *Shoah*. New Yorker Films, 1985.
LeBlanc, Larry. "Industry Profile: Stephen Posen." *In the Hot Seat with Larry LeBlanc*. http://www.celebrityaccess.com/members/profile.html?id=630&PHPSESSID=21hdlqtighrfqulao06p5driu1. Accessed 30 January 2013.
Liberman, M. M. "The Short Story as Chapter in 'Ship of Fools.' " *Criticism* 10, no. 1 (Winter 1968): 65–71.
Littler, William. "Glenn Gould: Inside the Mind of a Genius." *Toronto Star*, 9 October 1982, F1.
———. "His Curiosity Made Label of Pianist So Inadequate." *Toronto Star*, 5 October 1982, E1.
———. "The Quest for Solitude." In *Glenn Gould Variations: By Himself and His Friends*, edited by John McGreevy, 217–224. Toronto: Doubleday, 1983.
Lotz, Jim. *Northern Realities: Canada-U.S. Exploitation of the Canadian North*. Chicago: Follet, 1971.
Lyotard, Jean-François. *Lessons on the Analytic of the Sublime*. Translated by Elizabeth Rottenberg. Stanford: Stanford University Press, 1994.

MacMillan, Ernest, ed. *Music in Canada*. Toronto: University of Toronto, 1955.
Mansell, Darrel. "Glenn Gould: The Idea of South by North." *Iowa Review* 15, no. 3 (Fall 1985): 58–65.
Mantere, Markus. *The Gould Variations: Technology, Philosophy and Criticism in Glenn Gould's Musical Thought and Practice*. Frankfurt: Peter Lang, 2012.
———. "Northern Ways to Think About Music: Glenn Gould's *Idea of North* as an Aesthetic Category." *Intersections: Canadian Journal of Music* 25, no. 1–2 (2005): 86–112.
Mauer, Barry. "Glenn Gould and the New Listener." *Performance Research* 15, no. 3 (2010): 103–108.
McGreevy, John, dir. *Glenn Gould's Toronto*. John McGreevy Productions and Nielsen Ferns, 1979.
McGreevy, John, ed. *Glenn Gould Variations*. Toronto: Macmillan Canada, 1983.
McLuhan, Marshall. "New Media and the Arts." *Arts in Society: The Avant-Garde Today* 3, no. 2 (1965): 239–242. http://digital.library.wisc.edu/1711.dl/Arts.ArtsSocv03i2. Accessed 27 December 2023.
———. *Understanding Media: The Extensions of Man*. New York: McGraw-Hill, 1964.
McNeilly, Kevin. "Listening, Nordicity, Community: Glenn Gould's 'The Idea of North.'" *Essays on Canadian Writing* 59 (Fall 1996): 87–104.
Medvedev, Sergei. "The_Blank_Space: Glenn Gould, Russia, Finland and the North." *CTheory* 23, no. 2 (June 2000). https://journals.uvic.ca/index.php/ctheory/article/view/14603.
Mingus, Charles. *The Black Saint and the Sinner Lady*. Untitled liner notes, ITC 308 (insert A), Impulse! Records, 1963.
Moholy-Nagy, László. "New Form in Music: Potentialities of the Phonograph" [1923]. In *Moholy-Nagy*, edited by Krisztina Passuth, 291–292. New York: Thames and Hudson, 1985.
Monsaingeon, Bruno. *Glenn Gould the Alchemist*. DVD. Directed by François-Louis Ribadeau. EMI Classics, [1974] 2002.
Mowat, Farley. *People of the Deer*. Boston: Little, Brown, 1952.
Mudede, Charles. "The Turntable." *CTheory* (24 April 2003). https://web.archive.org/web/20191101211508/http://www.ctheory.net/articles.aspx?id=382. Accessed 27 December 2023.
Neumann, Anyssa. "Ideas of North: Glenn Gould and the Aesthetic of the Sublime." *voiceXchange* 5 no. 1 (Fall 2011): 39.
Nichols, Bill. "Documentary Reenactment and the Fantasmatic Subject." *Critical Inquiry* 35 (Autumn 2008): 72–89.
Nietzsche, Friedrich. *Beyond Good and Evil*. Compiled from translations by Helen Zimmernin and Walter Kaufmann. http://www.thenietzschechannel.com/works-pub/bge/bge-eng.htm. Accessed September 29, 2016.
———. *The Case of Wagner*. Translated by Walter Kaufmann. New York: Vintage, 1967.

Norden, Hugo. *Fundamental Counterpoint*. Boston: Crescendo, 1969.
Oliveros, Pauline. *Deep Listening: A Composer's Sound Practice*. New York: iUniverse, 2005.
Ostwald, Peter. *Glenn Gould: The Ecstasy and Tragedy of a Genius*. New York: W. W. Norton, 1997.
Owsinski, Bobby. *The Mastering Engineer's Handbook*. 4th ed. Burbank: BOMG, 2016.
Paddison, Max. *Adorno's Aesthetics of Music*. Cambridge: Cambridge University Press, 1997.
Parakilis, James. "How Spain Got a Soul." In *The Exotic in Western Music*, edited by Jonathan Bellman, 137–193. Boston: Northeastern University Press, 1998.
Payzant, Geoffrey. *Glenn Gould: Music and Mind*. New York: Van Nostrand Reinhold, 1978.
Pearlman, Judith. "The Idea of North." Director's introduction, *The Idea of Gould*. Cinematheque Ontario, Toronto, 26 April 2008.
Pearlman, Judith, dir. *The Idea of North*. Canadian Broadcasting Corporation and National Educational Television, 1970.
Perloff, Nancy. "Sound Poetry and the Musical Avant-Garde: A Musicologist's Perspective." In *The Sound of Poetry / The Poetry of Sound*, edited by Marjorie Perloff and Craig Dworkin, 97–117. Chicago: University of Chicago Press, 2009.
Phillips, Robert. *Canada's North*. Toronto: Macmillan of Canada, 1967.
Porter, Jeff. "Radio as Music: Glenn Gould's Contrapuntal Sound." In *Lost Sound: The Forgotten Art of Radio Storytelling*, 155–181. Chapel Hill: University of North Carolina Press, 2016.
Pousseur, Henri. *Electre*. Vinyl Record. Universal Edition UE 13.500, 1961.
Purcell, John. *Dialogue Editing for Motion Pictures: A Guide to the Invisible Art*. Burlington, VT: Focal Press, 2007.
Pryde, Duncan. *Nunaga: Ten Years of Eskimo Life*. New York: Bantam Books, 1972.
Roberts, John P. L., Eric Till, and Vincent Tovell. Interview, part 1 (video recording). 8 August 1984. Canadian Broadcasting Corporation Fonds, Item no. 393405. Ottawa, Library and Archives Canada.
Ryall, Anka, John Schimanski, and Henning Howlid Wærp, eds. *Arctic Discourses*. Newcastle upon Tyne, UK: Cambridge Scholars, 2010.
Said, Edward. *Culture and Imperialism*. New York: Vintage Books, 1994.
———. "Glenn Gould, the Virtuoso as Intellectual." *Raritan* 20, no. 1 (Summer 2000): 1–16.
———. *Orientalism*. New York: Random House, 1979.
Sallis, Friedemann. "Glenn Gould's *Idea of North* and the Production of Place in Music." *Intersections: Canadian Journal of Music* 25, no. 1–2 (2005): 113–137.
Salzer, Felix, and Carl Schacter. *Counterpoint in Composition: The Study of Voice Leading*. New York: Columbia University Press, 1989.

Sanden, Paul. "Hearing Glenn Gould's Body: Corporeal Liveness in Recorded Music." *Current Musicology* 88 (2009): 7–34.

Saydack, Roger. "GG: ST on LP." Listserv post, 11 February 2000. http://www.glenngould.org/f_minor/msg04587.html. Accessed 22 December 2023.

Schafer, R. Murray. "Open Ears." *Soundscape: The Journal of Acoustic Ecology* 4, 2 (Fall/Winter 2003): 14–18.

———. *The Tuning of the World*. New York: Alfred A. Knopf, 1977.

Scheper-Hughes, Nancy. *Death Without Weeping*. Berkeley: University of California Press, 1992.

Shelleg, Assaf. *Jewish Contiguities and the Soundtrack of Israeli History*. Oxford: Oxford University Press, 2014.

Shelley, Mary. *Frankenstein*. New York: Penguin Classics, 2007.

Siegert, Bernhard. "Das Hörspiel als Vergangenheitsbewältigung." In *Diskursgeschichte der Medien nach 1945*, edited by Irmela Schneider and Peter M. Spangenberg, 287–298. Wiesbaden: Westdeutscher Verlag, 2002.

Simonton, Dean. "Multiple Discovery and Invention: Zeitgeist, Genius, or Chance?" *Journal of Personality and Social Psychology* 37, no. 9 (1979): 1603–1616.

Skinner, David. "Divided Loyalties: The Early Development of Canada's 'Single' Broadcasting System." *Journal of Radio Studies* 85, no. 1 (May 2005): 136–155.

Skinner, Quentin. "Hermeneutics and the Role of History." *New Literary History* 7, no. 1 (Autumn 1975): 209–232.

Somerville, Janet. "The Gould Radio Documentaries: Some Birth-Memories." CD booklet included in *Glenn Gould's Solitude Trilogy*. Three compact discs, PSCD 2003-3, Toronto, CBC Records, 1992.

Spinelli, Martin. "Rhetorical Figures and the Digital Editing of Radio Speech." *Convergence* 12, no. 2 (2006): 199–212.

———. "Electric Line: The Poetics of Digital Audio Editing." In *New Media Poetics: Contexts, Technotexts, and Theories*, edited by Adalaide Morris and Thomas Swiss, 99–121. Cambridge: MIT Press, 2007.

Steffánson, Vilhjámur. *The Friendly Arctic*. New York: Macmillan, 1921.

Szwed, John F. *Space Is the Place: The Lives and Times of Sun Ra*. New York: Pantheon, 1997.

Taylor, Timothy, Mark Katz, and Tony Grajeda, eds. *Music, Sound, and Technology in America*. Durham, NC: Duke University Press, 2012.

Testa, Bart. *Spirit in the Landscape*. Toronto: Art Gallery of Ontario, 1989.

Thomas, D. K., and C. T. Thompson. "Eskimo Housing as Planned Culture Change." Northern Science Research Group Department of Indian Affairs and Northern Development, Ottawa, 1972.

Thompson, John. "There Is a Strong Visual Component in Radio." [Interview with Glenn Gould conducted in 1975.] *Intermédialités* no. 19 (Spring 2012): 181–187.

Thompson, Virgil. "John Cage Late and Early." *Saturday Review*, 30 January 1960, 38–39.
Till, Eric, and Vincent Tovell, dirs. *Glenn Gould: A Portrait*. Kultur Video, 1985.
Tovell, Vincent, dir. *Journey Without Arrival: A Personal Point of View from Northrop Frye*. Canadian Broadcasting Corporation, 1975.
Tovell, Vincent, et al. "Gould, the Communicator." Panel discussion, National Library of Canada, Ottawa, 25 May 1988, The Glenn Gould Archive. https://www.collectionscanada.gc.ca/glenngould/028010-4020.08-e.html. Accessed 20 June 2017.
Truax, Barry. *Acoustic Communication*. New Jersey: Ablex, 1984.
Tulk, Lorne. "Glenn Gould: Some Journeys into Isolation." CD booklet included in *Glenn Gould's Solitude Trilogy*. Three compact discs, PSCD 2003-3, Toronto, CBC Records, 1992.
Ultra-red. *Five Protocols for Organized Listening*. Self-published pamphlet. 2012. http://www.ultrared.org/uploads/2012-Five_Protocols.pdf. Accessed 27 December 2023.
van den Scott, Lisa-Jo K. "Geographies of Identity and Knowledge: Everyday Lived Experience and Features of the Home, Community, and Land, in a Post-Nomadic Arctic Hamlet." Doctoral dissertation, Northwestern University, 2015.
———. "Time to Defy: The Use of Temporal Spaces to Enact Resistance." In *Oppressions and Resistance: Structure, Agency, Transformation*, edited by Gil Richard Musolf. Bingley, UK: Emerald, 2017.
Walter, Arnold, ed. *Aspects of Music in Canada*. Toronto: University of Toronto Press, 1969.
Watts, Mary Jo. *The Idea of North* by Glenn Gould. Transcript of *The Idea of North*. https://web.archive.org/web/20010224012530/http://www.rci.rutgers.edu/~mwatts/glenn/ion.html 24 February 2001. Accessed 27 December 2023.
Wetters, Brent. "Allegorical Erasmus: Bruno Maderna's *Ritratto di Erasmo*." *Cambridge Opera Journal* 24, no. 2 (July 2012): 159–176.
———. "Darmstadt and the Philosophical Turn." PhD dissertation, Brown University, 2012.
———. "Idea and Actualization: Bruno Maderna's Adaptation of Friedrich Hölderlin's *Hyperion*." *19th Century Music* 36, no. 2 (Fall 2012): 172–190.
Whitehead, Gregory. "Out of the Dark: Notes on the Nobodies of Radio Art." In *Wireless Imagination: Sound, Radio and the Avant-Garde*, edited by Douglas Kahn and Gregory Whitehead, 253–263. Cambridge: MIT Press, 1992.
Williamson, Robert G. *Eskimo Underground: Socio-Cultural Change in the Central Canadian Arctic*. Uppsala: University of Uppsala, 1974.
Zerehi, Sima Sahar. "KTZ Fashion Under Fire for Using Inuit Design Without Family's Consent." *CBC News*, 25 November 2015. http://www.cbc.ca/news/canada/north/ktz-fashion-inuit-design-1.3337047. Accessed 15 December 2015.

Primary Source Materials

Gould, Glenn. "Idea of North | Interview Questions for James Lotz," 1967. Item 1979-20 4 94, Glenn Gould fonds. Library and Archives Canada, Ottawa.

———. "Idea of North | Transcript of James Lotz Interview, Tape 1," 1967. Item 1979-20 4 88, Glenn Gould fonds. Library and Archives Canada, Ottawa.

———. "Idea of North | Transcript of James Lotz Interview, Tape 2," 1967. Item 1979-20 4 91, Glenn Gould fonds. Library and Archives Canada, Ottawa.

———. "Idea of North | Transcript of Wally MacLean Interview, Tape 1," 1967. Item 1979-20 4 95, Glenn Gould fonds. Library and Archives Canada, Ottawa.

———. "Idea of North | Transcript of Wally MacLean Interview, Tape 2," 1967. Item 1979-20 4 98, Glenn Gould fonds. Library and Archives Canada, Ottawa.

———. "Idea of North | Transcript of Wally MacLean Interview, Tape 3," 1967. Item 1979-20 4 101, Glenn Gould fonds. Library and Archives Canada, Ottawa.

———. "Idea of North | Transcript of Frank Vallee Interview, Tape 1," 1967. Item 1979-20 4 117, Glenn Gould fonds. Library and Archives Canada, Ottawa.

———. "Idea of North | Transcript of Frank Vallee Interview, Tape 2," 1967. Item 1979-20 4 120, Glenn Gould fonds. Library and Archives Canada, Ottawa.

———. "Idea of North | Transcript of R. A. J. Phillips Interview, Tape 1," 1967. Item 1979-20 4 105, Glenn Gould fonds. Library and Archives Canada, Ottawa.

———. "Idea of North | Transcript of R. A. J. Phillips Interview, Tape 2," 1967. Item 1979-20 4 108, Glenn Gould fonds. Library and Archives Canada, Ottawa.

———. "Idea of North | Transcript of Marianne Schroeder Interview, Tape 1," 1967. Item 1979-20 4 111, Glenn Gould fonds. Library and Archives Canada, Ottawa.

———. "Idea of North | Transcript of Marianne Schroeder Interview, Tape 2," 1967. Item 1979-20 4 114, Glenn Gould fonds. Library and Archives Canada, Ottawa.

———. "Idea of North | Sketches of Form," 1967. Item 1979-20 23 82 1, Glenn Gould fonds. Library and Archives Canada, Ottawa.

James Lotz to Glenn Gould, 7 September 1967. Item 1979-20 34 24 14, Glenn Gould fonds. Library and Archives Canada, Ottawa.

Janet Somerville to Ron Solloway, 15 November 1967. Item 1979-20 34 24 18, 2, Glenn Gould fonds. Library and Archives Canada, Ottawa.

Contributors

Anthony Cushing received his PhD in musicology from the University of Western Ontario in 2013. In 2003, he had the distinction of being the first graduate student in music at the University of Southern Maine where he studied composition with J. Mark Scearce, Elliott Schwartz, and Daniel Sonenberg. His current research involves Gould and the *Solitude Trilogy* writ large, as well as mashups and counterpoint.

Christopher DeLaurenti is a composer and scholar who researches seldom-explored areas and composers of electroacoustic music. His installations, albums, and performances include *N30: Live at the WTO Protest November 30, 1999* (2000) and *Favorite Intermissions: Music Before and Between Beethoven Stravinsky Holst* (2007), as well as *Fit the Description (Ferguson, 9–13 August 2014* (2015) and *Return to the Cooling Tower, Satsop* (2025). He holds an MFA from Bard College and a PhD from Goldsmiths, University of London. Christopher has taught ongoing courses at Peabody Institute and the College of William & Mary while leading workshops and residencies at Harvard University, School of the Art Institute of Chicago, Duke University, and elsewhere.

Ethan Kleinberg is the Class of 1958 Distinguished Professor of History and Letters at Wesleyan University and editor-in-chief of *History and Theory*. He is the author of *Generation Existential: Martin Heidegger's Philosophy in France, 1927–61* (2006); *Haunting History: For a Deconstructive Approach to the Past* (2017); and *Emmanuel Levinas's Talmudic Turn: Philosophy and Jewish Thought* (2021). He is coauthor of the "Theses on Theory and History" with Joan Wallach Scott and Gary Wilder. His current book-length project is *The Surge: Temporal Anarchy and the Pursuit of Dynamic History*.

Mark Laurie received his MFA in documentary media from Ryerson University (now Toronto Metropolitan University) in 2009. His thesis film, *Pilgrimage to Solitude*, explored the personal geography of Glenn Gould. In 2017, to mark the fiftieth anniversary of Gould's radio program *The Idea of North*, Mark produced the documentary *Return to North: The Soundscapes of Glenn Gould* for the Canadian Broadcasting Corporation. It has been re-aired several times and was updated in 2023. Mark runs an orchard with his wife in Kamloops, British Columbia.

Markus Mantere graduated with a PhD in music from Brown University in 2011. Since 2021, he is a tenured professor in music history at Sibelius Academy in Helsinki, Finland. After his doctoral research on Glenn Gould, he has moved on to other areas of scholarly inquiry, such as the cultural history of pianism in Scandinavia, music philosophy, and the history of academic music research in Europe.

Lucille Mok is an educator and musicologist whose research interests include jazz studies, recording technologies, and the relationship between sound and the environment. She lives in Madison, Wisconsin, with a scientist, two kids, and three cats.

Paul Sanden is an associate professor in music at the University of Lethbridge, where he teaches musicology. His research regularly crosses disciplinary and musical-generic boundaries, drawing from musicology, performance studies, media theory, and other disciplines to investigate meaning formation in a variety of musical traditions, with a focus on the impact of electronic technologies on music's performance. Among other things, he is the author of *Liveness in Modern Music: Musicians, Technology, and the Perception of Performance* (2013), and multiple articles and chapters on Glenn Gould's recording and broadcast work.

Jeffrey van den Scott is an adjunct professor of musicologies at Memorial University of Newfoundland. From 2020 to 2024, he also served as a teaching assistant professor of Indigenous history. During 2018–2019, he was a postdoctoral fellow with the Tradition & Tradition Research Partnership. His current project, "Inuk in the City: Musical Identity-Work Among Nunatsiavut's Urban Inuit," examines the lives and meaning of music for Inuit living in city spaces, particularly considering how Inuit identity is so often tied to "the land." Jeff earned his PhD in musicology at Northwestern University in 2016 with a research project that examines the intersection of composed Canadian music and the culture of the nation's Inuit population. This study reveals the importance of the north in Canadian musical culture alongside a complex relationship between Inuit and Euro-Canadian populations, each of which expresses the desire to know the other.

Brent Wetters is an adjunct professor of music at Clark University and Worcester Polytechnic Institute. He holds degrees in composition from University of Michigan, the Ghent Conservatory, and Wesleyan University. He received a doctorate in musicology from Brown (2012), where he completed a dissertation on the Darmstadt Summer Courses titled "Darmstadt and the Philosophical Turn." His recent work has focused on a variety of topics, from Paul Celan's use of Franz Schubert's *Winterreise* to Gustav Mahler and his bicycle.

Index

Adorno, Theodor W., 151–152, 188
Agamben, Giorgio, 215
agoraphobia, x, 258, 263
Al Jaber, Sultan, ix
alcoholism, 49, 125, 274–275, 308, 312
aleatoric music, 6
Allan, Andrew, 32, 132, 167, 176
Amirkhanian, Charles, 76
Anderson, Tim J., 75, 88n35
Antarctica, 205, 238
anthropology, 215, 254–255, 262
arcticism. *See* Ryall, Anka
Arrau, Claudio, 178
Arviat, Nunavut, 53, 56, 63–64
audio production, 5, 11, 75, 91n85, 115–116, 117–118, 132, 139, 140–141, 168–170, 184n41
aural fatigue, 101, 122, 217–218n6
aurora borealis. *See* northern lights
auto-exoticism, 46, 48–51

Babbitt, Milton, 76, 196
Bach, Johann Sebastian, 84, 96, 114, 115, 156, 162n27, 179, 188, 301
  Art of the Fugue, The, 142n11, 152–153, 158
  Chromatic Fantasy, 153
  Die Kunst der Fuge (*see* Bach, Johann Sebastian: *Art of the Fuge, The*)
  Goldberg Variations, The, 3–4, 107, 181, 198–199, 301 (*see also under* Gould, Glenn)
  universality of, 152
  Well-Tempered Clavier, The, 109
Bachmann, Ingeborg, 174
Baffin Island, 53, 204, 280, 309
Baker Lake, 48, 256–259, 263, 291
basso continuo, 9, 13, 22, 26, 36, 37, 82, 99, 115, 121–127, 130, 134, 136–137, 142n11, 206
Bazzana, Kevin, 2, 4, 7–8, 23–24, 30–31, 39, 95, 96, 152
Beach Boys, The, 171
Beatles, The, 74, 171, 179, 263
Beethoven, Ludwig van, 96, 152, 156, 301
  sketches, 168–169
Benjamin, Walter, 166
Bennett, John and Susan Rowley
  Uqalurait: An Oral History of Nunavut, 51–53
Berberian, Cathy, 179
Berio, Luciano, 4, 74, 173–174, 178–179, 180
  Thema (Omaggio a Joyce), 173–174
Berlin Philharmonic, 79, 85
Bernstein, Leonard, 302
Berton, Pierre, 166
Bizet, Georges, 155

Blue Note Records, 75
Boulez, Pierre, 178
Brahms, Johannes, 96
  Intermezzo in A Major, op. 118, no. 2, 104–105, 109
  Piano Concerto No. 1 in D Minor, op. 15, 152
Breitsameter, Sabine, 80, 87n26
Burke, Edmund, 150
Burns, Robert, 252
Byrd, William, 96, 109

Cage, John, 117, 140–141, 180
Canada
  1967 Centennial, 5, 9, 46, 47, 71, 122, 148, 166, 210, 224, 294–295
  Department of Indian Affairs (*see* Indigenous and Northern Affairs Canada (INAC))
  Department of National Health and Welfare, 289, 305, 308–309
  Department of Northern Affairs and Natural Resources, 64, 229, 230, 289
  Indigenous and Northern Affairs Canada (INAC), 56, 231
  national identity, 145, 166, 211–212, 232, 234–235
  nationalism, 46–49, 122, 156
  Order of, 159–160
Canadian Broadcasting Corporation (CBC), 3, 5–6, 8–11, 76, 87n19, 96, 99, 100, 132–133, 140, 166, 171–172, 187, 210
CBC Content Sales and Licensing Division, 77
CBC Northern Services, 34, 47–48
CBC Radio, 11, 25–26, 71–74, 75, 77, 190
  Ideas, 5, 71, 108, 171, 294
  publicity department, 6, 294–295
  Sunday Night Stage, 32, 132, 167, 176

Canadian Conference of the Arts, 160
Canadian Museum of Civilization
  Glenn Gould: The Sounds of Genius (exhibit), 96
cannibalism, 215
Canning, Nancy, 75
Carroll, Jock, 98
Casals, Pablo. *See* Gould, Glenn: *Casals: A Portrait for Radio*
Chalmers, Floyd, 159–160
Chapin, Schuyler G., 196
Cherry, Colin, 134
Chilkoot Pass, 231
Churchill, Manitoba, 57, 61, 145–147, 204, 305, 307, 316. *See also* train: Winnipeg to Churchill
Cirauqui, Manuel, 73
Clark, Petula, 301. *See also* Gould, Glenn: *Search for Petula Clark, The*
climate change, ix, 2, 15, 208, 218n21
Coates, Peter A., 36
Cobbing, Bob, 75–76
cocktail party effect, 13, 134, 136, 139
Cold War, 166, 208, 211
colonialism, 16, 45, 49–50, 51, 52, 54–55, 63, 66, 131, 212, 234, 237
Columbia-Princeton Electronic Music Studio, 173
competition, 151–152, 156, 159–160
concerto, political implications of, 151–152
continuo. *See* basso continuo
contrapuntal music. *See* polyphony
contrapuntal radio, 6, 11, 23, 26–32, 38, 48, 50–51, 73–75, 78, 83–84, 97, 98–99, 100–105, 109, 115–117, 118–120, 135, 137–138, 141, 143n23, 153, 167–170, 181, 313
COP28 United Nations Climate Change Conference, ix

Copland, Aaron, 195
Coral Harbour, 124, 214, 286–287, 291–292, 305–308, 311, 315–316
Cott, Jonathan, 42n38, 190
counterpoint. *See* polyphony
Crandall, Jordan, 84
Culshaw, John, 195
Cushing, Anthony, 82, 83

Dahlhaus, Carl, 157
Darmstadt Summer Courses, 4, 172, 174, 180, 183–184n29, 184n41, 184n43
Davidson, Peter
  Idea of North, The, 3, 17n3
Der Spiegel, 175, 179, 300–302
development (musical), 127, 152, 156
digital audio, 73, 80, 81, 142n6
Diplome d'honneur, 160
DMCA (Digital Millenium Copyright Act), 78
Dodge, Charles, 76
dog sledding, 226–228, 258, 263
dystopia, 8, 205, 215

Eaton Auditorium, Toronto, 10, 100, 107
Edinburgh, Scotland, 146–147
Einstein, Albert, 234
Eldorado, viii, 213–214, 221–222, 224, 231, 232, 239
electroacoustic music. See *musique concrète*
electronic music *(elektronische Musik)*. See *musique concrète*
Ellesmere Island, 217, 227–228, 236, 309
Erasmus of Rotterdam, 173
Eskimo. *See* Inuit
ethics, 101, 148, 151, 153–155, 160, 189, 214–217, 220n46
  journalistic, 12, 113

Fink, Howard, 23–24, 29
form (musical), 27, 80, 101, 114–115, 119, 127–131, 134, 137, 140–141, 143n17, 143n20
Foss, Cornelia, 30, 42n34
Friedrich, Caspar David, 98
Friedrich, Otto, 30, 96, 193–194, 196, 199
Frisch, Max, 174
Fromm, Erich, 248
frontier, 40, 58, 122, 212–216, 218n19, 219n33, 220n41, 229, 262, 278–279, 284
Frye, Northrop, 100, 105
fugue. *See* polyphony
Fulford, Robert, 23, 25–26, 111–112n39

geography, 33, 97, 107, 145, 147–148, 225
Girard, François
  Thirty Two Short Films About Glenn Gould, 3, 41–42n28, 98, 99
Glass, Philip, 76
Glenn Gould Foundation, 98
global warming. *See* climate change
God (Old Testament), 216–217
Gould, Glenn
  Arnold Schoenberg: The Man Who Changed Music, 10, 182n6, 190
  Art of Glenn Gould, The, 10, 115, 190
  aversion to cold, 147, 310
  Casals: A Portrait for Radio, 2, 9, 11, 197
  contrapuntal radio (*see* contrapuntal radio)
  Dialogues on the Prospects of Recording, 10, 84
  eccentricities, ix, 2, 3, 300–302
  elephants, singing to, 98
  Goldberg Variations (1981 recording), 3–4, 181, 198–199

Gould, Glenn *(continued)*
"Hysteric Return," 38–39
Idea of North, The, 177
  commercial releases, xn1, 71, 76–77, 86n5,
  dining car scene, 10–14, 46, 57, 59, 83, 116, 123, 125–126, 134, 137–139, 140, 293, 299, 312, 313
  epilogue, 6, 8, 76, 85, 102, 104–105, 130, 131, 176, 177, 205–212, 213, 216–217, 300
  French title *(Idée du Nord),* 90n63
  genre of, 11–12, 15, 23–24, 101, 113, 166–167, 179–182
  internet streaming, xn1, 71, 77–78
  interview transcripts, 11–12, 15, 16, 45, 54–55, 58, 59–62, 76, 113, 128, 170, 209, 221–292
  library holdings, 76, 86n5
  prologue, 11, 13, 79, 103, 115, 122–124, 131, 134–137, 140, 172, 176–177, 191, 313
  radio broadcast, 26, 31, 71–75
  royalties, 77–78
  scene-by-scene analysis, 295–300
  sketch of form, 293
  soliloquy *(see* epilogue)
  stereo version, proposed, 89n40
  synopsis, scene-by-scene, 126
  television version (1970), 9–10, 100, 211–212
  YouTube uploads, 77–78, 90n63
Latecomers, The, 2, 11, 12, 76, 87n19, 89n45, 141, 143n17, 162n32, 188, 192, 197, 217n4
"Let's Ban Applause!," 157
painting of *(see* Movchan, Yana)
parodies of other musicians, 163n42
performance style, 96, 179
photographs of, 29, 98, 310
"Prospects of Recording, The," 177–178, 194–196
publication history, 200n16
Quiet in the Land, The, 2, 11, 12, 76, 141, 154, 162n32, 188, 192–194, 196–197, 198, 200n18, 217n4
  transcription of 33:42–36:21, 198
"Radio as Music," 5, 26–28, 127, 135, 141, 143n17, 143n18, 167–170, 176
retirement from performing, 3, 29, 39, 47, 84, 103, 301
Schoenberg: The First Hundred Years—A Documentary Fantasy, 11
Search for Petula Clark, The, 10, 100, 132, 140, 171, 177, 179
"So You Want to Write a Fugue?," 104
Solitude Trilogy, The, xn1, 2, 9, 15, 24, 27, 28, 29, 76, 98, 102, 143n17, 162n32, 188, 193–194, 199, 205, 217n4
Stokowski: A Portrait for Radio, 2, 9, 11
Strauss: The Bourgeois Hero, 9, 11
String Quartet, op. 1, 4, 140, 142n11, 175, 300, 302, 317n7
Grace, Sherrill, 51, 146, 160
  Canada and the Idea of North, 3, 49
Grange, Henry-Louis de La, 178–179
Grieg, Edvard, 34–35, 43n58
Grimley, Daniel, 34–35
Group of Seven, 35
Groupe de Recherches Musicales, 172–173
Guerrero, Alberto, 79

Habitat, 278, 283
Hancox, Rick, 106, 110n6

Hanslick, Eduard, 149, 155–159
Hardy, Thomas
  "1967," 165–166
harmony, 119–122, 126–127, 129–131, 138, 143n23
Harris, Lawren, 35
Harris, Mark Lee, 155
Hattersley-Smith, Geoff, 227, 228
Heble, Ajay, 84–85
Heile, Björn, 175
Helms, Hans G., 173
Henry, Pierre, 74, 117, 172
Henze, Hans Werner, 174, 183–184n29
hermeneutics, 148–150
Hewitt, Foster, 171
Hitler, Adolph, 215
Hjartarson, Paul, 35, 102
Hobday, John, 160
Hodgson, Jay, 171
Hoffmann, E. T. A., 157
Hogarth, David, 110n15
Honigmann, John and Irma, 262
Hörspiel, 117, 174–176, 179–180, 181, 184n32, 300, 302
Hui, Yuk, 77
Hunstein, Don, 98

Indigenous northerners. *See* Inuit
Ingold, Tim, 90n71
Inuit, x, 14, 16, 21, 36, 45–66, 67n4, 125, 138, 161n8, 191, 204, 212–213, 220n42, 224–225, 232–233, 237–238, 240, 256–259, 260, 262, 263, 264, 265–266, 267–268, 269, 270–271, 273–277, 284, 287–288, 289–290, 291, 292, 306–307, 312–313, 315
  "noble savage" trope, 51, 58–60, 62
  colonial attitudes toward (*see* colonialism)
  conception of time, 54, 291
  drum dances, 56–57
  gender roles, 51–54, 289–290, 313
  settlements, 46, 56–57, 64, 238, 256–257, 263, 267–268, 287, 289, 291, 306, 312
  stereotyping, 45–46, 52–56, 59, 237–238
Inuksuk, 59, 68–69n52
isolation. *See* solitude

Jaeger, David, 174
James, William, 85, 206–209, 245–246
Jessop, John, 28, 167–170, 182n3

Kagel, Mauricio, 174–175
Kant, Immanuel, 61–62, 150–151, 157, 161n17
Keithahn, Edward, 48
Kelman, Ari Y., 90n71
Kennan, Kent, 84
Kennedy, John F., 218n19
Kingwell, Mark, 137–138
Kirkpatrick, Smith, 176
König, Gottfried-Michael, 173
Kostelanetz, Richard, 27, 42n38, 76, 79, 81–82
Kramer, Stanley, 176
KSER 90.7 FM, 73, 87n16
Kusch, Martin, 149

Labrador. *See* Newfoundland and Labrador
Lachenmann, Helmut, 183–184n29
landscape, 34–35, 79, 97–99, 106–107, 110n6
Lanzmann, Claude, 106
Laurie, Mark
  Pilgrimage to Solitue, 95–109, 210
  Return to North: The Soundscapes of Glenn Gould, 107–109
Le Caine, Hugh, 177
Leacock, Stephen, 251

338 | Index

Leblanc, Larry, 30
Leigh, Vivian, 176
Leydi, Roberto, 173
Liberman, M. M., 177
Library and Archives Canada, 23, 96, 109n5, 156, 182n6, 223–224
Lieberson, Goddard, 195
lifeboat ethics. See ethics
Liszt, Franz, 301, 302
Littler, William, 29, 95, 99, 103–105, 109
Ljubimov, Aleksei, 147
Lotz, James, viii, 5–8, 9, 53–54, 58–61, 66, 124–125, 129, 130, 138, 184n38, 213–215, 217, 219n40, 221–241, 311, 317n2, 317n3, 317n10
Lumen database, 78
Lyons, Edmund Moubray, 274
Lyotard, Jean-François, 150–151, 161n17

Macdonald, John A., 122
Mach, Elyse, 29
Maclean, Walter "Wally," 5–8, 9, 12, 15, 37, 49, 60–61, 66, 76, 80, 82–83, 85, 102, 104, 129–130, 162n30, 176–177, 206–212, 213, 216, 224, 241–256, 311, 314, 317n2
Maderna, Bruno, 4, 173–174, 179, 184n43
  "Compositional Experiences in Electronic Music," 180–181
  I nvensione su una voce, 173
  Mahler, Gustav, advocacy of, 185n46
  Ritratto di Erasmo, 173–174
Maderna, Bruno and Luciano Berio
  Ritratto di Città, 173
Mahler, Gustav, 178–179, 182, 185n46
  "Des Antonius von Padua Fischpredigt," 98

Maine, 204
Mangolte, Babette, 106
manifest destiny, viii, 213
Mannis, Harry, 168
Mannoni, Octave, 237
Mansell, Darrel, 27, 29, 61
Marek, George R., 195
Martin, George, 171
Mason-Dixon Line, 204
mass media, 23, 236, 247–248, 264–265
McGill University, 226
McGreevy, John, 99
  Glenn Gould's Toronto (film), 98
McLuhan, Marshall, 28, 31, 32–33, 40n3, 73, 77, 143n18, 167, 222, 232, 285
McMaster University, 256
McNeilly, Kevin, 23, 30, 102, 153
Medvedev, Sergei, 147–148
Mehrländer, Klaus, 175
Mennonite religion, 2, 193, 197
Mingus, Charles, 75
Misericordia Hospital School of Nursing, 305, 310
Monsaingeon, Bruno, 151
moral equivalent of war. See James, William
Movchan, Yana
  painting of Glenn Gould, 98
Mowat, Farley, 48
Mozart, Wolfgang Amadeus, 96, 153, 156, 301
mushing. See dog sledding
musique concrète, 4, 15, 74, 88n30, 117, 142n5, 167, 172–180, 181, 183n22, 183n23, 300
Muskeg Express. See train: Winnipeg to Churchill

Nash, Knowlton, 8–9
nationalism, Canadian. See under Canada

nationalism, Nordic, 34–35
Neumann, Anyssa, 39, 150–151
New Viennese School, 179, 181
Newfoundland and Labrador, 1, 2, 192, 226, 246, 247, 260
Nichols, Bill, 107
Nicol, Eric, 251
Nielsen, Carl, 34–35
Nietzsche, Friedrich, 155–156, 217
Nightingale School of Nursing, 311
Norden, Hugo, 120–121
north
  deromanticizing, 49, 102, 131, 211, 250, 261–262, 273–275, 287–288
  future of, viii–ix, 105, 121, 126, 131, 205, 212, 219n33, 230–232, 238–241, 269–271, 277–278, 284–285
  going north, 1, 6, 15–16, 63, 130, 145, 147–148, 191–192, 205–206, 209–211, 215–216, 217, 229, 241–246
northern lights, 206, 243, 249, 306
northern listening, 15, 158–159, 248
Norway, 1, 35, 44n65
Nunavut, 46, 51–53, 55–56, 63–64, 204

Oliveros, Pauline, 74
opera, 74, 79, 101, 157–158, 313–314
orientalism. *See* Said, Edward
Orvig, Svenn, 226–227
Ostwald, Peter, 29
Ottawa, Ontario, 6, 222, 224, 226, 229–231, 234, 238–239, 262
  northerners opinions of, 229, 290

Pacsu, Margaret, 99, 103–105, 110n14
Parker, Dorothy, 231
Pascal, Blaise, 254
Pavlov, Ivan, 253
Payzant, Geoffrey, 50, 61–62, 101

Pearlman, Judith, 100, 311. *See also* Gould, Glenn: *Idea of North, The*, television version
Perloff, Nancy, 76
Phillips, Robert, 5, 7–8, 36, 54–55, 57–60, 62, 66, 83, 89n40, 103, 121, 123–125, 129–130, 135–136, 138, 191, 192–193, 212, 213–215, 224, 271–285, 311
Canada's North, 215
polar bear, 6, 36, 78, 81, 286, 307, 317n9
polar exploration, viii, 1, 21, 51, 206–207, 217n2
polyphony, x–xi, 13, 27, 38, 72, 78, 84, 104–105, 109, 115, 120–121, 133–139, 143n23, 153–155, 160, 170, 173, 178, 188–190, 195, 197, 199
Porter, Jeff, 83
Porter, Katherine
  Ship of Fools (novel), 176–177, 184n35
Posen, Stephen, 30
postmodernism, 150–151, 161n17
Potvin, Gilles, 47
Pousseur, Henri, 178
Protestant Reformation, 173–174
Pryde, Duncan, 48
psychoacoustics, 117–118, 132

Ra, Sun, 74
radio, 9, 24–28, 32–34, 38–39, 40n3, 71–85, 124, 128, 132, 166
Radiodiffusion-Télévision-Française (RTF), 142n5, 172
Rasmussen, Knud, 51
Reagan, Ronald, 218n19
Records and Recordings (journal), 178
Riesman, David, 248
Rivett-Carnac, Charles, 238
Roberts, John, 10, 160, 187
Rogers, George, 236
rondo form, 27, 127–130

Rossiter, Byron, 38
Rovaniemi, Finland, 146–147
Rowley, Susan. *See* Bennett, John and Susan Rowley
Rubenstein, Arthur, 76
Ryall, Anka, 50–51
Ryerson Polytechnic Institute, 167, 171

Said, Edward, xi, 50, 153–154, 188–189
Sallis, Friedemann, 82
Sanden, Paul, 142n7
Schaeffer, Pierre, 74, 117, 141, 142n5, 172–173
  Étude aux chemins de fer (Study with Trains), 172
Schafer, R. Murray, 23, 32–33, 36, 37–38, 40n3, 79–80, 82, 90n71, 145–146
Scheper-Hugues, Nancy, 220n46
Schlegel, Friedrich, 157
Schoenberg, Arnold, 84, 96, 138–139, 141, 156, 179, 181, 301–302. See also *Arnold Schoenberg: The Man Who Changed Music*; Gould, Glenn
  Piano Suite, op. 25, 114–115
Schöning, Klaus, 88n31
Schroeder, Marianne, 5–8, 9, 15, 17n10, 36, 52–53, 55–56, 59, 66, 78, 80–81, 82, 83, 90n68, 103, 123–125, 135–138, 184n38, 192–193, 214, 224, 286–292, 303–317, 317n10
Schubert, Franz
  Winterreise, 216–217
Scriabin, Alexander, 33, 43n55
Second Viennese School. *See* New Viennese School
semantics, 119–121, 128
semiotics, 99, 114–119, 127–128, 130–132, 134, 137–138, 140–141, 149–150

Service, Robert, 234, 246–247
Shackelton, Ernest, 22
Shakespeare, William, 132, 167, 249
Shelley, Mary
  Frankenstein, 203–204, 216, 217n2
Ship of Fools (film), 113–114, 176
Ship of Fools (novel). *See under* Porter, Katherine
Sibelius, Jean, 33, 43n55
  Fifth Symphony, 8, 22, 36, 50, 80, 85, 102, 104–105, 142n8, 206, 208, 210, 218n7
  Finlandia, 294–295
Sisyphus, myth of, 206
Skinner, Quentin, 149–150
social work, 256
sociology, 255–256
solitude, ix–x, 5, 13, 15, 22–24, 28–31, 33, 35–36, 38–39, 45–48, 49–51, 57, 59–63, 64, 66, 98, 102–103, 106–107, 114, 148, 154–155, 159–160, 188–193, 199, 204–205, 217–218n6, 217n5, 222, 235, 247–250, 254, 263–264, 267, 279–281, 287, 291, 315–316
Somerville, Janet, 5, 6, 75, 294–295
sound poetry, 75–76
soundscape (compositions), 14, 32–33, 37–38, 40, 79–80, 82, 167, 217n6
space, illusion of, 32–33, 36–37, 133, 139
Spinelli, Martin, 80, 83
St. Paul University, 230
Steffánson, Vilhjámur, 21–22, 40
Stockhausen, Karlheinz, 74, 88n30, 140, 173, 178, 180
Stokowski, Leopold. *See* Gould, Glenn: *Stokowski: A Portrait for Radio*
Strauss, Richard, 17n8, 109. *See also* Gould, Glenn; *Strauss: The Bourgeois Hero*

Studio di Fonologia Musicale di Milano della RAI, 4, 173–174
sublime, the, 39, 61–62, 150–151, 161n17, 179
Swingle Singers, 301

tactical media, 15, 71, 83–84
Tenney, James, 141
Testa, Bart, 110n6
texture (musical), 80, 84, 101, 103–104, 119, 131–139, 153–155, 197, 199
Thirty Two Short Films About Glenn Gould. *See under* Girard, François
Thompson, Manitoba, 147, 241–243, 246
Till, Eric, 187
Toronto School of Communication, 40
Toronto, Ontario, 1, 10, 25, 50, 60, 95, 97–100, 105–107, 146, 170, 171, 178, 212, 231, 247, 310
Tovell, Vincent, 100, 101, 103–105, 109, 110n15, 187
train
  rail building, 250–251, 253–254
  Winnipeg to Churchill, 5, 9, 22, 37, 103, 106, 122, 145, 177, 204, 212, 224, 241–243, 244–246
trio sonata, 78, 103, 122–124, 131, 134, 137
Tulk, Lorne, 9–11, 13, 27, 75, 79–80, 87n19, 100, 103–105, 110n10, 116, 118, 123, 132, 135, 169–170, 171–172, 176, 205, 309, 313, 314

Ultra-red, 74, 78
United States, 73, 204, 211–212, 219n40, 281
  Bureau of Indian Affairs, 233
University of Toronto music department, 177
Uptergrove cottage, 50, 105–107

Utopia, viii, 8, 49, 131, 154, 205, 213–216, 221–222, 224, 231–232

Vallee, Frank, 5–8, 12, 16, 36, 54, 56–59, 66, 76, 103, 123–125, 135–138, 184n38, 224, 256–271, 287, 311
Vallee, Mickey, 16
van Gelder, Rudy, 75
Vancouver Olympics (2010), 59
Vietnam War, 211, 281
Vogt, Ray, 12–13, 154
VU Metering, 79–80, 91n85, 136–137

Waddington, Geoffrey, 25
Wagner, Richard, 62, 155
  Meistersinger, Die, 4
war, moral equivalent of. *See* James, William
Weber, Carl Maria von, 39
Webern, Anton, 168–169, 176, 178, 181
Welles, Orson, 174
Westdeutscher Rundfunk (WDR) Cologne, 173–175, 179, 183n22, 300
Whitehead, Gregory, 74, 85
Whitehorse, 222, 230, 309
  squatters of, 229
wide-open spaces. *See* agoraphobia
Wiener, Norbert, 253
Williamson, Robert, 64–65
Wilson, Brian, 171
Wolff, Christoph, 162n27
World Soundscape Project, 32, 40, 40n3. *See also* soundscape (compositions)
World War I, 24, 218n14
World War II, 74, 172, 232, 303

YouTube, 77–78

Zen Buddhism, 314–315

www.ingramcontent.com/pod-product-compliance
Lightning Source LLC
Chambersburg PA
CBHW020121240426
43673CB00038B/548